the Valley Forge Winter

WAYNE BODLE

the Valley Forge Winter

CIVILIANS

AND

SOLDIERS

IN WAR

The Pennsylvania State University Press

University Park, Pennsylvania

Library of Congress Cataloging-in-Publication Data

Bodle, Wayne K.
   The Valley Forge winter : civilians and soldiers in war /
Wayne Bodle.
      p.   cm.
   Includes bibliographical references and index.
   ISBN 0-271-02230-2 (alk. paper)
      1. Valley Forge (Pa.)—History—18th century.
   2. Washington, George, 1732–1799—Headquarters—
   Pennsylvania—Valley Forge.   3. United States—
   Continental Army—Military life.   4. Pennsylvania—
   History—Revolution, 1775–1783—Social aspects.
   5. United States—History—Revolution, 1775–1783—
   Social aspect.   I. Title.

E234 .B63 2002
973.3'341—dc21   2002011741

First paperback printing, 2004
ISBN 0-271-02526-3

Printed in the United States of America

Published by The Pennsylvania State University Press,
University Park, PA 16802–1003
It is the policy of The Pennsylvania State University
Press to use acid-free paper for all clothbound books.
Publications on uncoated stock satisfy the minimum
requirements of the American National Standard for
Information Sciences—Permanence of Paper for Printed
Library Materials, ANSI Z39.48–1992.

FOR

Anne Phelan Bodle

AND

William H. Bodle

Contents

Acknowledgments

This book has been "in progress" for a long time. I have always heard that the most gratifying part of writing a book is the reckoning of the debts owed for its completion, and in this case there are many. This research was begun under the auspices of the National Park Service (NPS) as part of an interpretive planning project executed by a talented interdisciplinary group. Jacqueline Thibaut Eubanks, my colleague on the team of research historians and in writing the initial monographs, was instrumental in conceptualizing the project and in articulating our sense that the "real story" of Valley Forge was as much about civilians as it was about soldiers. Her work on questions of military supply and logistics and on the material culture of the camp also catalyzed our suspicion that a narrative organized around supposedly virtuous but inert soldiers stoically persevering through a "starving time" did little credit either to the army or to the truth. The other historians on our team, Michael Lawson, David Rich, and Harry Roach, were largely responsible for the almost embarrassing depths of documentary evidence from which we drew.

The NPS archaeological, architectural, and planning professionals who were the initial clients for the research were always supportive of our work, and they continually reminded us of the practical implications of "pure" knowledge. Helen Schenck and Michael Parrington, members of the University of Pennsylvania Museum archaeological team, were particularly helpful in this regard, as were the late John and Cherry Dodd, who studied the historical architecture of Valley Forge. Drs. David G. Orr and Brooke Blades, Park Service archaeologists, fought many a good fight on behalf of the more controversial implications of our research. The late Dr. John L. Cotter, of the Park Service and the University Museum, was supportive throughout, and never stopped believing that the work would one day appear in print. The members of the general management planning team from the Park Service's Denver Service Center gave us invaluable feedback, and took some heat from their superiors to incorporate our often revisionist interpretations into what would become the "official" story of Valley Forge. H. Gilbert Lusk was an ideal park superintendent during our travails. A history major at heart, Gil knew how to get budgets approved, and also gave us as much room to work as we needed. Professor John Shy of the University of Michigan served as the external referee for the research monographs, and his shrewd constructive criticism of the work was as indispensable to its long term success as his generous initial praise was to its immediate bureaucratic survival.

Back in academia—long before, during, and ever since my excursion into "public history"—I steadily accumulated other debts. Michael Zuckerman taught me almost everything that was worth knowing about how to think historically. He somehow discerned the voice of a practitioner trapped inside the florid writings of a graduate student pretender, and he did what he could to make room for that voice in the wider world. He saw in the draft chapters I sent him "the dissertation" that I only hoped to resume after "the project" was done, and he knew how to make it work out with the powers that be while I naively wondered, "Can you really *do* that?" That I was not interested in New England, eighteenth century towns, or even early America when I made him my advisor seems now like more of an ironic curiosity than anything else. Mike also steered enough opportunities to work in the real world in my direction—which did not begin or end with the Park Service assignment—to keep me going until things did work out.

The History Department at the University of Pennsylvania was a wonderful place to study in the 1970s. There I encountered every imaginable variety of "new" history. That I did not adopt *any* of them as my specific theoretical, methodological, or interpretive allegiance does not diminish the intellectual debt that I still owe them all. The good-natured intradepartmental contest of world views was both inspiring and creatively confusing to watch. Dr. Alfred Rieber, graduate chair at the time, was correct to warn us apprentices that the employment "market" was about to collapse disastrously, but also prescient to predict that it would eventually revive. I am only sorry that more members of my decadal cohort did not survive the catastrophe. Seymour Mandelbaum was more right than he probably knew to tell one seminar that if we *did* survive we would have to be able to literally reinvent ourselves scholastically—possibly more than once—and to challenge us to at least begin thinking about how we might *do* that. It worked for me.

Except for Mike Zuckerman, none of the department's early Americanists probably even *knew* me when I was a graduate student there, but they all have paid for that inattention in the long run. Richard Beeman agreed at a very late hour and on short notice to serve as a second reader for a student who he had had no real opportunity to instruct. He generously allowed a wallful of apprentice teachers to observe his American Revolution class one semester, where his *"to-the-edge-but-not-over-it"* pedagogical style showed me, at least, how far I still had to go in that area.

After an interval in another of history's "new" domains that I did not even hear named while I inhabited it—that of *"independent scholarship"*—I found my way back to academia and to Penn. The Philadelphia Center for Early American Studies provided that rarest of things in American culture, a chance to do something over, and a thing rarer still in academic life, an opportunity to repeat graduate school with new subfields without the formality of writing another dissertation. Richard Dunn returned to direct the Center after a year in England to find that he had inherited an office-and-library rat. He was gracious enough not to push me out of the nest until there was room at the next level. Indeed, Richard let me help drive the Center's bus once in a while even as he fretted that "the book" was not getting done. It was an unforgettable opportunity that I will always appreciate. Stephanie G. Wolf literally buttonholed me into attending the Center's seminars, and then guided me into the Center's society of fellowship. The Philadelphia Center—now the McNeil Center—has to be the most marvelous community in academic creation. Year after year it recruits new classes of scholar/fellows—young and old, accomplished and apprenticed—who are bright, funny, committed, and dedicated to research as a collective craft. It retains the energy and affection of so many of them that, during the years of my involvement with the institution, it has created an "alumni" network that is not just the most coherent, but doubtless also the *best organized*, of those in any disciplinary subfield. It would be almost invidious to attempt to list individually all of the members of that extended family who have listened to or contributed to the ideas in this book, but it would be even more objectionable *not* to name at least some of them.

Rosalind Remer shared an office with this project (and its various kin and progeny) for two years—as well as many a prank, snack, and field trip—and she has become, for me, the very model of a scholar's friend and academic soul mate. Her standards are as high as her support is constant and generous, and she knows more about more different things than anyone else I know. Steve Smith, of Fayetteville, called the next presidential election on the first day I met him and over the next few years he showed that this clairvoyance was no fluke. His passion for fun and productivity and his headlong commitment to ideas and liberty have been an inspiration to me. Roderick McDonald joined our crew at an early point. His refusal to abandon his "mates'" mess for academic high-table opportunities taught us all a valuable lesson. Bill Pencak published part of this study, Chapter 3, and has since written innumerable letters on behalf of its author. Billy Smith moderated a Center seminar on a draft of Chapter 4, and realized—probably from my impending collapse into his lap from exhaustion—exactly when to call off the chase. Ann Little has been a one-woman guardian of the moral economy of ideas ever since she first came to the Center's seminars as an undergraduate. I once had the good fortune to teach her in a graduate seminar, but I have undoubtedly learned much more from her in the years since then. Her redoubtable insistence that things must keep moving forward had its good effect, and her demonstration of that good principle in her own life and work have earned my great admiration. Neither the Center nor this book would have been the same without Anita Tien, Patricia Cleary, Aaron Fogleman, Simon Newman, Alison Games, Karin Wulf, John Majewski, Susan Branson, Jim Williams, Brendan McConville, Thom Wermuth, Donna Rilling, or Janet Lindman.

At the Center I also had the opportunity to meet and learn from many senior scholars. Linda Kerber, who was in residence during my first semester there, thought this project mattered literally from the first day, and she has waited with much more patience than I had any right to expect for me to try to prove her right. She has truly been a *godmentor*. John Murrin is the quintessential "wise man" to a generation of junior practitioners making their way in the early American universe. His students are fortunate that he brings them to Philadelphia, and his students are saint-like to share his intellectual generosity with everyone who he meets there. Jean Soderlund, Susan Klepp, Dallett Hemphill, Lucy Simler, Bruce Mann, Randall Miller, Frank Fox, Elaine Crane, Dan Richter, Mark Lloyd, Lisa Wilson, and Merrill Smith all contributed important ideas and support during the years that this work was in progress. Sandra Mackenzie Lloyd invited me to participate in a symposium on the American Revolution at Cliveden in Philadelphia, where I began thinking about some of the questions that led to the inclusion of Chapter 4 in this book.

I held a fellowship at the David Library of the American Revolution, and that remarkable oasis of primary source materials became an academic home away from home. David Fowler steadily built the collections there while allowing me to read or copy perhaps half of that trove. There I also met James Kirby Martin, who supported my work with a generous fervor that was compelling. I might still be promising to start the book if Jim had not begun to *insist* that I do so. Other repository-based fellowships—by allowing me to begin or work on other projects—actually helped to *delay* this book, but the continued learning that I accomplished under their auspices made it better for the delay. Individuals who I met along the way often deflected the book's interpretive course with questions, challenges to my glib assumptions, or new nuggets of data.

Alfred F. Young invited me to present papers to his early American seminar at the Newberry Library two years in a row—once on this project—and a number of sustained conversations with him about the work sharpened my understanding of its importance. No one ever ignored Al's reproving glare in a seminar except to his own intellectual detriment, or belatedly attended to the points that he was ultimately trying to make thereby without reaping a commensurate profit.

Peter Potter kindly took the project on at a critical moment and steered it to completion. Paul Blaum provided critical editorial advice, Eliza Childs expertly copyedited the final manuscript, and John Pankratz patiently extracted a usable jacket photo with minimal damage to the author.

Two readers for the Penn State Press furnished excellent suggestions for improving the study.

Opportunities to teach during the dry years, *post–job-crisis*, were critical to this work. Rick Beeman once loaned me his freshman seminar on the American Revolution at Penn, and Michael Katz, as department chair, gave me an opportunity to repeat that experiment. Edward C. Carter III and I co-taught his graduate seminar one fall, and he was gracious enough to let me do all of the fun parts. It was mostly due to Linda Kerber that I spent two and a half years at the University of Iowa, where I learned about teaching, research, and life, from a stellar array of colleagues who generously welcomed me into their midst. Roderick McDonald and Susan Klepp similarly brought me to Rider University for a fascinating semester and an opportunity to expand my course repertoire. My colleagues at Indiana University of Pennsylvania have made the last four years an intellectual adventure as well as a job. They have also continued to act as if they believed that this book was really "on the way," rather than just lost at sea somewhere. My research assistants at IUP, Doug MacGregor and Doug Bosley, kindly helped with the manuscript preparations.

Everyone who writes in specialized academic fields knows about the importance of non-practitioner friends—sometimes oddly called "laymen." They take you in in the middle of the night when surprise research trips lead you to their towns, or drag you out at the end of long hard days at the keyboard. They find new ways to ask the same old questions about "the book," and never act as if it might be the adult version of an imaginary playmate. Some even promise to *buy* a copy if one ever comes in their way. Janet and Joel Gray, Alison Smith and Steve Smith of Media, Sandy and Marilyn Wax, Barry and Margie Checkoway, Lynne Roddy Johnston, Lloyd Bodle, and Dave and Denise Bodle Greiner, did all of these things and more. Tom Small once made the mistake of promising to pay me on a fee-per-word basis to finish the project, at a rate that neither of us can even remember now. Chris Moore was kind enough to predict that the book would actually be read on American beaches some day, after which it became impossible *not* to finish it just to see if this would be the case! Owen Smith, Julie Gray, and Amay Smith—barely sprouts in the 1980s—are now making their ways toward or into adulthood in a world where the *"end of history"* has—for better or for worse—proved to be no more than a false start (or stop?). May they do a better job with both the world and with history than we have done. My parents, the late Anne Bodle and William Bodle, were already diplomatically *not* asking "so when are you going to finish it" long before most of the other people listed here even knew that I had *started* it. If only by that small gesture of humanity—but in reality for so many other reasons—they made it possible, and so are appropriately the subjects of the dedication page.

Wayne Bodle
Solebury, Pennsylvania
July 2002

A CHOROGRAPHICAL MAP, of the COUNTRY, round PHILADELPHIA. || CARTE PARTICULIERE, des ENVIRONS de PHILADELPHIE.

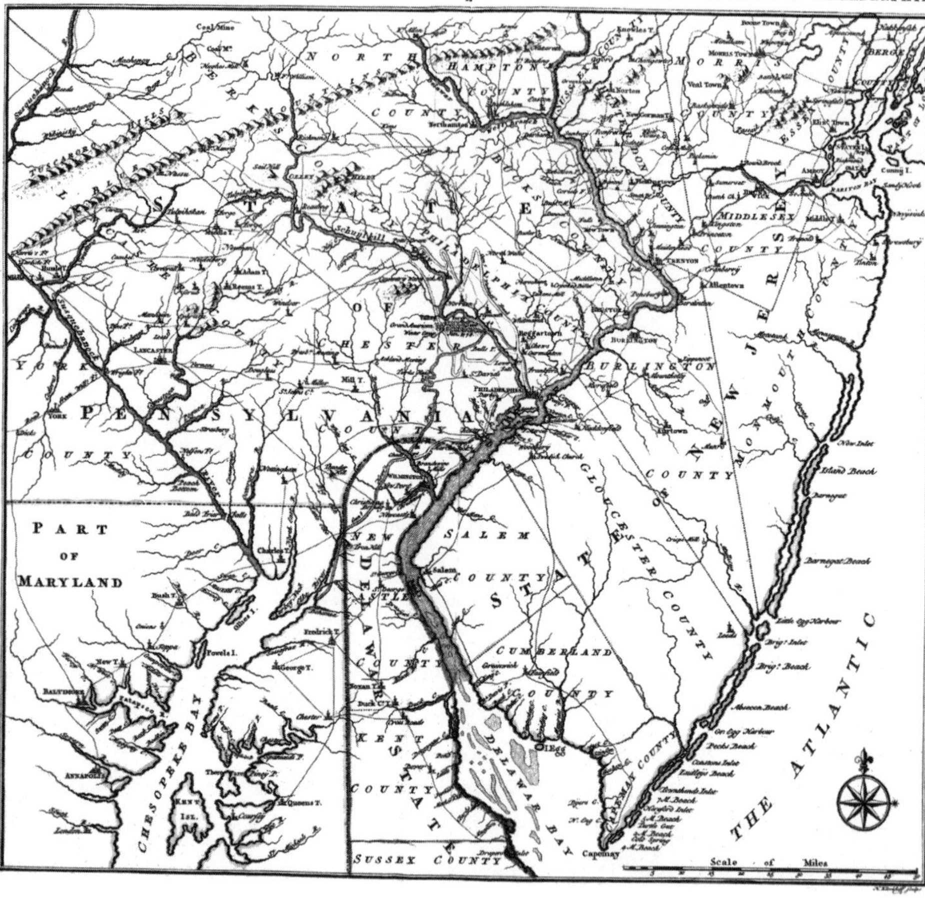

Introduction

"**W**hy do people always talk about Valley Forge?" This question arose during a chat with an associate dean of arts and sciences a few years back. The dean, an astronomer, politely inquired about my research during a visit to his office in connection with my job candidacy. When he learned that it was on Valley Forge, he revealed that he had grown up near Morristown, New Jersey—the other great winter encampment site of the Continental Army. His parents still lived there, he confided, and people back home always wanted to know why Valley Forge gets all the attention from the popular culture when it was colder at Morristown, the snow was deeper, supply shortages were just as great, and Continental troops even mutinied there? We both smiled at this paradox, and I admitted that there were no easy answers to his question.[1]

I began studying Valley Forge as part of a planning project for the National Park Service when the administration of Valley Forge was transferred from the state of Pennsylvania to the Park Service in 1977. Our research team was charged to discover what "really happened" at Valley Forge, in order to allow agency officials to write nonintrusive development plans for the park and to create accurate interpretive programs. In spite of the agency's best intentions, the culturally charged character of Valley Forge precipitated a few political explosions over what "what really happened?" really meant. A Golden Fleece Award nomination was floated by a local newspaper. A shrill protest resolution was passed by a national patriotic hereditary organization. A few angry letters arrived from anonymous taxpayers. Jealous allusions to Watergate-style analysis were inserted in an internal peer review document by agency insiders who had hoped to run the project themselves.[2]

At the end of the project I had a much better understanding of how Valley Forge was mythologized than of why. Ironically, the "ragged Continentals" may have been the unintended victims of their own commander-in-chief's political skill or rhetorical guile. General Washington sometimes exaggerated their weak and vulnerable condition to pressure the Continental Congress into supplying them better. In truth, I told the dean, I would happily surrender all of the florid honorifics that have been fixed on Valley Forge—the "birthplace of an army," the "crucible of victory," the "darkest hour of the war," or the "turning point of the Revolution"—to explore what happens when two armies descend on a diverse population in a divided community with complex and ambiguous historical experiences with war and peace.[3]

Now, 225 years after the event itself, this is the first comprehensive, book-length study of the Valley Forge winter based on extensive research in primary sources beyond the published papers of a narrow circle of national political institutions and military leaders. The book is not directly concerned with the mythological Valley Forge, but it is useful to acknowledge the continued existence of that myth. Who can deny the cultural power of soldiers' bloody footprints in the snow, or of Washington praying in the frozen woods for his army's deliverance? Two popular notions about Valley Forge, more abstract than those images, constrain our ability to understand the meaning of the event: the impression that the army spent the winter of 1777–78 in the wilderness, far removed from civilian society, and that its engagement with both its civilian host society and its military adversary was more metaphorical than material in nature. The pictorial iconography of the encampment has consigned Valley Forge to a hazy place in American memory and resists its recovery by the recent turn toward "social history." Most popular representations deny Valley Forge any *social* context at all, beyond that of ragged soldiers in an undifferentiated corner of the snowy wilderness. Paintings show Continentals huddled around campfires or shivering in huts on what looks like otherwise uninhabited terrain. Scarcely a barn, or a road-trace, or a hay wagon, or a corn row, or a domesticated animal, or even a fence line hints that anyone else has ever lived there.

Early works about the Revolution populated these desolate scenes with an austere human company huddled in scenes of heroic passivity. In the popular literature of Valley Forge, the Continental Army serves as little more than a giant, gaunt Greek chorus or a hapless prop in its own passion play. It arrives at Valley Forge stumbling over frozen, rutted roads, and then huddles there helplessly, before marching off on the road to victory. According to Harry Emerson Wildes's 1938 account, "the Revolution was won at Valley Forge." A "defeated, dispirited and tattered array came here hungry, cold and broken," he observed. "Washington led away the same men, drilled and disciplined into a confident army, in pride to victory." In Alfred Hoyt Bill's 1952 narrative, emaciated soldiers "stepped gingerly" over icy paths in the camp. By the next May, they could maneuver "with a speed and precision of which the brigades had been incapable two months before." In his study of the Valley Forge winter, Donald Barr Chidsey wrote that the troops hobbled into Valley Forge a "rabble of uncertain, lousy, sick, bleeding men." Six months later they marched away "with a swinging step, drums beating, fifes loud [and] ready to fight."[4]

In between these stark poles of capacity and incapacity, Wildes's "ragged barefoot volunteers huddled helplessly about their smoking greenwood fires." Chidsey's "shivering, sick, and red-eyed" troops "clung to that stump-studded hillside." To judge from this awkward mixture of artistic and literary conventions, American soldiers overcame a deadly combination of climatic hardship and abstract social adversity. The armies were engaged with each other more in an allegorical than a military sense; the one comfortably lodged in Philadelphia while the other shivered in the wilderness. Nor have civilians played compelling roles in these stories, other than as stock figures: the pacifist Quaker farmer; the Tory collaborator; or in Washington's account, oblivious politicians, writing hypocritical letters "by a good fireside" while the troops suffered. Such perceptions are reinforced by two providential mechanisms for the army's deliverance. The supposed arrival in the Schuylkill River in early 1778 of huge schools of American shad offered a secular bread and fishes metaphor to end a famine.[5] Then, according to most accounts, Prussian drillmaster Friedrich Wilhelm von Steuben came and forged a "horde" of men into "a real army," or "created a spirited army out of [a] ragged and demoralized mob."[6]

Academic historians, of course, have complicated and moderated this florid imagery. Long before there was a "new military history," they began to recover the colonial contribution to British eighteenth-century imperial wars. Today, scholars are more likely to emphasize British difficulties in projecting armed force over a 3,000-mile-long supply line, or the advantages accruing to the rebels from terrain and manpower reserves, than to divide American fighters into polar caricatures of "ragged hordes" and "backwoods marksmen" hiding to shoot from behind trees. Such historians as John R. Alden, Howard H. Peckham, Piers Mackesy, and Don Higginbotham have challenged the providential transformation myth of the Continental Army's development. Peckham—with specific reference to Valley Forge—has bluntly rejected the ferrous analogy of "forging a stronger army [by] applying heat to metal to harden it."[7]

Most of these caveats, however, are scattered in articles and book chapters devoted to broader issues. They have not commanded sustained attention within the professional or academic historical communities, or any deference in the popular culture. Indeed, the closer that professional scholars work to iconic elements of the Revolution, the likelier they have been to defer subtly to some of them. Robert Middlekauf's widely used synthesis of the Revolution, *The Glorious Cause,* for example, gives a respectful, or even an admiring, account of the Continental Army's performance during the 1777 Pennsylvania campaign, but then he defers to the old pictorial cliché, by concluding that Washington selected Valley Forge for its winter quarters because, in part, "it was remote from settled areas" and "out of the way of civilians." Middlekauf quotes Dr. Albigence Waldo's Valley Forge diary— one of two classic texts fixing the army's reputation as a crumbling horde— without noting that it was illustrated by a map showing Valley Forge's location in the middle of a densely settled commercial farmscape.[8]

Similarly, Don Higginbotham, a dean of modern Revolutionary military history, paints an army that was merely "touchy" in late 1777, rather than incipiently mutinous. But as they "huddled in tents and drafty huts beyond the Schuylkill," he writes, the soldiers confronted an "atmosphere" that was "marked by inaction, hunger, cold, and the absence of every necessity." John R. Alden acknowledges the resiliency of the American army in the 1777 campaign, but he then veers into romantic allegory by placing its members in "the Gethsemane of Valley Forge." Piers Mackesy notes that General William Howe's troops "spent the winter comfortably in Philadelphia," while their adversaries watched them in mere "discomfort" at Valley Forge. But then he adopts conventional imagery imposing a fortuitous passivity on the rebels. "The Americans suffered in their hutments through the harsh winter," he observes, saved mainly by Howe's indolence.[9]

Barbara MacDonald Powell, a careful student of Valley Forge imagery, has conceded that the "romantic haze surrounding the winter of 1777–78 will not likely be dispelled by any new historical research pointing out the 'real facts' of the encampment." That may not be a bad thing. Any event protean enough to inspire both a conservative "Freedoms Foundation" and Mao Zedong is probably doing cultural work important enough not to be cavalierly disturbed.[10] This book, however, meets Valley Forge on its own terms and literally on its own ground. Far from being set in a wilderness, the Continental Army's quarters were deliberately located in a settled area. Anything but the stoically passive recipients of deprivation and then deliverance, its members were effective agents in their own behalf. In 1777 they learned to perform one mission—conventional combat operations—that is the usual province of soldiers better than has been appreciated. During the next winter they adapted to another set of functions—serving as a partial proxy for faltering civilian political legitimacy—that armies have since come to dread, with grace and resilience. The army's relationships to its civilian host society and its British foe, rather than being literary or allegorical, were intimate, material, complex, and fluid.

One way to retrieve Valley Forge from mythscape into social space is to begin on the ground, at the juncture of the Valley Creek and the Schuylkill River in 1777, and to survey the surrounding region in geographical, economic, and demographic terms. Even scholars who do not describe the camp as being in a remote wilderness sometimes imply that it was in a barren area that could barely have sustained a combined civilian and military population in a good year. This assumption confronts a generation of scholarship depicting southeastern Pennsylvania as an important granary of the Atlantic world. The forge for which the settlement was named was an outlier of a broad band of ironworks extending from the Hudson to the Potomac rivers.[11] The complex of furnaces, forges, and iron-processing facilities on the upper Schuylkill River was critical to the American war effort. The British threat to them affected Continental tactics in 1777, and the need to protect them contributed to the British ability to capture Philadelphia.[12]

Valley Creek flowed north toward the Schuylkill River between two hills, Mount Joy and Mount Misery, draining a long and fertile floodplain known locally as the Chester Valley. Charlestown and Tredyffrin townships, on whose border Valley Forge was situated—along with Merion Township in Philadelphia County—formed a fan-shaped apron of land sloping gently southeast from the Schuylkill. Below the high ridges along these streams, Chester County was divided into wheat-and-cattle farms averaging about 130 acres each and owned mostly by English and English-speaking Welsh Quakers. Some Germans, belonging to the Reformed or the Lutheran churches or to one of several "pietistic" sects, lived among the English population, but Germans were more common in northern Chester County. Chester had at least 30,000 residents in 1777, and its population density was almost 50 persons per square mile.[13]

Much of the county was covered by highly fertile limestone soils, and its gentle slopes encouraged commercial farming. A generation before the Revolution, middling farmers in southeastern Pennsylvania sold between a third and half of their crops yearly. By the early 1770s, Delaware Valley merchants were sending vast shipments of wheat, flour, and breadstuffs into the Atlantic market and dominating the cereals trade with the Mediterranean world and the British West Indies. Farm sizes in the county fell through the eighteenth century as the spread of population from Philadelphia drove up the price of land. By about 1760, area farms reached their minimum efficient size for commercial grain production, and local inheritance, migration, and other cultural practices began changing to conform to this reality.[14]

Owners of smaller tracts within a half day's travel to the city turned to the intensive production of perishable foodstuffs for urban dwellers. A zone extending twenty miles west from Philadelphia sustained a "truck" farming regime for the production of milk, cheese, butter, eggs, poultry, orchard and garden crops, and hay. Farm families brought wagonloads of goods to the city twice weekly for sale on regulated markets. When the Continental Army tried in early 1778 to disrupt traffic to these markets, it turned a long-established pillar of rural prosperity in the region into a deadly contest.[15] The region between Valley Forge and Philadelphia was also the center of a grist milling industry. By 1777, dozens of scattered "country" mills were grinding wheat for domestic consumption, while a smaller number of "merchant" mills produced finer flours for the Atlantic export market. When war descended on the locality, these sites were critical resources in the struggle between two armies and the civilian community for subsistence, and their preservation and control became matters of great military importance. Although livestock were raised on all Delaware Valley farms, their meat was mostly produced for local consumption. Some surpluses were sent to the Philadelphia market, but Pennsylvania was not as critical an exporter of beef or pork to the West Indies as it was for grain and bread. Women on farms in the Brandywine Valley and in the townships along the Delaware

Detail, "A Chorographical Map of the Country, round Philadelphia," 1778, [1780], Bernard Romans b5/01/05. Courtesy of the Maryland State Archives, Special Collections (Huntingfield Map Collection).

River made butter for sale in Philadelphia and for shipment to the Caribbean. Cattle were driven to the area from the Chesapeake and New England for fattening on the river meadows along the Delaware.[16]

In late colonial America, as land near the Atlantic coast began to fill up, land prices rose, and some young people and immigrants either moved west or into seaport cities. Each region was affected differently by this phenomenon, depending on its geographical conditions, cultural characteristics, and relation to the Atlantic economy. Interregional comparisons are difficult, but the Delaware Valley negotiated this transition in ways that sustained its reputation as "the best poor man's country in the world." In Chester County, between a third and a half of the adult male residents on the 1774 tax lists disappeared from their townships before 1785.[17] Southeastern Pennsylvania became "a distributing center [for migrants] to the south and west." But while population growth fell from 5 percent a year in the 1750s to less than 2 percent by the 1760s, population densities continued to rise, and "more persons stayed home or moved only within Pennsylvania than moved out of the province."[18] To remain at home exacted a real cost in terms of economic adjustment and social stratification. Smaller numbers of people controlled increasingly large shares of the area's total wealth.[19] Contrary to traditional assumptions about the virtual universality of the "yeoman freeholder," Pennsylvania was home to growing numbers of landless residents in the eighteenth century.[20] As early as 1753, about 28 percent of the farmers in Marple Township in Chester County rented their land. A leading student of this phenomenon describes tenancy as a "strategy" that let the heads of families productively "bank" temporarily unused tracts that were reserved for the inheritance of children, while giving men who could not otherwise afford productive land access to Atlantic markets.[21] The percentage of rural tenants in Chester actually began to decline between 1766 and 1774.[22]

As rural tenancy began to decay in southeastern Pennsylvania, another economic regime emerged to address both the land and labor crises. Landed farmers whose children were not old enough to work, but who had seasonal labor needs because of the commercial wheat economy, rented dwellings and small pieces of land to "cottagers"—landless workers who practiced a mix of agricultural and craft occupations. The latter negotiated annual leases that gave them modest housing and garden plots. The laborers agreed to perform specified amounts of agricultural day work, at the discretion of the owners, for customary wages. This system gave landowners a flexible labor force for the planting and harvest seasons, while allowing cottagers to work on their own plots and to trade their craft skills on the local labor market. The system emerged by the 1750s, and it facilitated the growth of farms early in the family life cycle while fueling the region's participation in the Atlantic grain trade. For cottagers, it held few hopes of land ownership, and it meant frequent renegotiation of leases or relocation. But it checked the migration of workers from the region, and it may have retarded the growth of a discontented rural proletariat and thus slowed the velocity of revolutionary mobilization in Pennsylvania.[23]

Upper Philadelphia County, across the Schuylkill River from Valley Forge, north to the Berks County line, was hillier and less fertile than Chester.

The county had about 55,000 residents in 1777, almost 20,000 of them liv-ing in the city of Philadelphia. Thousands more lived in crowded suburbs on the "neck" between the Delaware and Schuylkill rivers. Population in the upper parts of the county, above the Perkiomen Creek, was more German and less Quaker than that of rural Chester County. Below the Perkiomen, the urban and export markets drove the local economy, as it did in Chester.[24] A historian of Bucks County on the eve of the Revolution called it "one of the most English, most Quaker, most rural, and most politically stable counties in Pennsylvania." Its population was between 18,000 and 20,000 persons in 1777, living on farms averaging about the same 130 acres that prevailed in Chester. Quakers dominated the lower half of the county. Coryell's Ferry was the northern portal to the region, through which most of the Continental Army entered Pennsylvania in the summer of 1777 and by which it left the area a year later. In the upper townships there were many German and Dutch settlers and churches. Farmers practiced wheat-and-mixed-farming culture like that prevailing in Chester. Those near the city carried garden and dairy goods to town, and when the war came to Pennsylvania, they intensified their efforts to defend this practice. This effort threw the local population into often violent conflict with the radical state government.[25]

Western New Jersey had rich loamy soils carved by tributary creeks and wetlands along the Delaware River. Its farmers enjoyed modest self-sufficiency, sending surpluses of wheat, corn, and meat to urban markets. In 1772, the counties opposite Philadelphia (Burlington, Gloucester, and Salem) had fewer than the 30,000 residents living in Chester County alone, concentrated near the Delaware. The population was mostly Quaker in Burlington County, but it shaded from north to south into a mix of English, Swedish, and Dutch settlers.[26] Across the Delaware River from Salem County lay New Castle, one of the "Three Lower Counties on the Delaware." These counties shared a proprietary governor with Pennsylvania, but "Delaware" had its own legislature after 1701. Settled by a non-Quaker English popula-tion mixed with Swedes, Delaware was pulled into Philadelphia's economic orbit by 1776.[27]

The northern counties on Maryland's Eastern Shore were also part of the "seat of war." By 1770, local planters had all but ceased growing tobacco and become part of "a vast wheat belt . . . in the northern Chesapeake, stretching from Kent County on the Eastern Shore through Cecil at the head of the bay across Baltimore [to] Frederick County."[28] At the northernmost navigable point on the Chesapeake Bay lay the village of Head of Elk, which provided the southern portal through which the British army entered the Delaware Valley. One historian notes that the route between that town and Philadelphia "reminded more than one visitor of the public roads leading to London." In 1777, British officers desperately wanted to see the corridor in those terms, although one later recalled it as a gateway to "the strangest country in the world."[29]

Strange or not, we can return by this path to Pennsylvania for a few final observations about the region. The rapid growth of Philadelphia after 1681 suppressed the growth of intermediate urban places within thirty miles of that city, but between 1730 and 1765, town planting resumed in the interior. The creation of Lancaster in 1730 was followed by the rise of York and Bethlehem in 1741, Reading in 1748, Easton in 1752, and Allentown in 1762.[30] These towns ran in a line from northeast to southwest, at twenty- to thirty-mile intervals, anchoring a tier of interior counties. Berks and Northampton County farmers practiced mixed farming less intensively than those near Philadelphia. The population of each county was about 80 percent German, with many Moravian pacifists settled around Bethlehem. Berks had almost 23,000 inhabitants in 1779, while about 10,000 people lived in Northampton below the Blue Mountains. Reading housed a major Continental supply base. The Lehigh Valley was far enough from the active arena of combat to shelter civilian evacuees of Philadelphia in 1776, sick American troops in 1777–78, and even the Liberty Bell, but Whig control was precarious enough that the radical state government kept power in the area only by the use of force.[31]

Lancaster County was a larger version of Chester, with a population of 35,000 in 1779. It had more German and Scots-Irish settlers, visible pockets of Mennonites, and fewer English-speaking Quakers than Chester. It contained even more limestone soils than Chester and its agricultural surpluses were thus somewhat larger. Farms were slightly larger than in Chester while settlement densities were lower. About 30 percent of the adult male population was landless by the 1770s and tenancy was common.[32] York County was a newly settled frontier offering land to immigrants who found the eastern counties filling up. Its 1779 population was 50 percent German and 30 percent Scots-Irish, with smaller pockets of English settlers. Local soils were less rich than the best parts of Lancaster and Chester, and the three-day trip to Philadelphia limited access to the Atlantic marketplace and generally isolated the county.[33]

Having mapped the "mythscape" of Valley Forge, and the terrain on which the episode occurred, it remains to populate the stage with soldiers and to sketch the design of the book. Chapter 1 is set a year before the Continental Army came to Valley Forge, with the collapse of American military resistance in 1776 and the threatened British invasion of Pennsylvania. It puts civilians on the stage first and shows them interacting with soldiers long before any armies arrived in their midst. The visceral panic that seized the Philadelphia region as the American army retreated across New Jersey was not simply a "natural" reaction, how *any* civilians would have responded in similar circumstances. Rather it was an expression of the continued imprint of Quaker culture on a plural society in which the Friends had long since become a demographic minority in their own colony while continuing to hold power.

In chapter 2, I narrate the campaign for Pennsylvania in 1777. Contrary to common belief, it is doubtful that even a small core of veterans stayed in the field after the surprise American Christmas victories at Trenton and Princeton, to serve as the foundation on which a new army could be built. Rather than preventing the dissolution of the army, Trenton delayed that event and shifted it to central New Jersey, where Washington could manage it more discretely. While raw new recruits trickled toward Morristown in early 1777, he had to conduct a charade of militias to "keep up the appearance" of having an army. These new troops fought ably in 1777. They escaped from the jaws of destruction into which Washington's planning placed them at Brandywine in September and made the best of his overly ambitious strategy for them at Germantown a month later. After Germantown, their officers expected more battles in which they hoped to prevail. They were shocked in October when the army was immobilized by the collapse of its supply departments. That collapse was precipitated by organizational changes in those departments made by Congress in 1777, but many soldiers attributed it to the indifference of Pennsylvania civilians to their welfare. In November, the army's ranks swelled with troops coming south from the victorious campaign against General Burgoyne at Saratoga. Inevitable rivalries between New Englanders who dominated the northern regiments and the Middle Atlantic and southern soldiers of the main army over their relative battlefield performances were quickly aggravated by the Yankees' fears that they now faced starvation in a biblical land of Goshen.

The decision in late 1777 for the army to go to Valley Forge is reconstructed in chapter 3. That decision was a compromise between the army's military needs and the political interests of Continental and especially Pennsylvania leaders. It deflected the army from a deployment in interior towns, a plan that enjoyed support from a narrow majority of the Continental generals as well as Washington's approval. The compromise put the army into the position of serving as a proxy for the police functions of civil government. In exchange, Washington insisted on state material support during the winter and a willingness by Congress to consider extensive military reforms.

In chapter 4, I examine the Pennsylvania campaign through the eyes of civilians. War was a *learning* experience for civilians, and Pennsylvanians—as the heirs of Quaker culture—had more to learn about it than did most Americans. Civilian responses to the invasion of 1777 were less intense or panicked than they had been to the phantom invasion scare the year before. Having learned that flight was not an effective measure, civilians tried other survival strategies. While they moved prudently from the path of the contending armies, curiosity and resignation kept most of them from headlong flight. The absorption of military jargon into civilians' vocabularies suggests their accommodation to war. The understandings of military culture that they forged constituted a half-knowledge that led the populace into both imprudent and effective behaviors.

The Continental Army's journey from Whitemarsh to Valley Forge and its first weeks in the new camp are examined in chapter 5. This period produced one of two demonstrably grave supply crises during the winter. General Washington openly questioned whether his force could be kept from mutiny or dissolution. While not questioning the severity of the hardships that the American troops faced, in this chapter I treat the crisis in the context of the compromises discussed above. Washington was provoked to the rhetoric of "dissolution" by his fear that politicians would renege on the conditions that he understood to have been attached to the decision to keep the army in the field. He used a misunderstanding with the civilian leaders of Pennsylvania's government, the undeniable shortage of supplies to feed the army, and a limited expedition from the city by a large body of British troops to reassert his own understanding of that agreement.

The winter of 1777–78, divided into one- or two-month intervals, is the topic of chapters 6, 8, 9, and 10. Each chapter begins by considering conditions at Valley Forge, treating the military situation; relations between the Continental Congress and the army; and questions about army morale, health, and military readiness. Each chapter then swings around the army's "crescent-shaped" winter deployment, beginning with its southern anchor on the Delaware River at Wilmington. The Schuylkill River divided the

Pennsylvania countryside into two zones. The army took responsibility for the west side, where its immediate security interests lay. The state agreed to keep 1,000 militia troops on the east side of the river. This arrangement faltered almost from the start. The most valuable evidence of civil-military interactions appeared along this axis. An examination of the army's northern "anchor" on the Delaware at Trenton and the war in New Jersey, from Burlington County in the north to Salem in the south, also form part of each chapter.

The visit to Valley Forge by a committee of the Continental Congress in February 1778 to discuss with Washington fundamental military reforms is considered in chapter 7. The committee's charge from Congress was broad and nonspecific, reflecting divisions within that body over military policy at this difficult period. The worst supply crisis of the winter, in mid-February 1778, coincided with the committee's visit. It allowed a critical mass of civilian leaders to see how vulnerable the new army could be to logistical disruption, owing to its size, its organizational complexity, and its increasing mobility. This coincidence sustained Washington's effort to achieve organizational reforms. The approval of those reforms thwarted a competing reform plan that Congress had also contemplated, one that would have given much day-to-day military authority to Washington's rival Horatio Gates. This previously obscure bureaucratic struggle, rather than the celebrated "Conway Cabal," was the main source of intramural political conflict within the military establishment in 1777–78.

In chapter 11, I follow the Continental Army from Valley Forge into New Jersey in June 1778 in pursuit of the evacuating British army. The Battle of Monmouth on June 28 was not decisive enough to prove the transformative effects of Friedrich Steuben's work with the Continental army. While the broad utility of that work is undeniable, the army never did enough fighting in the north after June 1778 to test Steuben's efforts on the battlefield. Their effect, rather, was to give soldiers a deeper identification with and pride in their craft, and thus to make them better able to withstand the rigors of military routine rather than the terrors of the British bayonet charge. This was appropriate because Washington's use of the army in the north for the rest of the war was a loosely adapted version of its deployment in Pennsylvania.

Chapter 1

THE SEAT OF WAR

I n late August 1776, barely six weeks after the American colonies declared independence from British rule, the military resistance needed to enforce that declaration faltered badly. A sense of euphoria—described by one historian as a *rage militaire*—had followed creditable battlefield performances against British regulars by New England militias at Lexington and Concord in April 1775 and by the new Continental Army at Bunker Hill that June. This optimism was reinforced in 1776 by military and political events. The British army under General William Howe withdrew from Boston to Halifax, Nova Scotia. Along the Atlantic coast, one royal government after another fell under the control of advocates of independence. In June, a fierce struggle between moderate and radical factions in Pennsylvania ended in favor of the latter, adding the political seat of the Continental Congress to the independence column and enabling that body to pass the Declaration.[1] Now, with the rebellion officially acknowledged, the military momentum that had sustained it evaporated. On August 27, 1776, the Continental Army under George Washington was mauled by its British counterpart, led by General Howe, on the Heights of Brooklyn on western Long Island. The Americans escaped destruction only by withdrawing to Manhattan under cover of heavy fog. Defeats at Kip's Bay on the East River on September 15 and at White Plains in Westchester County on October 28 pushed the colonial troops across the Hudson River. On

November 16 almost three thousand rebel troops were captured at Fort Washington in northern Manhattan.[2]

Accompanying this shift of military momentum was a sense of despair among American radicals and questions about the strength of the political will underlying the Revolution. After securing his headquarters in New York City, Howe sent troops into New Jersey to push the Americans south. On November 30, he offered pardons to rebels who swore oaths of allegiance to the king and thousands of New Jerseyans flocked to sign. Washington struggled to organize an orderly retreat toward the Delaware River, behind which he hoped to find refuge for the winter. By December 8 the Redcoats were in Trenton. Continental enlistments began to expire, and the army's effective strength plummeted by almost 25 percent within two weeks.[3]

With the rebellion's military sword being driven back into its political midsection, many Whig civilian leaders looked to their own protection. On December 12 the Continental Congress adjourned, resolving to reassemble in Baltimore as soon as it safely could. The new state government of Pennsylvania did not flee, largely because it was too internally divided over political and military issues to act in a coherent manner. By December 18 Washington was camped in Bucks County, Pennsylvania, in a mood of deepening despair. Blaming his predicament on the "defection" of the Middle States of New York, New Jersey, Pennsylvania, and Delaware, and on the "accursed" Continental policy of "short [term] enlistments," he wrote to his brother John in Virginia that unless his fortunes improved quickly the "game" was "pretty near up." It was the darkest hour of war, the moment when revolutionary resistance came closest to disintegrating.[4]

The headlong flight of soldiers and legislators badly eroded public morale, but members of Pennsylvania's civilian community soon recognized the approach of danger and began preparing for it. As early as December 1 they foresaw the movement of the war into their midst and began both to flee from its consequences and to exploit its diverse opportunities. The fear struck earliest and hardest in Philadelphia but it rippled out into the countryside. In early December about two thousand Philadelphia militiamen marched into New Jersey to oppose the advance of the British troops. Many civilians fled to avoid a battle for the city or the consequences of its capture. Seven years later Elizabeth Farmer, a young mother and the wife of a physician from Kensington, recalled the evacuation with detailed dread. Her husband hired a wagon, and on December 12 she packed her daughter Sally and much of the household's furniture into it and fled toward Pottsgrove. The local roads were so thronged with refugees on the first night that she had to "beg hard to get room at an Inn."[5]

From his roadside house at Trappe, in Providence Township, twenty miles northwest of Philadelphia, Henry Melchior Muhlenberg watched this sorry procession throughout December. On the seventh, the elderly Lutheran minister wrote in his diary, "today many conveyances went by filled with household goods and people in flight from Philadelphia." Six days later he noted that wagons loaded with the panicked evacuees "went by all day." Muhlenberg, like Mrs. Farmer, had heard that when the British troops captured Pennsylvania they would be rewarded with "three days' liberty to plunder" the area's civilians. On the eighteenth he reported that "men, women, and children are still fleeing the city for the country daily under unusually hard conditions."[6] Muhlenberg and his neighbors could take no country comfort in the plight of their city cousins. They were being inundated by this wave of human displacement. The minister's sons and other relatives fled from Philadelphia to Trappe, and on December 8, his children begged him to "send down our stagecoach and three freight wagons in all possible haste." Muhlenberg scoured the neighborhood but found that "most wagons . . . had already left for Philadelphia . . . to fetch friends or relatives." In mid-December he assured his demoralized parishioners that their Christmas services would be held as usual, but he could not help adding to his diary the prayerful injunction "God willing."[7]

Not everyone fled the city, nor did all civilians' view the approach of Redcoats with dismay. Sarah Logan Fisher, a Quaker and the wife of a prominent Loyalist merchant, stayed in Philadelphia, where she charted daily reports of Howe's advance with apparent relish while meditating uneasily on the possible consequences of his arrival. On December 8 she heard that the British had reached Princeton and she "stepped over to see neighbor Evans, who was in great distress for fear [that Pennsylvania's authorities] should force her sons to camp." The twelfth and thirteenth brought accounts of British warships in the Delaware River and news of a citywide curfew, but Fisher reported with grim satisfaction that "not . . . one person . . . that I knew" had complied with orders from Continental authorities to turn out to help build defensive fortifications north of the city. On December 17 she heard that the British were moving down the New Jersey side of the Delaware River and that "4,000 English soldiers were at Moorestown." Fisher approvingly noted rumors that while the Redcoats had "plundered those that they looked upon as rebels, [they] were civil and kind to them that were friends to government." But John Hunt, a Quaker lay minister from Moorestown, reported that "there was a talk of their coming to press men to go to war and we were in some fear of being tryd."[8]

Muhlenberg, Fisher, and Hunt observed different aspects of the evolving regional crisis and they were plugged into different strands of the verbal information networks of the day, but they and others agreed that the ebb and flow of military fortunes, and especially the physical movement of the war itself, were affecting the perceptions, moods, and behaviors of individuals and groups. They all suggested that the approach of danger catalyzed responses along already existing political lines. Pennsylvanians reacted to the shifting military situation by dropping their prudent masks of neutrality and displaying openly the political affinities they already harbored.

In mid-December Fisher noted that the rumored appearance of British ships in the Delaware River had put "a great damp to the spirits of some of our violent people," a term she contemptuously applied to ardent Whigs. A day later Muhlenberg acknowledged that "it is easy to judge how far [Whigs'] courage must have fallen." While Fisher credited comforting accounts of politically discriminating requisitioning by British troops in New Jersey, Muhlenberg heard "descriptions . . . of how inhumanly, barbarically, and horribly the British, and especially the Hessian, armies were ravaging in Jersey, raping defenseless wives and daughters, robbing, plundering, abusing aged, feeble, helpless persons." The political result was that "the strong spirits among the Independents had now lost everything they had and the Dependents took off their masks and let themselves bee seen and heard." Many Philadelphians "busied themselves praising to the skies the extraordinary virtues and unusual courtesy of the British officers and their troops." But Muhlenberg concluded that "there were all too many living witnesses whose marks spoke all too loudly of the inhuman atrocities committed in Jersey."[9]

Friends of the king were emboldened by the ascendancy of Howe's army in New Jersey and its likely appearance in Pennsylvania, while Whigs who did not choose to flee prepared to fight. In Chester County, Benjamin Abraham, a farmer from East Nantmeal Township, told his fellow drinkers at the Sorrel Horse Tavern that he was "intirely disaffected with the measures taken by the Honorable Continental Congress . . . [to] obtain the Libertys of America." Abraham's hearers "resented" these sentiments. Whereas a few months earlier such taproom bravado might have earned him nothing more than communal contempt, in the crisis of late 1776 the offended parties demanded that a county militia officer "take the rascal to a place of justice."[10]

Suspected Loyalists who might previously have been quietly tolerated or shunned by their neighbors were punished severely. John Johnson, a "thriving Philadelphia coachmaker," had his house ransacked by "rebels" in December 1776. He fled to nearby Jenkintown but returned with the British troops nine months later. Johnson's political views were probably already formed and well known by his neighbors. Other people's ties may have been shaped by the ad hoc responses of their fellow citizens to the exigencies of war. In November 1776, Washington sent agents to remove all boats from the Delaware banks to prevent the enemy from pursuing his army into Pennsylvania. Peter Partier, from the "Durham Lands" of upper Bucks County, lost three vessels and later told royal officials that this and other "grievous persecutions and abuses" had driven him to seek British protection a month later.[11]

In a few cases the arrival of war in Pennsylvania threatened to provoke armed conflict between the advocates of submission to royal authority and those who sought independence. In mid-December the Northampton County Committee of Safety warned its provincial counterpart that the residents of one township needed ammunition "to defend themselves against a number of disaffected persons who have combined together and threatened the[ir] lives." Colonel Henry Geigy of Heidelberg Township wrote that he had mobilized forty patriots "to atacke them tories [by] march[ing] against them before day where they was together in one house." The friends of the Crown were put to flight, but Geigy feared that they would inevitably return for revenge.[12]

The Council of Safety was spared open civil war in Pennsylvania. Even before it received Geigy's letter, two bold strokes by the Continental Army reversed the momentum of the war and drove the center of the conflict back toward New York City. Realizing that expiring enlistments and plummeting morale would dissolve his army at year's end without a shot being fired, Washington launched a desperate counteroffensive on Christmas night. Striking across the Delaware River from his retreat in Bucks County, his force of 2,400 troops overwhelmed a detachment of Hessians that Howe had left in Trenton to anchor a string of garrisons stretching across New Jersey to the Delaware. Washington then deftly eluded the British reinforcements and defeated another group of Redcoats at Princeton on January 3, 1777. As a result of these American actions, Howe withdrew his garrisons to a few posts east of the Raritan River.[13]

The Trenton-Princeton campaign has achieved legendary status in American folk memory as an example of the differences between "professional"

British and "popular" American modes of armed conflict. But if it featured important elements of tactical improvisation, it was not an early example of guerrilla warfare. Washington was from his youth an admirer of British military culture. Both his preference for conventional tactics and his penchant for bold initiatives under circumstances of real desperation fell well within the parameters of that culture.[14] Nor did the British reversals at year's end spare Pennsylvania from occupation. By December 13 Howe had concluded that further field operations before the spring were inadvisable. Satisfied with having dispersed armed resistance to royal authority, he decided to secure his quarters in New York City, limiting winter operations in New Jersey to a kind of pacification program that combined punishment of avowed Whigs and rewards to Loyalists with attempts to convince hesitant rebels or neutralists to accept the king's peace. To acknowledge this fact is not to discount the effects of the Trenton campaign in easing the trauma to civilians in the Delaware Valley in early 1777. As the experience of the beleaguered Whigs of Heidelberg Township shows, the encouragement of armed loyalism by British activities just across the river might have transformed an uncomfortable but stable adversarial relationship between the factions into open intramural violence. Pushing the war away from the Delaware River at year's end retarded the pace of the revolutionary process in southeastern Pennsylvania.[15]

Even with his stunning success at Trenton, Washington was able to persuade only a few troops to extend their enlistments beyond December 31 while Congress struggled to mobilize a new army. After Princeton, he marched this remnant to camps near Morristown in north central New Jersey, where he tried to keep them intact. Without his achievement at Trenton the army would have dissolved on the spot. This would not have prevented its replacement the next spring or resulted in the immediate loss of Philadelphia. But if British operations had not been pushed to the north, the experience of Heidelberg's Whigs might have prefigured that of Pennsylvanians generally during the winter of 1777. As it was, the reversal was accompanied by the same kinds of political changes, operating in the opposite direction, that had followed the British successes of late summer and early autumn. On December 27 Sarah Fisher lamented that the news from Trenton had "greatly elated our Whigs, and as much depressed the Tories." But Henry Muhlenberg exulted that the event had "given the Philadelphians another reprieve." Fisher watched Hessian prisoners being marched into Philadelphia and wrote that a curious throng of citizens had turned out to see the spectacle of these once-dreaded mercenaries in confinement. Muhlenberg heard that those prisoners had expressed astonishment at their "fickle treatment" by previously friendly New Jerseyans after their humiliating defeat at Trenton.[16]

The removal of imminent danger did not result in the immediate restoration of militarily quiet circumstances in Pennsylvania. Elizabeth Farmer remained with her daughter in Pottsgrove for six weeks. She found the evacuation so traumatic that she later vowed not to leave Philadelphia again if the British ever came back, but rather to "stay with [her husband] and take our share of the troubles." Henry Muhlenberg ended the year meditating sorrowfully on his "old, weak" constitution, his sick wife, his many kinsfolk, and even the soul of his country. "When they are all together," he wrote, "there are twenty-two souls under [my] roof." He still dreaded attacks by "roving bands" of British soldiers, who he had heard were only "thirty English miles" away in New Jersey and ready to act like "Cossacks."[17]

Early in 1777 the center of military operations remained in northeastern New Jersey, between the British headquarters on Manhattan and the Continental Army's threadbare camps in the hills of Morris County. A sense of what Pennsylvania was spared by the events of Trenton and Princeton can be had by considering the rapid intensification of intracommunal violence in Bergen and Essex Counties in New Jersey, and in Orange County, New York, in late winter 1777. In that crescent of settlements between the Raritan River and the Hudson Highlands, a dangerous "neutral ground" was formed by the ability of troops from both sides to operate, but the failure of either army to control the area. Civilian partisans on both sides in the struggle, both formally organized and entirely self-directed, exploited this vacuum to create the kinds of internecine havoc that Henry Geigy had hinted at in his letter from Northampton County.[18]

Military enterprise brought the Delaware Valley only a brief respite from the direct experience of war. In 1777 William Howe again campaigned for Philadelphia, not this time by inadvertence but as a matter of policy based on his hope that Pennsylvanians would welcome his men more warmly than New Jerseyans had in 1776. Washington again crossed the Delaware River, not in desperate retreat but rather in the calculated belief that the revolutionary capital could and had to be defended. Neither of these assumptions was borne out by events. The result was another inconclusive campaign in what began to look to both sides like a protracted war of attrition rather than a discrete contest that either could win decisively. For the rebelling colonies, from a narrowly military standpoint, the darkest times were almost behind them as they entered 1777. For the British government, the best chance of crushing the rebellion through armed force was probably gone forever.[19]

But for the civilians of eastern Pennsylvania and adjacent parts of New Jersey, Maryland, and Delaware, the months from July 1777 to June 1778 marked their turn to play host to the war within the Revolution. Considered as processes, the Revolution and its war operated everywhere in America between 1775 and 1783. Even places where soldiers intruded only briefly or barely at all—such as Concord, Massachusetts, where the fighting began, or Connecticut, which endured only coastal raiding and scattered intramural clashes—confronted forces of change that were both irresistible and irreversible. But only a few localities found themselves at the epicenter or "seat" of the war itself.[20]

What that meant, both to the people of those places and for the evolution of the armed struggle, is the subject of this book. John Adams came to believe that the war had been "no part of the revolution [but] only an effect and consequence of it." The real revolution, he famously reminded Thomas Jefferson in 1815, "was in the minds of the people, and this was effected . . . before a drop of blood was shed at Lexington." In 1818 Adams offered the more familiar formula of "Minds *and Hearts* of the People." For Adams "minds and hearts" had eighteenth-century connotations, but recent generations, sensitized by violent anticolonial conflicts, have seen these as linked faculties, just as subject to the kinds of power growing from the barrel of a gun as to those flowing from the pages of a pamphlet. John Shy has argued that the war occupied a "central position" in the lives of the revolutionary generation, to which it needs to be restored in our own historical memory. The war, he observes, was a "process which entangled large numbers of people for a long period of time in experiences of remarkable intensity."[21]

Elizabeth Farmer, Sarah Fisher, and Henry Muhlenberg would probably have agreed with the professor rather than the president. The harrowing events of late 1776 touched each of them and began to change them as well. Ideas and their human consequences may have shaped the Revolution in Adams's New England, where the fighting was short but lifespans were long, and cultural memories of generations of resistance to English interference were longer still. Sentiment may have been determinative in Jefferson's Virginia, where Whiggish rhetoric had long been the coin of the realm of colonial politics, and where planters had learned to define "slavery" as a synonym for their own indebtedness rather than a name for human chattelhood. But in the Middle Atlantic region, many people responded as much to perceptions of self-interest as they did to allegiances based on higher ideals or ideologies. These perceptions were often defined behaviorally by people's earliest direct encounters with combatants on both sides of the conflict, but they also had deep roots in regional historical development.[22]

The extreme panic and societal dislocation described above were not natural reactions: how any rational people would have behaved when faced with the approach of two armies. Late colonial America was a matrix of regional societies, each with its own experience of organized violence, and their responses to armed force varied widely. In New England, a region that was widely viewed as the implacable vanguard of revolutionary sentiment, which had born the brunt of colonial wars since the seventeenth century and where the militia was a deeply rooted institution, armed townsmen actually *converged on* Boston in 1775 when royal forces threatened their communities. New Yorkers—who had hosted four "Independent Companies" of British troops since the 1690s and who lived at the business end of the Hudson River corridor between the English colonies and French Canada—moved out of the way of danger with relative deliberateness in late summer 1776 when 32,000 Redcoats landed on Staten Island. Southerners, who had been creating coastal and backcountry, and slaveholding and small farming, regions-within-their-region for two centuries, reacted to the arrival of small contending armies after 1779 by turning on each other in civil war.[23]

War is a learning process and Pennsylvanians, because of the historical circumstances of their colony's development, had more to learn about it than did most of their contemporaries. Their complex social, political, and cultural inheritances from the Quaker "Holy Experiment" left them peculiarly vulnerable in the 1770s to both war and revolution. The political institutions created by the Quakers in the colony's first generation kept the Anglo-French imperial wars that wracked the Atlantic world from 1690 until 1750 much farther removed from the densely settled areas of southeastern Pennsylvania than from most other colonies. Their peacekeeping talents helped the Quakers to hold political power and social authority long after they became a minority in their own colony as a result of the non-English immigration tides in the mid-eighteenth century. The issues of war and ethnic accommodation endowed the Quaker polity with unusual flexibility and resilience and taught its leaders to find pragmatic solutions to the complex problems their constituents faced as a condition for staying in office.[24]

But war was always an Achilles' heel for any Quaker regime. With each cycle of global imperial conflict, the political tasks facing the Quakers became harder, and the durability of the solutions they devised seemed more tenuous. The Friends did a better job of absorbing and politically accommodating the thousands of Germans who reached Pennsylvania between 1717 and the 1750s than they did with the Scots-Irish Presbyterians who arrived between 1725 and 1770. They portrayed themselves as the party of "peace" and nonconscription and as dependable bulwarks against the unjust ambitions of William Penn's sons, who they claimed had abandoned their father's religious ideals to become selfish landlords. Germans, fleeing destructive warfare in central Europe in the early eighteenth century and the capricious demands of landlords, responded to these messages. Their votes helped the Quakers to control the colony's powerful legislative branch. By 1745 the Philadelphia-based, and largely Anglican, merchant-gentry who supported the Penn interest, often did not even seriously contest Assembly elections.[25]

Many of the later-arriving Scots-Irish immigrants settled farther to the west, on less fertile lands, more exposed to Indian attacks but less accessible to markets, than did the Germans. Their experience as tenants in Ulster inclined them to respond favorably to the Quakers' antilandlord appeals, but they rejected that sect's pacifism and its "charity" toward the Indians. The Friends relegated these latecomers to a few large and underrepresented western counties and tried to ignore their political demands, while relying on their "bellicose" reputation as a buffer against any Native American threats that could not be absorbed by diplomatic methods.[26]

During the decades leading to the American Revolution, the remarkable adaptive capacities of Quaker politics failed to meet the challenges of this increasingly turbulent pluralism. The celebrated "surrender" of power in the Assembly by a minority of strict pacifist Quakers in 1756, in the face of domestic and imperial pressures for active defense efforts during the Seven Years' War, did not end the Friends' political hegemony. Benjamin Franklin forged a coalition between pragmatic Quakers and many non-Quakers that preserved the colony's "quakerized" political culture. This group made enough concessions to imperial defense needs to spare the colony from internal violence between eastern pacifists and frontier settlers and to avoid political sanctions from British authorities. But it shunned all except the most limited forms of military and fiscal involvement with the Crown and continued to keep the physical impacts of war itself at bay from the colony's populous eastern counties into the early 1760s.[27]

When political systems become brittle or unresponsive, they are liable to crack. Franklin's legerdemain in defusing the potential military liabilities of the Seven Years' War was the last piece of political magic left in the old Quaker system. During the imperial crisis after 1763, the newly denominated Assembly party and its proprietary enemies fought bitterly over their rival projects to monopolize political power but ignored the meaning to Pennsylvanians of pressing issues like taxation or Parliamentary power. In a gross political miscalculation, Franklin went to London in 1764 to persuade the Crown to replace Pennsylvania's proprietary government with direct royal rule just as Americans began rioting to protest the Stamp Act. His campaign for "royal government" risked the chartered arrangements that had let the Quakers rule the colony as a minority and speeded their demise by destroying a main plank of the platform by which the Friends had kept the allegiance of German immigrants and others. After 1765 they could not credibly claim to be the true heirs of the liberal legacy of William Penn, as symbolized by his Charter of 1701. With many Scots-Irish alienated by the peace issue and most Pennsylvanians feeling the pressure of a severe postwar depression, political power in the colony might have been dislodged without an imperial crisis.[28]

After 1767 Pennsylvania's political system buckled. A new generation of younger, poorer, and previously excluded leaders representing exposed frontier communities, urban laborers and shopkeepers, and such disenfranchised religious groups as German Lutherans and Scots-Irish Presbyterians stepped into the breach to lead resistance to royal authority in Pennsylvania.[29] The Revolution, when it came to the Quaker commonwealth, was more socially divisive, and sometimes more violent, than in other parts of America. Nowhere else in America did issues of local control become so inseparably entangled with newer questions of imperial authority. In older colonies to the north and south, established elites led their own constituents in cautious resistance to the Crown. When rebellion came, they were generally able to keep it moderate.[30] In Pennsylvania, the rival elite factions, Quaker and Proprietary, ignored the imperial crisis for as long as they could. In 1776, they were pushed aside by resentful outsiders. Members of the victorious group—sometimes called the "Presbyterian party"—worked to build a new world of wider political opportunity for all men (but not of redistributed wealth), even as they shouldered the burdens of an intercolonial war effort against the British empire.[31]

These circumstances shaped the social and political dynamics of war when it reached Pennsylvania. The transition from the fading provincial regime of Quakers and Proprietary officers to the successor revolutionary government between 1774 and 1776 was tumultuous. Most Quakers were politically disenfranchised under the incoming regime by their refusal to swear the oaths of allegiance that the radicals demanded. Despite their villainized reputation in Whig propaganda, most Quakers were not active Loyalists. Many tried to ride out the storm, hoping for the return of peace and autonomy. Most of the much smaller group of Proprietary allies of the Penns, however, either left the state to join the British side or went underground.[32]

Although the resulting rump of political activists who dominated Pennsylvania's revolutionary government cannot be described as exclusively, or even predominantly, "Presbyterian," that denomination—comprising mainly the state's Scots-Irish frontier settlers and many city-based middling shopkeepers, artisans, and "mechanics"—united in resistance to the Crown more unreservedly than any other group in the commonwealth. Other ethnic and religious communities divided more evenly. German sectarian groups—Mennonites, Moravians, and a host of smaller societies—followed the lead of their original political mentors in the Quaker community into an alienated, apathetic, or pacifist detachment from the strife. The Lutheran and Reformed "church" Germans, on the other hand, leaned heavily toward independence.[33]

Historical clichés that portray Americans as dividing along class lines in their revolutionary allegiance have little serious explanatory power for Pennsylvania. Postwar Loyalist claims for compensation from the Crown for losses sustained make clear that George III had the support of carpenters and farm laborers as well as lawyers, clergy, and merchants. But in Philadelphia, a majority in the poor laboring and artisan communities, whose material security had declined steadily since 1750, used the crisis as a vehicle to assert more control over their fortunes. When these "mechanics" joined backcountry farmers, under the brokerage of the city's radical committees, the political grip of the Quaker-Proprietary alliance was shattered. Pennsylvania's new government supported independence, and the Revolution became official.[34]

Any government would have had its hands full organizing political machinery to replace the system that had been destroyed by the overthrow of the Quaker-Proprietary regime, even if the war were not imminent. Bringing stability to a superheated polity would have been difficult even if the radicals were not working at close quarters with powerful members of the national legislature. Some delegates to the Congress, including John and Samuel Adams of Massachusetts, encouraged or helped the radicals to overthrow the old Pennsylvania provincial government, but only because they needed the state's vote for independence. These men were far less radical than their local protégés, and the Congress hardly wanted an ongoing social revolution in the heart of its host city.[35]

The new state government had to rebuild its constitutional base while integrating diverse constituent groups, suppressing internal foes, maintaining surveillance over neutralists, and recruiting Continental soldiers from a society that had never fielded a permanent militia. It is natural to emphasize the innovative responses that the radicals made in meeting these challenges, but equally important is the weight of tradition. The political institutions that the Pennsylvania radicals forged were surprisingly similar, structurally at least, to the ones that they destroyed. Meeting in a state constitutional convention in July 1776, they created a strong, annually elected, unicameral legislature like the one the Quakers had wrested from William Penn in 1701. They yoked that Assembly to a plural executive branch, the Supreme Executive Council, that was, like its colonial predecessor, notable largely for its inability to dominate the legislature. Much of the political work of government was done by constitutionally ordained special committees or councils, including a Council of Safety that remained in session when the Assembly adjourned.[36]

Probably the most important, and certainly the most ironic, political inheritance of the radicals from Quaker Pennsylvania was the expectation by most members of the polity that government should protect its constituents from war. It was understood that in a revolutionary situation armies could not be kept out of the state, as the Quakers had routinely managed to do from the 1690s into the 1750s. But the new government was expected, as the Friends had done by an artful mixture of political surrender and reformation during the Seven Years' War, to provide a buffer against war's effects. Failure to do so would bring the legitimacy of any Whig regime into question or even precipitate its collapse. The panicked evacuation of Philadelphia in December 1776 showed how real a threat this fear was to Pennsylvanians. The need to protect civilians from war drove the complex negotiations between political and military leaders that brought the Continental Army to Valley Forge the following winter.

If war was a learning experience, the tumultuous weeks of late 1776 had taught many Pennsylvanians their first lessons: it is easier to flee combat than to hide from it; running away from one peril can lead you into the path of another; the approach of armies may not portend their immediate arrival. On December 11, 1777, just a year after she fled to Pottsgrove, Elizabeth Farmer prepared to execute her resolve to stay at home and take her "share of the troubles." Farmer was already viewing current events through the eyes of a person hardened by the dizzying fluctuations of wartime fortune. Although she "wish[ed] we had peace restored," she and her family were "in good health, Thank God for it." Then Farmer placed their predicament into perspective with a piece of army jargon whose very presence in her vocabulary bespoke the recent entanglement of civil and military phenomena, by suggesting how closely citizens were attending to the ways and words of their occupiers. The Farmers were, she reflected, "as easy as persons can be who live where the Seat of War is."[37] Their brush with military danger late in 1776 thus may have served for many Pennsylvanians as a kind of inoculation, summoning their worst fears about "Cossacks," then allowing them to stare them down. In the anxious months of early 1777, many of them undoubtedly made the same silent vows that only Elizabeth Farmer pronounced. When two armies returned to Pennsylvania later that summer, the state's civilians tried bravely to reprise their panic of 1776, but then they stopped—as if in embarrassment—and began to make their peace with war.

War was also a learning process for citizen-soldiers. Both armies moved constantly from one provincial context to another in an unhomogenized and imperfectly confederated society. For the rebels, it seemed as if their demographic composition changed as rapidly as they moved. The Continental Army that returned to Pennsylvania in July 1777 was a different organism from the one that had left there seven months before. It was composed mainly of new members serving under different terms and conditions, and quite possibly recruited from different social sources. Civilians perceived these changes, and this may have shaped their response to the troops they found once again in their midst. Soldiers spent most of the following year trying to comprehend, and learning how to navigate, social circumstances that few, except for the Middle Colonists among them, had ever encountered.

As for Washington and his officers, their brief sojourn south of the Delaware River in late 1776 alerted them that they would be operating in a peculiarly volatile environment if they ever returned to the state. In that year Continental authorities had fled the scene, and Pennsylvania's government was all but paralyzed. The radical Whig party that deposed the provincial regime in June 1776 quickly split into new "radical" and "moderate" factions over the state constitution, and these groups were struggling for power.[38] This was not a place where any but the most idiosyncratic of soldiers would have chosen to campaign. The Americans had such a general in Charles Lee, who saw in the American social structure, especially the backcountry hearth of Pennsylvania's radicals, sources of political strength that might prove invulnerable to conventional military power.[39]

Washington was made of different social, political, and military stuff. Although he campaigned wherever the military logic of his situation or the orders of his civil superiors took him, he tried to do so by methods as conventional as possible. But he had his own learning curve. At the start of his tenure as commander-in-chief in 1775, Washington arrived in Cambridge and castigated New Englanders as "an exceeding dirty and nasty people." He sidestepped the political consequences of this gaffe by diversifying the army, building a transregional chain-of-command between himself and the privates on the front lines, moving the army out of New England as quickly as possible, and learning to restrain his opinions on such politically sensitive matters.[40]

Washington was no more solicitous about Middle Atlantic warriors in 1776 than he had been about Yankees the year before. If he was no Charles Lee when it came to adapting military strategy to the native "genius" of his human materials, however, he had at least begun to appreciate the concept. He continued building an army that was "continental" both in the geographical range of its demographic sources and in the European inspiration for its operations. But he now paid at least intermittent attention to the fit between strategy and the politics of congressional and state relations, and between tactics and the social character of the communities he was operating in. This is illustrated by the way the 1777 campaign ended, with the Continental regiments awkwardly camped at Valley Forge. As the decision to move the army to that place shows, Washington had become capable of overriding both the technical preferences of his general staff and his own military instincts to serve broader revolutionary purposes that his highly political imagination compelled him to acknowledge.

Chapter 2

THE CAMPAIGN FOR PENNSYLVANIA

Before there was a new campaign for Pennsylvania, the Continental Army had to be completely rebuilt. The unexpected reversal of military fortunes effected at Trenton and Princeton enabled Washington to move his expiring army of 1776 from southeastern Pennsylvania into northern New Jersey, but it did not give him a solid foundation on which to build or train its successor. Far from preventing the dissolution of the Continental Army, as Revolutionary War legend suggests, the American victories in New Jersey merely delayed and shifted that event from one place to another.

Two images have bracketed and shaped our understanding of what Washington called his "new" army of 1777. The first depicts a small core of battle-tested veterans staying in camp over the winter to serve as badly needed sinews of experience, morale, and leadership for the new recruits. The second shows a twice-beaten band of "ragged Continentals" straggling into Valley Forge. Such epithets as "a defeated, dispirited and tattered array," a "rabble of uncertain, lousy, sick, bleeding men," or even a "half-starved mob" of "trappers and bookkeepers . . . farmers and fishermen," convey a sense of December 1777 as the Revolution's "darkest hour," and of Valley Forge as the war's miraculous "turning point," and thus frame the story of the coming winter.[1]

These images interact and resonate in complex ways both in real and in historiographical time. They are not mutually exclusive, but the truth of one implies the improbability of the other. A completely new army was likelier to meet a calamitous end than a carefully rebuilt one, but a saving remnant of hardy veterans might still be overwhelmed by more proficient foes. Any realistic account of the 1777 campaign, and of the events that followed it, should come to terms with these images and their implications, and if possible should try to sort them out.[2]

It seems reasonable that their New Year's triumphs might have inspired many soldiers to reenlist at Morristown, but the army's monthly strength reports suggest otherwise. Washington nominally commanded 11,000 men on the eve of Trenton (6,100 of them "present fit for duty"), but only about 2,400 took part in the raid on that town. No more than 1,400 soldiers stayed on long enough to fight at Princeton on January 3, and only a minority of those reached the new camps in Morris County. Few of those veterans, in turn, remained long enough into the new year to greet the enlistees who were being recruited to replace them. Washington spoke of having 800 New England Continentals in late January plus a "handful" of Virginians. In early March he estimated his corps of regulars at between 500 and 981 men.[3]

This should not surprise us. Americans had always raised new armies each spring for use in colonial wars. The reluctance of men to leave their farms or families for long periods and deep English reservations about dangers to liberty, property, and public safety from permanent or "standing armies" dictated resort to this familiar, albeit inefficient, procedure. New Englanders, who formed the foundation of the Continental Army in 1775 and still comprised its core a year later, were especially sensitive to this balance between liberty, interest, and safety. Sergeant Joseph White of Massachusetts, a member of the artillery corps, vividly described the pressures placed on the 1776 veterans to stay on at Morristown at least until their replacements could "learn how to handle the cannon." After General Henry Knox pleaded "in a pathetic manner" for his men to "stay two months longer," White bowed to his captain's wishes and even used his influence to detain some of his men, but he "engaged" only until March 1.[4]

From the evidence of the official record, White was not alone in departing that spring. In April Washington complained that his force had been "reduced to a mere handful of men," indeed, "reduced to a mere *nothing*." We should consider taking the latter phrase literally. His pressing warnings to Congress about the impact of manpower constraints on his ability to function effectively during 1776 finally moved that body to reluctantly authorize new terms of Continental enlistment for "three years or [during] the war."[5] For one more winter, however, like it or not and Trenton or no Trenton, the army had to be rebuilt virtually from scratch. We cannot discount the possibility that some 1776 veterans took advantage of the post-Trenton hiatus, or of lucrative recruiting bonuses, to retire temporarily to their homes before rejoining their units, but the core or cadre image seems overdrawn as a description of the force that took the field in June 1777.[6]

If anything, Washington had to publicly understate, not exaggerate, the thinness of his ranks. He desperately needed to let to Congress know his exasperation at the failure of the new levees to reach camp, but any letters he wrote might end up on William Howe's desk in New York City. He thus tried indirectly to alert public authorities to the real gravity of his position.[7] Less to protect his dwindling body of veterans than to preserve his camps as viable destinations for their laggard replacements, he borrowed militia and used them as substitutes for regular troops. He had no intention of entering the campaign with these troops, whose performance he had reviled through-out the fall. Instead, he rotated them around the Morristown area to "keep up [the] appearances" of an army and to "make small numbers appear large," to deceive the enemy while awaiting new recruits.[8] He succeeded in the lat-ter objective; some British intelligence estimates credited him with having more than 5,000 regular troops, but it was a lonely and desperate game. In late January Washington complained to the president of Congress that he could "not get a man [i.e., a recruit] to come near me." He could hardly believe that Howe did not see through his charade and launch an assault, and the contempt that he plainly conceived for Howe for this carelessness may explain his occasional tactical recklessness later in 1777.[9]

Finally in late April, just as the last veteran holdovers fell away, new enlistees began streaming into camp. By May 3 Washington had 2,600 reg-ular troops on hand, and three weeks later just over 10,000 men. He moved his headquarters from Morristown south to Bound Brook, where he tried frantically to train—or at least to discipline—these novices to military life for a campaign that he expected to begin any day.[10] The creditable perform-ance and steady demeanor of the army in that campaign thus seems even more remarkable in light of how literally new it was in May. The force that returned to Pennsylvania in August of 1777 was substantially less continu-ous with its predecessor but considerably better able to execute complex mil-itary operations than has been appreciated.

This circumstance cannot have been the result of formal training, which had barely begun during the seven or eight weeks they were afforded that spring by Howe's unexpected slowness in taking the field. Washington recognized the need for more systematic procedures, and he strongly condemned the "diversity of modes of training" he had observed throughout the army since 1775. He was also unwilling to lose even the tiny incremental benefits that recruits might derive from partial instruction just because a new campaign would begin soon. He repeatedly ordered his officers to exercise their men daily in the "manual and evolutions." Washington may have inadvertently disclosed more than he understood about this question in late May 1777 when he begged General William Smallwood to "improve all the leizure time your Brigade may have in manoeuvering and *teaching the men the use of their legs*." He almost certainly meant the fancy footwork required for close order drills, but Washington also described the one benefit that even green soldiers might gain from repetitive field exercise.[11]

The army of early 1777 was constantly in motion. This reflected Washington's desire to harass and contest the British troops in their New Jersey enclave near the mouth of the Raritan River, but it also derived from certain underlying ecological realities. There were not enough healthy troops around Morristown in January or February to build new camps large enough for the expected reinforcements. When the buildup of the army occurred all at once in early May, the existing sites could not hold 10,000 men. Washington wanted to give each brigade at least some training and discipline, so he continued the practice of rotating units in and out of the central camps near Morristown.[12]

It is hard to know how many miles a typical recruit marched between early May and late June, or how many more he had covered just to reach the army in New Jersey. Those numbers were substantial, however, and few roads in north central New Jersey were straight or level. Whether knowingly or not, Smallwood and his colleagues taught their men "the use of their legs," and the effects of this curriculum were considerable. Little is known about stamina in early modern war, but this mobility at least conditioned the tenderfeet, and its controlled adversity may have instilled high levels of group cohesion into new units. If the army could not be formally reorganized yet along the European lines that Washington had always envisioned, the logistical requirements for giving each of its units some drilling may have caused him inadvertently to invent a form of "basic" training that sustained it through its baptismal campaign while laying useful foundations for the later reformations of Friedrich Steuben.

Another factor that may help to explain the new army's cohesion, resiliency, and resourcefulness under camp and battlefield adversities during

1777 is its social composition. This is a complex and delicate subject because it requires the synthesis of fragmentary research and even more scattered primary evidence, and the dangers of interpretive caricature are high. Scholars have shown that after the demise of the *rage militaire* of 1775–76, popular willingness to face the British army on the battlefield declined rapidly, and it became increasingly necessary to use coercive means, supplemented by economic incentives rather than by patriotic or political appeals, to raise troops. A corollary inference has often been that this shift produced a significant decline in the socioeconomic status of the Continental force.[13]

Sketchy evidence from Morristown supports this hypothesis. Civilian neighbors of the regimental camps thought they discerned a somewhat rough and gamy "tang" emanating from those sites as the drilling of the troops began in the spring. Washington speculated in the middle of May that the incentives offered by Continental recruiting agents might now be "recommend[ing] the service to a lower Class of People." The generation preceding the war experienced increased socioeconomic stratification, especially in commercial port towns and their intensively developed agricultural hinterlands. Land prices rose, many independent crafts livelihoods stagnated, institutionalized "welfare" practices were established, and semipermanent populations of underemployed urban laborers and rural "strolling poor" families appeared in a society that otherwise seemed to be enjoying rising per capita material living standards.[14]

These were the social materials both of the political discontent that fueled revolutionary movements, especially in developed commercial regions like the Delaware Valley, and of recruiters' appeals to men whose economic security might improve in uniform. Many historians have tried to connect these phenomena, but definitive proof for such links will require detailed investigations of the social character of army cohorts on a comparative annual basis. To date, most such studies have been more conceptually insightful than comprehensive, and the precise chronological trajectory of social change in the army has not been mapped closely.[15]

How would the declining socioeconomic status of its members have affected an army's ability to survive ordeals that it had not been trained to encounter? Members of the "lower sort" may have brought different cultural perspectives to the business of using organized force to achieve political objectives than did their social "betters." Men whose lives featured economic and demographic instability or social marginality may have held more casual views about the sustained or purposive uses of violence than did members of the gentry elite or the emerging middling classes. Young men with fewer stable familial ties in civilian life may have been more willing to risk danger than the yeoman farmers who answered the Lexington Alarm. They were perhaps less likely to buckle when flanked and battered by disciplined columns of British infantry at Brandywine in September 1777 than their predecessors had been at Long Island the year earlier, or more easily induced to march all night in adverse weather against enemy strongholds like Germantown than were the veterans of the expedition to Trenton.[16]

We can also wonder if the *rage militaire* was not a cyclical *mentalité* rather than a one-shot psychological response and ask whether it might have animated different groups in a revolutionary society successively. If recruits reaching Morristown in May 1777 saw that moment as a discrete military "changing of the guard," by which a "lower sort" took up the mantle of military defenders of the Revolution from recently departed cohorts of "sunshine patriots," a class-based second wave *rage militaire* might have resulted. Such a mindset could have carried untrained troops through a punishing campaign and into the winter, rendering them into a formidable material for officers like Friedrich Steuben to polish and shine.

Much of this analysis is conjectural. We do not know indisputably whether the army of 1777 really wore a markedly different social face from that of its predecessor, much less how this might have affected its military performance. But the undeniably late assembly of the new army does challenge our understanding of the campaign that led to Valley Forge. It makes more plausible the classic images of a defeated rabble arriving there, ones that have dominated most popular accounts. Plausible or not, the narrative of the campaign that follows does not sustain such imagery. Morristown in early 1777, and not Valley Forge the next winter, was the real birthplace of a permanent Continental Army and the crucible of its prowess for the rest of the war. Valley Forge will have to establish other claims to historical significance.[17]

In July 1777 war veered back toward the Delaware Valley. After trying unsuccessfully in June to draw Washington into a decisive battle in New Jersey, General Howe loaded 14,000 troops onto transport vessels in New York harbor, setting sail on July 23. Howe left General Henry Clinton in command at New York with almost 7,000 troops, 3,000 of whom, however, were newly trained Provincials. The British fleet was sighted in the mouth of the Delaware Bay on July 29 and off the Virginia coast two weeks later. By August 22 intelligence reports placed it in the lower Chesapeake Bay. The

maneuvers of the Continental Army in response to these reports were similarly erratic. During late July, Washington marched his 10,000 troops back
and forth across New Jersey, trying to protect both the Hudson River corridor between Canada and New York and the seat of the Continental Congress
at Philadelphia.[18] On July 30 he committed the army to Pennsylvania by
crossing the Delaware River at Coryell's Ferry. By August 23 he concluded
that the British would land in the upper Chesapeake and attack Philadelphia, and he marched the army through the city to bolster civilian morale.
On the twenty-fifth, as the American troops reached Wilmington, Delaware,
the British left their ships eighteen miles away at Head of Elk, Maryland.[19]

Although these maneuvers may seem confused, they reflected concerted strategic priorities on both sides. Howe was struggling to execute a
complex campaign plan for the 1777 campaign, developed in concert with
ministerial officials in London the winter before. Washington was content to
let Howe take the initiative, but he considered it imperative that Congress
not be uprooted for the second time in eight months. For the British, the
main objective in 1777 was to sever the rebellion along the Hudson River
corridor, isolating New England from the rest of the continent. One British
army, under General John Burgoyne, would drive south during the summer
from Montreal, along Lakes Champlain and George, to Albany and then
down the Hudson Valley. Howe's force would operate from New York City
in some vaguely specified manner, partly in support of Burgoyne. He might
force his way up the Hudson, easing Burgoyne's way south. Or by campaigning elsewhere in the Middle Atlantic region, he would draw Continental
reinforcements away from that river. Secondary objectives were to dislodge
the Continental Congress from Philadelphia, to occupy the Middle Atlantic
states, and to gain material and moral assistance from the supposedly more
loyal inhabitants of the region. If Washington could be lured into risking his
army in a decisive battle in opposition to these goals, British strategists
expected to prevail.[20]

The exact mix between these strategic elements varied among parties
on the British side. Howe gave particular emphasis to the need to rout Congress, to succor loyal subjects in the Middle States, and to bring Washington
to a decisive battle. His proposals during late 1776 acknowledged some general need to aid Burgoyne, but when the Ministry denied his request for
15,000 reinforcements, he turned his attention to the south. On July 16,
after receiving reports from Burgoyne about his satisfactory progress toward
Albany, Howe decided to invade Pennsylvania by sea. Adverse weather and

Howe's doubts about his ability to navigate safely up the Delaware River to Philadelphia accounted for the slow progress of his fleet.[21]

After leaving their ships on August 25, the British troops paused to recover from the rigors of five weeks at sea while their scouts probed the local terrain. On the twenty-seventh they began marching cautiously toward Philadelphia. The armies moved north and then northwest into Pennsylvania, with the Continental forces staying between the city and the British. September 10 found them a short distance apart, with the Americans east of the Brandywine Creek at Chads Ford in Chester County, and the British in the hilly country west of that stream. Major General Nathanael Greene of Rhode Island calmly predicted to his wife that day that a clash would occur within a few days, and he described the American forces as being ready for action.[22]

Washington's arrangement of the army was based on his belief that Brandywine Creek was passable only at three fords, to which Chester County's road network connected. He massed his force at those places, extending six miles above Chads Ford to the forks of the Brandywine. On September 11, Howe left 5,000 troops at Chads Ford under the Hessian general Wilhelm von Knyphausen to feign a direct assault across the Brandywine. Howe and Lieutenant General Charles Cornwallis marched the rest of the army above the forks and found unguarded fords across both branches. The Americans skirmished with Knyphausen's force while Washington, girding for a frontal assault, ignored reports from military personnel and local civilians of Redcoats marching north. By three that afternoon Howe's force of almost 9,000 troops was poised on the right flank the American line. Having marched eighteen miles since dawn, they lost some time opening the attack. This delay allowed Major General John Sullivan of Rhode Island, who commanded the division on the right, to reorganize his men and let Washington reinforce Sullivan's outnumbered troops. The respite turned a likely rout into a desperately improvised and sharply contested American retreat.[23]

The outflanked Americans regrouped much more adeptly under hot fire than they had at Long Island the year before. Watching them desperately wheeling about to receive the assault, Lord Cornwallis reportedly observed to Howe that "the damn rebels form well," but this was only relative and grudging praise. American communications disintegrated and Continental units were repositioned quickly, using any available elements of terrain to form strong points. Washington rushed two divisions, under Major Generals

Lord Stirling and Adam Stephen, to the Birmingham Friends Meeting House, where they supported Sullivan's stricken troops and scrambled to block the British advance. When this position crumbled after two hours of intense fighting, Greene arrived with a third division to form a line in the woods behind the meetinghouse. They allowed the broken units of Sullivan, Stirling, and Stephen to fall back and conducted an impressive and professional retreat toward the village of Dilworth.[24]

Nightfall and the exhaustion of British troops kept Howe from extracting a decisive victory from the nearly fatal errors in the American plan. The Continentals suffered casualties of about 300 killed, 300 wounded, and 400 prisoners of war. British losses were estimated at 90 killed and 448 wounded.[25] The Americans were mauled, but they showed an impressive ability to exchange sustained fire with the best trained troops on earth. One student of the campaign has described the weeks after Brandywine as "a period of manoeuvring in which the Americans showed a resilience in defeat which was astonishing in an army of amateurs," and "a power of marching which put the British and Hessians to shame." The beaten army limped away to Chester on the Delaware River and on September 12 camped at the Falls of Schuylkill above Philadelphia. The victors buried their dead and rested on the battlefield for more than a day before pursuing the retreating Americans.[26]

The weeks after Brandywine were a contest of resiliency and marching power but also a clash of wits and conflicting purposes. Howe had not committed himself irrevocably to either seizing Philadelphia or else destroying rebel supply bases in the upper Schuylkill Valley. On September 14 the Continental Army crossed the Schuylkill and marched west to be better positioned to defend either place. A day later the British moved north toward fords on the Schuylkill that would let them threaten both targets. Early on the sixteenth their paths crossed in Chester County. Their resulting skirmish was beginning to turn decisively against the Americans when it was aborted by a torrential storm that flooded the battlefield and soaked the ammunition of both sides. Continental troops splashed west through flooded streams to Warwick and Reading Furnaces, where they replaced their ruined munitions. The British continued north to the Schuylkill River, sending a detachment to Valley Forge, at the junction of Valley Creek and the Schuylkill, to seize supplies and to burn the ironworks for which that settlement was named.

On September 18 Congress abandoned Philadelphia, resolving to meet wherever and whenever it safely could. The divided and beleaguered state government fled to Lancaster, after arresting and exiling to Virginia a group of Philadelphia Quaker merchants who symbolized domestic opposition to the Revolution. On the twentieth, 5,000 Redcoats attacked 1,500 American troops that Washington had left at Paoli under Pennsylvania brigadier general Anthony Wayne to observe the British camp. Surprising Wayne's sleeping men, the raiders ravaged them with bayonets, inflicting heavy casualties.[27] With this triumph, Howe's path to Philadelphia was clear. The occupation was effected on September 25, just a month after the British landed in Maryland, when Howe left 9,000 troops at Germantown and marched with 5,000 men into the city itself.[28]

The capture of Philadelphia ironically inverted the equilibrium of the campaign, giving Washington some measure of the initiative and Howe a difficult choice of responses. The British had lived from the countryside after their fleet left the Chesapeake in August. But now, with thousands of civilians to govern and 14,000 hungry troops to feed, Howe had to regain contact with his fleet, which had sailed around into Delaware Bay. Rebel forces blocked the Delaware River by holding fortified points at Billingsport in New Jersey, and at Red Bank and Fort Mifflin, facing each other across the river just below the city. Lines of floating log and iron obstructions called *chevaux de frise* were placed in the river to complete the blockade.[29] Howe needed to clear these barriers to open the river, but he could not afford to ignore a hostile army camped twenty miles north of his lines. Washington hoped to sustain the blockade by reinforcing the troops defending the forts and by threatening the city from above. On September 28, after Washington received preliminary news that John Burgoyne's advance toward Albany had been halted near Saratoga, his generals advised moving the army toward Philadelphia to "take advantage of any favorable opportunity that may offer for making an Attack." The next day the troops began marching slowly toward Germantown. On September 30 Howe detached two regiments to attack the American fortifications at Billingsport.[30]

At dusk on October 3, American troops paraded for the clash they had expected since Brandywine. Dividing into columns, they began their march along four country highways that converged in the village of Germantown. Washington planned a surprise attack at dawn, with American troops falling in waves on the enemy across a broad line. He hoped that if the British forces could be driven back, they would be unable to recover in time to stem an attack coming from several directions at once.[31] The assumption was a good one but its execution was flawed. The battle began at dawn in dense fog. The

British were shocked to be assaulted in their camp, and they fell back under heavy fire. But the Pennsylvania, New Jersey, and Maryland militia units on the flanks of the attack lost their way. Although unsupported on both sides, the Continental Army seemed to be on its way to routing the British forces. The attack unraveled when its two main columns, approaching along converging roads, failed to merge smoothly. Instead, one wing fell in behind the other in thick fog and smoke. With one division under friendly fire from behind, confusion spread through the ranks. As their ammunition ran out, many Americans hesitated and began to retreat. The delay, compounded by Washington's ill-advised effort to rout some British troops who had taken shelter in the stone mansion of Pennsylvania's chief justice, Benjamin Chew, allowed Howe's reinforcements racing from Philadelphia to counterattack. The discouraged Continental troops finally came to a halt late in the day at Pawlins Mill on the Perkiomen Creek, twenty miles northwest of Philadelphia.[32]

Germantown is sometimes popularly recalled as a second Continental failure in 1777, a defeat that offset American gains from the astonishing surrender by John Burgoyne to Horatio Gates at Saratoga, New York, on October 17. This perception frames the iconic image of a twice-beaten and badly dispirited American rabble-in-arms limping into Valley Forge in late December to begin its desperate winter of heroic endurance. It does not, however, accord with the virtually unanimous perception by American participants in that event. American accounts of Germantown reflected frustration for an important opportunity barely missed, but even the least sanguine analyses focused on the rebel army having "fled from victory." These accounts began shortly after the army stopped retreating and continued for a month. They reflect a surprising uniformity of perception among their authors. Soldiers' exposure to what one historian has called the "face of battle" gave them insights into the event that were unavailable to other close observers. These understandings formed the basis for an important collective expectation of what the future held for the army.[33]

Brigadier General George Weedon of Virginia acknowledged that "we got disappointed," but he also reported that the army had "no Objections to another tryal which must take place soon." Lord Stirling of New Jersey exulted that "this affair will Convince the World that we Can out General our Enemy, that we dare Attack them, that we can Surprise them, that we can drive them before us Several Miles together and that we know how to Retreat in good Order and defy them to follow us." He predicted that "the Enemy will find that after every Battle our Army will increase and their[s] diminish, this is fighting at such a disadvantage that they must soon be convinced that they can never Support the war in America." Major Benjamin Tallmadge of Connecticut wrote that the army had driven the enemy "from post to post" before misfortune reversed the verdict. Until the retreat began, he "expected to have been in Phila. by 10 o'clock." Lieutenant William Beatty of Maryland predicted that "we shall soon have another touch with them which will soon lessen their numbers." Jonathan Todd, a Connecticut surgeon, wrote, "hotter fire never was known" than at Germantown, but he said the Continentals were "preparing for another battle our army are in good spirits and are determined to see it out this fall."[34]

Optimistic accounts of the battle soon reached Congress and scattered auxiliary officials of the army. Charles Stewart, the commissary general of issues, wrote from Trenton of the "bloody and almost fatal to our enemy [clash] at Germantown." He reported that "the enemy feel most sensibly the Torys are near distracted not a smiling countenance in the City the Second Edition of Bunkers Hill is the term used by the British officers in their description," and he predicted that "a few days will produce the third." Eliphalet Dyer, a congressman from Connecticut, heard that "our troops before [the retreat] had behaved with the greatest spirit and bravery and [a] most Compleat Victory seemed in full prospect. Till this Unfortunate mistake occasioned by the fog snatched it out of our hands." Dyer observed, "we expect Another Attack will soon be made on the Enemy [I] hope we shall soon learn to beat them."[35] Nor did American assessments moderate with sober reflection. If anything, later reports showed growing satisfaction with the result. On October 8 Weedon wrote, "tho the enterprise miscarried, it was well worth the undertaking, as from [British] Accounts . . . their light infantry (the flower of their army) was cut to pieces." By the tenth, Colonel Mordecai Gist believed that "the laurels were fairly won and only modesty prevented our wearing them. We are now on our march to gain them a second time. Our troops are in good spirit and make no doubt of carrying the point—I shall take possession of the City Tavern [and] dance a minuet with Miss Footman."[36]

Significantly, the sanguine tone of letters coming from the American camp in the weeks after Germantown extended to their authors' expectations about the army's immediate future. The battle engendered feelings less of frustration over a missed opportunity than of a stubborn determination to maintain a relentless offensive posture. Jedediah Huntington, a Connecticut brigadier, wrote, "the Army is in daily Expectation of visiting [the enemy] again, and are not only in high Spirits but by best information, much Superior in Numbers to the Enemy." Henry Knox predicted that "we Shall soon have another brush with them in which we humbly hope for the blessing of providence—we are fully convinced that vigorous methods must be pursued." Governor Thomas McKean of Delaware understood that the British were "soon to be attacked again by General Washington and an army of more than double the number," and he predicted that "a month more will, in my opinion, give us peace, liberty, and safety."[37]

This anticipation of combat was no mere collective delusion. The army was on full alert between October 12 and 18. On the eighth, it began inching down toward Philadelphia, and by the sixteenth it was back at "the Grounds we occupied before the Action of the fourth."[38] The expectation of renewed battle was at a fever pitch, and circumstances suggested that another attack might be in the works. The army had again been reinforced, and, as before Germantown, there was news of significant military events in the Hudson Valley. On the twelfth, Washington learned that General Henry Clinton had led British troops north from New York City to attack the American stronghold in the Hudson Highlands in an effort to assist Burgoyne. Three days later Washington heard that Gates's army had dealt Burgoyne a crushing defeat. Either to justify his removal of troops from the Highlands to reinforce his position after Brandywine, or to avoid being upstaged by Gates, Washington may have felt pressed to maintain the offensive.[39] Washington's explanation for bringing the army back to its pre-Germantown camp was that the move would "divert the enemy's attention from the [Delaware] forts." In the view of most of his officers and in the judgment of many American political leaders, something more than a diversion was called for. Major Jeremiah Talbot informed his wife on the eighteenth that the army had been ordered to be ready to march the next morning, and he had no doubt about their objective: "I Expect Every Moment to hear the Action Begin, . . . I hope to Dine to morrow in Philadelphia."[40]

In truth, by mid-October Washington's conservative assessment of the situation was more accurate than the aggressive hopes of his subordinates. The opportunity for delivering a decisive blow to the British was not lost in the retreat from Germantown, but it withered steadily in the following weeks. If Howe had been loathe to credit the Americans for their escape at Brandywine, he showed no such hesitation after Germantown. On October 8 he urgently ordered Henry Clinton at New York to send large reinforcements to bolster his strength. He also hastened preparations to withdraw his army from Germantown and pressed his engineers to complete a line of redoubts across the north side of Philadelphia between the Delaware and Schuylkill rivers, behind which he intended to place most of his troops.[41] The circumstances that had favored the Germantown offensive were thus only apparently duplicated in mid-October. Washington's reinforcements might soon be nullified by the arrival of Howe's, and the possibility of another surprise would never really exist. Much as Washington wanted to match the victory at Saratoga by driving the British from Philadelphia, to have tried to do so by a direct assault would have been to court disaster. On the ninth, Howe removed his army from Germantown and placed it behind the new fortifications, and the campaign's basic strategic equation again changed. Jeremiah Talbot would not dine in Philadelphia the next day or any time soon. As it turned out, he was probably grateful enough if he dined at all.

The hope for renewed offensive operations never disappeared. It was occasionally voiced in the letters of army officers, while the always expectant Continental and state political leaders clung to their hopes for a southern Saratoga. The question of an attack was "agitated" by the general officers several times but received little support. There remain perplexing questions about the ten-day period after Germantown. This was the time when a second attack on the British army might have produced favorable results. Even without the element of surprise, the Continental army would have enjoyed some important advantages. Washington's reinforcements would arrive before Howe's, and an attack might catch the British without benefit of the fortifications they were struggling to build. It would have lifted pressure from the American forts on the Delaware and been consistent with the expectations of the American military establishment and its political constituencies.[42]

John Armstrong, the commander of the Pennsylvania militia, while assuring President Thomas Wharton of the state's Supreme Executive Council that another attack was "undoubtedly in contemplation," offered one answer to these questions: "It is impossible for persons at a distance to conceive," he lectured, "the time requisite to refit after an affair such as ours of the other day." In the confusion of the retreat from Germantown, many regiments had become scattered, and days were spent gathering stragglers. Moreover, the soldiers doubtless believed that they had earned a period for rest and convalescence. It would be presumptuous to judge the morale of the privates from the combative letters of their officers. Washington and his generals also could not have realized how brief an opening they would have for taking the initiative. It was not clear that Howe would withdraw his army to Philadelphia and concentrate on opening the river. The extent to which the British had been knocked onto a defensive footing at Germantown was not appreciated, nor was the imminence of Howe's request to his superiors at Whitehall to resign.[43]

These factors influenced Washington's inclination to proceed cautiously, but they do not explain the events of October 1777. To understand those events it is necessary to examine the organizations that performed the vital tasks of supplying the army with the food, clothing, shelter, and transportation that kept it in the field. Those departments had suddenly begun to unravel. By mid-December the army's logistical operations would be in complete collapse. As a result, the army would be crippled, and its normally invisible processes of supply would become evident. During the Valley Forge winter, the failure of the support departments would be in some ways the story of the army itself. In October those organizations remained behind the scenes, but their problems increasingly impaired the army's ability to function coherently.

Congress had reorganized the Commissary and Quartermaster Departments in May and June of 1777, as Washington was readying his new army for the field. These changes, intended to rationalize the procurement and transportation functions of the departments and to control the high costs that they entailed, did not translate well into the field. The veteran leaders of the departments, Commissary General Joseph Trumbull of Connecticut and Quartermaster General Thomas Mifflin of Pennsylvania, resigned in August and October 1777, at the beginning and at the very height of the campaign. Congress chose obscure members of Middle Atlantic merchant communities to run the Commissary Department, while it failed to appoint a new Quartermaster until March 1778. The new leaders of the Commissary failed to grasp the magnitude of their responsibility in feeding the army, and Trumbull did little to help them. The Quartermaster Department, which moved the army, drifted almost rudderless. These problems left the army essentially to its own devices in the Pennsylvania countryside.[44]

By mid-October army operations were suffering because of these logistic problems. There is no conclusive evidence that Washington would have attempted a follow-up attack in the aftermath of Germantown had the problems in his supply organizations not intervened. It is also impossible to know whether such an attack might have succeeded, but the weeks after October 4 offered the best chance to defeat the British on the battlefield in

1777. There was every motivation to seize the opportunity and much expectation that it would be done, but the experience of the supply departments suggests that the opportunity existed on paper only.[45]

By late October, with the British withdrawal from Germantown and Howe's decision to concentrate on opening the Delaware, the campaign's strategic balance again shifted. The American response evolved slowly and consisted less of a single watershed decision than a set of limited responses to specific needs and opportunities. The new American strategy had three elements: the redeployment of personnel to support the Delaware River fortifications, the modification of tactics to aggravate British logistical problems resulting from the blockade of the river, and efforts to resolve the organization and supply problems of the American war machine. It was imperative for the army to begin operating on a less mobile but, perversely, much more dispersed basis. If provisions could not be brought to camp, soldiers would have to be sent wherever there was food. On October 17, Congress warned the states that unless the army's needs were met "it will be impossible for the Troops to keep the Field." The supply crisis would occasionally be blunted, but never effectively nor long enough to remove it as a factor in the conduct of what remained of the campaign. In combination with the altered British strategy, the army's logistical problems shaped the anxious months between Germantown and Valley Forge.[46]

Small unit operations would become the new order of the day, both because they could better serve the new tactical needs and because they could be much better supplied on an informal basis. Washington detached part of the Pennsylvania militia under General James Potter to move into Chester County to sever communications between that area and Philadelphia. At Congress's request, the state called out more militia in Chester and ordered them to seize arms, clothing, and blankets from any people who refused to swear allegiance or who had assisted the enemy. In mobilizing the militia, state officials could not hide their lingering hopes for a grand offensive. It was "not too late to attack General Howe and drive him with disgrace from our country" they claimed, and they urged Pennsylvanians to emulate the New Englanders, whose swarming militia had overwhelmed Burgoyne. This bit of wishful rhetoric aside, however, the state leaders recognized the probable futility of such a scheme, and they admitted that if the militia had turned out earlier, the campaign might have already been over.[47]

By late October the campaign had become a war of nerves and supplies. Its focal point was the bottleneck in the Delaware River below the city and the forts that sealed it. The countryside for thirty miles around the city became a secondary theater of operations. Both armies remained entrenched and largely inactive: the British behind their lines in Philadelphia, and the Americans in their new camp at Whitemarsh, in the hills above the Wissahickon Creek thirteen miles from the city, where they had moved on November 2. As early as mid-October there were signs that the blockade was causing hardships in the city. Jedediah Huntington reported that the British had begun "to despair of removing the Obstacles to their Navigation in the Delaware—the Consequence is the[y] must leave Philad[elphi]a." On October 29 Washington sent Brigadier General James Varnum's newly arrived brigade across the Delaware to relieve Fort Mercer at Red Bank. He promised to send Potter another "large body of militia" to aid in disrupting convoys between the city and the fleet at Chester and ordered Potter to strip and dismantle all gristmills from Chester County as far south as Wilmington, Delaware.[48]

During early October British naval and marine forces began bombarding Fort Mifflin on the Pennsylvania side of the Delaware. By midmonth the island fort was under siege both from ships in the river and "floating batteries" in the back channels on the Pennsylvania side. Its tenacious defense and the difficulty of approaching it directly by land or water led Howe to consider seizing Fort Mercer, without which Fort Mifflin was untenable. On October 21 he sent about 1,200 Hessian troops under Colonel Carl von Donop across the Delaware. Late in the afternoon of the twenty-second, Donop reached Red Bank and launched a direct assault. He was met by withering fire, and after less than an hour of fierce fighting the attackers withdrew in confusion. The Hessians suffered casualties of 153 killed, including Donop, and more than 200 wounded. American losses were fewer than 40 killed and wounded. The night after the battle two British warships that had supported Donop ran aground. Both came under point-blank American fire from Fort Mifflin and from row galleys in the river. At noon on October 23 the *Augusta* exploded and at 3 P.M. the *Merlin* met the same fate. The concussions were felt throughout the Philadelphia region, stunning many of the area's civilians.[49]

As October closed, some American officers thought they saw signs of success from the new strategy. General Weedon noted that the enemy had moved cautiously on the river since their failed attack at Red Bank and predicted that if "our little forts [could] but hold out a month longer, and by that means prevent the Shipping from getting up, the Enemy, I think, will evacuate the City." Captain Matthew Irwin thought that "Howe can't winter in Phila without possession of our River. . . . I think he must soon retreat," but Jedediah Huntington expressed the obverse of this formula. Unless the Americans could "scare [the enemy] away . . . we must set down about them somewhere and watch them for the winter or fight them in their stronghold." As one officer wrote, "It is very evident . . . that if they cannot take [Fort Mifflin] they must either leave Philadelphia or starve." Washington was feeling his way, not always comfortably, toward a more dispersed and hazardous way of managing the army's interactions with the enemy and with area civilians. The logistical crisis continued to hamper American operations. One commissary reported at the end of October that provisioning the army was still a day-to-day affair, at the mercy of the weather.[50] Nor were the British likely to sit still and be starved out. Even as the defeat of the Hessians at Fort Mercer buoyed American spirits, British troops were carving out footholds on the islands behind Fort Mifflin. Weedon and Huntington, though posing the question from opposite perspectives, were both correct: the fate of the campaign would hinge on whether or not the forts could be held and the river kept closed until it froze. The first two weeks of November witnessed a massive British bombardment of Fort Mifflin. Washington had only limited options to resist the siege, such as making small detachments of reinforcements and harassing the perimeters of the city.[51]

The American army was reduced by its logistical problems to virtual immobility at Whitemarsh. During this period of inaction, the magnitude of the logistical crisis registered in the minds of officers and men. Battlefield expectations, which had built steadily during the late summer and early fall, collided squarely with the reality of limited achievements. And the reservoir of frustration and recrimination, which had been held back by the anticipation of success, overflowed. On the river, the eagerly awaited freeze that might yet have undone the enemy seemed to be taking forever. In the American camp northwest of the city, on the other hand, the army's winter of discontent had begun early.

Halting the army in a stationary camp complicated—even as it was intended to relieve—the emerging provisions crisis. Far-flung commissaries now had a fixed location to forward any goods that they might obtain, but the informal supplementary means by which troops had been supplied locally were impaired. This problem was offset by the detachments that were central to the new strategic order. While their headquarters remained fixed, more troops than before were operating in the belt of counties ringing the city, where they could help to feed themselves. This only mitigated the problem, however, and hunger continued to stalk the army. By November 3 the larder was once again bare. Ephraim Blaine, a commissary official, complained that there was "not one barrel of flour in Camp, nor any whiskey but what was seized from the sutlers."[52]

When Blaine voiced his complaint, the army had just reached Whitemarsh so the problem could be attributed to the move: rations were probably lagging nearby and the newly occupied area could provide supplies in the interim. With the troops at rest for a month, however, shortages were inevitable. As the prospect of combat diminished, soldiers had less to distract them and might be less tolerant of short rations. The two weeks after the army reached Whitemarsh were hungry ones. By November 16 the coincidental arrival of several wagon trains provided a rare three days' supply of flour and a large quantity of beef. The enthusiasm with which the troops greeted the food suggests that there had indeed been a severe shortage. "Thank God at last I had as much," commissary Thomas Jones exulted, "so as to Enable me to Cram their Guts full."[53]

November witnessed increasing friction within the army. There was little coherent pattern in this discontent, which reflected the normal experience of human organizations involved in complex cooperative enterprises in adverse times. Officers who a month before were predicting imminent offensives or dreaming of dances at the City Tavern found time to analyze the army's shortcomings and to demand their improvement. Some of the rancor reflected personality conflicts between officers. Colonel Daniel Brodhead of Pennsylvania congratulated Benedict Arnold on the victory at Saratoga, adding, "Since you left us your Division has suffered greatly and that chiefly by the Conduct of G[enera]l W[ayne], most of the officers are unhappy under his command." Others couched their frustrations over the stalled campaign in broader terms. Joseph Ward, the muster master general, felt the Americans had "act[ed] too much on the defensive" and had thereby "lost the fairest prospect of success and the best opportunity for defeating the British army." He thought the enemy should have been attacked soon after leaving Head of Elk and hinted darkly that another offensive had indeed been expected after Germantown but that "for certain reasons it was delayed." Jedediah Huntington wondered "what probability is there of recruiting our Army—Money will not do it for it has almost intirely lost its Value—how is it possible to Clothe our men—they have worn out their Blankets & other Clothing and I see no prospect of renewing them."[54]

Dissatisfaction was not confined to the army or to such abstract issues as inflation or civilian morale. The conduct of the local militia was harshly criticized. As early as mid-October John Armstrong, who had commanded those troops, warned President Wharton of Pennsylvania's Supreme Executive Council of a "very infamous falling off of the Militia which may with great justice be called desertion," which he said had become endemic after Brandywine. Samuel Hay, a major in the Seventh Pennsylvania Regiment, observed: "I suppose there is a new cargo of militia coming out; they may as well stay home, for not one fourth of them are of any use—about three fourths of them run off at the first fire and their officers formost. . . . There is no more regulation amongst what I have seen of them, than there is amongst a flock of bullocks." Mordecai Gist of Maryland raged at "the Boasted State of Pennsylvania whose number of [militia] enrollers amounted to 62,000 men now the Enemy are even at their Doors have turned out about 1,500 militia . . . whose time generally expires in about three weeks from the date of their arrival at Camp and during that time are subject to no law whereby we can bring them to support good order and regularity."[55]

The Pennsylvania government received its fair share of the abuse. The shortage of military clothing and blankets became an increasingly acrimonious issue as winter approached. The Supreme Executive Council was caught between its citizens and the army. The Continental Congress had pushed the state to furnish clothing and blankets since October. With the army shivering at Whitemarsh, Continental authorities exploded over the council's stated desire to restrict its county commissaries to gathering clothing from "such of the disaffected *as could possibly spare them*." The Board of War demanded that whatever the army needed should be seized "without paying a more scrupulous Attention to [disaffected inhabitants'] Comfort than these infatuated wretches have shewn to the Lives and Liberties of the loyal Citizens."[56]

The state was under heavy pressure from its own Continental officers not to take an overly punitive stance toward civilians. Major General Arthur St. Clair complained bitterly to the state's congressional delegate, Robert Morris, about the difficulty of operating in an area that had been "stripped almost Naked" and whose people were "already not a little jealous of the Army." Expressing the regional rivalry that was endemic in the American ranks, St. Clair wrote that the New England states "have never contributed a single blanket toward the general Supply of the Army." The state argued that clothing and blanket shortages were due largely to carelessness or to losses to "whores and rogues that went with the [army's] baggage." But one of its own officers admitted that "the generality of the people would much rather take a blanket from a soldier for half price than let him have one at double its value. The Devil will get half them yet." Anthony Wayne reported that Pennsylvania's troops were suffering as much as the rest of the army, and he lamented the state's honor, "which was held in high Esteem—but from the Supineness of some and Disaffection of Others—is fast Dwindling in that Consequence which I wish to see it hold."[57]

The army was also being stalked by payless paydays, the most dreaded decimator of military morale after empty camp kettles. On November 14 Henry Laurens, the new president of the Continental Congress, assured army Paymaster William Palfrey that he would soon receive part of the cash needed to pay the troops. Simultaneous crises in the supply of food and clothing had drained the Continental treasury and Laurens feared the "impending evil of being in arrears to the army." Nor would the provisions crisis completely abate. On November 23, Thomas Jones warned an aide of "the approaching calamity which I expect here every moment. Not a single barrel of flour . . . have I to deliver out to the troops this morning." Jones urged, "For God's sake exert yourself in this affair . . . or all's over."[58]

During these precarious weeks, the army continued to perform its mission, if in an increasingly adverse environment and with an inevitable decline of efficiency. While the main body of troops languished at Whitemarsh, the twin forts on the river withstood a brutal land and naval assault. Generally helpless to lift the siege, Washington made small detachments intended to aggravate the British supply shortages. These served morale as well as strategic or logistical purposes. Being included in parties sent into action relieved boredom, temporarily removed individuals from the distressed camp, and perhaps even minimized the formation of cliques or factions. General Charles Scott of Virginia, about to lead a patrol party to intercept convoys in Chester County, told a friend that he was in "High spirits and full of hope of bringing this most Horrid War to a Conclusion by Defeating Genl. Howe in a fiew days." Such boasting had been routine among the officers a month before, but by now these sentiments were unheard of. Scott's optimism may be attributable to the liberating effect of his imminent departure from the fractious camp.[59]

It must have frustrated many Continental soldiers to be both hungry and immobile at Whitemarsh while the state's forces played a disproportionately important—or at least visible—role in maintaining the blockade of the

Delaware River. These men had seen their expectations of successful offensive operations halted abruptly in mid-October by provisions shortages that many of them blamed, more understandably than fairly, on the citizens of one of early America's leading agricultural regions. One cruel result of the supply crisis was to place the campaign's outcome largely into the hands of Pennsylvania irregulars whose failure to turn out earlier, or to remain in the field longer, many soldiers thought, had put their welfare into jeopardy.[60]

There was a regional dimension to the intramural incidence and the occasional projection onto the local community of military frustrations. While at Whitemarsh in November, the army grew from 10,000 to about 16,000 men, with the arrival of five brigades from Horatio Gates's "Northern" army and from the garrisons in the Hudson Highlands. These troops had been raised by the same recruiting drives the previous spring, and they shared many social and demographic characteristics with the troops who had assembled at Morristown. But they possessed cultural differences and had experienced a very different 1777 campaign. Most were New Englanders or New Yorkers. While the main army barely held its own against Howe, the northern troops had humiliated Burgoyne. They had no feel for the subtle perceptions or behavioral insights by which their new comrades were putting their encounters at Brandywine and Germantown into perspective and pronouncing them accomplishments. This still-evolving "new" army would need much more homogenizing before it was truly "Continental."[61]

The army was the Revolution's only large-scale national institution, and during the course of the the war it operated in one local context after another. Much of the impressionistic evidence we have of the alienation of Continental troops from Pennsylvania citizens comes from the eloquent pens of New England officers. These men had been raised in the most literate corner of Anglo-America and were, because of their Puritan heritage, prone to express their frustration in colorful and often-judgmental biblical allusions. Coming from a society where the militia played almost sacred symbolic and political roles in the community, they could not easily understand the reluctance of Pennsylvanians to mobilize on their own behalf.[62] Farms in their region had been shrinking for decades as its teeming families divided finite amounts of land among generational cohorts that ran as high as eight children, and where outmigration from town or region, lives of "strolling" or transient poverty, dangerous seafaring careers, or poor relief in Boston had all become imaginable futures.[63]

In contrast, the Middle Colonies had recently blossomed into the breadbasket of North America and a leading provisions supplier to the

Atlantic and Caribbean worlds. Samuel Armstrong, a major from Massachusetts who joined the main army after the surrender of Burgoyne, saw the difference between Yankee and Yorker agricultural abundance and variety as soon as his regiment set foot in the Mohawk River Valley. On the half-mile-wide and table-flat valley floor the "wheat, Rye, Indian Corn, Oats Barley, [and] Pease" were, he remarked with undisguised wonder, "the greatest quantities I ever saw before in a place." This impression would have only increased as the troops campaigned their way down the Hudson River and across the "garden" state of New Jersey toward the Delaware Valley.[64] The spectacle of militia delinquents among local youths destined to inherit hundred-acre farms, or of citizens from a landlocked colony flitting around on the Delaware River in the state's perversely named row galley *Navy*, noisily harassing British men-of-war, must have been galling to Yankees.[65]

With the loss of Fort Mifflin on November 16, following two weeks of murderous bombardment, the campaign entered its final stage. Knowing that Fort Mercer was indefensible without its counterpart, Washington sent three generals to New Jersey to see whether it might be held anyway. On November 17 Howe ordered Lord Cornwallis with 3,000 troops to Billingsport with orders to march to Red Bank and compel the fort's surrender. Washington countered by detaching Jedediah Huntington's brigade and a division under Nathanael Greene to New Jersey, and he ordered John Glover's brigade, approaching from the north with reinforcements from the Hudson, to meet them there. Greene, commanding the American troops in New Jersey, found the fort abandoned, and he proposed to engage Cornwallis directly. Washington, who was again considering a general attack on Philadelphia, gave him broad discretion in the matter.[66] Greene's response to the prospect of combat after three weeks at Whitemarsh echoed Charles Scott's. He wrote to his wife that he "hope[d] to have the pleasure to meet [Cornwallis]" and predicted that "this excentrick movement will lengthen out the campaign for some weeks at least and it is possible may transfer the seat of war for the winter." Cornwallis was too strongly and cautiously disposed, however, to engage in anything more than a series of sharp skirmishes. He mopped up at Fort Mercer and returned to Philadelphia on November 25. Greene retired to Whitemarsh, and the 1777 campaign ended ambiguously and indecisively in New Jersey.[67]

Although the reduction of the forts opened the Delaware to British shipping and ended any hope of starving the enemy into submission, Howe could not provision both his army and the city's populace by that route alone. By disrupting trade to or foraging parties from Philadelphia, Washington could exploit civilian vulnerability and discontent. To do so required continuing the recent strategy of frequent detachments and small-unit operations. Skirmishing had been a regular feature of the army's regimen since early November, and the men seemed to have acquired a taste for the exercise. One cavalry officer described these encounters, mentioning "our General's rule; he sets no store by carbines or pistols, but rushes on with their swords." Another observer noted that the American troops "are generally successful" in detached skirmishes with the enemy.[68]

The opportunity for combat may have raised the morale of soldiers serving on detached parties, but it could not temper the sour mood at the American headquarters. The bleakest assessment of the situation was offered by General Louis Lebeque Duportail, a French engineer who would soon supervise the construction of the new camp at Valley Forge. Duportail, one of many European volunteers serving in the army, attributed what little success the Americans experienced that fall to the monumental stupidity of the British. He damned the American character in every particular he could think of, concluding, "in doubling our army, we would not double our strength by a great deal, we would triple our trouble."[69]

By this time, Washington was too deeply involved in plans to extract the army from Whitemarsh to attend carefully to soldiers' routine complaints. He was preparing to make decisions about where the army should move next and what activities it might undertake during the winter. Within a week he found that the politics of those decisions equaled in complexity any of the strategic or tactical choices he had made during the campaign.

Chapter 3

DOING WHAT WE CAN

As the army's supply systems deteriorated, conflicts over resources were inevitable. Decisions had to be made about the immediate future, and the declining material base near Whitemarsh made the situation more urgent. Despite the state government's self-serving incredulity that soldiers could be "starving for Want of Flour when the very Neighborhood of the Camp is at this moment full of Wheat," it was clear that a new location for the army had to be found quickly. The question was not a new one. In mid-November Jedediah Huntington observed that the general officers had been "agitating the Disposition of our Troops for the Winter and find ourselves, the more we canvass the matter, the more at a loss." Two weeks of food shortages, frustrating military setbacks, and internal disagreements over how best to address the larger crisis had done little to clarify the situation.[1]

The decision was not one for military leaders alone to make. The matter of the army's winter "disposition" comprised three distinct but inherently interrelated questions, each of which had important political dimensions. Where would the army spend the winter? What activities would it undertake there? And how could it be supplied with the material means to remain intact, much less to accomplish any mission? Three revolutionary constituencies— the state government, the Continental Congress, and the army— each had different answers to these questions.

Pennsylvania's leaders expected the army to remain as close to the British headquarters in Philadelphia as possible. Theirs was a precariously situated government, one whose political survival depended on vigorous opposition to the state's occupation. Pennsylvania had a large population of avowed Loyalists, many of whom had flocked to enemy protection, and an even larger group of pacifists, symbolized for outsiders by the seemingly ubiquitous Quakers. The state government was divided between a fragile majority of radicals who had overthrown the colonial Assembly in 1776 and written the most democratic state constitution in America, and a large minority of moderates who cooperated in the resistance to British arms while struggling to establish a more conservative frame of government.[2] The government's legitimacy depended on ensuring the safety of patriot civilians who had chosen to—or who in many cases had no choice except to—remain in southeastern Pennsylvania. The frontier Presbyterian-Philadelphia artisan coalition that displaced the Quaker-Proprietary regime in June 1776 had inherited the popular expectation that government should hold war at bay, or that it should at least buffer war's impacts on members of the polity. Keeping armies out of the state by 1777 was recognized as being impossible. The implied mandate of protection remained operative, however, and the only way the radicals could hope to meet it was through the army's cooperation.[3]

The Congress held a different but complementary position. Its members huddled in York, Pennsylvania, west of the Susquehanna River, hoping to recover their comparatively comfortable quarters in Philadelphia. During the fall the delegates remained overtly oblivious to the army's gathering logistical crisis and to their contribution to that calamity by attempting to reorganize the Continental Commissary Department just as the new army took the field. Congress was divided, largely along sectional lines, into loosely denominated "Eastern" (New England), "Middle," and "Southern" blocs, whose members disagreed over issues of revolutionary strategy, diplomacy, and finance.[4]

During the coming winter these congressional divisions would shape and complicate the army's material predicament. More immediately important, however, were the delegates' shared concerns and insecurities as the political authors of the Revolution itself. In November 1777 they anxiously awaited news from their commissioners in France about negotiations for a Franco-American military alliance. Hoping to capitalize on the credibility gained by Horatio Gates's victory at Saratoga, they finally overcame internal disagreements about the shape of the continental union to pass Articles of

Confederation to formalize the Continental government.[5] All the delegates feared that military setbacks to the main army in Pennsylvania or threats to the political legitimacy of that state's beleaguered civilian leadership might damage the revolutionary cause. Their focus on diplomatic, fiscal, and constitutional issues limited their involvement in strategic questions, but in the past they had not hesitated to meddle in military affairs in ways that reflected the enmity between the regional factional blocs.[6]

Concerning the disposition of the army at the end of 1777, however, congressional anxieties cut across, rather than along, regional partisan lines. Most members expected the Continental Army to remain on the offensive. William Ellery of Rhode Island, a moderate member of the Eastern bloc, thought American troops should "keep the Field this Winter" and said that they might even "intirely destroy Mr. Howe's Army." Cornelius Harnett of North Carolina, a southern moderate, was "not without hopes of dislodging Genl. Howe from Philadelphia this winter. . . . One bold push may yet retrieve all." William Duer, a conservative New Yorker who supported the southerners, felt that "we shall be able during the Winter to strike a bold Stroke ag[ains]t Mr. Howe." The president of the Congress, Henry Laurens, a South Carolina radical who voted with New England but who also maintained close ties to Washington, expected that "we shall infallibly be in possession of New York or Philadelphia or both before the expiration of January." On November 28 Congress voted unanimously to send a three-member committee to Whitemarsh to consult with Washington about "the best and most practicable means for carrying on a winter's campaign," which it described as "an object which Congress have much at heart."[7]

The army's stance on the question of winter quarters was, as Huntington's comments suggest, considerably less than unanimous. Washington had informally floated the question among his aides and general officers during the latter stages of the 1777 campaign. On November 30 he summoned his generals to a Council of War, where they discussed options at length but made no firm decisions. Instead, Washington asked the officers to place their opinions on the matter in writing. A day later he reported the results to Joseph Reed, his former aide and a Pennsylvania delegate to Congress. Stationing the army "from Reading to Lancaster inclusively, is the general sentiment," he wrote, "whilst Wilmington and its vicinity has powerful advocates."[8] Washington's artful summary concealed more complexity than it revealed. Eighteen officers answered his poll. Nine advocated retiring to various lines anchored by interior towns, which Washington grouped under

the rubric of "Reading to Lancaster." Seven respondents promoted cantonments at Wilmington, Delaware, twenty-five miles below Philadelphia on
the Delaware River. Two suggested encampments in huts nearer to Philadelphia. Washington described himself as "exceedingly embarrassed, not only
by the advice given me, but also in my own judgement," and he requested
Reed's views on the matter.[9]

Elements of the debates of November 30 echoed through the memoranda. They make clear, for example, that the generals had identified two
hypothetically complementary, but in fact at least potentially contradictory,
strategic objectives for the army's winter disposition. These were "covering"
the country near occupied Philadelphia and "recruiting" (or resting, refresh-
ing, and disciplining) the army. And they show that the three site options on
which the generals divided—Lancaster, Wilmington, and "hutting" in the
field—all emerged explicitly at the council. The memoranda comprised
efforts by the generals to harmonize or rank the strategic objectives and to
apply the results to the three alternatives.[10]

The patterns produced by those efforts are difficult to summarize
because the choices posed were not mutually exclusive. Most officers conceded
in principle the merits of both covering the country and recruiting the army.
But advocates of the Lancaster-Reading line tended to view "covering" in narrowly military terms of denying the British the material resources of the
Philadelphia hinterland, or—if they considered the political implications of
protecting or abandoning civilians—to subordinate them to the army's needs
for shelter. Henry Knox, the commander of Continental artillery, argued that
the "ease and safety" of the soldiers were "greater objects" than preventing
Howe from drawing supplies from the Philadelphia area. Peter Muhlenberg
considered "the preservation of the Army" to be of "much greater utility" than
"any small advantages" gained by confining the enemy near the city. George
Weedon wrote that covering "this, or any other spot, for the space of three or
four months, is not a motive sufficient to hazard" the army, "the Herculean
hinge on which American Independence turns."[11] These officers expected a
new campaign in 1778, saw the preparation of the army as the paramount need
of the winter, and feared that a disposition nearer to Philadelphia than Reading
might inexorably precipitate a winter campaign. A regional dimension in the
deliberations is suggested by the geographic origins of these men. The nine
advocates of interior cantonments included four Virginians, three New Englanders, and one European volunteer, but only one resident of the Middle
Atlantic states, where the war's most destructive fighting had occurred.[12]

The placement of the army at Wilmington attracted generals with different values, modes of analysis, and regional origins. Its advocates were more ambivalent about weighing the interests of their troops against those of Pennsylvania's inhabitants. They acknowledged that ideally the army would serve the needs of both constituencies. Indeed, they saw in Wilmington the relative possibility of doing just that. Nathanael Greene, of Rhode Island, explained, "we must have regard not only to the army but [to] the country." While denying any intention of "taking [military] measures from popular opinions," he emphasized the need to "preserve the confidence of the country." The Marquis de Lafayette, a recent French volunteer, used a similarly exhaustive analysis of competing variables to elevate the needs of "our present civil situation" for a "shining and perhaps bold" stance over the "prudent" military assets of the Reading line. He concluded that these "shining and perhaps military like" needs demanded sending the army to Wilmington.[13]

The most unambivalently political preferences for Wilmington were expressed by two Pennsylvania officers and one foreigner. John Armstrong, head of the much-maligned Pennsylvania militia, argued that the army's retirement to the Lancaster-Reading line would depress the "hearts of good men" everywhere, "sacrifice" Pennsylvania "in particular [and] without real necessity," and result in "an end to Government and the future aid of the militia." He recommended placing most of the army at Wilmington, with small detachments forming a "chain" northwest into Chester County. Pennsylvania brigadier Anthony Wayne concurred in stronger terms. The withdrawal of the army would not only disappoint the just expectation of Pennsylvanians for protection, he claimed, but it would deter other states from aiding in future campaigns, "least they should first irritate, and afterwards be left to the mercy of a more than savage foe." Frenchman Louis Duportail captured the gist of "covering the country" for officers who defined that objective politically by portraying the consequences of letting the enemy do the covering: "recruiting in this country," he mournfully recited, "extending himself in it, adding to the number of his partizans, in a word gaining the country."[14]

Two generals urged Washington to keep the army more closely engaged than it would be at Wilmington. Lord Stirling of New Jersey weighed the comforts that the troops "richly deserved" against the precarious security they would enjoy at Wilmington and the hardships they would impose on the war refugees swelling the inland towns. He decided that this equation required placing the army in huts in Tredyffrin Township in "the

Great Valley," west of the Schuylkill. James Irvine, a Pennsylvania militia brigadier, emphasized the negative effect on the future aid of his state of "disgust[ing] our friends" by leaving them at the mercy of the British. He urged that the army "take a strong position on the other side of the Schuylkill," in huts between twenty and thirty miles west of Philadelphia.[15]

Washington's summary of the opinions before him, then, did little justice to their complexity and contradiction or to their implications for the impending deliberations on the army's disposition. The summary may have revealed his own ideas, as he portrayed himself as "about fixing" on the decision. By calling the marginal preference for Reading-Lancaster "the general sentiment," lumping seven votes for Wilmington under the ambiguous phrase "powerful advocates," and ignoring calls for a hutted encampment, Washington perhaps identified with the desire of some of his most experienced commanders to elevate strategic considerations and the immediate needs of the troops over the political interests of the host government and its citizens. On the same day, he told Horatio Gates that the "most eligible" post would "afford the best cover to the Troops, and will at the same time cut off the Enemy from Resources of provisions." Washington's rhetoric more closely echoed the nonpolitical categories used by the Reading-Lancaster advocates than the civil and political terms employed by the rest of the generals.[16]

Whatever Washington's views, external developments soon altered the dynamic of the decision. By December 2 he learned of Congress's decision to send a committee to camp. He asked his generals for new memoranda on "the advisability of a Winters Campaign, and practicability of an attempt on Philadelphia." Those opinions gave him valuable ammunition with which to resist Congress's efforts to influence strategic decision making. Of the twenty-one replies received, seventeen generals spoke unequivocally against attacking Philadelphia. Two tempered their negative judgments with wishful scenarios under which they might recommend an assault. The two generals who supported an attack added strong reservations to their advice. On the broader question of a winter campaign, thirteen generals opposed the idea, five supported it, one equivocated, and two abstained.[17]

Washington was probably not surprised by the result of his canvas. But the poll revealed patterns that complicated his position. The five supporters of a winter campaign were all Pennsylvanians. Brigadier General Anthony Wayne and militia commander John Armstrong, who wanted to send the army to Wilmington, joined James Irvine, who voted for hutting west of Philadelphia, in recommending a winter campaign. And militia brigadiers

John Cadwallader and James Potter, who had not voted during the December 1 caucus, both supported the idea of a winter campaign. The Pennsylvanians reiterated their essentially political arguments about the need for the army to protect patriots, to sustain the spirits of timid or wavering citizens, and to uphold the army's reputation as the guarantor of revolutionary authority.[18]

From Washington's perspective this division complicated his ability to use the military expertise of his subordinates as a bulwark against strategic interference by his civilian superiors. The delegates from Congress came to camp to advocate a course their colleagues candidly acknowledged having "much at heart," but they also came hand-in-hand with the embattled civil authorities of Pennsylvania. Robert Morris was a delegate from Pennsylvania, and on the way to Whitemarsh he offered to President Wharton of the Supreme Executive Council to "execute any of your commands." The state had other representatives at or on their way to Whitemarsh. Reed and Cadwallader had served throughout the campaign as informal advisers to Washington and liaisons without rank between the army and the state government and its militia commanders. On November 28 the Council of Safety dispatched Assemblyman John Bayard and James Young to camp to investigate reports that Pennsylvania's Continental troops were more poorly clothed than men from other states. The same day, Congress sent two members to Lancaster to confer with the state on ways to improve the transportation of provisions to the army. With strategic and logistical issues so closely linked by recent events, the negotiations over the immediate military direction of the Revolution were bound to be complex.[19]

When they reached camp on December 3, the representatives of the civilian bodies quickly began promoting their various agendas. John Laurens, the son of congressional president Henry Laurens, and one of Washington's closest aides, posed for his father the stark terms in which the disposition debate had already been framed. "The question is," he noted, "whether we are to go into remote Winter Quarters and form a Chain of Cantonments in the interior parts of the Country leaving a vast extent of Territory exposed to the devastation of an enraged unsparing Enemy leaving the well affected to fall Sacrifice, and deplore our abandonment of them and the Country, or whether we shall take a position more honorable, more military, more Republican, more consonant to the popular Wish in a proper situation for covering the Country."[20]

Visitors to the army had their own answers. Elbridge Gerry, a delegate from Massachusetts and a strong advocate of a winter campaign, found the army to be "stronger than it has been this campaign." At their first meeting Washington gave the committee copies of the generals' opinions on winter quarters. Gerry observed privately that he had not "come to camp for the purpose of promoting this plan [for withdrawing to interior towns.]" He wrote that his committee had "large powers" and pointedly hinted that if a winter campaign was settled upon, its members might decide to "remain with the army" while it was executed.[21] The state committeemen also met with Washington on the third. Bayard and Young warned several generals of "the horrid Consequences that must follow" a retreat to the Lancaster-Reading line, "nothing less . . . [than] the loss of the states of New Jersey, Delaware, Eastern Shore of Maryland, and great part of this State." They found "our field officers in general are violently opposed to it and declare should such a measure be adopted they would immediately resign."[22]

On December 4 the congressional committee met again with Washington and received the second set of memoranda on a winter campaign and an attack on Philadelphia. Their deliberations on how to overcome the generals' objections to a winter campaign were disrupted by the sudden approach of the enemy. At midnight on the fourth, most of the British army left Philadelphia in two columns led by Generals Howe and Cornwallis and marched northwest through Chestnut Hill toward Whitemarsh. Washington had expected an attack all week, and the army was rested and equipped for the event.[23] The committees were treated to a demonstration of the army's strengths and liabilities—indeed, of its ability to undertake the winter campaign that they had come to Whitemarsh to promote. Howe found the Americans securely lodged in a heavily fortified camp that could be carried, if at all, only at the cost of unacceptably heavy casualties. Washington was unwilling to leave that ground, even for a battle his officers were spoiling for, because his casualties in the ravine in front of the camp would have been as heavy, and as impossible to justify, as Howe's would have been on the American redoubts. Howe thus settled for a methodical probing of the American position. On completing what amounted to a hotly contested inspection tour, Howe retired to Philadelphia, satisfied that he would be able to report to London that he had at least tried to provoke a decisive battle.[24]

The Americans were quick to claim victory by default, and the boasting, even derisive tone of their letters rivaled those following Germantown. Jedediah Huntington wrote that if many Americans had not been sick, "this time we might in all human Probability have prevented Mr. Howes ever returning to the city." Major John Steel Tyler of Massachusetts was disgusted to report the "disgraceful retreat" of the enemy. And Benjamin Tallmadge of Connecticut scornfully observed, "thus has the mighty Conquerors of America returned again to his [*sic*] stronghold with disgrace," and lamented "I am prodigiously mortified that the Thieves should go back without a confounded drubbing."[25]

Although indecisive militarily, the Whitemarsh skirmishes helped resolve the stalemate that had developed over the question of the army's winter disposition. Advocates of aggressive offensive measures saw in the episode reinforcement for their views. Elbridge Gerry regretted only that the British had been able to "puzzle our officers by their Manoeuvres," which he believed could have been prevented had the Americans initiated the attack.[26] Some of Gerry's allies in York reached similar conclusions, but his colleagues on the committee could have seen firsthand the perilously ill-supplied state of the army. Several observers insisted that a plan for an American attack on the taunting Redcoats had been "on the carpet" on December 8, but that there was strong opposition from many of the officers. The spectacle of generals unable or unwilling to pull the trigger on a response that most of them undoubtedly wanted to make probably convinced the committee that a winter campaign was impossible. But the wanton destruction of civilian property northwest of Philadelphia and immediately in front of the American camp may have also persuaded many generals that retiring to the Lancaster-Reading line would indeed subject many civilians to unacceptable depredations.[27]

This convergence set the stage for renewed deliberations, which began on December 9 and moved rapidly toward a decision. The final discussions were limited to Washington, his aides, members of the congressional committee, Reed and Cadwallader, and John Bayard of the Pennsylvania clothing committee.[28] Circumstantial evidence suggests that important compromises emerged from the discussions on December 9 and shaped the army's relationship with both political bodies and with the civilians of the Delaware Valley for the rest of the winter. On the tenth, the congressional committee wrote Washington summarizing their findings. They blamed the "general discontent in the Army and especially among the officers" for the open military resistance to the winter campaign. They proposed to address the problem with recommendations to Congress for officer's pensions, reforms in the distribution of military rank, and vague promises to improve payments for back rations. They acknowledged that an attack on Philadelphia was "ineligible" and advised that until the army could be reinforced, "such a Post should be taken . . . as will be most likely to aggrieve the

Enemy, afford supplies of provision . . . and [be] best calculated for covering the Country from the Ravages of the Enemy . . . as well as afford[ing] comfortable Quarters for the Officers and Soldiers."[29]

This formula relinquished plans for a winter campaign but otherwise did little more than restate the broad menu of desirable goals that had recently divided the generals into three broad camps. But evidence suggests that the discussions on the ninth more fully narrowed the boundaries of the decision. Joseph Reed, who was watching over Pennsylvania's interests, left for his home at Norriton that night. The next day he informed the Supreme Executive Council that the generals' plan to withdraw the army to interior lines for the winter had effectively been defeated. Washington, he wrote, "will not come into it, but take post as near the enemy, and cover as much of the country as the nakedness and wretched condition of some part of the army will admit." Reed conceded that the army could not "keep the field entirely" but assured Wharton that the plan had "been adopted principally upon the opinions of the gentlemen of this state" and would "give satisfaction to you and the gentlemen around you. If it is not doing what we would," he observed, "it is doing what we can."[30]

Reed later revealed that the new plan was crafted by himself, Nathanael Greene, and John Cadwallader as being "the most eligible [way] to quiet the minds of the people and cover the country." This statement is supported by a draft plan that Greene and the major generals presented to Washington on December 10. This complex design specified the order in which the brigades would cross the Schuylkill River. It also revealed, albeit obliquely, several elements of the decision reached the previous day. For example, it disclosed that a brigade of Continental troops would be sent to New Jersey to answer that state's importunities about its defenseless condition. That brigade would remain temporarily east of the Schuylkill, "to serve as a covering party" for the withdrawing army. The document also suggested that an understanding had been reached to allow the Continental Army to focus its attention on the area west of the Schuylkill, while the "whole of the Pennsylvania militia . . . act[ed] collectively" on the east side. This provision would increase the security and reduce the wear on the Continental troops by narrowing their sphere of responsibility and thus undercut objections to the revised plan by advocates of interior cantonments. One "Troop" of Continental cavalry would go to New Jersey with the infantry, while "the remainder of a Regiment" of horsemen stayed east of the river "to act with the Pennsylvania Militia."[31]

A broad framework was thus established for early winter military operations, but many details were left incomplete. The army had barely left Whitemarsh when the conditional nature of these arrangements became apparent. The vanguard, crossing the Schuylkill at Matson's Ford early on December 11, met a large British foraging party and retreated under heavy fire. Washington moved the army four miles north before crossing again on the twelfth at Swede's Ford. The troops halted in a narrow, wet defile known as "the Gulph," while final decisions were made about their destination.[32] On the thirteenth, Reed warned Wharton that the plan he had described three days earlier had "upon other advice been totally changed." He insisted that "a brigade of Continental troops [was to have been] left with the militia on this [east] side [of the] Schuylkill." Now, he complained, the "remains" of the Pennsylvania militia would cross to the east side, where the whole body, under General Armstrong, would only amount to "about one thousand militia, many without arms and without a single troop of horse."[33]

Despite quibbles about the details, most military officers understood after December 9 that a new plan had been adopted for the army. Elias Boudinot, the Continental commissary general of prisoners, told Wharton, "I am rather led to believe that we shall not see Winter Quarters this year." Jedediah Huntington wrote that the army would cross the Schuylkill that night to winter quarters, "but whether in the woods or in some town or towns I cannot tell you." Reflecting the frustration of high-ranking officers excluded from a seemingly endless decision-making process occurring virtually before their eyes, Huntington complained that "I don't like our Councils very well."[34] Pennsylvania's militia generals, James Potter and John Armstrong, expressed the same perception of the result with more satisfaction when both described the coming months as "a Winter's Campaign." Potter wrote before and Armstrong after the changes that incensed Reed, but both knew that Pennsylvania's parochial—if undeniably meritorious and strongly expressed—political interests had prevailed over the contrary ideas of many soldiers.[35]

For Pennsylvania's civil authorities, however, the possible demise of the agreement was a threat that had to be resisted. As late as December 13 Thomas Wharton was unsure that the army would remain near Philadelphia. The receipt of Reed's letter and the return to Lancaster of John Bayard turned doubt into alarm. On December 15 Bayard visited the council to request a joint conference with the Assembly "on the situation of the State, with respect to the Continental Army going into Winter Quarters." The two state bodies met that day and "unanimously agreed to remonstrate to Congress against the Army going into Cantonments." Their "Remonstrance" showed their belief that the army's intended destination in crossing the Schuylkill River was Wilmington. They complained that this would leave "the great part of this state . . . in the Power of the Enemy, subject to their Ravages." Underlying these fears was an explicit uneasiness about the tenuous state of the political ties between many Pennsylvanians and their leaders. "Nothing but the neighbourhood of the Army keeps [Pennsylvania's disaffected citizens] subject to government," the authorities admitted, and even good Whigs were in danger of becoming "discouraged & giv[ing] up all as lost."[36]

As revealing as it was of the precarious legitimacy of civil authority in Pennsylvania, the state's alarm was also the product of procedural inertia and difficult communications. Even as the politicians remonstrated, John Laurens assured his father that a field encampment, rather than cantonments in the interior towns, had been selected. The "precise Position" would be fixed that day, but Laurens insisted that it would cover "the Country we have just left—far enough from the Enemy not to be reached in a days march, and properly interposed between the Enemy and the most valuable part of the Country on this side Schuylkil." John Armstrong wrote that Washington "with the whole of the Army has now taken his Winter Position in [Chester County] so that the forbidding idea of Winter Quarters is now, I hope, fully laid aside."[37]

In explaining his decisions to his army, Washington drew rhetorical elements from Pennsylvania's three-week-long campaign to influence those decisions. He portrayed the interior towns as "crowded with virtuous citizens" who had fled the Philadelphia area and to whose burdens the army must not add. He pointed to the army's "firm friends" remaining in the area who would be "despoiled and ravaged by the enemy" and "exposed to . . . insulting and wanton depredation" if the army left the field. He borrowed from proponents of a field encampment the rationalization that the troops would be safer, if not more comfortable, concentrated in huts than dispersed in villages. And he appealed to the soldiers' patience, professionalism, and republican virtue, promising personally to "share in the hardship and partake of every inconvenience" with the army.[38]

The Pennsylvania remonstrance was not recalled, however, and its slow progress through the revolutionary bureaucracy prevented any smooth transition between the 1777 campaign and the ensuing winter. The remonstrance reached Congress on the seventeenth, the same day Washington exhorted his troops. The day before, Congress had received a report from its committee at camp that echoed the members' preliminary account of their findings to Washington and pronounced a winter campaign "ineligible." The documents were considered together on December 18. On the nineteenth, Congress forced the committee to divulge the generals' memoranda on quarters and on a winter campaign. That afternoon, as the Continental troops reached Valley Forge, it threw the issue back into Washington's lap by voting to send him a copy of the remonstrance. Its language suggests that Congress shared the state's fear that the army might leave the Philadelphia area. It asked for details about Washington's "line of cantonment," and especially how he would protect the area east of the Schuylkill and New Jersey. But beyond this residual disgruntlement, which reflected the belief of some members that an aggressive military stance was still possible, Congress deferred to Washington's judgment and turned back to routine legislative business. Before the day was over, Congress heard rumors that "the army are about putting in the Gulph Valley." Jonathan B. Smith, of Pennsylvania, gave the Supreme Executive Council the news, adding, "this is the wish of Congress as far as I can judge."[39]

The process by which the army's winter disposition was determined shaped the experience of civilians and soldiers in the Delaware Valley during the winter of 1777–78. Operating in close proximity to their congressional superiors, the army's leaders made a major strategic decision and a substantial commitment of military resources on explicitly political grounds. That decision left the army's fate tied closely, at least for the duration of the winter, to the legitimacy of the weakest and most divided state government in America. It is important to recognize what did *not* happen in revolutionary political councils as this process unfolded. The Continental Congress did not divide along sectional or ideologically based lines. Unlike the congressional split over command and strategy issues in the Hudson Valley, the Pennsylvania campaign did not provoke a clash between Eastern bloc radicals demanding a relentless offensive posture, supported by an outpouring of "virtuous" militia, and southern conservatives willing to sacrifice the comforts of the civilians of a "supine" state to give the army a chance to regroup and gird for ensuing campaigns. Rather, the evidence shows the Congress as a whole moving slowly from a consensus in favor of a winter campaign in late November to the grudging acceptance of a limited field encampment.[40]

Similarly, political forces within Pennsylvania did *not* divide over this issue in ways consistent with what historians have shown about the balance of power in that state. If they had, beleaguered supporters of the 1776 state constitution, clinging to power in both the Assembly and the Supreme Executive Council, should have led the fight for an aggressive military stance to shield the state's Whig citizens and to give the militia a center around which to rally. Conservative or moderate opponents of the constitution should have been indifferent to the matter—or perhaps viewed the crisis as an instrument for the downfall of the more radical regime. Instead, partisans of all ideological stripes within the fragile Whig coalition in late 1777 cooperated to assure the state maximum support from the army. The moderately radical Thomas Wharton, Jr., headed the council, balancing the open partisanship of the vice president, George Bryan. In the state's congressional delegation, the active radicalism of Daniel Roberdeau offset the avowed conservatism of Robert Morris.[41]

It was the state's agents at camp who best show the complex interplay of politics and strategy in this decision. Joseph Reed, John Bayard, and John Cadwallader had all been leaders of resistance to British policy since 1774, and each had risen to power through Philadelphia's politicized militia units. In spite of these ties, they were different actors, spanning the political spectrum from dead center to near right. Two were pragmatic supporters of the state constitution, but neither was in any real sense still a radical. Reed was an attorney and an instinctive moderate who began to diverge from the leftward drift of Pennsylvania politics in spring 1776 because of his belief that independence was consistent with the preservation of Pennsylvania's existing charter and assembly. He sidestepped these differences by accepting an appointment as adjutant general of the Continental Army in June 1776, and he remained in the field as a volunteer during most of 1777. But his cautious temperament led him to refuse an appointment as chief justice of Pennsylvania, from a reluctance to take an oath not to work for the revision of the state's constitution. He thus reached Washington's camp in early December with only lukewarm personal ties to the radical state government whose interests he undertook to represent.[42]

John Bayard was also tenuously connected to the standing political order in Pennsylvania. More willing than Reed to abandon the Assembly and charter in May and June of 1776, he began drifting away from the radicals a few months later. In October he chaired a public meeting in Philadelphia that adopted resolutions criticizing the new state constitution. In November he was elected to the new Assembly, but on a ticket pledged to resist the organization of the government and to demand the calling of a new convention.

Bayard's essential moderation is illustrated by the fact that historians have classified him as both "an Anticonstitutionalist mainstay" and a staunch "Constitutionalist." The latter characterization is more accurate, but when he reached Whitemarsh in December 1777, Bayard had long since given up the label of "radical."[43]

No such ambiguities colored John Cadwallader's politics. The son of a longtime activist in Pennsylvania's proprietary political establishment, Cadwallader adhered to the resistance movement longer than his more celebrated cousin, John Dickinson, but he shared Dickinson's deep conservatism. At a meeting chaired by Bayard in May 1776 to organize opposition to the Assembly, Cadwallader angered the crowd by attempting to moderate resolutions passed by acclamation. In June he offended the militia by refusing to poll his own "conservative . . . 'Silk Stocking' Battallion" on their support for the Assembly or for the extralegal committees. Two months later he opposed popular demands to allow the militia companies to elect their own officers. Early in 1777 he refused a commission as a brigadier general in the army rather than swear not to take steps detrimental to the constitution. He came to Whitemarsh with such contempt for the state regime whose position he worked to protect there that he told Reed that its government could not be changed "without another Revolution."[44]

We might ask why, then, Cadwallader helped to broker a compromise on the winter placement of the Continental Army, the failure of which might have precipitated such another "revolution" against the radical government that he abhorred? Or why Reed or Bayard, with their more tempered ambivalence about the implications of government-as-constituted in Pennsylvania, joined in that effort? The answer lies largely in the ambiguities of the situation. All three men, and others like them, were groping along complex situational paths in late 1777. Whereas past or impending milestones on those paths can be useful guides to understanding their reaction to events, they are no more than that. The intensity of their commitment to such views as Cadwallader's expression about "another Revolution" can be wondered about, but they should not be blithely presumed. It was impossible for anyone to predict how the struggle over the state government would evolve in the immediate future, or how it would intersect with the equally opaque course of the war. The state officials at Whitemarsh were only hedging their several bets by supporting a position that would constrain the ability of the British army to ravage the state while protecting its citizens of various whiggish loyalties.

Finally, the decision that brought the army to Valley Forge, however political its premises may have been, was not imposed on the army by either the state or Continental political bodies. The intervention of state agents deflected the decision from the course it would have taken if the generals' written memoranda had been the only consideration involved. But the ultimate decision was undoubtedly Washington's to make. Cornelius Harnett, who had supported the congressional scheme for a winter campaign, advised a constituent that Congress knew "no more of the Intentions of the Army than you do, until some event or Other takes place, Congress have very wisely determined to put it in Genl. Washington's power to keep his own secrets." This stand was largely disingenuous, as Harnett acknowledged in the next sentence when he mentioned the "Committee of Congress now at Head Quarters." But it seems probable that even the committee understood its arrangements with Washington there to have been more of a general framework than a fixed settlement. And their colleagues' acquiescent response to the embittered Pennsylvania "Remonstrance" suggests that they saw matters the same way.[45]

Joseph Reed's alarm, Thomas Wharton's petulance, and the Remonstrance itself show that the state's agents had a more rigid interpretation of the decision reached at camp than Congress did. But the Remonstrance was ultimately, by its timing alone, more of an ironic or even a seriocomic element embedded within the broader deliberative process—an argument counterproductively continued after the point is won—than the decisive factor by which the state's leaders coerced the army's winter disposition. Washington agreed to keep the army in the field for the winter because he came to see, however grudgingly, that the fears expressed by state and Continental leaders about the political implications of an army withdrawal had some foundation. Undoubtedly, too, he realized intuitively that the troops who had performed so tenaciously—if with such bitterly disappointing results—throughout the fall, would be able to withstand all the challenges and hardships imposed on them by that compromise.

Although the civilians of the Delaware Valley were much more conscious of the destruction wrought northwest of Philadelphia during the confrontation of the armies at Whitemarsh than of the concurrent deliberations between Washington and the politicians, the latter had more far-reaching consequences for them. Those consequences were neither simple nor uniformly distributed among the area's population. For all individuals, the continued presence of an American army in the region meant a different kind of winter. For some, that difference involved more danger, more damage, or more pressure on their ability to remain aloof from the conflict. For others, it included more protection or more ability to exploit the perverse opportunities of war. For most, it offered more of both elements than a Continental withdrawal would have done.

For members of the military community, an encampment rather than cantonments meant more danger, not more opportunities. Washington reluctantly embraced the need for the army to help secure the legitimacy of Pennsylvania's government by serving as a symbol, if not a surrogate, for civil authority, but he worked hard to delineate that role as narrowly as possible. When he placed the army at Valley Forge, he insisted on a literal interpretation of the division of military responsibility with the state along the Schuylkill River. When that division proved unworkable in fact, he clung to it as an increasingly hollow fiction, rather than commit the army to a hopelessly debilitating or counterproductive police action spreading across the region. And before winter fully began, Washington took an early dividend from the inaptly timed and ineptly phrased Pennsylvania "Remonstrance" by using it to extract from the Continental Congress a commitment to military and logistical reforms he considered imperative to the army's long-term welfare.

December 19, 1777, the day the Continental Army reached Valley Forge, is burned into the American imagination, where it resembles a passion play more than a historical event. In that play, the army is a giant, hobbled, gaunt, and silent Greek chorus, making its entry into some undifferentiated corner of the snowy American wilderness, to await with patient virtue—but little innate military competence—its providential deliverance by the arrival of spring and the patient work of a comedic Prussian drillmaster, Friedrich Steuben. It is impossible to take seriously both this image and the course of the 1777 campaign. The army was certifiably badly kept by the end of the year, and its members were clearly much the worse for wear for their recent troubles. December 19 found them on the threshold of yet another logistical crisis and—based on the record of the army's previous movements—no one could have predicted when the supply lines might begin flowing again. As for their appearance, the troops may well have merited one scholar's condescending epithet "as ragged a band of scarecrows as ever graced a cornfield" because their stock of replacement clothing had long since dried up.[46]

But the army was not in its death throes. This image contrasts appealingly with the equally facile one of British officers and their Loyalist hosts, comfortably lodged by the warm fireplaces and bright lights of Philadelphia, torn only between the theater and the ball for an evening's entertainment.

Together with the portrait of the Continentals marching briskly out of the hills along the Schuylkill six months later, on their way to chasten their corrupt, luxury-loving foes at Monmouth, it brackets Valley Forge like a pair of alabaster bookends. It suggests reassuringly that deliverance does happen, and that there is justice somewhere in the universe. But it also poses impossible questions of historical explanation.

The army that lost two battles in Pennsylvania during the 1777 campaign was a larger, more cohesive, more resilient, and quite simply a much better force than the very different one that somehow managed to close 1776 by winning two battles in New Jersey. If the logistical collapse that halted its progress early in the 1777 campaign betrayed the organizational fraying of the Revolution, it also hinted at the army's steady evolution toward operational stability and combat effectiveness. No longer the spontaneous outpouring of communal and familial bands of 1775 that had moved about very little and could thus be subsisted informally from a friendly New England countryside, its new recruits had literally as well as figuratively begun to outrun their material resources when they assembled from eight states at Morristown in late spring of 1777. The army's sheer mobility increased its metabolic needs and made it harder for its faltering commissaries to bring enough food and supplies to what had now become a relentlessly moving target. In leaving its New England cradle and beginning to become truly "continental" in its composition, the army had also begun in a very real sense to become nobody's particular responsibility. Until civil and military leaders learned how to equip them with supply departments adequate to their growing capabilities, the troops would always operate at the end of a short logistical tether, and months of relative material comfort would often be interspersed with weeks of harrowing physical hardship.

No better testimonial to the army's military improvement can be found than that of the enemy's heavily barricaded deployment in Philadelphia at year's end. For William Howe, the lessons of Trenton and Princeton had been brutally reinforced at Germantown. By late 1777 he knew better than to carelessly leave detachments of drunken Hessians to roister in exposed positions, as open invitations to the kinds of small, symbolic military successes that count so heavily in dire revolutionary straits. This Christmas, the king's German mercenaries would carouse safely behind a line of strong fortifications north of the city.

Of the three questions posed by the disposition debate, only the first—where would the army go?—had been decided by the negotiations at

Whitemarsh. The second—what would it do there?—was at best a vague understanding, subject to different interpretations by the various interested parties. And the third—how would the army be sustained?—had only been finessed by that debate. When he sensed that his superiors might be content to let the last question remain unanswered, Washington implied that the entire decision about disposition could be reopened. In late December he angrily warned the Revolution's civilian leaders that his long-suffering but possibly mutinous troops might yet leave the state or else impose more directly on its citizens; that they might—to invoke his colorful parchment sound bite that got them better fed that winter, while fixing forever their image as a hapless, stumbling rabble—"starve, dissolve, or disperse."[47]

The troops did their best to give their commander-in-chief a credible human prop. As they built their camp, they filled the damp, wintry evening air with derisive hoots and catcalls, animal imitations, and ominous, politically charged chants warning "no bread, no soldier." Historians and popularizers who have woven these fragments of the army's voice together with Washington's more eloquent warnings about "dissolution" to paint it as a sullen "rabble-in-arms" have mistaken its actual character. Its vocal performance on arriving in camp—like its military performance throughout the fall—were marks of its cohesion and discipline, of its likelihood of staying together rather than hints of its incipient disintegration. Indeed, the chanting was perhaps intended more for the benefit of the army's neighbors in the local community than for its officers. The soldiers were as inclined to blame the inhabitants of America's "bread" colony for their short supplies as they were army commissaries, and it was clear to them that they had been kept on Philadelphia's frozen doorstep more for political than for strategic reasons.[48]

The appropriate note of benediction for the dutifully observed American celebration of Thanksgiving was sounded by Joseph Ward of Massachusetts, the army's muster master general. Ward was as responsible as any man for monitoring the army's organizational metabolism, and he saw more silver than lead lining the clouds of war when he wrote to his friend Samuel Adams on December 17. Although he had been a vigorous critic of the campaign's progress, Ward hardly sounded like a man listening for the army's death rattle. Rather, he beheld in the day's hardships the hand of "Providence . . . administering a political and moral physic to this people." While admitting that there would "not be much feasting here" for the next day's Thanksgiving observance, on the whole he thought that "we have infinite cause for gratitude supreme."[49]

Chapter 4

In order to understand how civilians experienced an eighteenth-century military campaign, it is helpful to recall how one was processed by Revolutionary War soldiers. Continental officers, like Joseph Ward, could conclude a disappointing campaign, like that of 1777, with hopeful outlooks—if not always in happy moods—because they had well-structured frameworks for measuring almost everything that happened around them, and because they inhabited an organizational culture designed both to create and to reinforce such frameworks. American troops rose and dressed each day and then fell in to hear "general orders." Dictated the night before at headquarters, these remarks addressed an endless stream of housekeeping details, but they also formed a kind of paternalist narrative in which the commander-in-chief cajoled army members, reminded them, warned them, placated them, and sometimes tried to amuse them. Read this way, these orders served as an interpretive vehicle. The general described the big picture to men whose daily routines exposed them to only small parts of it. After these were read, brigade and company commanders appended their own daily orders, mixtures of local detail and narrative weaving an intermediate picture together with the big one.

This educational system was, to be sure, only partly effective. Even higher-level officers often had only fragmentary knowledge of what was happening around them. To an army, campaigning in a strange country could feel like going around in endless circles. James Varnum wrote the epigram for the Continental Army's blurred vision of Pennsylvania when he called it "this Tory Labyrinth." But even a labyrinth encourages trained actors to try to move in as straight a line as possible. Soldiers communicated through peer networks, seeking to reduce the confusing events they were experiencing to so many explicable deviations from norms they had been prepared to internalize. Putting the best face on a complex situation—as the American officers did in their post-Germantown discourse—was a normal part of this rationalization process. Verbalizing anxieties inherent even in triumph was also normal. In November 1777 British major general Charles Gray tempered his satisfaction over the capture of Philadelphia by recalling the campaign as being "as hard an exertion as ever was made by any army, through the strangest country in the world." Labyrinths can disorient those who navigate them successfully almost as much as they do those who lose their way.[1]

What the soldiers did differed only in form, not function, from what their civilian neighbors were trying to do. Making sense of chaos is a universal human need. If having too coherent a mental map for measuring or anticipating reality can make apparent winners and losers feel equally uneasy, having one that is too little articulated can be even worse. Eighteenth-century civilians got no general orders each day; in 1777, most of them did not even receive newspapers regularly. They had no training in how to live, as civilians, in what military men called the "seat of war." What knowledge they did have, as Elizabeth Farmer discovered in late 1776, was likely to be dysfunctional. For Delaware Valley civilians, even more than for soldiers, the early years of the Revolution were a learning experience. If civilians did not have as many formal mechanisms to structure their learning as did military personnel, they were not atomistic, isolated actors wandering in the wilderness either. As the Pennsylvania campaign proceeded they taught themselves and each other to survive, to understand, and sometimes to exploit the exigencies of war.

Evidence of civilians learning the obvious and eternal lesson of war—that it was hell—and displaying the modern psychological response of "flee or fight" is easy to come by. Elizabeth Farmer's 1776 resolve to "stay and share the danger" if the war ever returned to Pennsylvania was a rhetorical position. It may have been widely shared, but for it to become a behavioral norm, the lessons of 1776 had to be relearned and reinforced. British troops approaching Pennsylvania from the south by water in August 1777 beheld scenes like those they might have seen from the north had Howe broken through over land eight months earlier. From the decks of British warships moving up the Chesapeake Bay, the shores of northern Maryland had an eerily empty appearance. What signs of human activity there were did not convince the Redcoats that the Quaker provinces would be more hospitable than New England or New York, as Howe believed. Colonel Charles Stuart informed his father, Lord Bute, that although the Eastern Shore of Maryland showed signs that it might "return to obedience," on the western side people seemed "very averse to a reconciliation."[2]

But it was the deserted character of the countryside that most struck the invaders. When the king's troops landed at Head of Elk on August 25, Hessian General Leopold von Heister noted that this "well-built village" contained a "large magazine" of military supplies, but "there was not a single human being there." Charles Stuart wrote, "most people whether through fear or disaffection left their houses." Finding caches of unprotected property belonging to presumed adversaries, royal troops readily claimed them. Francis Downman, an artillery officer, wrote on August 27 that he had met neither friend nor foe: "The country is quite deserted [but] . . . cattle and other things have been met with and found very acceptable." Howe forbade "any kind of marauding," but Downman thought "it is not in anyone's power to prevent this where there is so large an army and such a mixture of troops."[3]

Impressions of easy pickings from an empty countryside were gradually dispelled by more disturbing signs. Charles Stuart feared the lack of resistance had lured the British into "our usual carelessness," and he concluded that if an "active enemy" had materialized, "our Corps wou'd be destroyed by detail, without a possibility of supporting one another." On August 31 two Redcoats were "found a little way from the camp with their throats cut. It is supposed they were plundering and were set upon by some lurking rebels." Other British occupiers continued to note the deserted character of the area, which some attributed to the "false representations" of the Whigs who, one said, had "terrified country people out of their senses."[4] But some of their peers decided that they were not operating in so abandoned a country as others believed, or thought that the silence of the countryside portended danger and not submission. General von Heister called the situation "critical": "We are going into a country where there is a numerous hostile army in front of us, and where we shall be surrounded by inhabitants that are badly disposed towards us. . . . The place we have left [behind] no longer belongs to us but to the enemy. We face the rebels on all sides when we pitch a camp. . . . What would happen if the good fortune the army has hitherto had should have forsaken us? Oh, what a detestable picture."[5]

When Redcoat columns entered Pennsylvania on September 3, they began to encounter distinctly unshy people in front of them as well behind them. Having pronounced all absentees "rebels," they reasoned that those who approached them must be friendly. On September 10 Hessian Captain Johann Ewald wrote with wonder that the inhabitants near Kennett Square, Pennsylvania, "are generally Quakers, who since they did not want to participate in the war, did not flee, but arrived in crowds and asked for protection." The battle of Brandywine was fought the next day, and after it ended "several well disposed inhabitants . . . arrived at camp" to warn the British that the roads to Chester were filled with retreating Americans. "These people," Ewald wrote, "could not express sufficiently their astonishment that [we] had allowed this great number of wagons to move off so peacefully." The accuracy of British assumptions about the politics of their visitors is questionable, but it must have occurred to at least some of them that when civilians presume to become tactical advisers and critics, armies are not operating in a civil or a political vacuum.[6]

These soldiers' accounts of civilian behavior are interesting, but they complicate our task of trying to penetrate the civilian *mentalité* to view the invasion of Pennsylvania from the inside out. They tell us much about the military template for evaluating the local environment as a factor of war, but only at the cost of making it harder to judge scarce civilian testimony. We need as soon as possible to set them aside to interrogate the considerably more refractory civilian evidence on its own terms. For a variety of reasons, Brandywine may be as good a place as any to begin this process.

If flight before moving armies seems like a commonsensical civilian response, we should especially expect to find battlefields devoid of civilian bystanders. Although eighteenth-century soldiers sought to avoid harm to noncombatants, armed clashes were hard enough to control without having to account for the safety of spectators. But actions could begin so abruptly and envelop space so unexpectedly that civilians imprudent enough to remain in the neighborhood of armies sometimes found themselves unwillingly on the inside looking out. This was the fate of many Pennsylvanians when the rebels and Redcoats squared off across the Brandywine Creek on September 11, 1777. Their accounts support directly neither the notion of war as a universal hell nor that of early modern combat as a festive entertainment.

Eight-year-old Sarah Frazer was "at school as usual" that morning in Thornbury Township when musket and artillery fire were heard in the distance at about nine o'clock. Her teacher stepped outside briefly and returned to tell the class, according to Frazer's later recollection, "there is a battle not far off, children you may go home." As Sarah led her brother and sister toward their house along the Chester Creek, their mother raced toward them on horseback. Far from stopping to attend to her children, she rode past them toward the battlefield to inquire after their father, Lieutenant Colonel Persifor Frazer, who was involved in the action as a member of Anthony Wayne's Pennsylvania brigade. Mrs. Frazer came home briefly later in the day but soon "was off again and did not return till dark." Neither of these behaviors, pedagogic or parental, fits neatly our ideas about the responsibility of adults for the well-being of children, or of the probable behavior of civilians in close proximity to combat.[7]

Nor, for that matter, does the response of Sarah's father. Colonel Frazer emerged from the day's clash unscathed, but before coming home he assisted a wounded soldier from the battlefield. He returned late at night to a sleeping household and draped his bloodstained greatcoat over a staircase banister before retiring. When Sarah rose the next day and saw the coat her "murder shout" filled the house. Her father emerged from his room, but rather than staying to comfort her, "as soon as his horse was prepared" he "mounted and rode off to the army." Frazer was captured a few days later, and he spent the next winter in a British prison. His wife, Mary Worrall Frazer, was left in a form of de facto responsibility for the household's welfare that the recent historiography of this generation of American women has made quite recognizable to us. But the experience of children with these phenomena has gone unnarrated.[8]

Another youth, twenty-one-year-old Joseph Townsend, was living on his parents' farm in East Bradford Township when the war came virtually to his front dooryard on September 11. Like many observers of the invasion scare of the previous year, Townsend's account suggests that the approach of two armies to an already divided community altered people's demeanor along lines of their prior dispositions toward the war. Whigs "thought it advisable to remove their families, stock and furniture to a distance. . . . Others being of a different opinion, were disposed to remain at home and risk the danger." Most of Townsend's neighbors were Friends "who generally believed it right to remain at their dwellings, and patiently submit to whatever suffering might be their lot." Washington and several of his generals took up quarters in the houses of the evacuees, which, Townsend recalled years later, "afforded an opportunity to spectators to view them."[9] Members of the Birmingham Monthly Meeting arrived at their meeting house on September 10 hoping to worship there one last time before the building became an American field hospital. But Continental officers were already rearranging the space and the best the Friends could do was to get permission to move some of the benches outside for their meeting. They spent some time in silence, after which a "female Friend" spoke about a visitation "from a kind of Providence" and the members discussed where they would meet after that day.[10]

A day later the community was visited by a different kind of "providence" in the form of a pitched battle between two armies. Despite having been moved by the previous day's peace testimony, Townsend recalled from the perspective of old age that he and other local youths "possessed of curiosity and fond of new things" had rushed toward the Brandywine Creek to see what would happen. They found themselves among "many like ourselves, but no intelligence could be obtained." They repaired to the alternate meetinghouse their elders had chosen for the "week day meeting," until new "disturbances" in the distance enticed many members to abandon the service. The youths met some neighboring women who said English troops were coming, murdering all before them. They discounted these reports but soon saw hundreds of red-coated soldiers emerging from the nearby woods, until the "fields were literally covered over with them," with their bayonets flashing in the sun. Townsend and his brothers decided to go home to protect their sisters but, disappointed when the armies did not cross their parents' farm, they again set out for the Brandywine. They met Sarah Boake, an area farmwife, "who had been as curious as ourselves and who had been among the soldiers as they marched along." Boake "encouraged" the young men to see for themselves, "saying what fine fellows they were, and to use her own expression 'they were *something* like an army.'"[11]

Townsend and his friends obtained permission to cross the lines and to enter the army's perimeter. They proceeded, somewhat awestruck, through "a crowd of military characters," until they reached a handsome house, into which "divers of the principal officers came . . . who manifested an uncommon social disposition." They were repeatedly asked the whereabouts of the Americans, which allowed Townsend's brother, William, to assume the delighted role of the neighborhood know-it-all. Much of this inquiry was in search of routine military intelligence, but some of the questions, such as those asking "what sort of a man Mr. Washington was," went beyond the merely technical. William Townsend, having been at Washington's headquarters, played his opportunity to the hilt, which seemed to "check their ardour." One of Joseph's examiners acknowledged "in some rapture" that the

Quakers "have got a hell of a fine country here, which we have found to be the case ever since we landed at Head of Elk." Years later Townsend recalled, "most or all of the officers who conversed with us were of the first rank, and were rather short, portly men, were well dressed and of genteel appearance, and did not look as if they had ever been exposed to any hardship; their skins being as white and delicate as is customary for females who were brought up in large cities or towns."[12]

By this time, Joseph Townsend had "become familiar" with the Redcoats, and he recalled that since "no danger or difficulty [was] to be apprehended from them, my curiosity or ambition was increased." He recruited a friend, and they plunged deeper into the vortex at the edge of the battlefield. Finding themselves near the front lines, they were surprised to hear the firing intensify, and Townsend, although "under no apprehension of danger . . . concluded it best to retire, finding that my inconsiderate curiosity had prompted me to exceed the bounds of prudence." His companion refused to be dragged away so Townsend retreated alone. As he reached a fence line, a German officer ordered his company to enter the field and flourished his sword over Townsend's head to make him help take down the fence. Joseph complied reflexively, until he realized that he was becoming more of a participant than a passive observer. His qualms about "being active in assisting to take the lives of my fellow beings" prompted him to sneak away ashamedly. Townsend eventually found himself standing on a hill with a mixed group of officers and civilians watching the progress of the battle. The observers included General Howe, "a large, portly man, of course [*sic*] features," who "appeared to have lost his teeth."[13]

After four hours, with shadows lengthening and the battle ebbing, the youths prepared leave. But since "admiration and curiosity had been the order of the day," Townsend "proposed to some of my companions that we should go over to the field of battle and take a view of the dead and wounded, as we might never have such another opportunity." His friends reluctantly complied, and they suddenly found themselves in a scene of human carnage. They were drafted to carry wounded men to the field hospitals and watched an amputation in progress. Townsend left only when told that the British army was "fixing the Picquet Guards" and that if they did not leave immediately they would be compelled to spend the night within the lines.[14]

On the way home the youths crossed another hazy boundary between reality and the altered states of perception in which they had spent much of the day. Their immersion on the British side and the momentum of events persuaded them that "there was not the probability of an American under arms in the whole neighborhood." But two of their party, "talking rather freely on the defeat of the American army," were challenged by a Continental scouting party, who opened fire on them, wounding one Simon Kerns in the thigh. The youth was carried to a nearby house where he lay "groaning and lamenting in a most grievous manner," and Townsend and his friends began to rue their "imprudence or inconsiderate conduct": "The novelties of the day were now damped. . . . Imagination was worked up to a great height and our fears were as great as we could bear, such was the dilemma that we were in. I considered that it had overbalanced all we had seen . . . to pursue the public road home was dangerous, from the expectation that the aforementioned scouting parties of the military were lying in wait for us and that we might be fired upon or otherwise taken up and carried before the prevailing power to answer for our conduct."[15] The boys finally snuck home through moonlit fields and woodlots, where Townsend received "a severe reproof" from his sisters. He lay in bed wondering "what might be the consequences of that day's expedition when it came to be known that we had shown such an attachment to and familiarity with the enemies of our country, and which the American forces were contending against."[16]

From the perspective of old age, Townsend did not offer answers to this or any other questions he may have asked himself that night. If he had reflected, he might have concluded that a battlefield was not a civil or political vacuum accessible only to soldiers; that it was easier for noncombatants to enter than to leave one; or that there was such a thing as an "eye of the storm" at the center of an armed engagement that could be safer than either the front lines or the ambiguously defined rear areas. He might also have observed that to be within the boundaries of a battle was to become a participant in it whether one intended to or not; and that one's safety there depended on random factors, such as an individual's value as a source of intelligence, or his or her impulsive demeanor toward unfamiliar authority figures.[17]

The outcome of the Brandywine clash did politicize the identities of some civilians in southern Chester County, especially those who had ties to the retreating American forces. The Frazer family found itself the object of frequent British attention in the days after the battle. Major Frazer came home on September 12 to find two self-invited houseguests who fled upon his arrival, men who, he concluded, must be "dreadful good-for-nothing Tories." On the advice of friends in the army he made himself scarce, leaving

Mary home with four children, a servant, and three slaves. Anticipating trouble, she began dispersing the family's valuables around the neighborhood and in the nearby woods and gardens.[18] On the fifteenth, a wagon train of British foragers approached the farm. The family scattered into the woods, leaving Mary and a young slave girl to confront the troops. One British officer asked "in broad Scotch . . . 'where are the damned rebels?'" She replied that she "knew of no Rebels—there was not I believed a Scotchman about the place." Mary Worrall Frazer, the daughter of an English Quaker married to a Scot, here invoked a complex constellation of images embodying a tradition of deep antipathy between English and Scottish Britons, centering on the abortive Jacobite uprisings of 1715 and 1745. Her target "flew into a great rage" and poured forth "abusive language" on her. The troops were ransacking the lower levels of the house, and Mary watched in helpless fear, mixed with resentment, as her neighbors gathered at the edge of the property to witness the spectacle.[19]

The commanding officer, a Captain De West, entered the house, drove off his drunkest and most violent troops, and personally conducted a thorough search and confiscation tour. He was contested by Mrs. Frazer on a closet-by-cupboard basis and compelled to negotiate with her over the propriety of each step in the search. She rebuffed De West's demand that she recruit her husband to join the British side, claiming that she would reject him if he showed any willingness to betray "his country." Mrs. Frazer may have ended the day sadly wondering which "country" she meant. Her personal sorrow fixed on the loss of "two little glass cream buckets with ladels,—the most beautiful little things . . . they were brought from England by my Grandfather Taylor." Her other mortification was the return of her starving dependents from the nearby woods and the realization that she did not have enough left in the house to feed them![20]

Persifor Frazer, meanwhile, was captured, possibly on the same day, at a nearby tavern by another Scotsman, General James Grant. Ironically, Frazer deployed precisely the same cultural weapons that his wife had, and to the same intended end: resistance to British authority. But he gave the double-edged verbal blade an opposite twist. When Grant heard Frazer's name and remarked "that is a Scotch name . . . and should not be the name of a rebel," his prisoner archly reminded him, "England has called other men rebels besides those who resist her government in America." Frazer was not released for his insolence, but Grant let him retain his horse and sword as badges of favor and perhaps of ethnic solidarity.[21]

It is doubtful that Grant and De West had an opportunity to compare notes on these incidents. Even if they had they would not have found themselves consulting with their American counterpart, General James Varnum. But had they done so they might have agreed that Pennsylvania's "labyrinthine" character extended down into its most basic social units, the family and household. The marriage in 1766 of Persifor and Mary Worrall Frazer illustrates the social components of Pennsylvania's "internal revolution." Her English Quaker forbears helped build the province in the 1680s. His immigrating Scots-Irish parents typified demographic trends that transformed Pennsylvania's social and political landscape during the generation after 1730. These changes did not bring the Revolution to Pennsylvania, but they helped to form the state's cultural character during the 1770s. Political tensions between Quakers and Scots-Irish Presbyterians shaped the development of resistance politics during the 1760s, and in 1777–78 they sharpened the conflict between moderate and radical Pennsylvania Whigs. British officers trying to police such a population would have known little about these matters, but as occupiers they had many opportunities observe the myriad political meanings of "Britishness" in its colonial dimensions.[22]

Ambiguities embedded in that internal revolution colored encounters between civilians and military personnel even when they did not invoke ethnic antagonisms. On September 30, four days before the battle of Germantown, Thomas Livezey, a prosperous Quaker farmer and miller from Roxboro Township on the Wissahickon Creek not far from Germantown, emerged from his orchard and met a small party of armed horsemen on the road. The group included Joseph Reed and John Cadwallader, two powerful Pennsylvania moderate revolutionaries who had important ties to both the Continental Army and the state government. Alienated by the radical drift of that government but alarmed by the vulnerability of the revolution in their state, both men served with the army as volunteers during the campaign, advising Washington and helping to coordinate a response to the British invasion.[23]

Neither man was uniformed that day, and Livezey did not immediately recognize them. As he tried to negotiate this precarious encounter, the horsemen began asking him pointed questions about the whereabouts of any "rebels" in the neighborhood. Presuming that he was dealing with an armed party of nonuniformed English cavalrymen, he answered cautiously that he had seen none but had "heard" there were some "on the other side of Germantown." Livezey then made a mistake by invoking the name of a prominent Pennsylvania Loyalist, asking them whether they knew Joseph

Galloway, which both men said they did. At this point, he suddenly recognized Reed and perceived the wrong turn the discussion had taken. Wanting to find a tactful way of letting his inquisitors know that he knew who they were but realizing to his "surprise" that he "did not know how to do it," Livezey was fumbling for words when his wife called from their house that she "had heard that Joseph Reed and Cadwallader were seen a little before near there." He thought this would be "a good opportunity" to acknowledge their identity. For some reason, however, he decided that the best way to do this would be simply to warn them that they—Reed and Cadwallader—had been seen in the neighborhood.[24]

The party rode off, but three nights later Cadwallader returned to arrest Livezey. This second encounter produced another impassioned discussion, with all pretenses about identity dropped, but it quickly deteriorated into an argument about who had said, done, and understood what at their roadside meeting. Livezey was reduced to seizing Cadwallader by the hand, trying to persuade him that he had not "informed" on him to a party of "English Horse," and that by telling Joseph Reed that one "Reed" was in the neighborhood he had merely been trying to facilitate their "escape," rather than basely contriving at their "capture." Cadwallader rejected the explanation and arrested Livezey's sons. A month later, Livezey was still trying to undo the damage. He was apparently in hiding, but he had heard that it was "propagated" in General Washington's camp that he had been an informer and, worse than this, that Washington was personally "angry" with him. In genuine anguish, he sought both to convince Cadwallader of the propriety of his conduct and to persuade him to lay the case before Washington.[25]

This episode is recorded in unusual detail, but at least some of the same ironies were embedded in every encounter between soldiers and civilians during the Pennsylvania campaign. Their potential consequences were riskier for civilians, who were less likely to be armed and more likely to be harmed. But such encounters were fraught with hazardous ambiguity for soldiers as well. Livezey's narrative nicely captures the confusion and dissonance inherent in these incidents for all parties; with actors realizing that they should do something to defuse a potentially lethal encounter but not knowing quite what to do, or if they knew what, not realizing how to do it. In such moments the best of intentions could precipitate the worst of tactical responses, and anxious innocence might provoke more suspicions than red-handed culpability.

If they were fortunate enough to escape arrest, as Thomas Livezey was, or to avoid random violence, as Simon Kerns was not, civilians might learn to process the signs and situations of war, and by doing so, begin to protect themselves from its dangers. Sustained or coherent narratives of such experiences are rare, but by exploring even a few we may be able to gain insights into how they worked in a wider range of cases.

One such narrative is that of sixteen-year-old Sarah Wister. Wister's family, like Elizabeth Farmer, fled Philadelphia in late 1776 when it seemed likely that war would come to Pennsylvania. Unlike Farmer, her parents stayed in the country at the farm of their kin, the Foulkes, in Gwynedd Township, Philadelphia County, when the immediate danger passed. Beginning in late September 1777, after the British occupied Philadelphia but before the battle of Germantown, Sarah recorded her experiences in a journal meant for her friend Deborah Norris, whose family remained in the city. Sarah's parents were moderately Whiggish in political persuasion, so the American soldiers who controlled the countryside and who began frequenting the Foulke farmstead were not avowed enemies. But to a Philadelphia teenager, armed and uniformed Virginians or Marylanders were almost as culturally alien as Redcoats.[26]

As a party of Philadelphia militia "pushed into the house" on September 24, Sarah withdrew in fright, "not having presence of mind eneough [sic] to face so many of the Military," but when she "call'd reason to my aid my fears were in some measure dispell'd tho' my teeth rattled and my hands shook like an aspin leaf." Wister acknowledged "the terror we were in [as] we expected to be in the midst of one Army or tother." She advised Norris to "summon up all your resolution call Fortitude to your aid" but quickly admitted that "courage" was "what I stand in need of myself but unfortunately have little of it in my composition."[27]

Sarah made no entries during the two weeks surrounding the battle of Germantown on October 4, noting that "nothing happen'd worth the time and paper it wou'd take to write it," but two months later she exclaimed, "the battle of Germantown and the horrors of that day are recent in my mind." During the interval between the battle and her writing she began to organize, evaluate, and give names to the phenomena she observed and her feelings about them. In the process she seemed to gain some control over her reactions. On October 19, she, her younger sister Betsy, and their friend George Emlen "went about a half mile from home where we cou'd see the [American] army pass" on the way to the northern outskirts of Philadelphia.[28] Wister anticipated and defiantly parried Norris's reproval, observing that "thee will stare at my going but no impropriety in my *opine,* or I wou'd not have gone." She wrote that they had "return'd with excellent appetites for our breakfast," and—on discovering that Maryland General William Smallwood and his staff had taken quarters with her family—she and Betsy quietly retired to prepare for flirtatious "adventures." She concluded: "How new is our situation. . . . I feel in good spirits tho surrounded by an Army the house full of officers yard alive with soldiers." Indeed, Sarah observed with almost self-reflective wonder that their guests "eat like other folks, talk like them, and behave themselves with elegance, so I will not be afraid of them."[29]

During the next several weeks, as the focus of the campaign shifted to the naval siege of American fortifications on the Delaware River below Philadelphia, Wister and her girlfriends began to regard the American soldiers more as objects of playful romantic conquest than as potential ravagers or oppressors. She recorded the marital status, appearance, demeanor, and rumored fortune of a small platoon of aides-de-camp with grace, humor, and deadly effect. Captain Furnival had "excepting one or two the handsomest face I ever seen," while Finley was "wretched ugly." Major Stoddard sat at the table and helped her to "divert" her infant brother, but Dr. Diggs was "a mighty disagreeable man." Major Letherberry was "a lawyer, a sensible young fellow and will never swing for want of a tongue," while another officer was "very bashful, so much so he can hardly look at the ladies." On October 27 an awkwardly tall army chaplain, "thin and meagre" without "a single personal charm [and] very few mental ones" came in and "fell violently in love with [Elizabeth] at first sight, the first discover'd conquest," leaving Sarah to wonder why she had "not charms sufficient to peirce the heart of a Soldier."[30] On October 31, when the household learned that the army would march from the neighborhood that day, Wister described their withdrawal in reasonably technical detail then interrupted herself to observe "how Militaryish I talk no wonder, when I am surrounded by people of that order." When their houseguests left the next morning, Sarah observed that she was "very sorry for when you have been with agreable people tis impossible not to feel regret when they bid you adieu," and she predicted that "when they leve us we shall be immur'd in solitude."[31]

By early December Wister was "all alive with fear," when the British thrust toward the American camp convinced her that "we shall be in the midst [of] it heaven defend us from so dreadful a sight . . . it will be sufficiently dreadful if we are only in hearing of the firing." But two quiet days and the return of Stoddard restored her nerves. Sarah monitored her own resilience. She sat in a chair "so low spirited that I could hardly speak the dread of an engagement . . . (if a battle should ensue)." Then she noticed that she "did not feel half so frightened as I expected to be, tis amazing how we get reconcild to such things six months ago the bare idea of being within ten aye twenty miles of a battle wou'd almost distracted me and now tho' two such large armys are within six miles of us we can be cheerful and converse calmly of it."[32]

An event that day helps to explain why. The family "distinctly heard platoon firing," and after running to the door, they concluded that the two armies were finally engaged. Wister reflexively acknowledged that she was "in the horrors." But it is impossible to read her journal without observing the cognitive and emotional growth of a girl who three months before had been unable to distinguish American horsemen from British because both "wore blue and red," but who could now glibly categorize types of engagements six miles away by the cadences of their musket discharges. Stoddard left the next week to rejoin the army, but not before Sarah observed his composure briefly cracking when he interrupted a typical "silent fit" by "clasping his hands and exclaiming aloud 'oh My God I wish this war was at an end.'"[33]

Stoddard's place in the household was taken by two more soldiers, Captain Lipscomb and Mr. Tilly, and the Wister and Foulke girls began plotting new conquests. When an evening tea turned to talk of politics ("a subject I avoid") they adjourned to the grounds. The moon shone with "uncommon Splendour," their spirits were "high," and Sarah "proposed a walk." When they reached the road they heard hoofbeats and voices, "a party of Lighthorse said one, the English perhaps [le]ts run home," but Sarah insisted "no, no, [let's] be heroines." The intruder was only Major Stoddard, who was not quite ready yet to exchange his pleasant billet for a cold log hut and who had returned to the Foulke farm to spend a few more days before the winter began.[34]

As the 1777 campaign drew to a close, Wister and her friends conspired with Stoddard to punish Tilly for his annoying habit of playing wretched music on his flute. They found a realistically painted wooden figure of a "British Grandadier" in the attic, set it up in the doorway, and tricked Tilly into answering the door. The stricken dandy fell for the ruse and "bolted" into the nearby woods. He sheepishly returned half an hour later to a howling household—a "full assembly of girls and officers"—and to Wister's bemused judgment that his "fright, confusion and race had not divested him of his beauty." When the troops decamped for good on December 19, she noted in her journal that she was feeling "a differe[nt] kind [of sorrow] from what I felt some time since." They would "not see many of the military now," she lamented, "we shall be very intimate with solitude . . . after so much company I cant relish the idea of sequestration."[35]

It would be an error to dismiss Wister's account as a mere record of girlish coquetry, a diverting break from the "real" business of war. For civilians—whether schoolchildren unceremoniously dumped onto battlefields or aging millers accosted by sly horsemen in orchard lanes—sorting out visceral sensations and matching names with confusing phenomena *was* the real business of war, and doing it well or badly could make the difference between sacrifice and survival. Wister's account is important not for its precocity but rather for its articulate continuity. It is unusually comprehensive and cumulative, and almost uniquely self-reflective in its treatment of the civilians' learning process.

More often than not in the fragmentary record we see people making all the wrong decisions; individuals violently cut down along the unpredictable trajectory of comprehending warfare. Monumental stupidity born of ignorance or naiveté knew no bounds. Mans Hellms, a Swedish farmer from the Raccoon Creek neighborhood along the Delaware River in New Jersey, below Philadelphia, boarded a British man-of-war anchored in the river near his homestead in October 1777. When asked what he was doing, he replied that he "was only curious to see how things were managed there." Lord Howe's tars promptly arrested Hellms as a spy, and although they released him when he became sick, he died soon after going home. Henry Janes, an Irishman married to a Swedish woman from the same Lutheran congregation as Hellms, lived in Penn's Neck. He was a local magistrate under New Jersey's Whig government and housed a troop of militia who disrupted commerce between inhabitants and the fleet. Janes rebuffed a written entreaty from the British commander to change sides and then allowed his guests to stand behind his house and fire on the sailors when they came ashore to trade. He too was cast into the hold where he sickened, and he too was carried to his house to lie on his deathbed.[36]

Even the minister who buried these men was not above folly. After American troops repulsed the British and Hessian assault on Fort Mercer on October 23, Reverend Nicholas Collin toured the fort, which became instantly famous as the site of a rare rebel victory in a frustrating campaign. The exhausted Americans were not holding an open house that day, however, and some "rascals" accused him of being a spy. Collin regarded the Whig friends who were with him as a badge of protective identity, but the fort's commander was more interested in the fact that he was "mak[ing] drawings of the fort." Collin was arrested and threatened with being hung on the spot. Because he could quote "international law" and because he was willing to sign a parole, the reverend lived to tell the tale. But the rest of his journal suggests that he never really came to terms with what he called "this unhappy war."[37]

Residents of the Delaware Valley needed to collaborate with each other to make at least provisional sense of events because it was impossible for any one individual to collect enough information to even partly understand what going on. Sarah Wister's determination to keep her journal; Thomas Livezey's belief that General Washington was angry at him and his insistence on doing something about it; and Joseph Townsend's pained realization that his "familiarity" with the British troops would inevitably "come to be known" to his neighbors, all suggest the efforts of civilians to communicate with each other and to reduce ambiguity by collective effort. If the subtext of the learning process was gossip and rumor, the text itself was pure noise. For civilians, the informational culture of war was aural before it became oral. They heard and felt the percussive and concussive effects of combat and waited for strangers to bring the latest news.

Henry Muhlenberg, the elderly German Lutheran minister and diarist from Trappe, recorded small arms or cannon fire on more than a quarter of the days in which he made entries in his conscientiously kept diary, between September 7, when the campaign neared his neighborhood, and November 14, when the British troops broke the American blockade on the Delaware River. The first entry was almost offhand in nature: "the firing of cannon . . . in the distance." Within a week, on the morning of the Brandywine engagement, however, he recorded "heavy and long continuing cannonading some thirty miles away on Brandywine *Crick.*" By September 16 Muhlenberg could distinguish the intensity, the different kinds of weapons, and the proximity of the percussion: "a sharp skirmish with field pieces and small arms about fourteen miles southwest of us on the other side of the Schulkiel."[38] But the pattern in the noise, if any, remained maddeningly elusive. On the afternoon of September 28 there were "fourteen heavy cannon shots," unaccompanied by any other sounds that might have clarified the nature, location, or meaning of their source. October 4 brought "some field cannons," while the ninth began with a "heavy cannonading from the direction of Philadelphia." Visual evidence was useless in defining the campaign's progress. On September 24, Muhlenberg saw "several high columns of smoke" on the horizon but heard no weapons firing.[39]

By mid-October the artillery battle for control of the lower Delaware River climaxed in intensity, but the regularity—or perhaps the resulting comprehensibility—of the noise seems to have dulled Muhlenberg's inclination to report it. On the eleventh, twelfth, sixteenth, and seventeenth he routinely recorded "cannonading" but failed to comment on its source or meaning. Only a "blast or roar which shook our house" on the twenty-third and was followed by a palpable silence reengaged his imagination. By then he was more inclined to conjecture (instead of wonder) than he had been a month earlier. Muhlenberg pronounced it "probable" that "the powder magazine in [Fort Mifflin] was ignited and blown up," a phenomenon that could, he reassuringly noted, easily "cause a concussion in the distance like that of an earthquake."[40] After that comforting dash of expertise Muhlenberg made only a few perfunctory observations of firing "again" from the river. But when an Indian volunteer serving with the Continental Army came to his house on November 7 with news that put much of this cacophony in perspective, he tacitly acknowledged having heard "considerable cannonading" constantly between October 15 and 24. And between November 7 and November 14, when the artillery siege on the river reached its crescendo, Muhlenberg's literary silence suggests that he had simply stopped paying attention to it.[41]

Muhlenberg was well situated to gain intellectual control over the invasion crisis because his residence was located at the convergence of two major roads leading from Philadelphia to the Continental storehouses in the Reading area and his pastoral role made his house a gathering place for civilians and soldiers. From the first days of the campaign his journal was studded with reports of the passive receipt of news, rumor, and information, mixed with much more occasional active efforts to sort, process, evaluate, or act on it. It is "reported" that "the British army is working its way closer and closer to Philadelphia and Lancaster." The British "are expected to make their way to Frantz Crik and are said to be only seven miles from there." An "intelligent *gentleman* told me where the British army is encamped and conjectured that a division will cross the Schulkiel near us." His son "brought us the news that the American army left Philadelphia yesterday and marched across the Schuylkill." A British camp "could be seen, I was told, through a fieldglass." It "was reported that the British were crossing the Schulkiel . . . and that the battle would take place in this neighborhood."[42]

In a countryside filled with "thieves, robbers, and marauders," where "parents [were fighting] against children, children against parents, brother against brother [and] neighbor against neighbor," Muhlenberg's spirits slowly began to crack.[43] The daytime chatter of muskets and booming of field pieces played counterpoint to a nocturnal symphony of raps on his door and clatters in his barnyard that brought dangers closer to hand. There was the "man with a flint" who walked into Muhlenberg's bedroom on September 19 to demand bread, and the American troops who pounded on the door two nights later "as if they wished to break it," but then asked only for "fire." There was the "old English neighbor" who came in the middle of the night to beg the minister to intercede on his behalf with General Maxwell. There was the fearful rapping on October 3 that roused the household but produced only "two riderless horses" in the barnyard.[44]

His grown children urged him to flee to safety, as they had during the invasion scare of late 1776. Then he had then waited stoically along the Reading Road watching the rest of the region stream by his door; now he began to consider evacuating. But the heavy rainstorm that aborted the "Battle of the Clouds" trapped him and his wife at home as they were "taking counsel." His old resignation began to reassert itself and a degree of activity crept into Muhlenberg's mode of processing news and rumor.[45] That day he "received the news" that the British army was moving on the other side of the Schuylkill and responded that "certainly it is to be conjectured" that they would attack the Americans.[46] He "learned" that the fourteen heavy cannon shots that had been fired without accompanying sounds of battle had come from the American camp where troops were celebrating the news that General Burgoyne's army had been halted near Saratoga. Two weeks later, when Gates's troops defeated and captured Burgoyne's men, he was able to identify the ensuing celebration from the American camp as a *feu de joie,* a patterned sequential firing of thousands of small arms.[47] A few days later he was "fetched" to help bury a parishioner and he passed near the American camp, where he sorted through army scuttlebutt with precision and detachment. The word in camp was that the British would leave Philadelphia to guard against American efforts to exploit the defeat of Burgoyne. If true it was "probable," Muhlenberg decided, that they would "hasten on board ship, and sail to New York." He was prepared to credit "the good, gracious, and merciful God" for such an act of deliverance, but he cautioned that "the report is almost too good. It requires confirmation."[48]

The regional rumor mill never stopped operating during the fall, and Muhlenberg's diary continued to be filled with accounts in which "we learned," "it was said," "reports were received," and a grammatical catalogue of passive receptivity. By mid-campaign a more active vocabulary was emerging. When the house-rattling explosions of October 23 shook the area, "everybody" was "curious"—the term that seemed so callow in Joseph Townsend's narrative from Brandywine but so deadly in the case of Mans Hellms—to know what had happened. Muhlenberg was quick to correlate the rival conjectures that circulated with the political identity of their believers.[49]

By late November, when agents of the American Quartermaster's and Commissary Departments inquired about his cellar and barns, Muhlenberg could readily distinguish the import from that of the routine, opportunistic military intrusions he had learned to tolerate throughout the fall. He guessed—accurately enough, as it turned out—that "the American army will establish winter quarters in this region."[50] On December 11, he only feigned surprise to learn that "[enemy] officers have singled me out for revenge and [say] that they will have me captured by their dragoons at the first opportunity." He rebuffed "partisan insinuations" from "false accusers," affirmed his decision not to leave the area, and resignedly wrote in his journal: "what a difference there is between peacetime and wartime, especially when hostilities are pushed to extremes." A week later, as the army marched toward Valley Forge, Muhlenberg entertained perhaps his five hundredth visitor of the fall, a friend from the backcountry. That night he remarked, in a tone suspended between smug condescension and weary incredulity, "for the first time in his life he had heard a cannon."[51]

Muhlenberg's wonder was probably not feigned. Delaware Valley residents were surrounded by sound, and the noise of war became for them a kind of currency, to be heard, exchanged, doubted, compared, and above all comprehended. Christopher Marshall, an aging, disillusioned Whig living in the temporary Pennsylvania capital of Lancaster, recorded many kinds of information—reports, rumors, visual phenomena—all of which he sorted, analyzed, and categorized as truth or lies, significant or meaningless. But he struggled with nothing so much as noise and what his neighbors were saying about noise. On September 19 some "people came out on the hill near our place in order, its said to hear the firing of the cannon between our people and the enemy, but I could not say that I heard any." A month later it was "said" that "a very heavy cannonade was heard on the outside of this Town, most part of this afternoon." The next day his neighbors "remarked" on "a constant heavy firing all this forenoon, which was distinctly heard near twelve." By this time Marshall almost seemed to be straining toward the city, until he indeed "heard a heavy firing from [the] E. S. E.," which he predictably "apprehended . . . to be platoon or brigade firing."[52]

But he had to rely on rumors to record the explosions of the British transports on October 23, and a real earthquake that rattled the area on November 22 seemed to muddle Marshall's new confidence in his aural faculties.[53] He was soon growling that "some people pretended to have heard a firing of cannon this morning" and complaining that "this is a strange age and place in which I now dwell, because nothing can be had cheap but lyes, falshood and slanderous accusation." At some point during the autumn, the roar of war became for civilians a perversely comforting thing: an index of the distance, direction, or intensity of danger and a counterpoise to the whisper of war in the form of hearsay and gossip from passersby and partisans. The absence of the first kind of sound only magnified the effects of the second; the midnight door-pounding that Muhlenberg came to dread or the swirl of rumor that drove Marshall crazy.[54]

Most of this evidence comes from the countryside, from regions under Continental control or contested between rebels and Redcoats, but Philadelphia was also an integral part of the civilian arena of war, sharing its anxious culture of knowledge, ignorance, conjecture, debate, inquiry, and interpretation. Despite the efforts of both armies to patrol their perimeters, the membrane separating the occupied city from its beleaguered hinterland was always much more porous than either side wished. Philadelphians and their rural neighbors were players in a puzzle game, with both holding fragmentary answers that interlocked imperfectly with each others' half-articulated questions. In seeking to create a collective picture of the war the wonder is perhaps not how badly they did it, but how they did it at all.

Elizabeth Drinker, the wife of a prominent Quaker merchant who was arrested and exiled to Virginia by the state government just before the city fell in September, at first tried to keep the occupation at bay by focusing on her responsibility as the de facto head of a household that included as many as ten persons. Like many of the region's civilians, she measured the ebb and flow of war as much by sound as by sight and paid attention to most phenomena in proportion to their nearness to her house. As late as October 2, a week after the arrival of the Redcoats, she observed almost proudly to her diary that she had "not yet exchang'd a word, with any of the new comers." But her attention was inexorably pulled outward, first by the discovery that her loft window offered a good view of the battle for control of the Delaware

River, and then by the realization that events in her neighborhood were affected by developments beyond its borders. As early as September 27 she climbed into the loft to watch a naval skirmish on the river.[55]

At first she made no systematic efforts to correlate or analyze the strange phenomena relating to the occupation. But after the Battle of Germantown on October 4 and the devastating skirmish at Red Bank three weeks later, Drinker's reportage became more wide ranging, sharply focused, and even analytical. Rumors swept through town that an American division would attack when most of the British army rushed to Germantown and a "double guard" was thought necessary. On October 14 there was "much talk" of a rebel attempt to "enter the City." Two nights later the inhabitants met "to regulate a Nightly Watch," an old Philadelphia police custom that had been "drop'd for some time," but one that citizens now thought desirable to reestablish.[56] By mid-October Drinker was noting in her journal when she did not hear "certain" accounts or "Perticulars" of the sounds of war.[57] Later that month, as the rebel bottleneck on the river and the blockade of area roads began limiting supplies of food for civilians, Drinker observed, "the people round the Country does not come near us with anything" and the "Amricans" [sic] turned back people who went into the country to buy food.[58] She presumed when October began that mysterious British efforts to "number the Inhabitance" reflected their acceptance of a military responsibility to feed civilians "in case provisions should be scarce." A month later, with hunger at hand, she recorded Hessians "plundring" the townspeople for the first time.[59]

Drinker seldom stirred far from her home. A mid-December stroll a few squares over to Jane Bartram's dry goods shop in Market Street was a rare venture beyond her neighborhood. By early November, however, some members of her household began cautiously exploring the perimeters of the occupation apparatus. On the seventh her daughters Sally and Nancy walked "up to Philipss Rope-Walk to see the Redoubts which are errected thereabout." With at least some military information now coming from her own dependents, Drinker's consciousness fixed as sharply on the periphery as in her own neighborhood or hearth. Ironically, when the British capture of the American forts on the lower Delaware in mid-November brought the campaign to a close and lessened military activity in the region, her attention to the details of war began to peak.[60]

On the seventeenth, she noticed that the British troops were "busyly employ'd geting up the *Cheveaux-de-Frise,*" using a naval word for river obstructions that she might not have recognized earlier. On the nineteenth she interrupted an account of visiting friends to note that "G[eneral] Corn Walace left this city the Day before Yesterday," and that "he designs for the Jersyes." On the twentieth she clambered into the garret window to see burning vessels from the American fleet. She could distinguish "cannon and small arms" fire and began to report minor skirmishes in distant places.[61] The invasion of her house on November 25 by an "enraged, drunken" officer who swore, waved his sword, and "stole" her servant girl, Ann, was a traumatic experience for her, but she quickly wrote off the loss and resumed watching the progress of the occupation, with growing bitterness at the harm British plundering was doing to civilians; the "enormitys . . . committed by those from whome, we ought to find protection." She followed with interest talk in early December that part of the British army would leave town on "some secret expedition" and expressed surprise when the orders were "countermanded." When the troops left on the night of the fourth but returned without explanation four days later she accurately concluded that the development "carrys no very agreeable appearance with it."[62]

By mid-December Drinker could cast the minutiae of home economics in the jargon of an army logistics officer. Her son Henry had "gone a Forageing," probably for the household larder. She had stubbornly resisted the intrusion of an army lodger into her house by pleading her status as an unprotected female and the sole provider for a large household. Now, with the campaign ending, she faced up to the inevitable. She listed her criteria for an acceptable boarder, negotiated with a likely prospect, and on December 29 she closed a deal. Major John Cramond had "now become one of our Family," she wrote, hopefully invoking what may have been the only relational term that eighteenth-century mothers and generals shared. She put the best face that she could on a potentially calamitous event. He "appears to be a thoughtful, sober young man," she reported, "which is a great favour to us." For Drinker, at least, the martial and the maternal dimensions of the autumn occupation crisis had belatedly come to an ironic kind of closure.[63]

Robert Morton was, like Drinker, a Quaker, a dependent of one of the "Virginia Exiles," and initially at least a tacit supporter of the British. But while Drinker stayed at home protecting her family and piecing together her own understanding of the occupation order, Morton roamed the streets with a restless abandon that recalls the peripatetic Joseph Townsend at Brandywine. Unlike his country counterpart, however, Morton was serving as the eyes, ears, and legs of an immobilized household, protecting family property on the lower Schuylkill River and gathering resources. His mobility—and the amount of time he spent along the edges between the city and its hinterland—gave him a unique ability to integrate the events of the autumn into a coherent picture. Morton compulsively watched the soldiers, of course, like most Pennsylvanians did, but more important, he spent large amounts of time watching his fellow citizens watch the soldiers.

Morton began the campaign by invoking, albeit inverting, the civic judgment that Drinker reached at its conclusion when he derided the Continental Congress for abandoning Philadelphia. "Thus we have seen the men from whom we have received, and from whom we still expected protection," he sneered, "leave us to fall into the hands of . . . a barbarous, cruel, and unrelenting enemy." When British troops arrived on September 26 he hailed them as liberators but wrote that parts of the city "already begin to show the great destruction of the Fences and other things, the dreadful consequences of an army however friendly." Within days the ravages of the occupation had struck members of the Quaker exile community, and Morton made the first in an endless series of increasingly frustrating applications to British officers for protection from the "friendly" troops.[64]

Both in his capacity as an intermediary between Quakers and Redcoats—and undoubtedly as a "curious" youth, too—Morton began perambulating the contested borders of the city, from the Middle Ferry on the Schuylkill to "Plantation" at Gray's Ferry, to Province Island near Fort Mifflin, to Hollander's Creek on the south end, then up the Delaware riverfront to Kensington and west along the new British earthworks across the neck above town.[65] Everywhere he went he saw physical destruction, and he constantly watched for signs of the civilians' reactions. At the Middle Ferry on October 4, while the battle of Germantown raged, he saw a group of citizens standing with thirty British Light Dragoons watching American troops on the opposite bank. The next day he went up to Germantown itself to "collect if possible a true acco[unt]" of the battle. The Americans, he learned, had attacked "with an unusual firmness" and had driven the British troops back before their assault became unglued. At Howe's headquarters Morton met an aide who was "enraged" that citizens had not warned the Redcoats about the attack, and who hinted that a large swath of countryside might be depopulated as punishment. As he left he caught a glimpse of Howe himself, who did "not answ[er his] expectations" any more than he had impressed Joseph Townsend three weeks earlier.[66]

Morton visited a British army hospital and an American prisoner billet, comparing the medical care offered at each. He and several "gentlemen" went to Hollander's Creek, where they watched British and American vessels preparing for battle. He noticed the apathy of some citizens responding to a fire at a stable where the Hessians were lodged.[67] All the while he was recording the "cannonading" that frightened rural Pennsylvanians, and by mid-October he, too, could identify "platoon firing."[68] He noted constricting food supplies, rising prices, and "a prospect of starvation."[69] Like Drinker, he correlated these phenomena with increasingly aggressive British requisitioning. Some Hessians came "on a foraging, or rather plundering party," and a neighbor's unguarded vegetables stood, in Morton's venomous phrase, "a silent spectator to their infamous depredations."[70]

The word "plunder," in fact, began to haunt his discourse, and as it did his strategic and political judgments shifted. He catalogued the Hessian debacle at Red Bank on October 23 under the rubric "the important effects of despising the American army." The devastating explosions of two British warships on the Delaware elicited, he noted, "the great amazement of the inhabitants and the disappointment of the soldiery."[71] A day later he predicted that "the ravages and wanton destruction of the soldiery will, I think, soon become irksome to the inhabitants . . . who are now almost satiated with British clemency.[72] He hurried to his parents' country house on the Schuylkill and spent three days removing its fences to prevent their destruction. But on November 1 he cut short an account of his "particular affairs" to resume a detailed critique of both British treatment of Pennsylvania civilians who relied on their protection and of the British army's tactical proficiency. On the second he walked along the Schuylkill River on his way to the British camp and remarked that American troops on the other bank seemed to be "clean and neat." When the American forts on the Delaware fell in mid-November, his attention focused less on the prospect that Philadelphians would now be supplied by the British fleet than on the "perseverance" of the rebel defenders.[73]

Indeed, just *because* of his alienation toward the occupying troops, Morton's account of the fleet's arrival included details that escaped the notice of other informants in the city and the attention of historians ever since. On December 1, as more British transports reached the wharves, he disclosed that "a contest has subsisted in this City since the arrival of the fleet, concerning the legal Paper Currency." The ships carried British merchants, who moved into shops abandoned by Whigs, hoping to profiteer from a captive market of hungry, politically reliable Philadelphians. They demanded hard currency for their badly needed goods but ran headlong into resistance from the city's "most respectable inhabitants," who used "all their influence to support" the credit of "legal" paper money. This effort was spearheaded by the town's loyal or pacifist women, who were "determined to purchase no goods with hard money." Others, including greedy Loyalists, "enemies of the British constitution" who had stayed in the city, and even some members of "our Society" of Quakers, Morton sorrowfully observed, were freely spending hard money. In doing so, he implied, they were "purchasing momentary gratifications at the expense of the Public" but subverting the only realistic means of sustaining a viable political economy in a restored regime.[74]

In this sketchy account, Morton may have revealed an important but entirely unappreciated episode in civil-military relations during the British occupation of Pennsylvania. Standard accounts of the monetary dynamics of the war juxtapose abundant, if depreciating, Continental paper money, whose credit depends on the fate of the rebellion itself, against scarcer but strategically deployed British "specie"—gold and silver coins. Most Whigs, however grudgingly, accept the former as a necessary surtax on the Revolution's success, whereas Loyalists revel in (or with) the king's coin. The disparity in value between the two currencies becomes a strategic resource for British commanders and a lever with which to pry the critical neutralist community away from the rebellion.[75] The scenario Morton hinted at does not reverse this equation so much as expands it to include the ties some Pennsylvanians felt to the old colonial regime. The "legal" paper currency that the townspeople were struggling to "support" was not Continental money, but the old Pennsylvania provincial currency. Morton disclosed that "the friends of government and others have been collecting this legal tender for several mo[nth]s past, expecting that in those places in the possession of the British Army it will be of equal value with silver and gold." That hope had been rebuffed by the community of British merchant interlopers, and— with British commanders staying above the fray—the fate of the project now depended on solidarity among citizens.[76]

This imbroglio suggests an interesting wrinkle in the broad British strategy to subdue America, for which Howe had recently risked Burgoyne's army, and indeed the entire 1777 campaign plan, in hopes of reaping the political benefits of the widely presumed "disposition" of most Pennsylvanians to "return to their duty." Pennsylvania experienced the most clear-cut internal revolution in America in 1776 when its old Quaker and Anglican, proprietary and "popular," elites were swept aside by an emerging cohort of previously disenfranchised radicals. General Howe's advisers were no more likely to understand the precise meaning of these developments than their field officers could have appreciated the subtleties of ethnic insults in the taverns or farmyards of Chester County, but those meanings were critical to his hopes of making any strategy based on mobilizing disaffected Americans work in the field.

To the Quaker and Anglican gentries hoarding the old colony money, expectations for its acceptance as a currency went far beyond their hopes for a fiscally buffered occupation winter. Rather, these expectations suggested the specific meanings that those communities attached to the very idea of the "restoration" of "government" in America. They implied the restoration of *their* government—as it had been established between 1681 and 1718; perfected from then until 1755; and nurtured through the turbulent upheavals of revolutionary politics until June 1776. The efficacy of Pennsylvania's paper currency issues after 1722, and their linkage to the colony's Loan Office and to Quaker patronage regimes had been, after the preservation of peace, the most effective tool the Friends had for keeping political control of the province in the face of waves of non-English immigration.[77] The state's displaced elites saw the Loan Office notes as both an evocative symbol of normalcy and a critical test of the occupiers' good faith. General Howe's support of the English merchants, however, showed that he had a somewhat more limited definition of "restoration" and a far more expansive one of "government," than most Pennsylvanians could have imagined. He could not realistically hope to force the London traders to accept old colonial money to curry favor with friendly inhabitants who had stayed in or fled to the city, while requiring them to pay opportunistic neutral civilians who came to town with country produce in hard specie.

The political task facing the British Army in Pennsylvania was not one of dividing and conquering—the internal revolution had already done that—but rather of gluing together a diverse and shattered polity. Now, before Howe could even unpack his transports, the silent monetary struggle reported by Morton showed what a difficult if not hopeless task that might become. The decision went to the new merchants and rural suppliers. The city grandees had already made almost irrevocable political commitments and, in a literal sense, they had nowhere else to go. The market people in the countryside were not only a critical element in Howe's plan to feed civilians, but their willingness to risk traveling the roads with their goods might have the ancillary virtue of draining the habitat of the Continental Army of agricultural resources.[78]

Howe could not know about the political bargaining that was occurring that week at Whitemarsh between the American army and state and Continental political leaders. But if Washington took literally, rather than just seriously, the implications of the deal he had struck and tried to stop the trafficking in country produce sustained by the currency imbalance, his army might be placed into an untenable relationship with its civilian neighbors. A nominally "rebel" force would become the police arm of the de facto incumbent political regime, reaping all of the thankless liabilities of such a role. The imperial army, meanwhile, might have the temporary luxury of acting the part of an insurgent, by encouraging the region's inhabitants to defy restrictions placed on their "liberty" by the local authorities. Howe was perhaps incapable of thinking in such creative tactical terms, but he knew which side of the city lines both his bread and his butter were coming from. Sterling money remained the coin of the realm in Philadelphia, and the project to "support" the provincial notes died quietly.[79]

Robert Morton's diary shows that he had a subtle political imagination far beyond his tender years. But the end of the 1777 campaign found him at wits end. He despised the liberators who he had once seen as his saviors; he was appalled by the divisions within the Loyalist and Quaker polities; and he was perhaps even beginning secretly to admire the rebels who still held his stepfather captive in Virginia. During December his observations became increasingly perfunctory. Then, on the next-to-last day of the year, the season's first ice obstructed the Delaware River, six weeks too late to spare the Continental Army from enduring its bitter ordeal at Valley Forge. Several British transports still waiting to reach the city docks broke loose, and one was forced onto the New Jersey shoreline. Morton closed the year by noting, with barely a hint of bitter glee, that the vessel had quickly been "plundered by the inhabitants, who came down in great numbers to participate in the plunder."[80]

Borrowing martial vocabularies was, for civilians, perhaps a step along the way toward adopting military behaviors. Delaware Valley civilians had learned many things during the four months since their communities had been invaded, but the campaign's close deprived them of many of their newfound and hard-won aural and visual cues. The boom of cannonading ended, and the chatter of small arms fire faded, to be replaced by the same eerie silences that had unnerved British soldiers on their journey up the Chesapeake Bay. After the New Year, citizens' encounters with soldiers bore more resemblance to Thomas Livezey's deadly verbal jousting with Reed and Cadwallader than to

Joseph Townsend's callow banter with pale-faced and portly Redcoats. And the relatively safe interstices that Townsend somehow found in the battle of Brandywine had few palpable counterparts along the muddy roads where Bucks or Chester County farmers sought to traffic harvests of peace for the coin of war. Having learned, after a fashion, to live with war, civilians now had to adapt that knowledge to survive perilous circumstances that were as different from war as they were from peace.

Chapter 5

STARVE, DISSOLVE, OR DISPERSE

T he army's first two weeks at Valley Forge shaped its experience there. They also fixed its reputation, and that of the winter itself, for the next two centuries. The Continental logistical situation, never more than barely adequate from mid-October on, worsened steadily after the Americans crossed the Schuylkill River on December 11, until the army's ability to function as a coherent entity was openly questioned by its own commander-in-chief. The movement of the army from Whitemarsh to Valley Forge, which the main body reached late on December 19, triggered another provisions crisis by severing the fragile communications and transport links by which large amounts of food were brought to the troops. Once again the crippled support departments struggled to service a moving target. One commissary officer bemoaned the "approaching calamity that threatens our Army for want of Provisions," and he grimly predicted that the army would "not be able to Exist one week longer."[1]

The trials of late autumn had taught commanders to recognize patterns of incipient disaster and allowed them to experiment with hastily improvised remedies. As in November, most of the troops were now placed in a rugged site that could be further fortified against enemy attacks and one that furnished an anchor for an increasingly dispersed supply network. It remained necessary, for both tactical and ecological reasons, for large parts of the army to be detached from this main body. By such a disposition, small parties could serve limited strategic purposes, such as guarding key towns, harassing enemy movements, and protecting "well-affected" segments of the population. This denied the British the easy enjoyment of the fruits of their campaign successes and distributed the troops closer to the remaining available food supplies. Thus the system of informal self-requisitioning that had always supplemented the operation of the regular supply departments, and had filled the breach when those departments faltered, could be maintained despite progressively diminishing local resources.

Washington moved quickly to implement this plan. In essence, the army was trading places with the Pennsylvania militia, which had assumed responsibility for the region west of the Schuylkill during the army's immobilized weeks at Whitemarsh. The militia troops, numbering fewer than 1,000 men, crossed to the east side with orders to disrupt communications between the city and Bucks and Philadelphia counties. They would continue using the dispersed, small-unit tactics that they had labored to execute during the autumn. Their commander, John Armstrong, planned to sweep the areas near the city to collect all cattle remaining "convenient to the enemy" and then to divide his command into small mobile parties posted at "common duty stations." These patrols would be supplied and directed from a central camp, but they were ordered to stay in motion and to hold "every capital road" in the area.[2]

Washington worked to establish a similar screening operation west of the Schuylkill to contain British foraging parties, to discourage public cooperation with the enemy, and to support a small cohort of intelligence officers and their civilian spies. His priority for regular army units, however, was to collect them at the new camp; establish their quarters there; and determine their strength, condition, and material needs before deciding on detached duties. He thus withheld a small group of militia to anchor this network until more permanent arrangements were made. General James Potter, with 300 Pennsylvanians, was sent toward the lines. He established his quarters at the village of Radnor, and, with the support of Colonel Daniel Morgan's regiment of Virginia riflemen, deployed his men in small parties along major roads linking eastern Chester County with Philadelphia.[3]

Behind this temporary screen the soldiers began building a secure camp. The well-worn campaign tents were pitched for temporary shelter, and troops scoured local hillsides and woodlots to retrieve raw materials for the "log city" that would provide their winter housing. Army engineers were ordered to survey the terrain in a broad triangle between the Schuylkill

River and Valley Creek and to mark out for the brigade officers their troops' assigned living areas. Wood-cutting teams were directed to save sections of tree trunks suitable for hut construction, and three generals were appointed to receive proposals for new methods of roofing the huts.[4] While the army labored, in Thomas Paine's vivid simile, "like a family of beavers," Washington turned to issues of strategy and army organization. On December 19, fearing that the British would seize Wilmington, from where they might "countenance the disaffected" on both sides of the Delaware and menace the upper Chesapeake Bay, he ordered General Smallwood to march with his division to Delaware to fortify the town and anchor the circular blockade he was trying to erect around Philadelphia to the river.[5]

It was critical to Washington's ability to manage the army that effective control be maintained from headquarters and that all detached personnel operate on specific assignments. A scattered deployment might serve as a cover for loitering, desertion, or marauding unless steps were taken to control the flow of military and civilian traffic. A porous blockade around Philadelphia might be tolerated on the grounds that conditions precluded anything more effective. If the perimeter of the American camp proved equally permeable, however, the army's security would be threatened and its relationships with Congress and the state compromised. By late December it became clear that the army had hemorrhaged manpower during its exodus from Whitemarsh to Valley Forge. Unattached soldiers and commissaries were roaming the countryside, unleashing their whims and resentments on friend and foe alike, crippling the ability of legitimate functionaries to perform their duties and arousing the fury of the local populace. General Anthony Wayne, a resident of Chester County, was besieged by old neighbors and acquaintances complaining of their treatment at the hands of soldiers. Even the families of militiamen had been "stripped" and insulted, Wayne complained, and he predicted that many of these men would abandon the service to defend their homes.[6]

A situation where half-uniformed soldiers roamed the countryside was creating a brigand's paradise for self-appointed guerrillas. Parties of armed men calling themselves "volunteers" were patrolling roads near the city, indistinguishable from army detachments, stopping and looting civilians and soldiers alike. Major John Clark, the supervisor of Washington's small spy network, complained that this "set of Gentry" who "infect[ed] the public roads" was "no better than as many highway robbers." One rogue had stopped one of Clark's agents and challenged the authority of the pass he was carrying. Clark and Wayne both predicted that the situation would ruin the army unless it was be halted immediately.[7] Washington recognized that the straggling and illegal behavior of army members were partly a rational response to acute hunger and to the many failures of the political and military machines, but he could not afford to condone it. His expressions of outrage became daily features of his general orders, and he sent officers into the countryside to round up stragglers; required commanders to make "constant rollcalls" to account for their men; promised severe punishment to soldiers caught away from camp without passes; forbade troops to carry weapons except when on duty; and lectured the army daily on the need for discipline.[8]

Washington's decision to pull in the Continental units and rely on militia for patrol duty reflected his recognition of the political sensitivity of having tired, frustrated, and resentful troops operating among a fractious citizenry of mixed loyalties. Using Pennsylvanians to keep civilians and Redcoats apart would, it was hoped, minimize the chance of provocative clashes by the attachment of the troops to their fellow citizens. Incidents that did occur could be referred to the state as an internal matter. Events soon conspired, however, to undermine this arrangement. There were simply not enough militia to do the job. Washington began receiving insistent requests from John Armstrong for reinforcements east of the Schuylkill. Armstrong reported that as soon as he reached the east bank he found the people were "beginning to Crowd upon me from the Delaware side" demanding protection. Until Washington could detach units to secure a military anchor on the Delaware above Philadelphia like the one he had made at Wilmington, Armstrong's responsibility would extend from the Schuylkill to Trenton. He began to implore Washington to send General Potter to join him.[9]

Washington could not accede to these reasonable requests. By January 1, as part of his agreement with Thomas Wharton on the number of militia the state should provide, he suggested that he would not need to use any state troops west of the Schuylkill. Meanwhile, Potter's skirmishers were needed for what was becoming a dangerous military situation in that area. Instead, Washington detached several companies of Continental light horse to help Armstrong. These troops were ordered to patrol the roads leading into Philadelphia, to watch enemy troop movements, and to intercept goods and supplies going to the British army. They were posted along the Ridge and Germantown roads, allowing the militia to extend their reach to the northeast into Bucks County. The initial reports that Washington received were discouraging. John Jameson, who commanded a company of Virginia dragoons, wrote that he had too few men to cover both roads. He concluded that it was impossible to keep the "market people" away from the city. Opportunistic civilians had adapted easily to his patrols by going on foot, inquiring of neighbors for the whereabouts of American cavalry, hiding in each others' houses, and slipping off "through the Plantations" as soon as the American patrols had passed.[10]

Meanwhile, Washington received ominous reports that the enemy was stirring in Philadelphia. John Clark wrote that army engineers were building entrenchments along a road leading north from the Middle Ferry and preparing 300 horses on the city common. On December 20, 1,000 British troops crossed into New Jersey to "let the Country People have the benefit of the Market" by suppressing militia activity that interfered with the trade. A party of Hessians with 100 wagons also probed west of the Schuylkill River toward the village of Darby, where they loaded hay and rye straw and returned to town. Clark lamented that if he had any troops he "could have caught them easily."[11]

Clark may have helped to provoke this enemy foraging expedition. On December 19 he sent an agent to accost British scouts, feign Tory sentiments, and warn them that Washington was sending a large body of troops to Darby to occupy that town for the winter. British provisions reserves, while not as critically short as those of the Americans, had plummeted to less than 120 days' supply at current consumption levels. With an ocean at his back, a 3,000-mile supply line, and thousands of restive civilians to control, Howe could not depend on the avarice of area farmers. The Continental Army's struggle to hack out its camp in Chester County offered the last safe opportunity to restock his larder before the winter set in.[12] Washington urged James Potter to destroy the hay at Darby and speculated that if this provoked the British into coming out in force to remove it first, the American patrols might have "an opportunity of cutting off a party" of enemy foragers. On December 21 he ordered Clark to give Potter and Morgan early news of any expected British sorties so that he could send reinforcements. Clark reported the same day that a large expedition was expected to come out soon to "plunder" in Darby, Marple, and Springfield Townships to the south and southwest of Philadelphia.[13]

Washington, who was justifiably nervous about his hungry, restless troops in their still-unfortified camp, may have imputed more urgency to this intelligence than Clark intended to convey. He seized the occasion to try to mobilize at least part of the army to contest the British movement, but two of his brigadier generals suggested that such a mobilization was not possible. Jedediah Huntington of Connecticut wrote dryly that "fighting will be far pref[erable] to starving," but he noted that his own brigade was completely out of provisions. Huntington hinted at unrest among his men, which he said he had done his best to quiet, and he predicted that stealing from civilians might become prevalent if the shortages continued. James Varnum, Huntington's camp neighbor and fellow New Englander, observed that it was a "very pleasing Circumstance to the Division under my Command, that there is a probability of their marching," but he said that his men had been without provisions for three days. Varnum also alluded to difficulties in controlling his troops, observing that "the Men must be Supplied or they cannot be commanded." He even allowed himself a veiled criticism of Washington for his well-known scruples against imposing martial law on recalcitrant citizens and hinted at the need to remove the army to a state that could better meet its material needs than Pennsylvania had done so far.[14]

This implied reopening of the debate over the army's winter disposition offered the worst possible circumstance for Washington to learn that Pennsylvania's government was still complaining about the political compromises he had imposed on that debate. On the afternoon of December 22 Washington was drafting a letter to the president of Congress, enclosing Varnum's and Huntington's reports and observing, almost matter-of-factly, that "unless more Vigorous exertions and better regulations take place in [the Commissary Department] and immediately, this Army must dissolve." He said that he had been unable to respond to an expected enemy movement across the Schuylkill River that morning because of a lack of provisions, and he implied that his army was the presumed object of this movement.[15] Washington was closing a technical discussion of disputes over rank among the general officers when he received a copy of Pennsylvania's "Remonstrance" against the army's presumed intention to march to Wilmington. Thrown off guard by the implied critique, he sarcastically wrote that it would "give [me] infinite pleasure to afford protection to every individual and to every Spot of Ground in the whole of the United States." He observed that the decision about the army's winter quarters had cost him more "reflection or consideration" than any circumstance in "my whole life," and he carefully reviewed his efforts to protect the entire region.[16]

Washington then calmly resumed trying to measure, and if possible to contain, the British foraging excursion to Darby. That morning Howe led

8,000 troops—well over half of his effective force—together with 500 wagons, across a new pontoon bridge over the Schuylkill and marched them down the Darby Road. The troops deployed in a continuous line for more than four miles. At Darby, the column fanned out into a flank guard, and the wagon detail began gathering hay and forage behind this shield. Hessian General Wilhelm von Knyphausen was left in command of the 6,000 British and German troops still in the city. Intelligence reports that began pouring in confirmed the broad outlines of John Clark's prediction of a limited foraging excursion.[17]

This fact had propitious tactical implications. Unless Howe changed his mind or was preparing a ruse, the camp at Valley Forge would not come under direct attack. Because the army's formal organizational structure was paralyzed by hunger, sickness, and the presence of nearly 3,000 men unfit for duty for lack of clothing, any effective American response to Howe's "grand forage" would have to be made outside of that structure. On the evening of December 22 Washington ordered each brigade to detach eight officers and "fifty privates, all picked men" under the command of "a good partizan Captain." These troops were to be "fit for annoying the enemy in light parties," and each man would receive forty rounds of ammunition.[18]

By the next day the effect of these detachments was felt along the perimeter of the British expedition in sufficient weight to undermine traditional images of a Continental Army disabled by logistical shortcomings during its first days at Valley Forge. The force that Washington assembled to resist the enemy incursion into the countryside was undeniably a makeshift weapon. Virginian Daniel Morgan knew skirmishers, and he was under no illusion that these were the genuine article. On encountering fifteen parties fresh from camp, he found that each considered itself to be under separate command. He reported to Washington that he would try to advise these detachments, but he felt that he could not command them "even if we were engaged." James Potter complained of the same problems and said that the reinforcements had reached the lines without proper rations. Potter seemed no more eager than Morgan to add the problems of commanding these forces to his existing responsibilities. After finding "pickets" or guides for them, he sent them toward the British lines, but he had no great expectations for them.[19]

These judgments, while not categorically unfair, were only first impressions. Potter admitted grudgingly that the new parties had embraced the spirit of their mission with enthusiasm. One detail, after scouting all night, met a group of British light horse beyond Darby and pursued them lustily before breaking off the chase. Potter observed that the British were generally keeping "pretty close" to their lines and concentrating on the haying operation. Indeed, the Redcoats were anything but contemptuous of the patchwork net that Washington had fashioned to contain them. An aide to Howe wrote on December 22 that "some rebel dragoons and a few hundred of Morgan's riflemen are swarming around us."[20]

Morgan told Washington that several captains had "put themselves under my Command" and reported that "I took charge of them, fixed upon a place of rendezvous," and turned them loose to cover the enemy lines. They were "by no means fit for scouts," he complained, "being taken promiscuously from the reg[imen]ts, when they ought to have been pickd men." Their lack of supplies rendered them "almost useless," and they were so prone to straggle that Morgan believed that if the British were "any ways interprising" they could have captured two Americans for every man they lost. But one party had driven a troop of enemy cavalry into a swamp, where ten men and a dozen horses were captured. Despite his willingness to catalogue their faults, there was in Morgan's tone something of the stern but proud parent, anxiously watching the first steps of an eager child. Several parties patrolling north of Darby Creek had not been heard from when Morgan wrote his report on Christmas Eve from Springfield Meeting House. Far from assuming the worst, he speculated that "perhaps they have done something clever."[21]

The detachments represented almost a tenth of Washington's able-bodied force, and in his cautious view their operations called for the supervision of a general officer. Providentially, as a result of the troops' vigorous scouring of the countryside near the camp and the arrival of fresh supplies from Armstrong's foragers east of the Schuylkill, the provisions crisis had eased slightly, allowing Washington to detach more reinforcements. He ordered Lord Stirling to proceed with a force of unspecified size to Potter's outpost. When he reached Radnor late on December 23, Stirling learned that Morgan had advanced that morning with the previous day's detachments and part of Potter's militia toward the enemy lines. He found the front quiet despite a few scattered incidents of firing. The British were keeping close to their lines, fully occupied with the removal of hay and forage from the islands between Darby and the Schuylkill. The air of crisis ebbed gradually once the American detachments were reinforced and the limited objectives of the British expedition became apparent. The situation developed into a stalemate, punctuated by random clashes between mounted parties on both sides. American intelligence confirmed Howe's intention of keeping his forces concentrated and avoiding outbreaks of fighting that might delay or disrupt the party's stated mission of stripping the area behind his lines.[22]

With the situation stabilized, the American troops used the opportunity to do some foraging of their own. Howe's defensive lines along the Darby Road left much of the adjacent countryside exposed. Stirling found many more foodstuffs than he had been led to believe would be available in the area. He began loading captured enemy wagons and sending them to camp, and he urged headquarters to send him as many more vehicles as could be spared. Stirling predicted that he would "make a very good forraging tomorrow," and—recognizing Washington's well-known sensitivity about military intrusions into civil affairs—promised that "no force will be used while limetive measures will answer the purpose."[23]

Washington was delighted to learn that what had begun as a desperately improvised defensive measure was yielding an unexpected flow of food for the army. On Christmas day each brigade was ordered to furnish a lieutenant and eight men for service under the commissary general, and to unload three baggage wagons for the use of the foraging parties. Washington concurred with intelligence estimates that Howe probably would not attempt any offensive measures, but he insisted on receiving prompt "notice of the least movements." His aide, Tench Tilghman, doubtless voiced the sentiments of the entire army on the first anniversary of the battle of Trenton when he added to these orders the wish that "we could put them in mind tomorrow Morning what happened this time twelvemonth."[24]

Stirling, Potter, and Clark combined to bombard Washington with the intelligence reports he had requested. The British foray seemed to be paying dividends all along the city's perimeter, as farmers hurried toward town with their goods, on the pragmatic calculation that they would be better compensated for property voluntarily tendered than for items forcibly seized by either side. The fear that 8,000 British troops would sweep back through the city's western apron, raking before them everything of military value, became prevalent among area residents.[25] But three days' provisions were sent from Philadelphia on the twenty-fourth, leading John Clark to predict that Howe would march home soon. By the twenty-eighth, reliable news of the British retreat was at hand. Howe's force, which had withdrawn from Darby the night before on reports that Washington had sent 3,000 troops toward the lines and was following in person to lead an attack, lumbered across the

Schuylkill over the Gray's Ferry and Upper Pontoon bridges, dismantling those structures behind them. The expedition yielded more than 200 tons of hay and several hundred cattle and sheep for the British. Weary American skirmishers hounded the enemy wagon trains all the way back to the bridges.[26]

The containment mission to Darby was a perfect example of why the American army had remained in the Philadelphia area and a down payment on the bargain Washington had forged with state and Continental political leaders at Whitemarsh: to keep the army in the field to uphold revolutionary authority and the legitimacy of the embattled state government. After Howe's troops returned to Philadelphia, Washington dismantled his improvised force. He ordered Stirling to bring his troops back to camp as soon as he was certain of the finality of the British retreat. James Potter predicted that the enemy would "Bless themselves and sit down in peace this winter in the City." By January 5 Potter's brigade had disbanded and its few remaining men joined Armstrong east of the Schuylkill. Potter insisted on a winter furlough, and Continental troops assumed responsibility for the west side of the river. John Clark asked for a leave to visit his family, and he offered to do any errands that Washington needed in Lancaster and York on his way home.[27]

Clark's offer was timely. By the end of the year Washington was doing a brisk business with the political bodies in both towns. As the crisis along the lines near Darby played out during Christmas week, Washington resumed his quarrel with Congress and with the Supreme Executive Council over the latter's protest that the army was abandoning the state. On December 23 he began another angry letter to Henry Laurens. "Fresh, and more powerful reasons oblige me to add," he intoned, "that I am now convinced, beyond a doubt that unless some great and capital change suddenly takes place in [the Commissary Department] this Army must inevitably be reduced to one or other of these three things. Starve, dissolve, or disperse, in order to obtain subsistence in the best manner they can." "Rest assured Sir, he insisted, "this is not an exaggerated picture, but that I have abundant reason to support what I say."[28]

Washington recounted his efforts to mobilize the army when he learned that the enemy was moving from Philadelphia: "behold! to my great mortification, I was not only informed, but convinced, that the Men were unable to stir on Acct. of Provision, and that a dangerous Mutiny begun the night before . . . [which] with difficulty was suppressed by the spirited exertion's of some officers was still much to be apprehended." A commissary had been brought forward who told Washington that there were no cattle in camp and only twenty-five barrels of flour. As a result, Washington could only "send out a few light Parties to watch and harass the Enemy, whilst other Parties were instantly detached different ways to collect, if possible, as much Provision as would satisfy the present pressing wants of the Soldiery."[29] He couched the matter in personal terms. His "own reputation [was] so intimately . . . affected by the event," that he felt justified in resorting to strong language. "Finding that the inactivity of the Army . . . is charged to my Acc[oun]t, not only by the common vulgar, but by Those in power," he complained, "it is time to speak plain in exculpation of myself." "With truth then I can declare," he raged, "that no Man, in my opinion, ever had his measures more impeded than I have, by every department of the Army." He reviewed the poor performance of the supply agencies, reminding Congress that the 1777 reorganization of the Commissary Department had been made "contrary to my judgement, and the consequences thereof were predicted."[30]

Washington reserved his harshest words for Pennsylvania's government, which he accused of insensitivity to the condition of the soldiers, of laboring under delusions about the performance that could reasonably be expected of the army, and of outright duplicity. "I can assure those Gentlemen," he sneered, "that it is a much easier and less distressing thing to draw remonstrances in a comfortable room by a good fire side, than to occupy a cold bleak hill, and sleep under frost and snow without Cloaths, or Blankets." Having vented his wrath in two seething pages that his aides had to correct just to make them coherent, Washington offered recommendations to resolve the problems he had identified. These included a pension plan to encourage officers to stay in the service and the appointment of another committee from Congress or the Board of War to confer on military reforms.[31]

Washington's "starve, dissolve, or disperse" letter has figured more prominently than any other evidence in accounts of the disabled state of the Continental Army at the start of its sojourn at Valley Forge. It has achieved wide citation in the literature but has received little analysis of its contents or context. But the letter cries out for such analysis. Our problem is one of finding ways of taking it seriously without automatically taking it literally. Its claims need to be compared with the best available evidence from other sources, and its broadest intent and ultimate effect must be carefully scrutinized.[32] Washington's introductory statement that "fresh and more powerful reasons" required a recapitulation of the points he had made the previous day suggests a rhetorical device designed to explain his suspension of those arguments on the receipt of Henry Laurens's letter on December 22 and his reintroduction of the subject a day later. He doubtless availed himself of the twenty-four-hour interval to scour the camp for evidence of the army's debility, but little new information can have turned up overnight. Indeed, depending on the time of day when Washington began his counter-remonstrance, he may have already received messages from the lines near Darby with intelligence that the British foray had been temporarily checked by the special detachments, or from east of the Schuylkill River informing him that large amounts of beef and clothing were on their way to camp.[33]

Washington's treatment of the British foraging expedition and his efforts to respond to it showed impressive skill. By withholding the fact that he had advance intelligence of the limited nature and extent of the thrust, and noting only that "a body of the enemy [was to have] crossed the Schuylkill this morning," he was in a position to depict the event in any terms he deemed suitable to the points he wanted to make. With Congress contemplating an army immobilized by logistical deficiencies for which it bore some responsibility, and now facing an aroused and offensively minded enemy, Washington had the rhetorical initiative. He used it with the confidence of a man who has no reason to fear that his portrayal of the situation will be challenged. Thus his assertion of amazement at being "not only informed, but convinced" of the immobility of his troops, as well as his incredulous depiction of his discovery of the empty magazines. Far from worrying that armchair generals in York might wonder how a commander could be ignorant of such circumstances until they stopped him in his tracks, Washington pressed on assuredly. He failed to mention that the British foraging expedition was a perfect example of the "movement in force" that, it had always been understood, could not be prevented by a wintering American army. And he drew on a largely unappreciated talent for literary embellishment to evoke images of a "dangerous Mutiny" at camp, suppressed only with great difficulty, from the ubiquitous grumbling and rancor that had characterized the army's discourse since it came to a halt at Whitemarsh nearly two months before.[34]

Washington's only sources for this "mutiny" were reports by Jedediah Huntington and James Varnum of December 22, alluding to derisive vocal discontent and asserting their inability to mobilize their men. Traditional accounts of the army's first days at Valley Forge, drawing largely on the published diary of Connecticut surgeon Albigence Waldo, feature colorful expressions of discontent from members of the rank and file. Of contemporary observers, however, only Washington saw fit to treat these as mutinous, and then only in this report to Congress. Such expressions can just as easily be understood as showing the army's cohesion, or even its good humor, under circumstances of undeniable hardship that it was equipped and prepared to endure, than of disintegration. Indeed, some soldiers displayed almost a well-fed equanimity during this trying period. Lieutenant Samuel Armstrong's Massachusetts regiment reached Valley Forge on December 19 with enough food on hand to "Eat like Insatiate Monsters," with pie for desert, which they consumed "'till our Guts began to Ake." Armstrong admitted that the army's movement soon thereafter dislocated the precarious commissary system and the troops endured a hungry Christmas week before the supply lines were restored. But he observed that the "Men never bore up with such bad Usage before, with so little Mutiny . . . and indeed there was more mutiny among the Officers than among the men."[35]

In fact, most of Washington's angry letter to Laurens, after its opening paragraph and before the last several, was a matter of embellishment; portrayals of fact and circumstance more or less true depending on the context in which they were considered. The allusion to his own "reputation" warned adversaries that he was declaring a combative personal stake in the matter. His attack on Pennsylvania authorities gave equivocators an opportunity to wonder if they might be overreacting to pressures from the state. The heart of the matter, however, lay in Washington's implicit threat that if the complex, multifaceted question of the army's winter disposition was still an open one, then it was open in all of its component elements. In bringing the army to Valley Forge instead of seeking urban quarters in interior Pennsylvania, Washington believed he had erred, if at all, in the direction of the political leaders' desire for a winter campaign. If the bickering over that decision continued, however, to the exclusion of serious consideration of the related questions of supply and strategy, then the decision itself might be reopened. In his letter of December 22 Washington hinted at the possible dissolution of the army. In less than a day he hardened his stance. The continuance of the army at Valley Forge would soon be untenable without some "capital change" in its system of material support.

His very elaboration of terms underlined the gravity that Washington attributed to the matter. It had come to a choice between "starvation"—which wouldn't have been contemplated by armed men in a fertile country—and dissolution or dispersal. Washington was not given to a scattershot or redundant rhetorical style, and the latter options had distinguishable implications. "Dissolution" might be read as tantamount to abandoning even the pretense of concerted military resistance to the British presence in the Middle States, with furloughed troops streaming, singly or in undisciplined groups, toward their homes. This, after all, is what had happened the previous winter after the unexpected victories at Trenton and Princeton, and the rebellion, far from collapsing, had revived the following May. "Dispersal" was an uncertain concept, but it had about it a firm basis in recent reality. Washington had already detached a large part of the army to Wilmington for the winter, and he would soon send a sizable contingent of cavalry to Trenton. He had discounted the feasibility of breaking the army into detachments for strategic purposes only the day before, but he had been experimenting with less extreme variations on that principle throughout the fall campaign. In the harried imaginations of state and Continental authorities, "dispersal" must have conjured images of the army leaving the front lines to claim shelter in the towns where it already had logistical footholds, such as Reading and Easton, or perhaps even in their own overcrowded refuges at York and Lancaster. Alternatively, the grim options implied under the rubric of "starve, dissolve, or disperse," could be obviated entirely if Congress showed a reasonable appreciation of the material disabilities its soldiers were facing. That appreciation could be most effectively demonstrated, Washington suggested, by an early resumption of face-to-face discussions at Valley Forge.[36]

There is something ironic and genuinely poignant in the spectacle of Washington's crisis-management style, based on a comparison between the early months and closing weeks of 1777. He spent much of his energy at Morristown orchestrating a charade of militias to "keep up the appearances" of maintaining an "old" army that really *was* dissolving to deceive the enemy. That deception bought Congress enough time to get at least a small part of the promised 75,000-man "new" army into the field and gave Washington time to begin organizing it. Now in the last month of the year, Washington labored to convince the same Congress that those very troops—which six months in the field at their head had made clear to him were not going anywhere—might literally evaporate into thin air without comprehensive reforms. Historians—as much as William Howe, John Hancock, or any of the officials working for or with them—have accepted both of these charades, with subtly distorting effects on our understanding of the war.

While he waited for Congress's response, Washington lobbied Elbridge Gerry on behalf of his proposal for a new consulting committee on military reforms, and he corresponded with the governors of several states pleading for their "exertions" to recruit troops and to stem the flow of officers' resignations.[37] He continued to monitor developments along the lines near Darby. As these developments began to cohere into a reliable image of the enemy's strength, location, and intentions, an ambitious scheme emerged at the American headquarters. Its inception is profoundly obscure and its existence has barely been acknowledged in most histories of the Revolution. The plan may have been the product of Washington's imagination, or that of his aides or generals. It centered on the old siren song of an attack on Philadelphia and surely had roots in the tangible yearning among many officers that the anniversary of the battle of Trenton should not be allowed to pass without celebration or repetition. A conditioned military response may also have resulted from the realization that Howe had once again become dangerously separated from his Hessian allies.

Whatever its origin, the idea was soon sketched on paper. Its central premise was the realization that if Howe, with more than half of his army, could be trapped outside of Philadelphia, the diminished garrison in the city would be dangerously vulnerable to assault. The plan contradicts the notion that the defeat at Germantown disabused American strategists of their fondness for elaborate maneuvers. The enterprise would begin with a feigned attack on the left wing of the British outpost at Darby by the troops under Lord Stirling that were in the area. They would "keep up the appearance of an Attack" and harass the enemy as much as possible. If Howe took the bait, the main army would cross the Schuylkill and advance in two columns down the east bank toward the British fortifications north of Philadelphia. The light horse on the west bank would divide, with half of it patrolling north of the British position at Darby to screen the movement of the main army, and half crossing the river to trail the columns as a rear guard, leaving detachments to cover the fords and ferries from Swedes Ford down to the city.[38]

As the army approached the Philadelphia fortifications, a shock corps composed of sixty men and eight officers from each brigade would rush forward to seize the redoubts, forming a "Chain of Centrys" across the city neck. Once the lines had been breached the right column of the main force, under General John Sullivan, would file off along the Schuylkill, seizing the four main ferries and cutting the floating bridges at those places adrift from the west bank. This wing would be responsible for holding these crossing points to frustrate Howe's attempts to battle his way back over the river to relieve the beleaguered garrison.[39] The larger left wing would force its way into the city to release American prisoners and "demand a surrender of the Enemys Arms under promise of good Quarter in case of compliance, and no Quarter if opposition is given." The plan envisioned John Armstrong's Pennsylvania militia recrossing the Schuylkill to the west bank "the Moment our lodgement is made," to reinforce Stirling's outnumbered detachment in case Howe chose to turn on him rather than fight his way back into town. Stirling would also be joined by General Smallwood's brigade, which would rush up from Wilmington, and hopefully by a Saratoga-like outpouring of Middle Atlantic patriots who would be "pourd in to Crush Howe before he could recov[e]r. from the Surprise or regain his Ships."[40]

This bold design presumed such a degree of precision and organizational dexterity on the army's part that skeptics might well conclude—if only in light of Washington's simultaneous depiction to Congress of its crippled state—that it was indeed the result of a sugar-plum reverie gone awry or a holiday-induced overindulgence in hemp or Madeira at American headquarters. The scheme was never communicated to Congress, nor to Smallwood, Armstrong, or any of the other individuals on whose performance it would have depended. Such skepticism would be more credible if there was not evidence that Washington sounded out some of his general officers on the advisability of attacking the enemy at exactly this time.

The consultation was carried out informally, by word of mouth, among a number of key individuals. General John Sullivan reported that he had discussed the question of an attack with "some of the General officers which I thought most capable of advising" on the matter. The details of the project were kept carefully guarded, and the outline implied a direct attack upon Howe's expedition.[41] The tone of the responses was polite but unenthusiastic. The generals could "by no means advise for or against an Attack," but in their view Howe had a formidable force with him and he was "possessed of very Strong Grounds." If Washington was determined to attack they were "willing to Risque their Lives and Fortunes in the attempt," but they believed that it would take the army at least two days to get into a position to give battle.

A successful assault aimed at the bridgehead between Darby Road and the Philadelphia peninsula would destroy the enemy, but if it failed the attackers would be pushed into the Schuylkill. On the whole, the generals thought there was more to be lost than gained from the venture. While they would cheerfully vote to attack Howe if he approached Valley Forge, they could not advise taking the offensive. Sullivan acknowledged the gravity of these objections, but he felt "so weary of the infernal Clamor of the Pennsyl-vanians" that he was in favor of "Satisfying them at all events, and Risquing Every Consequence in an action," which might, even in the case of a defeat, at least teach Congress to "censure with more caution."[42]

This puzzling, shadowy episode bore no fruit. In light of the faint trace that it left in the contemporary documentary record and its utter absence from the literature of the Revolution, its significance resists analysis. It is difficult to determine, for example, what relation the proposed attack that Washington dangled before his generals bore to the one that he sketched in the "Intended Orders." He may have kept knowledge of the real nature of the proposed operation confined to his closest aides, while proffering a more conventional plan to his generals as a way of maintaining security while ascertaining their overall offensive inclinations.

What meaning can fairly be attributed to the fact that any American assault could have been contemplated in late 1777? The plan appears to con-tradict Washington's depiction of his troops as being on the bitter brink of dissolution. If Congress had learned of the project, its members might have wondered how the army could have been so inert on December 22 on the first news of the British foray, and yet be thought equal to a full-scale assault on a heavily fortified city only three days later. On the other hand, the ven-ture might be taken as presumptive evidence to refute any suspicion that Washington's threat to dismantle the army was a bluff or a political bargain-ing chip. In Washington's military personality a gambler's instinct played minor counterpoint to an essential tactical conservatism. The former was usually unsheathed only when rational cause for optimism had been exhausted. That he even considered an all-out attack may suggest that he seriously doubted the tenability of the position in which the collapse of the commissary and the obtuseness of state and Continental leaders had placed him, and that he was ready to risk everything, as he had the year before, on an unexpected and improbable venture. Or he may have been wrestling with John Sullivan's exasperated conclusion that it would be worth risking defeat if that were the only realistic way of forcing political leaders to acknowledge the harsh material straits of the army.

It cannot be asserted with finality that the plan was not put into motion. At least two British observers wrote that Howe had notice on December 27 that Washington was moving toward Darby with 3,000 rebels, in consequence of which the British commander hastened his prepa-rations to withdraw to Philadelphia. The intelligence may have been leaked deliberately to speed the enemy withdrawal or to observe the British reaction to it. Had Howe moved troops up from Darby Road near Gray's Ferry to reinforce his left wing, rather than retracting that wing, the signal might have been given to execute the hazardous march to the redoubts north of Philadelphia. But Howe reacted as a majority of the American generals predicted he would, and the "Surprise" died in obscurity.[43] Instead of a full-dress reenactment of the triumph at Trenton, the rebels settled for a Christmas Eve dumb show, replete with elements of comic relief but otherwise devoid of military consequence. John Bull, a Pennsylvania militia commander, marched his men down the Frankfort Road to the redoubts north of the city and lobbed a few shells noisily but harmlessly over the earthworks, before scattering back into the night. The British put their army into winter quarters, and the Americans settled down at Valley Forge to determine how they could hold theirs together.[44]

Chapter 6

TRUBLESUM TIMES FOR US ALL, BUT

WORS FOR THE SOLDERS

olitically if not materially, the army's fortunes improved
almost immediately after Congress's receipt of Washington's letters of December 22 and 23. Although tangible
results would not be felt at camp for a month, their blunt language had a galvanic effect on many congressmen. Pennsylvania
delegate Daniel Roberdeau informed President Wharton of the
"grim news" from the army concerning its food supplies. General
Washington "speaks out for the first time," he reported and—con-
veniently neglecting Washington's denunciation of state authorities—observed that he blamed the Commissary Department for
the shortages. Roberdeau noted that Pennsylvania was "in an
excentric way to provide flour and fat Cattle." If it did not, he
wrote, "I have no other prospect but that the army will be reduced
to the necessity of abandoning their post and disperse."[1]

Congress referred Washington's letters to a committee consisting of the members of the Board of War plus three of its own
members. This group was "fully empowered to take the necessary
measures for supplying the army with provisions and other necessaries." Its deliberations are hard to reconstruct because of the
skeletal nature of the records that have survived, but the impact of
Washington's outburst is unmistakable. His warning about the
dissolution of the army swung the pendulum of congressional
opinion away from the interests of Pennsylvania. Roberdeau
lamented that his "situation" had become "extremely delicate on

this occasion, the ruin of our Army, or the interference with the police of the State I apprehend will be the alternative set before me."[2]

By the new year the matter was out of the state's hands. The new committee pressed the Supreme Executive Council to furnish food and supplies or else face the army's withdrawal from Pennsylvania. Congress had "received such unexpected and distressing Accounts . . . relative to the Situation of the Army," it explained to Wharton, that emergency measures were needed. The committee "deplore[d] the Necessity" of resorting to seizures from the inhabitants on its own authority because such measures would "give Umbrage" to civilians. It would take that step, however, unless the state found other ways to forestall the shortages. "Your Excellency will therefore judge," it intoned, "in what Manner the Concurrence of this State is to be procured."[3]

Congress, meanwhile, moved quickly to implement interim measures while it sought long-range solutions to the organizational and provisions crises. It voted to award the troops in camp a month's "extraordinary pay" to compensate for their hardships and asked the officers to forego the extra rations to which their ranks entitled them and to accept the balance in cash. On the last day of the year, Congress entertained a motion to appoint a committee to go to camp to confer with Washington on any means of promoting "a speedy reformation in the army."[4]

Washington turned his attention to urgent matters relating to the army's security and reorganization. He pressed for accurate returns of the regiments, both for internal control purposes and for transmission to the states to bolster their recruiting drives. And, in anticipation of a visit from congressional representatives, he collected memoranda from officers and staff department heads on the problems they faced and their recommendations for reforms. These provided him with information to lay before any inquisitors who might arrive from York, and they also served to tap some of the frustrations that were festering within the officer corps.[5]

Continuing detachments needed to be made both for strategic and subsistence purposes. Because of severe shortages of forage near the camp and the irreplaceability of horses, Casimir Pulaski was ordered to take the cavalry to Trenton to find winter quarters there. This detachment would provide for the security of that town, but Pulaski was enjoined to avoid unnecessary wear and tear on the animals and men and to train and reorganize them for the coming campaign.[6]

By bits and pieces some of the subsistence pressure on the commissary eased as companies whose enlistments expired prepared to leave camp. This was, however, a mixed blessing because these troops had to be provisioned for their trips home.[7] Although the supply crisis was largely blunted by the end of the year, Washington knew the situation could recur. He had little choice but to act as if solutions could be found to these logistical problems. Whenever the pressure of immediate emergencies slackened, he tried to focus his attention, and that of his subordinates, on the campaign that would resume early in the spring.[8]

On January 1 Washington wrote to Congress to resume his advocacy of comprehensive military reforms. He adopted a tacitly conciliatory tone because he wanted to help Congress accomplish some of the steps he was asking it to undertake. He therefore recommended that the legislators appoint Colonel Udny Hay, a deputy quartermaster at Albany, to the vacant post of quartermaster general. He had no prospective candidate for adjutant general, however, and was thus temporarily obliged to detain Colonel Timothy Pickering in that post, preventing Pickering from taking his seat on the new Board of War.[9]

Washington's confidence that he had seized the initiative from Congress and from the state was not misplaced. As he composed his conciliatory letter to Henry Laurens, the new president was writing him that Congress had been aroused by the army's plight. Laurens attested that Washington's messages would "have the desired effect" with his colleagues. Had he been privy to Laurens's other correspondence, Washington would have had even stronger reasons to believe that he had gained the army a hearing with Continental leaders. Laurens confided his distress to Governor William Livingston of New Jersey in a highly emotional letter. Within a few days, he averred, Livingston would "be informed . . . that our whole System is tottering, and God only knows whether we shall be able to prop it up half the first Month of the approaching New Year." "My heart is full my Eyes overflow, when I reflect upon a camp 1/4th and more of Invalids for want of necessary covering—an Army on the very verge of bankruptcy, for want of food—that we are Starving in the midst of plenty—perishing by Cold and surrounded by Clothing Sufficient for two Armies, but uncollected." There was providentially, he thought, "some hopes now of having this necessary work performed in a few Weeks," but the harm to the army from neglect had already been and would continue to be great. Laurens then introduced a theme that would dominate his view of the crisis for weeks: that it had now become necessary for Congress to broaden its purview from the "great outlines of public business" and "descend even to the executive parts of the Duties of Clothier General, Quarter Master General, Commissary General, &c., &c., &c."[10]

At the army level, this "descent" had long since been made. Down through the ranks from headquarters into the huts, officers found themselves becoming unusually involved in the daily details of military maintenance. Jedediah Huntington's wry lament that generals had "become sope boilers, oilmen, tanners, and the Lord knows what" overstates the case. But the duties imposed on everyone drawing rations deviated glaringly from the martial imagery that had led many officers to seek commissions in the first place. Autumnal visions of a short, victorious campaign culminating in cele-bratory balls at the City Tavern dissolved in the snow and mud of winter into the grim realization that there was more than enough mundane camp duty to go around. While Washington waited for Congress to respond to his request for comprehensive reforms, January became a month of relentless tinkering with the burdened systems of supply.[11]

The trough in the supply curve that accompanied the movement of the troops to Valley Forge was the deepest of the campaign. By the end of the year, however, there was some evidence that a fragile balance had been restored between need and supply. This equilibrium stemmed from no single development but rather from the cumulative effects of processes that increased the flow of provisions available to the army and others that reduced the demand on those supplies. In connection with the deployment of the Pennsylvania militia on the east side of the Schuylkill, John Armstrong swept that area just before Christmas. He found the country there "picked clean" and complained that he was "beholden to the highway for a Christmas din-ner," but his efforts yielded large numbers of cattle. Meanwhile, the special commissary detachments that Washington sent out on December 22 con-ducted similar operations west of the Schuylkill. Moreover, the foraging activities of both armies at year's end disclosed supplies that might otherwise have remained hidden. As people frantically attempted to get their goods to city markets before they could be seized, American patrols had increasing opportunities to do just that on local highways rather than in area barnyards.[12]

These were only emergency measures, however, intended to bridge the chasm between need and supply until the commissary system could be reestablished. As the army settled at Valley Forge, the dynamic between local and long-distance supply mechanisms swung back toward equilibrium. The establishment of the new camp reanchored the logistical network. By the last week of 1777 the army was once again stationary, and commissaries could focus on procurement without wondering whether the provisions would go astray between the point of purchase and the itinerant regiments. In early

January food and clothing from New England began arriving in camp. One Massachusetts officer was pleased enough with the "large supplies of provisions" from home to predict that "those difficulties [food shortages] are at an end." A Connecticut private found the provisions "very poor," but he conceded that they were "better than we have had [some] time back." Jedediah Huntington congratulated his father on Connecticut's performance. She had "exerted itself beyond most, if not any, of her Sister States," he exulted, but he warned that she "must do more than her Part." Huntington was not sanguine that the shortages had been permanently abated. "We live from Hand to Mouth," he wrote, "and are like to do so, for all anything I see."[13]

Augmenting the army's food supply at Valley Forge only partly relieved its plight. Beyond the political implications of Washington's rhetoric, he was stating a simple ecological truth when he contemplated the dispersal of the troops "in order to obtain subsistence in the best manner they can." The number of troops that could be kept at camp could not exceed the number that could be fed there. The rest would have to be redistributed in proportion to the availability of resources.[14] That distribution was effected through a variety of means. The detachments sent to Wilmington and Trenton were made with specific reference to subsistence as well as strategic purposes. Unintended developments contributed to the same outcome. The inevitable incidence of death and desertion as well as the departure of troops whose enlistments had expired had negative implications for the army's combat readiness, but opposite ones for its ability to subsist. The detachment of small parties sent to thresh grain or collect food also relieved the strain on the central commissary. John Armstrong was far from being alone in finding himself "beholden to the highway" for his Christmas dinner, and undoubtedly for many more after that.[15]

The stabilization of the supply situation did not inaugurate an era of good feelings at camp. Indeed, January was a month of watchful waiting reminiscent of November at Whitemarsh. The emergency of December kept written communications official and to the point, but once it was blunted, old antagonisms and disagreements surfaced. Much of the discord was fleeting and idiosyncratic, but there were a number of recurrent themes. Washington encouraged the general officers to include constructive criticisms and suggestions in their memoranda. Their favorite topic of complaint concerned questions of rank and seniority. There were many private disputes, but the officers found a common target in Congress's decision to promote Thomas Conway, an Irish volunteer, from the rank of brigadier to that of major general, to accompany his appointment to the new office of inspector general. Conway's appointment and promotion were bound up—in Washington's mind at least—with a political struggle for control of the army. Many generals seized on Conway's promotion as a vehicle to express discontent with the conflicting systems used by Congress and the states to distribute rank and other privileges.[16] The disputatious demeanor of the generals set the tone for camp life and provided many bad examples for their subordinates. On January 1 some officers protested the scarcity of liquor in their ration. Washington ignored their complaints and pointedly excluded officers from his offer of a "gill of spirits" to noncommissioned officers and privates to celebrate the New Year.[17]

The contentious mood in camp became endemic by mid-January. Relative inactivity compounded its causes. By the twentieth, most of the huts had been completed; the project to build a bridge over the Schuylkill River at Fatland Ford stalled because of a lack of equipment to raise the heavy timbers; and frozen ground hindered progress on the fortification of the camp's perimeters. With more time on their hands, the troops had increased opportunity to express their antagonisms and discontent. As they sat in their huts or returned to camp from command detachments, many soldiers were able to write to family and friends for the first time in months. Their anxiety to relieve the concerns of loved ones only slightly exceeded the relish with which they sought unjaded listeners to whom to address their complaints.[18]

Many junior officers followed the example of their elders in wrangling over promotion. In addition to these intramural antagonisms, there is evidence of the hostility that many troops had developed toward the locality and its inhabitants. Jedediah Huntington wrote his father about the consequences of the interaction between the civil and military communities. "Any Army, even a friendly one," he noted, "if any can be called so, are a dreadful Scourge to any People—you cannot conceive what Devastation and Distress mark their Steps." By early 1778 the Continental Army could hardly have been called "friendly" toward the belabored population among which it found itself restlessly encamped. Five months of enforced intimacy with Pennsylvanians—coinciding with a precipitous decline in their own well-being—had inclined many soldiers, whether fairly or not, to see a causal relationship between the two phenomena.[19]

John Brooks of Massachusetts angrily surveyed the scene of the army's plight. When he considered the "unequal distribution and scanty allowance of provisions," he had no trouble discerning the roots of the problem. The former, he allowed, was the fault of the army's Commissary Department, but "the cursed Quakers and other inhabitants are the cause of the latter." Brooks indulged in the regional derision that was widespread in the anything-but-homogenized Continental Army, observing, "the States of Pennsylvania and Maryland do not seem to have any more idea of Liberty than a Savage has of Civilization." Surrendering to unbridled disdain, he wondered what New England's fate would have been had its citizens "Shown the same Disposition towards Gen[era]l Burgoyne, which the cringing, nonresisting ass-like Fools of this State have done towards How[e]."[20]

Brooks's litany was singular chiefly because of his facility with the vocabulary of disparagement. Many of his fellow soldiers, especially the New Englanders, shared his distaste for local civilians. The seemingly equivocal response of many Pennsylvanians toward the invasion of their state incited in some of their putative defenders a spiteful ambivalence toward the war's impact on the locality. One officer reported disbelievingly that a pair of shoes purchased near the camp cost a soldier a month's pay, and he attributed this inflation to the avarice of the "banditti inhabiting Penn[sylvani]a [who] openly refuse [continental currency] as a tender." "'Tis beautiful," he gloated, "to see the vestiges of war thro' their plantations." He continued: "What the English began the Americans have finished—the dutch the Welsh and the scots and the quaking gentry hailed brother Howe a welcome guest but ruin and devastation indiscriminately befel the friend and foe. Military power that so long deprecated evil must soon take place in the vicinity of our army to curb that spirit of dissention now prevailing throughout the state. The sufferings of the inhabitants are intolerable, but they may thank their own perversity."[21]

Pennsylvania's large and diverse population of religious dissenters from war became particular targets for the invective of the frustrated soldiers. The Quakers, as the largest and most visible segment of that population, stood proxy for much of the offhand bigotry directed at those presumed to be "disaffected" from the patriot cause. This reflected the provincial background of the troops, many of whom could not have distinguished among the myriad sects inhabiting the state, much less between conscientious and cynical pacifists. Variations of such phrases as "Quaker" or "quaking" served as easily available epithets for frustrated men who would happily have found substitutes had these not been readily at hand.[22]

This facile resort to derogation obscures a wide diversity of viewpoints among soldiers. Many, such as Jedediah Huntington, eschewed emotional comments altogether, choosing to regard the refusal of Quakers to support the war as an uncontrollable fact of professional life. John Clark, whose responsibilities as the former head of the army's intelligence service gave him unique insights into the habits of civilians, suggested that nine out of ten Quakers would "be happy" to provide intelligence in exchange for exemption from active military service or from fines for refusing that service. Even the hard-bitten John Brooks believed that he saw signs that the "*Thees* and *Thous,* who have had their Wives ravish'd, [and] houses Plunder'd and burn'd, are now ready on any party's making a Sally from the City, to take their Arms & oppose them."[23]

Some Pennsylvania officers were scarcely less critical of their state than their comrades. Colonel Richard Butler castigated the "blind supineness of the state" for allowing its troops to languish in the energetic but overburdened care of Anthony Wayne. Nor was Pennsylvania alone in feeling the sting of its natives' disenchantment. Captain William Gifford, a New Jerseyan "wish[ed] with all my heart our State wou'd make better provisions for our Brigade, respecting clothing and other necessaries than they do." He added, "If they had any idea of the hardships we have and do undergo . . . they Certainly wou'd do more [for] us than they do." John Brooks tempered his venom when he weighed Massachusetts's contribution to the ragged spectacle that its "bare footed, bare leg'd, bare breech'd" regiments presented against Pennsylvania's responsibility for their meager rations. Nevertheless, his judgment fell heavily on his state. "Where the fault is I know not," he mused, "but am rather inclin'd to think our g[enera]l Court has not done everything that might be expected of them." Brooks railed, "If it be for want of foresight in our Rulers, the Lord pity us: But if it be thro' negligence or Design, is there not some chosen curse reserv'd for those who are the cause of so much Misery?"[24]

General Enoch Poor laid the plight of his New Hampshire troops almost as bluntly in the lap of that state's council. "I am every day beholding their sufferings," he lectured its governor, "and every morning waked with the lamentable tale of their distresses." They looked to him for relief, he observed, and Poor made it clear that he in turn looked to the state:

> If any of them desert how can I punish them when they plead in their justification that on your part the Contract is broken? That you promised and engaged to supply them with such things as were requisite to make them comfortable here, and the situation of their families tolerable at home, this they say they had an

undoubted right to expect. You promised they should be supplied with the common necessaries of life at a reasonable rate . . .
instead of which they must now give [extravagant prices] . . .
which vile extortions if permitted they say must inevitably
reduce their families to a starving condition [or] to a dependence
on the cold hand of meek eyed charity alone.[25]

Poor begged the state's authorities to relieve the material concerns of
their troops. Their right to expect the soldiers to discharge their responsibilities, he implied, would depend on such relief. If the matter were neglected,
he would "shudder and tremble at the consequences—nay it will be impracticable to keep them much longer in the field." Jedediah Huntington made
similar points with Connecticut authorities. In forwarding his men's gratitude for the clothing sent them, he articulated their anxiety about the situation of their families. They knew that war-induced inflation was forcing up
consumer prices not only in Pennsylvania but at home as well. They believed
that their families were suffering almost as much as they were, and they were
not inclined to tolerate it for long.[26]

It was a source of particular vexation to many soldiers that the people at
home had no realistic appreciation of the circumstances under which they
labored. John Brooks's tirade was provoked by a friend's innocent observation
that he was "not so *sanguine* about matters in this Quarter" as he had once been.
Brooks wondered how the man could have ever been sanguine. Ichabod Ward, a
Connecticut sergeant, was similarly strained to place the army's achievements
into a context that would be comprehensible to the citizens at home. Ward
wrote to a friend to allay "the unesyness thare seems to be att hum concerning
the Solders." He had heard "that some are very unesy because that we have not
kil[d] all the Enemy thay wonder what we are about forty shillings a munth and
Nothing to Do." Ward wished that the army's critics could "undergo half so
much as one of us have this Winter . . . that those grumbling att Solders New
what they undergo."[27] Ward's halting command of written English contrasted
glaringly with Brooks's literary acrobatics. Between them, they may have
bracketed the army in terms of eloquence. It is unlikely that they ever knew
each other, but they shared a bond of experience that irretrievably separated
them from their friends at home. In the end, it was the barely literate Ward who
wrote the epigram to which Brooks, Poor, Huntington, Washington, or anyone
in the army could have subscribed. "I can tell you Sr," he assured his home-
bound friend, "it is trublesum times for us all, but wors for the Solders."[28]

By the evidence then, the army's first month at Valley Forge was fraught with rancor, disgruntlement, and frustration, which were widespread through the ranks and which found expression in both intramural and external outlets. The camp was recognized as a good place to avoid, and many key staff officers made themselves as scarce as possible.[29] It is too easy, however, to make a case for the ill-tempered, fractious disposition of the army at the expense of equally important components of its character. Its image as a disorderly rabble-in-arms, sullenly waiting its "Prussianization" at the hands of Friedrich Steuben, has fed too freely on picturesque but idiosyncratic evidence of this kind. The army had a surly and contentious streak that was one of the underpinnings of the collective intransigence that held it stubbornly together in the face of adversity. The colorful terms in which it found expression, however, have frequently masked its coexistence with a hitherto uncelebrated strain of innate discipline.

That discipline gave coherent shape to the contentious individualism of the troops and—in the absence of an armywide level of formal organization comparable to that of contemporary European armies—made it a militarily useful quality. It never found sufficiently distinctive or evocative forms of expression in traditional sources of evidence and has thus been eclipsed in the army's historical reputation. The discipline that the army did possess was more remarkable for what it prevented than for what it visibly accomplished. By late January 1778, the army had continued for several months to function on a tether of logistical disarray that might have disintegrated many of the more outwardly regimented European forces. It was not until mid-February, when the supply system again tottered and then briefly collapsed, that the troops were pushed toward outright disorder. For the moment, at least, the Continental privates remained a contentious group of men, but by no evidence a mutinous one.

It fell to some officers to recognize the discipline that the men could not articulate on their own behalf. Many were struck by the restraint with which soldiers accepted their hardships. Jedediah Huntington told Governor Jonathan Trumbull that Connecticut's troops, despite their open concern for their families, had uniformly acquiesced in their own plight. "Every Hardship and Distress," he beamed, "they have encountered and endured without Murmurs or Complaint." Richard Butler believed that the "Private men [were] the best in the world Else they would Mutiny and Desert in Bodys, I think they have more virtue than half the Country." John Brooks eulogized: "no men ever shew more Spirit, or prudence than ours. In my opinion nothing but

Virtue has kept our Army together thro' this Campaign." John Laurens summarized the view from headquarters. "Our men are the best crude materials
for Soldiers I believe in the world," he told his father, "for they possess a
Docility, and patience which astonish foreigners—with a little more discipline we should drive the haughty Briton to his Ships."[30]

That "little discipline" consisted, to judge from the army's mixed success during the preceding campaign, less of individual self-restraint than of
coordination between units in close order maneuvering under fire. Failures
in this area had caused the army's greatest problems throughout the war. It
could cover great amounts of ground quickly and efficiently in forced
marches. Once engaged, moreover, individual units repeatedly proved their
ability to stand and fight bravely if not always effectively. It was in complex
close-order drill, which determined an army's ability to adjust to sudden
changes in combat situations, that Continentals had proved consistently
inferior to the British. The army's near-rout after its right flank was turned
at Brandywine and its disastrous failure to form a smooth junction between
converging columns at Germantown were the hallmarks of its deficiency.
The hot fire maintained by Nathanael Greene's division while covering the
Brandywine retreat and the spirited assault that had opened the Germantown attack, conversely, were the symbols of its strength.

These problems were well understood at headquarters and corrective
measures were under discussion long before Steuben arrived at Valley Forge
in February 1778. This fact has gone unrecognized because Thomas Conway—a foreigner far less savory to American revolutionary sensibilities than
Steuben—contributed to the discussion. Conway returned to Valley Forge in
late December as the newly appointed inspector general. Finding other generals drafting memoranda to Washington on the reform of the army, he proposed to detach several officers from each regiment to Pottsgrove to be
drilled in a new set of maneuvers. They would then "spread the instruction"
through their units. Conway claimed to have seen 200,000 men trained in
European armies by this method in fewer than three months. Washington
had no intention of being dictated to by a man who he was about to declare
his "enemy," but Conway had outlined the germ of a "logarithmic" method
of improving the army's drill system that Steuben would employ to his eternal credit, and to the army's benefit, later that winter.[31]

Comprehensive improvements in the army's drilling technique would
await Steuben's full-time assignment to the task in March. These discussions,
meanwhile, benefited their participants by counteracting raw boredom. In a

culture of war where fighting is at best an eight-month-per-year affair, a wintering army is almost by definition a dispirited institution. Aside from preparing for the next campaign and doing what they could to confine the enemy in Philadelphia, there was little in the daily routines of camp life to give the troops a sense of purpose, much less of progress. A palpable feeling of suspended animation spread from headquarters down through the ranks and into the huts. Except for troops with command assignments that took them away from camp, time hung heavily. A soldier could write only so many letters to friends or loved ones before realizing that, as one general forlornly expressed it, "barren is the Camp of news."[32]

Even detached duty could become dull and routinized. One officer wrote from Wilmington that he was suffering from a cold caught while ice skating on the Brandywine Creek! "We have great Diversion at that Sport," he reported, "some days upwards of 50 men on all day." Such dubious pleasures did not dispose most men to remain in a cold camp if they could escape. Soldiers were deserting from Wilmington every night, the officer wrote, which he attributed to the mistake of stationing Maryland troops too close to their homes. But detached duty offered some soldiers an opportunity for involvement in activities customarily associated with their occupation, such as marching, riding, or fighting. Service on detachment, more importantly for our purposes, often brought ordinary soldiers and civilians into contact—and sometimes outright conflict—with each other.[33]

It is convenient to imagine the Continental Army in terms of the conventional notion that it "spent" the winter of 1777–78 *at* Valley Forge, but the reality of its deployment was much more complex. Valley Forge was most importantly the site of "Head Quarters." It housed by far the largest single contingent of troops and officers, it was the heart of the logistical system, and it was the place from which orders came and to which most intelligence was sent. Before the systematic training of the regiments began in late March, however, and to a lesser extent thereafter, many important elements of the army's winter mission were conducted along the far-flung perimeter of the British garrison at Philadelphia. The army perched in a broad, crescent-shaped configuration along that perimeter. The crescent was thickest at its center, at Valley Forge, and tapered in either direction toward anchoring points on the Delaware River below Philadelphia at Wilmington, and, more tenuously, above the city at Trenton.[34]

The post at Wilmington was hobbled by a supply situation nearly as bad as the one at Valley Forge, by an acute shortage of horses for scouting and security details, and by the poor turnout of area militia. Smallwood's troops staged the army's biggest coup of the early winter by looting the stranded British brig *Symmetry* on January 1, but the outpost's chief military value was defensive. Indeed, Washington seized the town largely to prevent the British from doing so. The presence of armed Americans in Wilmington forced the enemy to move warily past it on the Delaware River, constrained their mobility southwest of Philadelphia, and provided much intelligence about enemy movements. The post protected the supply and reinforcement lines to the army from the southern states via the Chesapeake Bay, and it theoretically afforded protection to Whigs and discouragement to Tories in Delaware's three counties and in Salem County, New Jersey, across the river. After the excitement of the brig's capture passed, the garrison settled into a period of relative quiescence. Both the problems and the pleasures of life there reflected those at Valley Forge. Smallwood observed that his troops, like Washington's, were "pennyless, and are dissatisfied and clamorous." Between alarms provoked by the movement of enemy ships on the Delaware, they passed the time as well as they could. Whenever they saw the opportunity, many of them deserted and went home.[35]

In Pennsylvania, the detachments were small, mobile, scattered, and frequently mounted, and their responsibilities were more varied than at Wilmington. They had more frequent contact with the enemy and almost constant interaction with civilians as a result of their efforts to enforce the embargo between the city and its hinterland. For administrative purposes, and by tacit agreement between the state and Washington, the area was divided by the Schuylkill River, with the respective spheres designated as "west" and "east" of the river. Responsibility for covering the west side was assumed by the Continental Army and was carried out by small rotating patrols from Valley Forge. These parties operated largely autonomously, but their overall supervision after Lord Stirling returned to camp in late December fell to Captain Henry Lee of Virginia, who commanded a company of dragoons. Lee took charge of John Clark's intelligence service in January and assumed responsibility for disrupting trade with Philadelphia west of the river and for the camp's security.[36]

Like many officers whose duties involved regular close contact with civilians, Lee recognized the impossibility of completely segregating them from the enemy. He also developed a keen appreciation for the local inhabitants' point of view, for the unfairness with which the war imposed upon them, and for the need to find flexible solutions to these problems. He drafted a plan for consulting with the farmers in his area to mutually determine the amounts of food and forage they could realistically spare for the maintenance of his patrols. Individuals who agreed to deliver their surplus goods to his quarters would be paid for them and given a "protection" for the rest of their crops. This would relieve the Continental wagon service, Lee reasoned, and farmers would be "eased from the dread of the forage masters, whose general injudicious conduct afford[s] just cause for murmers and complaint."[37]

It is doubtful whether Lee's project was ever implemented, but it would have been greatly appreciated by local inhabitants. Continental authorities later acknowledged that "plunder" and "abuses" were endemic within a radius of "three miles in every direction" from the camp between December 26 and January 6, after which the regular supply system stabilized. This was a conservative estimate of the spatial and temporal boundaries of the looting that accompanied the move to Valley Forge and the collapse of the Commissary Department.[38] John Lesher, a forgemaster at Oley, twenty-five miles northwest of Valley Forge, complained to state authorities that he considered himself "no more master of any individual thing I possess," due to his frequent losses to American soldiers and foraging teams from the Continental wagon service. Lesher endorsed the idea of making requisitions proportional to the needs and resources of civilians, as an alternative to the actual behavior of American troops, who "under the shadows of the Bayonet and the appellation [of] Tory act as they please." Farmers in his neighborhood were so discouraged, he wrote, that they were threatening not to plant their fields for the coming season. From Trappe, six miles north of the American camp, Henry Muhlenberg could not find transportation because most wagons and horses had been pressed into service for the army. By late January, Muhlenberg observed, there was a shortage of animal fodder "over almost the whole [of Providence] Township" because of continuous Continental requisitioning in the area.[39]

Considerable evidence suggests that the decision to concentrate Continental resources west of the Schuylkill was initially effective in suppressing rural trade with the city there. Howe's army, like Washington's, became relatively quiescent during the early weeks of 1778. Having retired to winter quarters at the beginning of the year, well stocked with supplies seized on their late-December forays, the British were generally content to let the area's inhabitants assume the risks of the road with whatever supplementary foodstuffs they were willing to sell. Johann Ewald, a Hessian captain attached to a jaeger corps assigned to patrol the inner periphery of the city, observed that by the middle of January "Washington began to make the highways around Philadelphia so unsafe with [detached] parties . . . that the country people no longer dared to bring provisions to market." The result, Ewald reported, was a precipitous rise in the "already too high" prices of beef, poultry, milk, and sugar.[40]

By the end of January, Ewald revealed, British commanders found it necessary to resume "partisan warfare activities . . . to protect the country people going to market." Such activities included a more aggressive policy of British patrolling on both sides of the Schuylkill. These patrols generally found themselves "surrounded by spies," however, who helped the Continentals frustrate British tactics. Somewhat more effective were the counterrevolutionary measures organized with the help of—and often on the initiative of—local inhabitants whose political sympathies lay with the Crown. Many of the area's Loyalist inhabitants fled to the protection of the British army in the city. A few organized auxiliary militia units to work in cooperation with regular British army patrols to terrorize their Whig neighbors.[41] Jacob James, from Goshen Township in Chester County, joined the British side a few days before the battle of Brandywine. He served as a guide for the Redcoats and worked as a freelance intelligence officer during the autumn. On December 1, 1777, he received a warrant from General Howe to raise an "independent troop of light dragoons" among his neighbors. By early January, James unleashed his guerrilla squadron on his enemies. Within six weeks this group had become a scourge to the friends of the revolutionary government in Chester County and a source of protection to Loyalists and opportunistic neutrals, and it had come to the alarmed attention of Continental authorities.[42]

Covering the area east of the Schuylkill, along a broad circular line around the city between that river and the Delaware near Trenton, was even more complicated. The region was much larger than its western counterpart. The freeze-and-thaw cycle on the river made communications, supply, and support between the area and Valley Forge hard to sustain before Sullivan's Bridge was completed over the Schuylkill at the camp in early March. The river reduced the threat to the camp from the east, but it complicated the task of disrupting British foraging there, especially when it came to keeping "country people" from carrying their produce into Philadelphia for sale. Nominally these responsibilities belonged, by agreement between Washington and the state, to the one thousand militia troops Pennsylvania had promised to keep on the east side of the river. But the state contingent never approached that number, and reinforcements of Continental troops were required throughout the winter to keep the district under even precarious control.[43]

Washington detached several mounted companies to patrol the roads leading northwest from Germantown in late December, but in general he tried to keep operations east of the Schuylkill as autonomous as possible in order to focus his attention on the security threat west of the river. Major John Jameson, the ranking officer with the Continental detachments, was ordered to direct his requests for support to Casimir Pulaski's cavalry garrison at Trenton. With Jameson's troops along the Schuylkill and Pulaski on the Delaware coordinating Continental efforts, the area covered by the Pennsylvania militia would hopefully be reduced, and the state troops might be stiffened by their placement between two more experienced forces.[44] Events conspired from the start to subvert this hope. Pulaski had his hands full just establishing his outpost at Trenton. Coordination between the undermanned militia and the Continental detachments in the area was poor from the beginning. Washington repeatedly had to attend personally to problems arising east of the Schuylkill. He declined to appoint a commander with overall authority there for fear of legitimizing Continental military responsibility for that district. The relationship between the state and Continental forces was thus plagued constantly by noncooperation and mutual distrust, and the intended isolation of the city garrison from the rural population suffered accordingly.

Colonel Walter Stewart, the commander of a Continental foraging party that swept through lower Bucks County from Old York Road to the Delaware River in mid-January wrote that the area was being drained of provisions for the benefit of the city. "I can assure your Excellency," he informed Washington, "not less flour than is sufficient to maintain Eight to Ten Thousand men goes daily to Philadelphia, carried in by Single Persons, Waggons [and] Horses." What could not be accomplished by stealth was sometimes being achieved by force, as farmers turned to paramilitary methods to thwart the restraints of martial law. A drove of cattle had reached the city the previous week escorted by "a Small Party of armed country men." Hardly a day passed, "but a Number gets into that place by different roads on this side of Schuylkill."[45]

Washington professed to be "amazed" by the leakage besetting the blockade on the east bank, but none of the individuals responsible for that operation shared his surprise. Some members of the militia contended that their Continental counterparts were actively complicit with the trade. James Potter, who directed militia affairs in the area while the state looked for a replacement for General Armstrong, confirmed the existence of a "smart trade" between the city and the countryside. He blamed the problem mainly on Continental officers, who had given passes to their "favorits . . . in Consequence of which waggons loaded with flower . . . go into the City." Potter angrily insisted that this practice would "put it out of my power" to stop the marketing.[46]

Washington began an immediate investigation of the charges. His aides informed John Jameson of the substance (but not the source) of the allegation and asked him to "minutely inquire" into its accuracy. Jameson was ordered to select some reliable "countrymen" to "tamper" with his own horsemen, to see whether any of them were accepting bribes. A dragoon captain stationed near Germantown arrested a wayward subordinate, Hofman Lowrey, who "under the character of being one of my horsemen rob'd a number of Poor people—takes provisions from the poor—and Sel's it for hard money to others." This revelation corroborated the partisan observations of one British officer responsible for patrolling the city's boundary. Lieutenant-Colonel John Simcoe, commander of the Queen's Rangers, charged that "the rebel patroles, who came to stop the markets, were considered by the country people as robbers."[47] Despite the wrongdoing revealed within their ranks, Continental officers adamantly insisted that the militia were responsible for the abuses. The state troops "run away on the least alarm," one complained, allowing the country people to "keep going to Market constantly." He echoed Potter's embittered language, concluding that it was "not in my power to Discharge the duty of an officer on this post at present" because of the militia's dereliction.[48]

This recrimination was a byproduct of the awkward joint operations east of the river. An examination of the region from the perspective of militia leaders yields unique insights into the social dynamics of war, revolutionary allegiance, and civil-military relations. In the middle weeks of January the command of the militia was transferred from two veteran generals, John Armstrong and James Potter, to John Lacey. Lacey, a twenty-three-year-old ex-Quaker who had grown up in Bucks County, possessed an unshakeable enthusiasm for the Whig cause, but these assets were offset by his inexperience and by his local political baggage. Lacey had served in the Pennsylvania regiments at Ticonderoga during 1776, where he incurred the wrath of the state's most powerful general, Anthony Wayne. On returning to Bucks

County, Lacey found that "a radical change had taken place in the Political sentiments of my Neighbours and acquaintances" during the invasion scare of 1776. "A sullen vindictive and malignant spirit semed to have taken hold of a large portion of the People of this County," he recalled, "whose Hostility to the Revolution was too apparent not to be noticed, and semed only waiting a good opertunity to brake forth openly in favour of England, and against their own Country." His Loyalist kinsmen tried to lure him into the interest of the Crown.[49]

During the months before the war returned to the state in summer 1777, a muted contest of intimidation and intrigue took place between the Whig and Loyalist factions, who, Lacey believed, were of almost equal size but decidedly unequal virtue. Putting aside his resentment of Wayne and much of the state's conservative Whig establishment, he accepted a commission to organize and command the Bucks militia. After the 1777 campaign, Lacey's troop parted like "a Band of Brothers," and he returned to his father's farm in Buckingham Township determined to wait out the war. He received threats against his life from old neighbors and found Bucks County Whigs "seeking hiding places." When state authorities offered to promote him to the rank of brigadier and asked him to replace Armstrong and Potter, Lacey considered refusing the assignment, before reluctantly agreeing to try to restore order to his fractured community.[50]

Lacey reached the militia's camp at Graeme Park, on the border between Bucks and Philadelphia counties, in mid-January. The camp was in a "deplorable condition"; its equipment was scattered; his six hundred green recruits were confused, demoralized, and leaderless; and local residents were busy trading with the British. Lacey was immediately importuned by "dozens" of inhabitants from the Germantown area for passes to carry flour into the city. His troops were scheduled to be discharged on February 1, and their replacements showed no signs of turning out. He decided to move his camp several miles back into the country to await reinforcements.[51]

Lacey's inability to police his district was so complete that the British did not even think it necessary to contest his presence systematically. Their patrols came out of the city four or five miles every day but retired without offering any threat to his force. The British units patrolling east of the Schuylkill on "market days" had a largely ceremonial or symbolic role, assuring marketeers of their availability for protection if necessary. Simcoe reported that a tacit system of "private signals" evolved among civilians, who hid overnight in the woods until his corps approached and then proceeded into the city under escort. This freed Howe to concentrate his military resources west of the Schuylkill River, where Continental patrols were having some success in cowing Loyalists and neutrals and in maintaining the blockade.[52]

It is significant that Washington—on being confronted with evidence of this breakdown in the army's performance—did not act more forcefully to reorganize the division of labor or authority east of the Schuylkill. Any effort to do so might have complicated the delicate relation between the army and the state government or risked accepting fuller Continental responsibility for that area. The merits of the Continental and militia officers' cases against each other seem to have been equally valid. There was evidence both of army criminality and of a disposition on the part of the militia to avoid close involvement in contested areas near the city. It was only clear that the arrangements made to disrupt trade between the city and its hinterland in a critical geographical sector were malfunctioning. Washington's choice to tread gingerly in search of solutions reflected the limited options available to him and the implicit liabilities all of them carried. Aside from investigating allegations of Continental complicity he left the matter in the state's lap. He asked James Potter to take the "most immediate coercive measures" to combat illicit trade and to give him information about any individuals who were granting passes to civilians, and he instructed John Jameson to cooperate with Potter in carrying out the blockade. When Lacey took command of the militia, Washington admitted that a complete suppression of this traffic was impossible and urged him instead to "make an example" of a few obviously guilty parties.[53]

In settling for a token effort to resolve the problem, Washington accepted the consequences of adhering to the division of state and Continental responsibility along the Schuylkill River as the best part of a bad bargain. His chief security problems lay west of the river, where the bulk of his army was precariously camped. Washington had reserved his best dragoon units and most effective skirmishers for service there. The parties of light horse that he sent to reinforce the militia were merely the best of the few effective troops left. Even these were kept close to the river, so they could be recalled quickly if the enemy threatened to move against Valley Forge. Further detachments were out of the question. Although the army's subsistence situation temporarily stabilized during January, its functional immobility due to shortages of shoes and clothing quietly worsened. The 2,900 troops Washington had reported unfit for duty for want of clothing on December 23 had risen in barely a month to almost 4,000.[54] Any attempt to provide more Continental coverage east of the Schuylkill would have drawn strength from other parts of the city's perimeter. The effect might have been to spread the leakage plaguing the embargo effort from one part of the city's perimeter to its entirety. From a political as well as a tactical standpoint, confining the inefficiency to one area was preferable to its wider distribution. In future debates over the performance of the army's mission, it would be useful to be able to point clearly to the militia as the real source of the problem.

The army had remained tenuously in the field for the winter at the behest of state authorities, conditionally committed to executing their policy of resisting British exploitation of southeastern Pennsylvania. In Washington's priorities, however, that objective was secondary to the security of the Continental army, to its comprehensive reorganization, and to preparations for a new campaign. The state's inability to muster a force sufficient to uphold its part of the bargain, and the fact that many Pennsylvanians were openly trading with the British, largely shaped and justified Washington's adherence to his priorities.

The failure of the Continental cavalry to establish a strong outpost at Trenton contributed to the problems in the area east of the Schuylkill. Politically, a Continental military presence in Trenton constituted at least a token response to Congress's expressed desire for the army to shield parts of New Jersey adjacent to Philadelphia. Strategically, a force there might function as a Continental "hinge," linking and reinforcing the makeshift assemblage of militia troops struggling to blockade Philadelphia. Its mere presence might have helped to suppress overt Loyalist activity in Burlington County, New Jersey, and in Bucks County, Pennsylvania, or even stimulate the turnout of militia in both places. By discouraging disaffected citizens near the Delaware River, an effective dragoon base at Trenton would relieve Pennsylvania's troops of some pressure to protect Bucks County Whigs and allow them to concentrate in the center of the region between the Schuylkill and Delaware rivers.[55]

Obstacles to quartering the cavalry at Trenton began to emerge, however, before the four companies rode into town. Far from helping to pacify the immediate area and extending support across the Delaware, the cavalry had to resort repeatedly to headquarters for assistance. The disputes that attended its placement at Trenton pitted army imperatives against militia needs, local wishes against state priorities, soldiers against civilians, and parts of the Continental establishment against each other. The mere rumor that Trenton had been chosen for the cavalry's winter base unnerved the town. The unsavory reputation that dragoons enjoyed disposed residents to question the "protection" that the measure was intended to afford them, and local authorities begged Washington to abandon the plan. Having garnered the wages of Hessian patronage in 1776, they were dubious about the advantages of the American variant. Far from securing the town, they argued, a cavalry garrison would tempt the enemy to belabor it.[56]

Washington, who had witnessed and even participated in the previous year's ravages upon Trenton, was sympathetic toward the local viewpoint, but he was not inclined to let it interfere with his own perception of the army's needs. He stood by his forage master's opinion that the town would "afford a sufficiency of forage" against the magistrates' insistence that it would not. Admitting that his petitioners were "of a contrary opinion," he assured them that they would "find [themselves] deceived," but he implied that he might alter the plan if he were mistaken.[57] When the four companies of light horse reached Trenton on the night of January 8, they were astonished to discover that there was "not a load of Hay in Town." Indeed, General Pulaski told Washington, he had only with the "greatest difficulty" been able to find even temporary shelter for his troops and none at all for the horses, which he sent several miles into the countryside.[58] Washington responded to these problems with the weariness of a man who had to attend personally to every piece of important army business, and a tone that suggested he would not be of much help in resolving them. If forage could not be found at Trenton, he suggested moving the cavalry inland, but if the problem was merely "a little difficulty that may at first occur in procuring the most desirable Quarters," he was not disposed to hear about it. Pulaski decided to split his detachment into three groups, sending two companies to "Flemingtown," two to "Pennytown," and keeping a small guard of dragoons under his own command at Trenton.[59]

The cavalry's failure to secure a viable base of operations at Trenton subverted the army's mission of depriving the British of a supplementary source of provisions in the ring of farm communities surrounding Philadelphia. Instead of a strong Continental "hinge" between thinly stretched Pennsylvania militia and New Jersey's irregulars operating along the Delaware opposite the city, the post became a weak link. State troops in both parts of Philadelphia's hinterland were unsupported, and their resistance to the flow of supplies there was minimal or token. The British garrison remained comfortably supplied during January. This left Howe's troops with little incentive to venture beyond the city's heavily guarded fringes to risk encounters with American skirmishers, and perhaps—by their predictable acts of soldierly depredation—to alienate would-be friends of the king in the local community.

The opposition to the cavalry garrison at Trenton might have allowed Washington to redeploy that force to better achieve his tactical objectives. If, as one officer reported, his troops were sustaining their horses with forage ferried across the Delaware from Bucks County, why did they did not return to Pennsylvania to brace its tottering militia? There is no evidence that Washington considered making such a redeployment. In addition to the outcry that this might have elicited from Congress over the abandonment of one of its constituent states, Washington had a valuable relationship to consider with New Jersey's governor, William Livingston. Livingston had been singular among his colleagues in his personal concern about the plight of the army, and he had gone to considerable lengths to assist Washington the previous winter at Morristown. Livingston, moreover, took seriously the value of a strong Continental garrison at Trenton, as a significant contribution to the military security of his state.[60]

Washington, a determined proponent of the long view when desperation did not require heeding the short, was responsive to this kind of cooperation. By mid-January the critical supply shortages had been temporarily blunted, leaving him with the precarious luxury of looking down the road. He already envisioned the likelihood that the next campaign would shift the seat of war back toward New York, in which case the army's dependence on New Jersey would be as great as it currently was on Pennsylvania. The strategy of containing the British in Philadelphia was essentially a conditional commitment, dependent on effective cooperation among the army, Congress, and the state governments. Washington was not willing to significantly impair the regional disposition of Continental forces he had made, at the long-term expense of the army's welfare, to make up for the inability of Pennsylvania to fulfill its commitments. He continued to encourage the militia commanders of Pennsylvania and New Jersey to resist enemy depredations in their states. Beyond that, however, his energies were shifting by late January to the war's next phase, and to preparations to formulate and implement the military reorganization measures on which the success of that phase would depend.[61]

Chapter 7

THE STONE WHICH THE

BUILDERS HAVE REJECTED

The specially appointed investigating committee from Congress that Washington had requested finally arrived at Valley Forge on January 24, 1778. The delegates—Francis Dana of Massachusetts, Nathaniel Folsom of New Hampshire, John Harvie of Virginia, Gouverneur Morris of New York, and Joseph Reed of Pennsylvania— represented a rough geographical balance within their parent body and a wide range of temperaments and political orientations. They carried a broad but indefinite mandate to initiate reforms in the military establishment. Congress had directed them to:

> concert with [General Washington], to form and execute a plan for reducing the number of batallions in the continental service . . . to remove officers in the army for misconduct, negligence, or incompetency, and to appoint others in their room until the pleasure of Congress can be known; to remove all just causes of complaint relative to rank . . . to determine and report . . . to Congress, their opinion of the necessary reinforcements for the cavalry, artillery, and infantry and the best mode of obtaining them . . . and in general, to adopt such other measures as they shall judge necessary for introducing oeconomy and promoting discipline and good morals in the army.

Any confusion about the committee's mission that was embedded in this broad mandate was magnified by last-minute changes in its membership. The delegation initially included three members of Congress (Dana, Reed, and Folsom) and three officials from the new Board of War. The board, however, decided it could not interrupt its own work of reorganization and asked to be excused from going to camp. Congress accepted the "sundry reasons assigned by General Gates," the board's new president, and chose Morris and Charles Carroll of Maryland in place of the board members.[1]

It was widely recognized in York and at Valley Forge that the board's reluctance to participate in the mission stemmed as much from tensions between Washington and Gates following the Conway affair as from the press of the board's work.[2] James Lovell, a delegate from Massachusetts, offered the word "ostensible" to modify the given reason for the alteration of the committee's membership. Richard Peters, the board's secretary, implied that "Congress have thought it most prudent considering the State of Parties at Camp to keep General[s] Mifflin and Gates here." The machinations underlying the committee's makeup were less fully understood in the army, but the discordant implications of the maneuvering were clear enough. Jedediah Huntington observed that members of the board had been expected to participate in the conference, but he wrote, "I fancy they don't like us well enough to come."[3]

The particular yet open-ended instructions the committee carried reflected the fact that it comprised almost a quarter of the active membership of Congress. One delegate complained that the American states were content to "have their Business managed by a snug set indeed," which numbered barely twenty members in attendance at York. In sending so large a part of its membership to attend the army, Congress was fulfilling, after the fact, President Henry Laurens oft-repeated complaint that it had been compelled to "descend" into the minutia of day-to-day military management. To spell out in binding detail what it wanted the committee to do might have been counterproductive. Instead, the delegates divided Congress into two bodies: one to oversee the reorganization of the military establishment and the other to attend to the "great outlines of public business," of which many delegates were fond and which some, like Laurens, considered their "proper sphere." Decisions requiring legislative action would await the consideration of the whole body. In the meantime, the committee established itself at Moore Hall—a country mansion two miles north of Washington's quarters—which became the forum for the transaction of the army's political business.[4]

In the absence of a detailed record of the daily proceedings of Congress, the letters of its members provide the best evidence of their view of the committee's role. In their letters the delegates are almost at a loss to explain the committee's purpose in any definitive terms. To John Henry of Maryland it was only clear that the army was to "undergo a reformation" and that a committee had been "appointed on that Business." Abraham Clark of New Jersey stressed a more narrowly defined objective: "As the Reduction of the battallions is become necessary, a Committee of Congress . . . are going to the Army for that purpose." Other members combined broad and specific imperatives. "The Business of the Committee," Pennsylvania's Daniel Roberdeau observed, "are to reform the army by reducing the Regiments and introducing discipline." James Lovell of Massachusetts felt the deletion of members of the Board of War destroyed the committee's effectiveness, but Laurens reported that the committee had been "stripped of all their intended Military Coajutors" without dismay.[5]

The potential for conflicts between civil and military interests seldom lay far below the surface. John Witherspoon of New Jersey saw a growing tendency toward insubordination on the part of some soldiers as the chief obstacle to the committee's success. "Our Officers are infected with such a seizing thirst for Rank and Pay," he grumbled, "and there is sometimes such a Want of Firmness in Congress that there is Danger of their throwing Things into Confusion." But Laurens arrived at an opposite conclusion. "Nine Brigadiers," he observed, had "made an humble Representation of injury which they feel from an undue promotion of General Conway" that Congress had "treated with the Contempt of lying on the Table." He complained that "such a display of Wisdom & Justice may provoke a resentment exceedingly detrimental to the service." Reducing the number of understrength "paper" regiments, which might allow Congress to dismiss dozens of the marginally talented "supernumerary" officers thought most prone to complaining, was among the highest priorities of most congressmen.[6]

Whatever their divided views or halting efforts to explain the committee's purpose, the delegates were disposed to give it broad discretion in carrying out their common objective of reorganizing the army. Laurens depicted the imprecise but apparently wide authority vested in the group for the Marquis de Lafayette. "The powers of this deputation," he observed dryly, "are ample, I will not say unlimmitted."[7] This fact was not lost on Washington, and during the fortnight between the committee's appointment and its arrival at camp he drove his aides in the task of "preparing and digesting matters" for the committee in anticipation of its work. These prepa-rations consisted mainly of collecting and abstracting data on the army's strength and on the state of its current and foreseeable material supplies, and digesting ideas for reform drawn from the detailed memoranda that he had received from many officers since arriving at Valley Forge. This work paid off handsomely in the detailed statement of concerns and recommendations Washington placed before the committee at its second meeting. This thirty-eight-page "Representation to the Committee of Congress" provided an agenda for the conference. By offering the delegates a comprehensive account of the army's deficiencies and proposals for their removal, Washington placed himself in a strong position to influence their deliberations.[8]

The "Representation" was a carefully polished tract, keyed to the con-cerns Congress had articulated in its resolution establishing the committee, incorporating enough hard evidence to resonate with information the mem-bers could gather for themselves by walking through the camp, and sprin-kled with ideas that Washington had solicited from his subordinates. It was, Washington wrote, "submitted to consideration and I shall be happy, if [the proposals] are found conducive to remedying the Evils and inconveniences we are now subject to and putting the Army upon a more respectable foot-ing." Above all, Washington insisted, "Something must be done, important alterations must be made; necessity requires that our resources should be enlarged and our system improved." He retreated from his rhetorical predic-tion that the immediate dissolution of the army would follow from a failure of reform but held out the grim alternative that without reforms "[the army's] operations must infallibly be feeble, languid, and ineffectual."[9]

The first item on Washington's agenda quickly became the most con-troversial: a request that the disgruntled officers be more firmly attached to the service by the adoption of a "half pay and pensionary establishment." Washington was sympathetic to Congress's desire to be rid of bad officers, but he was even more interested in being able to retain competent ones. According to his plan, officers who remained in the army for the duration of the war would receive half of their pay annually for the rest of their lives. Their widows and orphans would also receive pensions, and officers would be allowed to sell their commissions, as they could in most European armies. Washington acknowledged that the plan would arouse "capital objection[s]" on such grounds as its cost and especially from ideological opponents of the idea of a "standing army," but he defended the plan on practical grounds. He decried the frequent resignations of qualified officers and ascribed the "apathy, inattention and neglect of duty, which pervade all ranks" to the financial insecurities of military service. He also pointed out that making commissions "valuable" would offer a way to exact obedience from officers, by holding over them the threat of dismissal and the consequent loss of their investment in the office.[10]

In response to the perpetual difficulties presented by the inability of the states to fill their troop quotas, Washington proposed annual drafts from the militias of each state. After a year of compulsory service, draftees would be encouraged to reenlist by means of cash bounties. The "Representation" also outlined a new "establishment," or system of organization for the army as a whole. In deference to Congress's desire that the awkward and expensive arrangement of unevenly "completed" units be "reduced" and made more uniform, Washington proposed folding the current ninety-seven "paper" battalions into eighty new ones, organized into uniform brigades and divisions. The new arrangement also provided for the establishment of an office of inspector general to devise a uniform system of maneuvers for the army.[11]

Washington described the "lavish distribution of rank" among members of the support staff departments as a major cause of dissatisfaction in the army. He suggested that all posts that required commissioned officers, such as quartermasters and paymasters, be filled from the line, and that those officers base their claims to pay and promotion solely on their performance there. Commissaries, forage masters, and wagon masters should be drawn from civilian personnel and hold no army rank. Washington described irregular promotions as a source of endless disputes and proposed "some settled rule of promotion, universally known and understood," but with enough flexibility to allow rewards for exceptional merit or performance. The "Representation" closed with commentaries on each of the army's support departments—the quartermaster, clothier, commissary, medical, engineering, and other services—carefully enumerating their shortcomings. Washington made it clear that he saw improving the performance capabilities of these agencies as a precondition to the army's ability to function effectively in the field.[12]

The "Representation" provided the committee with a broad framework on which to base its inquiry. The record of the group's deliberations is fragmentary, consisting mainly of the sparse minutes that it kept, the official correspondence it issued, and the private letters of its members. The committee made no comprehensive report to Congress. Rather, it took actions and made recommendations on a piecemeal basis, both during its stay at camp and after its members returned to York, but the impact of Washington's views is clear in the tone and substance of the deliberations. The group made a fumbling start in its first session with a divided decision to recommend Major General Philip Schuyler of New York for the vacant office of quartermaster general, a nomination that failed in Congress.[13] It then plunged directly into the critical deficiencies of the Commissary Department. Concluding that the department could not be managed satisfactorily by its current head, William Buchanan, the delegates recommended that Jeremiah Wadsworth of Connecticut be named commissary general of purchases in his place. Pursuing Washington's oblique criticism of the "extravagant rage of deputation" in the supply departments, the members ordered the heads of those agencies to submit detailed lists of the numbers, names, stations, and salaries of each of their assistants.[14]

The committee's early sessions established a momentum that it sustained during its first week in camp. At its third meeting the group took up Washington's proposal for a new "arrangement" of the battalions, and—in the terse language of the minutes—"settled it." Perhaps feeling flushed with their progress, the members put the controversial half-pay pension plan on the table that day. There were, however, strong and sharply divided sentiments in Congress on this issue. Whether Washington's arguments for the measure elicited any debate is unclear, but the matter was—as noted in the minutes—"not concluded."[15]

The expeditious way these issues yielded to the committee's mediations reflected the care with which its agenda was prepared at headquarters in the weeks before the conference. It was also, however, a function of the nature of the questions themselves. All the problems the delegation took up initially were amenable to executive or recommendatory action. The nomination of department officials and the adoption—pending the approval of Congress—of a paper "arrangement" for the army were among the tasks that the committee had been expected to undertake. The group's assumption that it had "settled" such matters was sometimes premature. It could, nevertheless, congratulate itself after four days of work that, within the bounds of its resources and authority, it had moved expeditiously to address several difficult problems that Congress had taken only passing notice of for months.[16]

Then the committee moved on to problems of an entirely different order of complexity and tractability. It was easy enough to fill long-vacant offices or to dismiss demonstrable incompetents and to replace them with better agents or to ordain, on paper at least, new relations among the divisions and brigades. The main business of the delegation, however, would be more complex and time-consuming. If the army could have subsisted on magazines of flour or herds of cattle voted into existence with the summary authority with which new arrangements of regiments were decreed, the committee might have returned to York within a fortnight. Instead, before the end of their first week in camp the members recognized that the causes of the army's travail ran much deeper than they had originally believed. When the delegates "took into consideration the scarcity of provisions" on January 31, it marked a significant departure in the relationship between Congress and the army. It was only then that a quarter of Congress's members took leave of the rarefied air of the "great outlines of public business" that Henry Laurens had called their "regular Sphere." As they did so, a subtle but powerful change began to take place in the intellectual chemistry of the national legislature.[17]

The committee's introduction to the complexities of the logistical breakdown began with its examination of the lists of deputies it had requested from the supply agencies. The group spent a day pouring over returns from the Commissary of Issues for the Middle Department and the forage master general. The minutes do not reveal what they thought or said, but we can infer the dismay of the members of a legislative body of barely twenty members responsible for the political management of the Revolution when confronted with graphic evidence of a sprawling entity of hundreds of men that was required to supply the material wants of the military machine.[18]

The group adjourned over the sabbath, its members perhaps sobered by this glimpse of the true dimensions of their task. Gouverneur Morris chose to "improve" the rest day by writing a melancholy letter to his old friend John Jay in Paris. "Congress have sent me here in Conjunction with some other Gentlemen to regulate their army," he mused, "and in Truth not a little Regulation hath become necessary." Whether there remained enough strength in the political foundations of the state to sustain its military branch seemed doubtful to Morris. "The mighty Senate of America is not what you have known it," he opined. "The Continental C[urrency] and C[ongress] have both depreciated, but in the Hands of the almighty Architect of Empires the Stone which the Builders have rejected may easily become the Head of the Corner."[19]

Morris's fears provided a fit prologue for the committee's work. Throughout February—a period during which the army's support departments again faltered and then lurched through the severest supply crisis of the fall or winter—the group's proceedings played a restless counterpoint between measured consideration of issues of formal army organization and direct intervention to maintain the failing logistical systems. The delegates were treated to a display of the army's material vulnerabilities so dramatic and timely that a cynic might have guessed that it had been arranged for their benefit. From the Continental horse yard, situated between the committee's outpost at Moore Hall and Washington's headquarters, the stench of dead animals wafted through the air. In the camp the fear of riot or worse hung almost as palpably as the stench. The pitch and tone of letters from army officers rose through progressive degrees of anxiety until they bordered on hysteria. Only the terse entries in the committee's minute book maintained their previous tenor; one so relentlessly devoid of emotion or urgency that it is necessary to resort to the occasional private letters of its members to know that they even grasped, on a visceral level at least, the real gravity of the crisis.

The committee laboriously digested evidence of the debility of the supply departments even as the latest emergency bore down on the army. On February 3 it summoned Ephraim Blaine, a deputy commissary of purchases, and questioned him on the "State of Provisions of the Army and recd his return of Meat purchased." It also took returns of "rations drawn," but its attention was still fixed on the December provisions crisis rather than the graver one that was developing just outside its door. The delegates received proposals for the reorganization of the "Provision Department" from Blaine on the fifth and met with him on the seventh, but it was not until the thirteenth, when they "Conferred upon the starving condition of the Army," that an awareness of the immediacy of the crisis crept into their official records.[20]

The committee's spare minutes do not do justice to either its concern or its comprehension of the situation. After examining Blaine and comparing reams of data concerning the army's consumption of food with evidence of the availability of supplies, the delegation was so disturbed by its findings that it wrote at length to Congress. The members' genuine alarm is clear from the contrite tone of their report. From their initial understanding of the amounts of food issued by the army's commissaries, they observed, "we had presumed that there must have been some mistake or Fraud, a detection of which would have enabled us to make a considerable saving." After examining the available evidence, however, they could "not find any considerable difference—the large issues being satisfactorily accounted for in the number of Continental Troops to be fed."[21]

With this transformation in its thinking on an issue critical to the army's survival, the committee's role and function, both in relation to the army and within the Continental establishment, underwent a subtle alteration. For the duration of the crisis, the delegates were almost as much active participants in the operation of the military machine as investigators or reformers of it. This shift fell well within the parameters set out by Congress, but it had important implications for the functioning of the committee, and for the relationship between Congress and the army. As the provisions crisis threatened to overwhelm the army, the delegates found themselves—like passengers on a foundering vessel—struggling side by side with the crew to try to stabilize the situation.

Both collectively and individually they communicated with the governors of neighboring states, urging them to expedite their efforts to increase the supplies of food to the army. The direct effect of these interventions is hard to measure. The immediate crisis had abated by February 20, before most of these appeals reached their intended targets. But the effect of the emergency on the committee, and on its relationship with Congress and the army, is unmistakable. Because the committee had better access to reliable information about the army's condition than the Congress did, its dependence on that body decreased. Committee members became more willing to challenge decisions emanating from York, whereas Congress found itself increasingly dependent on its delegates for information.[22]

These changing relationships spilled over into the other business on the committee's agenda: the reorganization of the army. The delegates struggled to maintain a distinction between their ad hoc intervention in the supply crisis and the reorganization itself. The latter project was more fully embedded in their mandate, and when they had time to analyze the situation at all, they tended to treat the collapse of the supply system as merely a terrifying distraction. In asking the governor of Maryland for help they characterized their mission at camp in terms of broad army reformation and lamented, "During the Progress of this important business the critical situation of the army on the score of Provisions hath filled our minds with Apprehension and Alarm."[23] To Washington, or to anyone who viewed the progress of the war from the army's perspective, the supply crisis was anything but incidental to the larger problems at hand. This was a perception that the committee members would reach only gradually. The opportunity to place their hands directly onto the machinery of supply in a circumstance of desperate necessity contributed materially to their ability to do so, and in the process it reinforced Washington's credibility with the group on a broad range of military issues.

The conference proceeded even as hunger tore at the fabric of the army. Between emergency discussions with harried commissaries and sessions spent drafting frantic appeals to neighboring governors, the members considered a variety of organizational issues. Their decisions repeatedly reflected and often plainly adhered to Washington's expressed views. They accepted his request for a draft to fill up the regiments. They opposed an initiative from Pennsylvania's delegates in Congress for an immediate assault on the British garrison in Philadelphia. They recommended reorganizing the army's Engineering Department "agreeable to the Gen[era]ls plan" and addressed a forceful, if deferentially worded, dissent to Congress's decision to implement the Board of War's proposal for a mid-winter invasion of Canada, instead endorsing Washington's private views on the question. The committee also "settled" a new plan for the orderly promotion of officers, taking its language almost verbatim from the "Representation." The committee did not limit itself to a rubber-stamp role, and when they felt called upon to do so its members could assert vigorously their own ideas. In general, however, the group's stay at camp effected a stronger basis for cooperation between Congress and the army by combining the unique perspectives of both.[24]

The effect of this process was clearest in the committee's role in reorganizing the Quartermaster's Department, which illustrates the degree to which the group used its access to reliable information to mediate effectively between Congress's expectations and the army's needs. It also shows Washington's ability, as a provider and orchestrator of that information, to achieve a higher degree of leverage in influencing organizational decisions in the political sphere than he had previously enjoyed. The delegates recognized the centrality of the quartermaster and his office to the success of any other reforms. They warned Henry Laurens that this department was the cog "on which not only the future Success of your Arms, but the present Existence of your Army immediately depends." Any continuing dislocation of the army's transportation or logistical functions would undermine or destroy its performance. "The Influence of this Office is so diffusive through every Part of your military System," they counseled, "that neither the Wisdom of Arrangement, the Spirit of Enterprise, or favourable Opportunity will be of any Avail, if this great Wheel in the Machine stops or moves heavily."[25]

No single question occupied more of the committee's time or attention, except for the supply crisis, than the search for a solution to the problems of the Quartermaster's Department. Its initial attempt to to bring the rudderless department under control through the nomination of General Philip Schuyler of New York as quartermaster general foundered in Congress. Schuyler lay under a cloud of allegations that he had contributed to the loss of Fort Ticonderoga the previous July, and he was pressing Congress for a court martial to clear his name. Congress barely took notice of the nomination, observing only that the committee had "represented the necessity of appointing, without delay, a quarter master general" but neglecting to enter Schuyler's name in its minutes.[26]

The committee's choice of Schuyler was a bad beginning to its efforts to reorganize the department. The day before receiving the nomination, Congress entertained a proposal from the Board of War that threatened the integrity of the department itself. The board reviewed the "situation" of the department, emphasizing its financial weakness and offered Congress two plans, either of which would have greatly increased its influence over this vital part of the military establishment. It asked Congress either to appoint "an Officer of rank, Activity and well acquainted by experience, with the business of the department . . . with power to arrange the Department, with the approbation and concurrence of the Board of War," or else to divide the department into four parts. Under the second plan, the quartermaster general would be stripped of most of his supply and procurement functions. He would handle little or no money, and he would share with the board the supervision of three subordinate officers, who would perform most of the functions traditionally under his jurisdiction, including the procurement of military equipment, the provision of wagons to transport the army's goods, and the collection of forage for its horses.[27]

Congress had postponed consideration of this ambitious proposal, but news of the committee's selection of Schuyler quickly brought the board's project back into view. It was moved that the board's first alternative, the appointment of a quartermaster general subject to its own approval, be adopted, and that the nominee "be directed, in concurrence with the Board of War, to prepare a new arrangement for that department, to be laid before Congress for consideration." On February 5, Congress instead adopted the board's second alternative. The decision sharply restricted both the authority and autonomy of the quartermaster general. The elimination of his power over public funds and the creation of subordinate staff officers to handle the department's most important functions reduced that official almost to the status of an agent of the board stationed with the army.[28]

The board's effort to seize control of the quartermaster's department marked the pivotal thrust in that organization's political offensive, one that paralleled Washington's efforts to expand his influence over congressional decisions relating to the army, which were then culminating in the Conference Committee's deliberations at camp. The board, which was reorganizing under the leadership of Washington's bitter rival, Horatio Gates, and his former quartermaster general, Thomas Mifflin, had embarked on a series of initiatives aimed at enlarging its role in military affairs. Congress—as the Revolution's only national-level political institution—became the forum in which the efforts of Washington and the board collided.

In January, the board secured from Congress broad powers to establish an independent network of provisions magazines for the army; to appoint superintendents to administer a purchasing, processing, and transportation system for those magazines; to set prices for wheat and flour; to call on Washington for military assistance in support of its activities; and to investigate the state of Pennsylvania's supply efforts. These powers permitted the board to compete with the Commissary Department in provisioning the army. The board followed this success by pushing through Congress its plan for an invasion of—or "Irruption" into—Canada. This move suggested that its ambitions were not limited to sharing responsibility for the army's support services, but rather that it hoped to participate in strategic decision making as well.[29]

The board's remarkable success in securing congressional approval for these enterprises resulted from several phenomena. It was able to manipulate Congress's perception of itself as a body nearly overwhelmed by its heavy workload. Henry Laurens's letters alluding to Congress's forced "descent" into the minutia of routine military business illustrate its increasing sense of loss of control over its own affairs.[30] The effect created in the minds of delegates by Washington's depictions of the army's plight also fueled Congress's tendency to delegate power haphazardly. His "starve, dissolve, or disperse" letters dislodged a real vein of fear in Congress and led, as he hoped they would, to the appointment of the Conference Committee. There was no way, however, of limiting the effects of Washington's reports. By unleashing on already hard-pressed delegates a fair—but in many respects an embellished—portrait of the army's material jeopardy, Washington deployed a many-edged sword. It is not surprising that Congress responded by availing itself of whatever remedies it could find. The Conference Committee was surely the first of these, but the Board of War was another. If only to foster a desperately needed division of administrative labor, Congress began delegating wide responsibilities by referring some military problems—and with them military authority—to the board.[31]

The inclinations, temperament, and political ingenuity of the board itself should not be overlooked. The strong animosity between Washington and several of its members—especially Gates and Mifflin—is obvious. Even more important was the role of organizational relationships. The new board was a body very much on the make in 1778. Recently victorious generals seldom leave the field for powerless desk jobs. Horatio Gates, with Mifflin and Pickering, left few avenues unexplored in their search for a significant role in Continental military affairs. In assembling their initiatives the board's members proved to be astute readers of the intricacies of navigating in troubled congressional waters.

The most apt but perhaps also the most charitable explanation for Congress's approach to policy making here is that it showed considerable confusion and that the delegates were subject to unusual degrees of suggestibility. At Washington's request they sent a committee to camp to confer with him on army reforms. Unable to agree on a comprehensive statement of its business, however, they failed to give that body a clear mandate. If the Board of War had other proposals, they were willing to experiment with them, even if they might conflict with the committee's initiatives. Congress most of all was seeking results, and—unsure of its ability to get them—it was hedging its bets. The board shrewdly discerned this mood and played to it in grasping for control of the Quartermaster's Department. It touched a perennially exposed congressional nerve by alluding to the matter of fiscal prudence. "Large sums of money are immediately wanted for the business of this Department," it warned, inviting Congress to wonder whether those funds would be better entrusted to itself or to an agency impeached of incompetence by no less an authority than the commander-in-chief himself. The ingrained fear of waste had proved effective in 1777 in persuading Congress to reorganize the Commissary Department. The board was not mistaken in assuming that it would do so again.[32]

While Congress completed its work on the Quartermaster's Department the February provisions crisis broke over the heads of the army and the committee at camp. Its members turned from decisions about nominations for the various support departments and involved themselves in desperate efforts to feed the troops. Both the committee and Washington worked in ignorance of the changing political situation in York. On February 7

Congress directed President Laurens to notify the committee of the new arrangements for the department and to ask it to confer with Washington to provide a list of nominees for the "several departments" that would comprise the new agency. At this point fortuitous circumstances ensured that the proceedings at York and Valley Forge continued in isolation from each other. Rapidly deteriorating weather swelled the rivers and inundated the region's roads, severing communications between the two points. The Susquehanna River became impassable between February 6 and 12, stranding Laurens's letter between Congress and the camp. The committee did not learn of Congress's decision to reorganize the Quartermaster's Department until the thirteenth. During the interval, largely because of its experience with the supply crisis, it began to rethink its position on both the state of the army and on the needs of the department.[33]

The weather was also, ironically, the principal agent in the sudden collapse of the army's supply systems. Even personal travel about the camp became difficult, and the movement of goods through the region came to a complete halt. By February 12, the army was reported by two brigadier generals to be on the brink of disbanding. The committee, concerned about the long silence from York on its nomination of Schuyler to be quartermaster general, began to cast about for other candidates. It summoned Nathanael Greene to Moore Hall and conferred with him about the appointment. Greene had just been ordered by Washington to lead a large foraging party into eastern Chester County to strip the countryside there in a desperate attempt to keep the army intact. He called on the committee on his way out of camp, but the discussions led to no firm conclusions about the department.[34]

After with meeting Greene, the committee urged Congress to resolve the quartermaster situation. It attributed the apparent delay to the possible miscarriage of its January 28 letter but admitted that it might have resulted from some "disapprobation of [Schuyler]." At a loss to explain the silence from York, the delegates began crediting unfounded rumors. They lectured Congress on the reasons why deputy quartermaster Henry Lutterloh, who they had heard was under consideration, was unqualified for the post. To reinforce their position, they hinted that "a character has presented itself, which in great degree merits our approbation, judgement and wishes. We have opened the subject to him, and it is now under his consideration." They could not name their new candidate before receiving his consent but hoped to be able to do so soon.[35]

When it received notice of Congress's decision to divide the department on February 13, the committee treated the news almost as cavalierly as Congress had its own nomination of Schuyler, by recording its receipt in its minutes but otherwise ignoring it. This resulted partly from the press of the supply crisis, which reached its worst dimensions between the twelfth and fifteenth, but it may have also reflected a calculated decision to play for time in the hope that the consequences of that decision could be averted. The delegates' response to Congress on the fourteenth avoided the issue altogether, concentrating instead on the plight of the army. The interval provided by the severance of communications with York gave them a chance to reconsider their politically inept decision to nominate Schuyler. Congress would soon be in receipt of their tacit acknowledgment of error in the matter, and of the news that they were preparing another nomination. Nathanael Greene, who had probably made known to them both his reluctance to accept the office and his conditions for doing so, would not return to camp until February 22.[36]

The committee resumed its contrapuntal round of balancing questions of long-range organizational significance and those of immediate import to the supply emergency. It wrote to Governor George Clinton of New York "for aid in procur[in]g or transport[in]g Provision." But at Washington's request it also reviewed the instructions given by the Board of War to the superintendents appointed to operate one of the provisions magazines and a contract that had been awarded. It "reported agt" the contract, terming it "unnecessary and unreasonable and exhorbitant." The issue related only peripherally to the committee's mandate, but their response suggests the delegates' deepening divergence from the recent sense of Congress toward the board's multiple initiatives in military affairs.[37]

Congress, meanwhile, waited with mounting impatience for the committee's nominations for the four posts in the new quartermaster's office. On February 20 it ordered Laurens to repeat its request, but the next day it softened the tone—if not the substance—of its stance on the question. Spurred by "intelligence this day received from camp, that alarming consequences are likely to ensue from a longer delay of appointing proper persons to fill the several offices in the quartermaster's department," it voted to allow the Conference Committee, in concert with Washington, provisionally to make the "proper appointments" for the department "forthwith."[38] Although it had been wrought in the belief that no time should be lost on such formalities as recommendations or approvals, this decision's ironic effect was to give the committee the one resource it needed most: time itself. By February 20, before receiving news of Congress's latest desires, the delegates were feeling constrained by their implicit obstruction of that body's intentions. Nathanael Greene had not returned to camp, and the delegates had been unable to develop a coherent plan to offer in opposition to that of the board. Without such a plan there was little hope that Congress could be dissuaded from implementing the board's proposal.

Anticipating Congress's impatience, the committeemen sought another delay with yet another noncommittal reply. They acknowledged receipt of the resolve of February 5 and observed obligingly (if somewhat condescendingly) that the subject was "very important." They "only wait[ed]," they explained, "some further information when we shall do ourselves the Honor of laying our sentiments before Congress on the material Alteration proposed in this Office." By the twenty-fourth, the shift of initiative to the committee was confirmed when it received news that Congress had decided to let it staff the department. The delegates reacted magnanimously by hesitating to exercise the "Powers which Congress have thought proper to intrust us with" without its informed concurrence. Despite this rhetorical deference the group assured Laurens that it would make "all the necessary Arrangements . . . to put matters in such a Train as will produce desirable circumstances." By now the committee was working furiously with Washington to convince a reluctant Nathanael Greene to accept the appointment.[39]

By February 25 the committee had exacted a sufficiently strong commitment from Greene to propose his name to Congress. Armed with a formidable candidate and with its own recent, rueful experience in keeping the army supplied, it launched a deferentially phrased but devastating critique of the Board of War's plan to divide the department. Such a step, it argued, would involve the subordinate officers on which it relied in "interference with each other, infinite Confusion, and a Variety of Controversies, which must be terminated by the Commander in Chief." It riddled many of the arguments on which the Board had relied, noting, for example, that what the board labeled "petty expenses," actually amounted to enormous outlays. Indeed, the committee neatly reversed some of the most persuasive points that the board had tried to make with the cost-conscious Congress. Far from saving money, it observed, the dispersal of spending authority among several officers would increase the chances for fiscal abuse. Adverting to the "Administration of Affairs heretofore," the members dissected the widespread malfeasance of the old department and left it to the "Wisdom of Congress" to infer the consequences of any reorganization that left its successor's powers under an agency including the previous incumbent, Thomas Mifflin. "Upon reconsidering this Business in all its Connections," they soothingly predicted, Congress would "see a Propriety" in placing the department under "one controuling superintending Power."[40]

Having demolished the underpinnings of the board's proposal for reconstructing the department, and by implication Congress's wisdom in acceding to it, the committee presented its own plan. The department would be managed by a quartermaster general (Greene), who would assume full responsibility for all of its traditional functions and by two deputies on whose appointment he had conditioned his own acceptance. The three men would share a fixed commission of 1 percent of the amount of their total expenditures. Greene would remain with the army and would handle the overall administrative responsibilities while one deputy managed procurement activities and the other kept the department's accounts.[41] Congress lost no time in acceding to the committee's plans. On March 2 it withdrew its approval of the board's quartermaster scheme and replaced it with the one offered by the committee. Greene was allowed to retain his rank in the army and Mifflin was ordered to "make out immediately and transmit to Congress and to [Greene] a state of the preparations for the next campaign."[42]

The abrupt reversal was a marked setback for the Board of War. With the abandonment of its intended annexation of the powers of the Quartermaster's Department, its attempt to influence day-to-day military affairs was substantially impaired. As was the case with the evolution of the board's offensive, its demise occurred simultaneously along a broad front. The state of Pennsylvania resisted the act authorizing the board to establish independent magazines from the time of its passage, insisting that the board's agents would interfere with the prerogatives of the state and the liberties of its citizens. Under fire from the state and the army, the board spent too much of its time and energy defending the project. By mid-February, with the army desperately close to dissolution, the board suspended these operations temporarily, perhaps as a cynical way of proving their indispensability. Meanwhile, the board's second venture, the Canadian "Irruption," failed even more unequivocally. The board had only indirect control over the operation, but it bore a heavy responsibility for its success or failure as its main initiator. When the Marquis de Lafayette, Congress's choice to lead the invasion, reached Albany in mid-February, he found a complete lack of local preparations. By March 2 Congress ordered the board to suspend the project, acknowledging that it had been rendered "not only hazzardous in a high degree, but extreamly imprudent."[43]

Congress's reversal on the Quartermaster's Department thus completed the collapse of the board's search for a wider role in military operations. There is no evidence that the board waged any effective struggle on behalf of the measure after its passage. By the time the proposal met resistance within the army, Horatio Gates and his allies were too busy trying to salvage their system of purchasing magazines to defend their other ventures. The board's political offensive decayed largely as a result of its own inertia. It had been broadly but not very deeply conceived, in a climate of institutional opportunism fostered by the convergence of a hesitant Congress with an unexpected crisis that overwhelmed the army's established mechanisms and procedures. Washington's efforts in December 1777 to influence Congress had inadvertently paved the way for the initial success of the board's initiatives. As those efforts matured at Valley Forge in February 1778, however, the board's brief ascendancy began rapidly to recede.

The truncation of the plan to dismantle the Quartermaster's Department was the Conference Committee's most important accomplishment at Valley Forge and the one that best illustrates its role in the evolving relationship between Congress and the army. Armed with reliable information from its long stay in camp, and with an awareness of the fragility and interdependence of the army's logistical systems gained by its experience during the provisions crisis, the committee was in a strong position to counter the board's arguments with credible ones of its own. It displayed both political ingenuity and stamina in delaying its reaction to Congress's adoption of the board's plan until it could retreat with grace from the disastrous nomination of Schuyler by the diligent recruitment of Greene.

Washington's exact role in the evolution of the committee's position on the Quartermaster's Department is uncertain. He supported, if he did not orchestrate, its resistance to the idea of dividing the department and removing it from his control. He pressed Greene to accept the leadership of the department, undoubtedly realizing that no other outcome could better ensure the demise of the board's plan. The committee's work was the constant focus of his attention from the day of its arrival in camp until arrangements for the department were "settled" at the end of February. Thereafter, Washington began to concentrate increasingly on supervising preparations for the 1778 campaign. His role in the decision was an extension of his broader involvement with the committee from the time of its appointment. He acted as a provider and a manipulator of information, and as the self-appointedly "humble" submitter of ideas and recommendations. Beginning with the carefully thought-out preparation of the "Representation" to the committee, he was continually ready to inform the members, to guide their perception of the problems that they undertook to solve, and to interpret for them the meaning of those solutions to both himself and for the army. In this respect, he had a decisive effect on the group's work.[44]

Some committee members stayed in camp until early April, making arrangements or refining decisions they had reached earlier.[45] Many of the committee's proposals were not formally introduced in Congress until the late spring or summer of 1778, and some were not acted on until long after that.[46] In an important sense, however, the effect of the group's stay at camp was more immediate, if difficult to measure precisely. On their return from Valley Forge, the committee members provided Congress with an infusion of hard information on the state of the army and an enriched appreciation of the scope and complexity of the military enterprise itself. For at least the duration of the current session, Congress comprised a membership a quarter of whom were familiar with army operations on a working basis. These members constituted a core for whom there could no longer be any credible basis for arbitrarily dividing public business into spheres designated as "broad outlines" and "particulars." The June 1777 reorganization of the Commissary Department—which more than anything else precipitated the collapse of the army's supply system the following fall—had been an almost paradigmatic example of the kinds of public policy that proceeded from such a division. The aborted sundering of the Quartermaster's Department, to which Congress reflexively turned in an attempt to repair that dislocation, narrowly missed becoming another such example.[47]

Chapter 8

THE LORD'S TIME TO WORK

February began quietly at Valley Forge and along the lines between the American camp and Philadelphia. Both sides were only sporadically engaged, as they had been since the British withdrew from Darby in late December. Although the presence of Maryland troops at Wilmington complicated the importation of goods from England and New York, the British garrison remained relatively well supplied. Its consumption of foodstuffs stockpiled during the foraging of Christmas week was balanced by the ease with which "market people" were able to circumvent the blockade of the city. A British lieutenant colonel wrote his brother that his winter quarters were "peaceable, and in some degree tolerable, at least in comparison with what might have been expected." Prices were high, he observed, but this fact was itself "so tempting that the [Americans] cannot prevent the people's supplying the market." He inferred that it was equally difficult to "prevent [the rebels] getting supplies of all things they want" from the country without adopting more aggressive tactics than Howe seemed inclined to do. In practice, the Americans faced serious local disadvantages. The Continental Army enjoyed equal or better access to the farms of southeastern Pennsylvania than the British did. Indeed, its experience in the state showed that it could not survive without consuming their resources. Its very need to do so, however, worked to alienate the army from the producers of those goods.[1]

This dynamic was rooted in a political economy in which the depreciating paper currency on which the rebel army relied was outperformed in regional markets by British specie. When Continental supply and transport systems failed, it became necessary to feed the regiments with supplies obtained, voluntarily or otherwise, locally. The weakness of the Continental currency required a reliance on coercive methods, which reinforced the initial preference of the country people to trade with the British. Once this cycle was established it operated with an accelerating momentum to the advantage of the British. If people were willing to bring their goods to town, it was unnecessary for Howe to send his foragers into the countryside. This lessened their exposure to rebel attacks and reduced the likelihood that predictable incidents of soldierly excess would compromise the advantages of a reliable treasury. As more marketeers swarmed onto the roads leading to Philadelphia, rebel operations shifted from a competitive to a preventive or even a punitive emphasis. Beginning with the disequilibrium between the currencies, the Americans lost at the start of the winter many of the tactical advantages that might otherwise have accrued to a "native" army.[2]

Washington recognized the dangers inherent in this dynamic, and he struggled with diminishing success to prevent its establishment. During the fall he hesitated to implement the martial prerogatives that Congress had granted him to seize provisions from the inhabitants for fear of initiating just such a cycle of communal disaffection. As the campaign evolved after Germantown from a pitched contest between two relatively compact armies into a dispersed regional struggle, however, it became harder to control the behavior of the small, mobile detachments on which Continental strategy relied.[3]

When the army was temporarily reconcentrated at Valley Forge in late December, the collapse of its support departments forced an open, if fairly tacit, resort to draconian measures to assure its survival. Then, after the beginning of the new year, it became harder to control the frustrated, resentful, and increasingly disenchanted army. When the camp was established strategic detachments were again deployed, and control became less a question of official policy than of individual responsibility among field-grade officers, many of whom were wont to perceive in the local populace a menacing strain of indifference or even antipathy toward their own welfare, and to return those sentiments with a vengeance.

By the end of January it was recognized at headquarters that the consequences of communal disaffection were a serious threat. Continental food supplies were momentarily stable, but it was understood that those supplies might fail again at any time. Hoping to capitalize on the entrepreneurial spirit the flourishing British markets had aroused in the area's populace, Washington decided to establish an informal emporium of his own. He announced that a traveling market would rotate around the perimeter of the camp, close enough to its center to discourage wandering by the soldiers but sufficiently far away to minimize security risks.[4]

The wording of his proclamation notifying the "good people" of Pennsylvania and adjacent states of the opening of the market indicates that Washington recognized just how far the alienation between the army and its neighbors had progressed. He found it necessary to assure prospective suppliers: "That the Clerks of the market are inhabitants of this State, will attend on the respective days and at the places before mentioned. Whose duty it will be to protect the Inhabitants from any kind of abuse or violence that may be offered to their persons or effects—and to see that they receive pay for their articles according to the prices hereafter mentioned." The advertisement further promised that "All persons coming to the markets . . . for the purpose of supplying them—or returning from the same, may depend [that] their carriages shall not be impressed or otherwise detained."[5]

The goodwill Washington hoped to reap from this measure was aborted even before the proclamation circulated in local newspapers. The sudden collapse of the Commissary Department in mid-February forced the army to resort to the widespread seizure of provisions and other goods and sent waves of farmers onto area roads in an effort to get their property into Philadelphia ahead of the American foragers. In the face of starvation and the possible dispersal of the army, local goodwill became a dispensable luxury. Washington found it necessary to order the army to strip the countryside in front of the camp. For the first time, the order omitted his customary injunctions to leave friendly residents with at least enough resources to sustain their families during the winter.[6]

At Valley Forge, the surly mood of the soldiery carried over into February. By that time, dozens of officers had their resignations pending or were considering leaving the service. Pleading with Robert Morris to support the plan for lifetime half-pay pensions proposed by Washington, Tench Tilghman observed that after the army reached Valley Forge, officers "came in crouds" to headquarters seeking permission to resign. The officers' discontent was reinforced by their realization that the army's interests hung in the balance in political deliberations to which they had no real access. Jedediah Huntington of Connecticut lamented that generals and privates alike waited helplessly to learn what conclusions the Conference Committee would reach. "It may be the Lords time to work when we are at the weakest," he suggested hopefully, "I am sure [that] we seem to be doing but very little for ourselves."[7]

Some officers, unwilling to trust their interests to the deliberative process or to the Lord, addressed themselves directly to Congress. Brigadiers Enoch Poor and John Paterson, who feared that charges of neglect of duty against them stemming from the surrender of Fort Ticonderoga during the 1777 campaign might be settled by the recommendation of the Conference Committee, wrote to Henry Laurens to demand immediate court martials. Lachlan McIntosh of Georgia, who feared that two members of his state's delegation in Congress might seek to have him "reduced" (i.e., removed) from the state's remodeled Continental roster, warned his old friend Laurens that political motives underlay the maneuver and hinted that Laurens's influence in York might spare him such a fate.[8]

For otherwise "friendless" officers, Washington was as much an object of first resort as a source of final appeal. Except in moments of profound vexation, he was almost tirelessly willing to entertain petitions and other requests for favor from members of the army. In his self-proclaimed guise as the guardian of the common rights of every man under his command, he was bombarded with requests for special consideration from his officers.[9] While he generally listened sympathetically to grievances, the precariousness of the army's situation made it difficult for him to resolve most of them. Instead, Washington contrived to turn the petitioning process itself into a mechanism for the diffusion of discontents. Even when disappointing petitioners, he was often able to blunt their anger by acknowledging their grounds for complaint or by emphasizing his commitment to the principles of fairness itself. By willingly listening to complaints, Washington used his office as a buffer for the amelioration of dissatisfaction.[10]

It would be misleading to suggest that most of the army's internal discourse reflected clashes of self-interest. For every officer who probed the system in search of personal advantages, others politicked on behalf of their fellows or subordinates, both from motives of humanity and for the wider good of the service. Pay shortages were a particular source of complaint within the ranks. Cash—unlike food or other supplies that were procured from the states at large—was essentially an item of government issue, and shortages were usually interpreted as a sign of indifference on the part of politicians toward the soldiers. Washington told Henry Laurens that the distress in camp for want of money was "not easily described." George Weedon sought out the paymaster general to solicit funds for one of his regiments that was about to complete its service and go home. He couched his request in terms of the public good, pointing out that he wanted to leave his men "perfectly satisfied, as [we] have hopes of their re-enlisting after a while provided they can be paid up to the time of their Dismission."[11]

The New Englanders for whom Jedediah Huntington intervened were in worse straits. Having joined the main army from Peekskill the previous autumn, they had not received any ration money since that time and lacked a paymaster to keep their accounts current. Still worse was the situation of a Maryland regiment stationed at Wilmington, where the paymaster had received a "great quantity of money" but refused to issue it to the troops because his predecessor had not prepared adequate payrolls. The unit's commander begged Washington to "relieve the Affairs of the Regiment from their present state of Confusion and Irregularity."[12]

The most serious consequence of the army's material shortages and organizational deficiencies was the slow but steady erosion of the force itself. Morale problems could be checked or incidents of contention blunted on a case-by-case basis, but only at the cost of daily desertions, or resignations, and individual decisions not to reenlist. In early February, a British spy in New York told Henry Clinton that Americans were crossing the Hudson River every day "on furlough." Disgruntled New Englanders were not alone in their resolve to escape from the miseries of camp life. Pennsylvanians, "uneasy" about the scanty supplies of clothing that they were receiving, were deserting "by the dozen" according to Jedediah Huntington. James Varnum informed Alexander McDougall that despite the astonishing patience of many of his men, the overall situation was "gloomy, as Desertion becomes very prevalent."[13]

The collapse of the supply departments in mid-February descended on an army that was already reeling from the effects of the earlier shortages, and one whose internal cohesion was being threatened, but not subverted, by conflicts over resources. The "second Rupture," as one commissary official termed it, emerged with a suddenness that must have stunned all but the handful of individuals who understood how tenuously and superficially the December breakdown had been papered over. While the contours of the crisis were inherent in the material deficiencies of the Commissary and Quartermaster's Departments, the collapse itself was triggered by a sudden outbreak of bad weather that began during the first week of February and continued for most of the month. By February 5 the Schuylkill River had become almost impassable because of high water, and the regional road network was largely awash. The next day Washington informed Casimir Pulaski in New Jersey that food supplies at Valley Forge were "nearly exhausted, and the army is reduced literally to a starving condition."[14]

The Conference Committee simultaneously came to realize that the supply problem was an ongoing emergency, not an isolated past event. It warned Congress that "this army has been fed by daily supplies drawn from the country at large." Unless those supplies continued, the troops would soon have to "disband, live upon every Quaker in the country—or perish." This formulation amounted to an inelegant paraphrase of Washington's prophesy that the army might have to "starve, dissolve, or disperse." Washington had by now narrowed the options to the grim specter of dissolution. In a letter dated February 7, he warned his commissary general, William Buchanan, that the previous occasional deficiencies "seem now on the point of resolving themselves into this fatal Crisis, total want and dissolution of the Army." He told Henry Champion, an army purchaser in Connecticut, that the situation was the "most Melancholy that can be conceived." While supplies had once been merely "very deficient and irregular," the "prospect now opens of absolute want, such as will make it impossible to keep the army much longer from absolutely dissolving."[15]

Although the situation was certifiably grave during the first week of February, Washington was partly indulging his penchant for graphic embellishment in order to stave off a full-fledged disaster further down the line. Between rhetorical sallies, his letters to Buchanan and Champion suggested that he believed that the army might hold out for another month under the existing circumstances. For several days after sending these letters, he returned his attention to routine army matters, making no further references in his correspondence to any "fatal crisis." On February 9 he wrote to General Benjamin Lincoln, adding almost casually that nothing "of importance" had taken place of late.[16]

If Washington was exaggerating the extent of the emergency at its outset, he was also being wildly optimistic in suggesting that the army could survive for another month. The weather continued to worsen and the movement of supplies in the area became impossible. By the twelfth it appeared that Washington's worst fears would indeed be realized. Almost resignedly, Jedediah Huntington and James Varnum scribbled their pessimistic conclusions on the condition reports from the camp guards that they sent to their respective major generals. "I have nothing to add, my Lord," Huntington informed Lord Stirling, "but that the camp is in a melancholy condition for want of provisions, and that there is a great danger that the Famine will break up the army." And Varnum warned Nathanael Greene, "the situation of the Camp is such that in all human probability the Army must soon dissolve."[17]

The crisis provoked a desperate flurry of activity to press any remaining provisions from the already ravaged region. Washington ordered Greene and General Anthony Wayne to strip the area west of the Delaware between the Schuylkill River and the Brandywine Creek for between fifteen and twenty miles inland. Wayne was a Pennsylvanian from a neighboring area, and recruiting him for this task was probably seen at headquarters as a way of making these measures more politically palatable to that state's authorities. Greene and Wayne took with them between 1,500 and 2,000 men, including almost half of the fully clothed and otherwise ambulatory troops left in camp. It was understood, however, that even under the most favorable circumstances, these measures would not meet the army's needs. It was also necessary to drain the few magazines that had been established in the region for the opening of the spring campaign. Washington ordered Ephraim Blaine, a deputy commissary, to go to Head of Elk, Maryland, the main storage point for food supplies and military stores coming from the south, to bring whatever goods were left in the magazines there back to Valley Forge.[18]

This decision in essence mortgaged the army's future to its immediate needs, but given the deadly implications of the emergency it was unavoidable. Washington again indulged in the rhetoric of dissolution, but now with abundant corroborating testimony. He notified Governor Livingston of New Jersey that the army was "on the point of a dissolution for the second time this year." Although he disapproved of the Board of War's intention to operate an independent provisioning organization in competition with the Commissary Department, he pleaded with the board's superintendents to expedite their efforts. Without their earliest relief, he exclaimed, "no address or authority will be sufficient to keep [the army] long together.[19]

These efforts to secure provisions disarranged the regional deployment of forces that had been made to contain the British army in Philadelphia. It was necessary to use regular troops not only for foraging purposes but also to move provisions from area magazines to Valley Forge. Washington sent Henry Lee, whose corps had anchored the detached patrols covering the area west of the Schuylkill, into Delaware to seize supplies and to protect the southern convoys coming from Head of Elk. While the troops under Greene and Wayne in eastern Chester County temporarily helped suppress enemy activity there, they left the area long before Lee returned from his mission. The result was a dangerous gap in the camp's security network and an open invitation to civilian inhabitants to carry any goods they were able to conceal from Greene into Philadelphia.[20]

The effects of this disarrangement extended to the wings of the army's sprawling disposition at Wilmington and Trenton. Those garrisons depended on magazines that would now be emptied. The distress at Valley Forge was "beyond anything you can conceive," Washington told William Smallwood, by way of explaining that Henry Lee would soon arrive at Wilmington to "tap" the magazines at Dover and Head of Elk, "a general mutiny and dispersion is to be dreaded." He consoled Smallwood with the disingenuous observation that "you are in an abundant country [and] I imagine you might furnish yourself from the resources of it." The removal of Continental stores from Trenton and its vicinity similarly undermined Pulaski's efforts to use that town as a base of operations to support militia activities both in southeastern Pennsylvania and in New Jersey.[21]

The army's activity at the start of the crisis stirred the region. Some Pennsylvanians thought it signaled the long-awaited start of a wave of military enterprise. A Lancaster resident reported rumors circulating in that town that Greene was moving to join Smallwood at Wilmington and triumphantly concluded "thus we see a new campaign opening." This illusion was rapidly dispelled for anyone in direct communication with the army. John Laurens depicted for his father the actual implications of the movements: that they had narrowly pulled the army back from the "brink of ruin" itself. "By extraordinary exertions, by scraping from distant scanty magazines and collecting with parties," he wrote on February 17, "we have obtained a temporary relief, and have hopes [of] such further supplies as will save us from the disagreeable necessity of dividing the army into cantonments."[22]

John Laurens's optimism that the crisis was over was more hopeful than definitive. A day later one commissary officer expressed doubts about his own safety among hungry and clamorous troops, while another forlornly declined to predict when it might be possible to "afford . . . a plentiful supply." At least a trickle of food had begun to reach the camp, however, and the most critical moment had passed. By the twentieth, Jedediah Huntington reported, "we begin to be in better supply." The next day Washington reverted to the past tense, speaking of "a time when the army *was* nearly experiencing a famine." Commissary Ephraim Blaine noted that "Col. [Thomas] Jones has a good supply for the present and [I] hope it will continue until the middle of March." Jones was less sanguine. While he thought that the new supplies might "pass us on for a few days," he was already bracing for "our next cry." If provisions did not continue arriving in timely fashion, he predicted, "we shall have the same jigg over again."[23]

The tenuous rescue of the army was effected at a real cost to itself and to its host community. By tightening the screws of oppression on the local populace, Washington was able to force it to yield small but crucially important amounts of supplies, and by emptying carefully hoarded magazines in adjacent states he secured a sufficient reserve to wait out the weather-related disruption of the supply departments. The seizure of goods eroded civilian goodwill, despite attempts to guarantee timely payment for appropriated goods. Washington's effort to establish a marketplace near the camp was aborted. The army's grip on the Delaware was weakened, and the opening of the spring campaign was jeopardized by the consumption of resources on which they depended. Before the foraging parties had been recalled to camp, an embarrassed Washington had to beg the region's residents to "exert themselves to prepare Cattle for the use of the Army during the months of May, June, and July next," just to replace supplies that had been consumed.[24]

The effect of the crisis on the army defies easy characterization. In light of Washington's repeated expressions of doubt about whether he would be able to maintain control over the troops, we might ask whether disorder became prevalent during the depths of the famine. Considering his penchant for rhetorically embellishing his correspondence when the interests of the army depended on it, his testimony may require some corroboration. He had, after all, alerted Congress to the overnight eruption and precarious suppression of a "dangerous mutiny" during the food shortages of late December, an event that no other observers characterized as such. During February, however, such corroboration was abundant.[25] Commissary officials were particularly fearful that they would bear the brunt of the frustrations of hungry troops. Thomas Jones wrote almost daily to his absent superior between February 15 and 18, bemoaning his chances of living until he could resign on March 1. The trepidations of Commissary Department officials, however, might be attributed as much to the workings of their consciences as to the demeanor of the troops. Except for a few severe verbal floggings from general officers, they emerged from the crisis relatively unscathed.[26]

More disinterested informants expressed similar fears about the maintenance of order. When Francis Dana, a member of the Conference Committee, made an incredulous tour of the camp on February 16, seeking to confirm the alarming testimony that the committee was receiving at Moore Hall, he beheld what he took to be an army in the throes of incipient mutiny. The previous day, he reported, "Col. Brewer's regimt. rose in a body and proceeded to Gen. Patterson's Quarts. [and] . . . laid before him their complaints and threatened to quit the army." Paterson had calmed them only by the "prudent conduct" of allowing them to "go out of camp to purchase meat as far as their money would answer" and then to offer certificates for which he would be responsible. John Laurens may have had the same episode in mind when he told his father of the "most alarming situation" in which the army lay. He wrote that "the soldiers were scarcely restrained from mutiny by the eloquence and management of our Officers."[27] It bears noting, however, that neither of these accounts alleged anything more than occasions of severely strained decorum, and that both emphasized the ultimate maintenance of discipline. There are quite simply no documented cases throughout this period of large-scale collective disorders. When Nathanael Greene returned to camp in late February he used a similar incident to illustrate the "patience and moderation" that he believed the troops had "manifested under their sufferings [which] does the highest honor to the Magnanimity of the American Soldiers." He reported that a delegation of starving troops had come "before their superior officers and told their sufferings in as respectful terms as if they had been humble petitioners for special favors; they added that it would be impossible to continue in Camp any longer without support."[28]

On balance, the best picture that can be drawn of the temper of the army during this period is a mixed one. As in the late December emergency, there seems to have been at least a temporary lull in internal conflict as the crisis reached its full pitch. This perhaps resulted from the concentration of individuals on just staying alive, with its attendant lack of opportunities for conducting disputes or at least for committing them to paper. There is also less evidence of verbal antagonism toward local civilians during this period than during the better-supplied weeks of January. There were fewer cases of derogatory allusion to the state's ethnic or religious communities, and those that occurred were less vehement than before. Anthony Wayne begged Thomas Wharton to get shirts for his men "if you strip the Dutchmen for them." John Paterson offhandedly mused that it would not be prudent to "expect great things from this Sanctified Quaking State." If the silence of the record accurately reflects the army's actual demeanor, it may signify a short-term indifference by the soldiers to the sources of the crisis. They may have turned on their own errant suppliers in times of real shortage and bothered to reflect on their external causes only during intervals of better supply.[29]

There was also a discernible vein of benevolence afoot in camp during the crisis. Some soldiers took a humorously detached view of their own predicament. "The army you know," wrote one dragoon serving on detachment in New Jersey, "is the Vortex of small fortunes and wo betides him who makes no Provison for a wet Day—while we are under every disability, in the field, to take advantage of the times, or even to keep the old ground good." Others kept sight of the fact that the hardships of war bore as heavily on civilians as on themselves. A group of Virginia officers circulated a subscription during the emergency and raised fifty pounds for a Philadelphia widow who had helped American prisoners there. "Any little matter that gentlemen chuse to contribute," they proclaimed, "cant fail of being acceptable and will be considered as a grateful acknowledgment on their part for the voluntary benevolent part she has acted."[30]

While the troops at Valley Forge struggled with the mid-winter famine, an increasingly violent conflict spread through the region between the army's crescent-shaped deployment and the Philadelphia lines. The "stationary" garrison at Wilmington was relatively less involved in this conflict than the other American detachments. Its defensive and intelligence responsibilities required that it cleave to the Delaware River, anchoring the right wing of the Continental position. As the winter wore on these essentially passive imperatives combined to turn the post into a microcosm of the main camp at Valley Forge. It suffered from the same bleeding away of manpower; its officers wrangled over promotions; and its privates chafed over missed paydays. Its harried commissaries suffered from the same inability to meet their responsibilities as did their brethren at Valley Forge, and they often met the same unhappy fate at the hands of their hungry charges.[31]

In the area between Valley Forge and Philadelphia, the face of war began to wear a look of unrelieved civil calamity. As the continuing demands of two armies for food, forage, and clothing reduced fixed stocks of those commodities, prices mounted and competition over goods became less amicable. Increasingly, to live in the region between the contending sides was to be drawn, voluntarily or otherwise, into the conflict.

Until events associated with the February famine forced him to modify his approach, Washington adhered to the strategic division of the area into spheres divided by the Schuylkill River. The river provided the main axis of security for Valley Forge. Despite Henry Lee's efforts to gather geographical intelligence for the area during January, Washington considered his knowledge of the region to be badly flawed. In late February he recruited surveyors among the officers from Pennsylvania to make a "General Draught" of the countryside. Until he felt better informed about the geographical complexities of the area he resisted occasional overtures to expand the scope of Continental responsibility to the eastern side of that river.[32]

It remained an article of faith within the army that the Continental detachments west of the river were performing their function of preventing trade between the city and its hinterland more effectively than were the Pennsylvania militia on the other side. By early February the provost's guard at camp fairly bulged with hapless civilians seized on area highways with items of contraband presumed to be intended for Philadelphia's markets. With no state courts sitting in the eastern counties, some of these people were tried by regimental courts martial. They received makeshift penalties that were as arbitrary as their proceedings were irregular. One Thomas Butter was tried for attempting to carry flour to Philadelphia and sentenced to receive 250 lashes on his bare back. Thomas Ryan was convicted of bringing mutton and a bull toward the city. He was fined £50 and ordered confined in the guardhouse until the money was paid for the "use of the sick in camp." William Maddock and Joseph Edwards were presented for trying to drive cattle to the enemy and both were fined £100. Another wayward drover, Philip Kirk, was sentenced to be held in a jail somewhere in Pennsylvania until the enemy left the state, and then to have his real and personal estates confiscated! John Williamson and David Dan were found guilty of driving cattle to the city and each received 250 lashes, while Daniel Williamson drove some sheep there and was let off with a mere 200 stripes.[33]

The efficacy of Continental patrols was vigorously questioned by Joseph Reed, the state's only delegate on the Conference Committee. On the contrary, Reed insisted, the "intercourse on this [west] side Schuylkill tho on acct. of the River more easy of Interruption is the greatest." He belabored regular troops with the same allegations that it had become usual to lay against the militia: they were few in number, in constant need of refreshment, and "so corruptible that we should delude ourselves if we depended on their Exertions." Reed had recently helped to broker that "dependence," but now he wanted to put the whole business of blockading the city into the hands of the militia, which he noted, "improves . . . every day." He cautioned against crediting criticisms of the state forces by Continental partisans. "It is fashionable to blame them," he noted, "and it is sometimes carried to a blameable length."[34]

Nathanael Greene's observations as the head of the foraging expedition sent into Chester County in mid-February are more damning to army interests than Reed's openly political views. His reports conveyed a portrait of matters there that was inauspicious in every respect. In spite of the concentration of Continental resources in that district, he found it anything but pacified. "The face of the Country," he observed, "is strongly markt with poverty and distress," and his initial efforts to collect supplies were therefore "inconsiderable." Whigs, he concluded, constituted only a small minority of the population, and they lived in such fear of retaliation from their Tory neighbors that they were stubbornly reluctant to cooperate with the American army, or even to supply him with intelligence. He remarked with amazement on the ability of Jacob James's new provincial corps, which numbered about one hundred citizens, to suppress the county's Whigs and to protect the marketeers. The latter, Greene ruefully noted, had already carried into the city "all the cattle and most of the best horses" in the area.[35]

Because of the emergency at camp, Greene had neither the time for making fine distinctions among local attitudes nor the opportunity for the politically useful but time-consuming work of making new friends for the army or protecting its existing ones. A careful reading of his observations, however, suggests a more complex picture of the political and social fabric of the area. The countryside was apparently neither so absolutely drained of resources as it initially seemed to Greene, nor so sharply divided into dominant Tory and submissive Whig camps as his comments appeared to imply. Rather, there was a large and essentially self-interested middle group of inhabitants whose guiding principal lay in the protection of their own lives and property. Six months of intimate experience with the conflict, moreover, had made this group increasingly sophisticated at the business of doing just that, especially by hiding their goods from the intrusive attention of army foragers.

In less desperate circumstances, the existence of this group might have offered a valuable opportunity for winning some of its members to the insurgent cause by a discriminating application of intimidation and force. Henry Lee had experimented with just such a policy during his brief command in the area in mid-January. Greene, however, was operating under the specter of a famine at camp, and his explicit orders were to strip the area bare. His discovery that despite Lee's presence in the neighborhood a brisk trade with the city was going on constituted an implicit indictment of the failure of Lee's more lenient approach.[36] Lee was sent to Delaware to remove stores from that state's magazines and to provide security for the increasingly important Continental supply line from the southern states to the army. Greene, meanwhile, found that by cracking down harshly on its residents he could squeeze significant amounts of resources from what had initially looked like a completely barren district. "The Inhabitants cry out and beset me from all quarters," he reported, "but like Pharoh I harden my heart." Finding two men on the road with provisions intended for the city markets, he "gave them an hundred [lashes] each by way of example." He promised, "I determine to forage the country very bare. Nothing shall be left unattempted."[37]

His progress was obstructed at every step, however, by the ingenious ability of the inhabitants to conceal their property. Greene reported almost daily that the district had been gleaned only to find more goods in practically every defile and copse that he came to. "Our poor fellows are obliged to search all the woods and swamps after them," he complained, "and often without success." To forestall this frustrating game of hide-and-seek, Greene began to invoke martial prerogatives of his own devising, by refusing to give receipts for property found concealed, and in one instance by ordering the arrest of civilians caught indulging in these obstructive practices. After five days in the field he revised his initially gloomy estimate of the availability of forage and conceded that it was "really plentier than teams" with which to carry it back to camp. At the end of the assigned duration of the expedition, Greene reported that there remained enough supplies in the area to make it "necessary for me to continue for a few days longer," and he noted that "we want nothing but Waggons to make a grand forage."[38]

As the expedition dispersed through eastern Chester County, its defensive needs and logistical imperatives began to clash. The original detachment of between 1,500 and 2,000 troops slowly fragmented into numerous smaller parties. On February 17, Anthony Wayne broke off with between 400 and 800 men to cross the Delaware at Wilmington and extend the forage along the river in New Jersey across from Philadelphia. Small patrols were sent into Goshen Township and the area between the forks of the Brandywine Creek in search of cattle. Although the British army made no concerted efforts to contest his presence in the area, Greene had to assign increasing numbers of his own troops to protect these foragers and wagon details.[39] Twenty privates were detached under a "good officer" and for two days remained missing in suspicious circumstances. Unable to believe that they had been captured, Greene worried that the officer had been seized by his own men—many of whom were, he said, "Virginia Convicts."[40]

Greene's observations during his twelve-day sojourn through Chester County offer an exceptionally revealing portrait of the civil context of the Valley Forge encampment. Despite the open concentration of Continental efforts west of the Schuylkill, that area remained manifestly unsubdued and unpropitiously disposed toward the army's welfare. An increasingly bold Tory minority was arming to subdue an already cowed and even smaller Whig minority, and in the process enhancing the ability of the self-interested middle group to act effectively on its own behalf. Because of the economic disequilibrium between the currencies of Continental and British forces, the actions of the latter group inherently and increasingly tended to favor the British side.

Greene's reports sharply revealed the disadvantages under which the Americans operated. In the area Washington had chosen to dominate—west of the Schuylkill—he was barely able to do so, and then only by resorting to the politically alienating exercise of authority. The confiscatory policy that Greene was trying to implement made little if any distinction between the allegiances of inhabitants. Seized goods were paid for with receipts that carried such little presumed credit that many of the army's unwilling suppliers scornfully refused them. Whatever property could not be transported back to camp was destroyed in order to keep it out of British hands.[41] Meanwhile, it became necessary to act as if the forestallers—most of whom undoubtedly belonged to the apolitical middle group—were in fact, to use Anthony Wayne's colorful phrase, "Toriestically inclined." Henry Lee's more discriminating approach, which entailed some hope of winning the confidence of these neutral civilians, was abandoned under the pressures of the emergency. As for the area's nervous Whig minority—for whose sake the army had largely agreed to remain in the field for the winter—few measures for protecting its members from their reprisal-minded neighbors seem to have been considered.[42]

Instead, with Lee on an extended assignment in Delaware and Greene's detachment back in camp by the end of February, the lower reaches of the district west of the Schuylkill were effectively, if only temporarily, abandoned to British control. Greene's last report from Providence Meeting House was hopeful in its prediction that before he left the area would be "pretty well gleaned." In light of his initial judgment, that it had been barren at the start of his expedition, and especially considering his own rueful observation of the ability of locals to conceal their property, this optimism may well be doubted. Until the army's strength and operational effectiveness could be substantially rebuilt, Washington's policy toward the area would necessarily depend on the questionable assumption that it had been rendered militarily valueless by Greene's harsh efforts. The region would continue to be an object of paramount concern for the security of the camp, but for the time being the American army gave up any pretense of being able systematically to protect, or even to police, its remaining inhabitants.[43]

This strategic change reflected a broader shift of military resources in response to the February subsistence crisis. Troops sufficiently healthy and equipped to operate in the field were still needed to cover the country west of the Schuylkill, but it was more important that they protect the army's vulnerable supply lines from the north and south. Removing troops from the city's periphery to drain the southern magazines meant that Continental efforts to control the region near the city were temporarily abandoned. General Howe did not find it necessary to contest Greene's foraging expedition through the district, doubtless realizing that its latent effect would be to increase the flow of supplies to the city, as residents took whatever they could hide from Greene into town as soon as the army withdrew. Instead, Howe sharply increased British support of civilian traffic on the east side of the Schuylkill, where Continental resources were more constrained. By early February, Washington's firm adherence to the division of responsibility between state and Continental forces along the Schuylkill River had borne disastrous fruit in the form of a virtually unimpeded flow of people and goods into the city, especially from lower Bucks County.[44]

Exploiting the lack of effective military resistance in the area, the British army helped to establish several corps of provincial troops like Jacob James's company in Chester County. One of these units, captained by Richard Hovenden, was composed of sympathetic civilians and, reportedly, American deserters. Operating under the occasional guidance and protection of regular British detachments, the corps tried to subdue the neighborhoods where its members had once lived, to succor its Tories, and to suppress its Whigs. Although Thomas Wharton and some others chafed under the knowledge that the state had failed to maintain 1,000 militia troops in the field throughout the winter, other members of the state's Whig establishment were less hesitant about blaming the Continental Army for the conditions around Philadelphia. Joseph Reed fumed that the political consequences of the provincial corps' ravages would be worse than the military ones. He warned that "no person conspicuous in civil or military life not with the army or at a great distance will be safe" unless the state met terror with terror by enlisting a similar corps. "Even good Whigs [will] begin to think Peace at some Expense desirable," he complained, unless the traffic between the enemy and Pennsylvania civilians was stopped. Reed predicted that during the spring the state could expect to "lose some of [its] best citizens"—perhaps envisioning himself—and he made it clear that he did not believe that regular army forces could protect the region against partisans or British marauders.[45]

Under pressure from the Conference Committee because of the ineffective blockade of the city, Washington sought ways of assisting the militia without removing Continental troops from other important stations. His initial efforts involved a series of rhetorical devices, organizational changes, and tactical decisions aimed at invigorating the Continental detachments already operating east of the Schuylkill. He urged their officers to step up their efforts to arrest and punish some "notorious offenders" among the market people, making an example of them. He also ordered John Jameson to assist the militia in disabling gristmills along the Pennypack, Frankford, and Wissahickon creeks, thus reducing the availability of flour and the temptation of civilians to carry it to town.[46]

As he investigated the causes of the ineffectiveness of the Continental patrols, however, Washington found that they only began with problems of insufficient manpower. A trusted officer foraging in the area wrote that the "length of time [the patrols] have been on that station has made them too well acquainted with the girls and people from town, who I fear seduce and make them commit things highly improper, such as seizing flour . . . from one person and delivering it to their favorites." Jameson reached similar conclusions, and he asked for "a sett of fresh men." These reports persuaded Washington that civilian marketing was flourishing in a climate of Continental corruption nourished by what one aide-de-camp described as "too intimate connexions between the Soldiery and Citizens" of the isolated district.[47]

This conclusion defined the problem but it did not offer any obvious solutions. If anything, it suggested the necessity of reducing the Continental presence in the area and increasing the reliance on militia forces, a difficult step and one that would be unacceptable to Pennsylvania's political leaders. The evidence also suggested that the abuses went beyond the mere incidence of ubiquitous wartime favoritism. Jameson complained that it had "not been in my power to prevent [trade] with the men that are on this side the River unless I could be with them day and night as they are a set of the greatest Villains I ever heard of." In addition to opportunistic ladies' men, Jameson's miscreants included thieves, bribe takers, and outright highwaymen. He had identified two of the latter, but he had "not as yet confined them as there are not three of the men that I could with any degree of safety trust my life with."[48] Despite this evidence of Continental complicity, Washington continued to emphasize the responsibility of the militia for the area east of the Schuylkill. One army officer was replaced as a result of the allegations, and his successor began a more ambitious effort to apprehend the marketeers. When Casimir Pulaski wrote from Trenton that three troops of New Jersey mounted militia were willing to cross the Delaware to serve on the lines north of Philadelphia, Washington seized on the idea as a practical solution to an all but intractable problem, and he asked Governor Livingston to loan him the troops.[49]

Washington continued to press Pennsylvania to help police the area. He lectured Thomas Wharton on the dependence of the joint military effort on the state's effective participation. He refrained from criticizing the new militia commander, John Lacey, but he did complain that "[the militia] have by some means or other dwindled away to nothing." He discounted the ability of regular army troops to take up the slack and asked Wharton to furnish "some hundreds more" than the originally stipulated one thousand men. "We find the Continental troops," he acknowledged, "(especially those who are not Natives) are very apt to desert from the piquets." The militia had indeed all but disintegrated. For most of the first half of February, Lacey's band numbered between sixty and one hundred men. New classes of recruits had been called out in four western counties, but none had reached his camp at Warwick in Bucks County. Lacey was forced to collect his men into one party and retreat from the city because more active duty was impossible in their "weak and scattered condition."[50]

Although Lacey's conduct embarrassed Wharton, puzzled Washington, and infuriated Continental officers serving east of the Schuylkill, it was undoubtedly prudent. He was, in essence, keeping his own men under detention, although he occasionally must have wondered whether he was not himself their detainee. In a letter to a political patron, thanking him for his support, he painted a grim picture of his band:

> I do by no means approve of the conduct of the militia. They ought to be men who govern their conduct by principle but unhappily for America and themselves they fall far short of that character, they are constantly stealing from the inhabitants and

from one another, we dare not leave the least thing in their sight nor even in the care of the guards or we are sure to have it stolen, our discipline is very bad and impossible to enforce it with the present officers, unless you form in them new ideas and new souls as their whole study is to be popular with them and taking their part. Such conduct never fails to miss the desired object.

As for their military value, he lamented, "I am not able to do any good in proventing [*sic*] the intercorce between the city and Country. [The market people] come and go as they please."[51]

Lacey was not exaggerating his weakness or its effect on the military situation in Bucks County. The commander of the Continental troops guarding a fulling mill at the county seat of Newtown watched helplessly as residents traded openly with the British. "It is surprising what numbers of people pass to Philadelphia from this and other places Daily," he observed. "I am informed they carry on marketing little inferior to former times—there being no guards on the road between here and the city."[52]

With stoic patience but little conviction Washington pressed the state to help stabilize the situation. He informed Lacey that a "considerable reinforcement" was on its way and cajoled him to make his men "more active in their duty." So precarious had the situation become that he was willing to avail himself of the spirit of brigandage that the militia had begun to display by allowing its members to keep any goods seized from the market people. He required only that militarily useful horses be sent to camp, and that any forfeitures take place under a commissioned officer to prevent the "privilege" from being used as a pretext for stealing from innocent inhabitants. He insisted that the militia should "ramble through the woods and bye ways" as well as the "great roads," and "fire upon . . . those gangs of mercenary wretches" who were trading with the enemy. Increasingly, Washington looked to the use of deadly force to accomplish what numbers could not. He demanded subjects for exemplary discipline, and he called for the arrest of "great offenders" who might be liable for capital punishment.[53] This resort to cajolery, reprisal, and material incentive failed to revive the militia. As late as February 15 Lacey's troop had not been enticed from its retreat in central Bucks County. His command was reduced in strength, he plaintively told Thomas Wharton, "to almost a sipher," and he did not feel "safe in our camp," much less nearer to the city. Even when the long-promised reinforcements arrived the situation did not improve. Of 600 men then in camp, he reported, only 140 were armed, and Lacey flatly refused to resume patrolling until more weapons were provided.[54]

East of the Schuylkill, meanwhile, conditions rapidly assumed the character of an open civil war. Encouraged by the collapse of armed resistance in the area and by the Continental Army's immobility and preoccupation with foraging on the west side of the river, the British began to ravage the area. The new provincial corps spearheaded the operation, which was explicitly intended as an assault on revolutionary civil authority in the unprotected zone. On February 3 the corps marched out the Frankford Road to Oxford to support some Tory "peasants [who] . . . had informed us that they intended to seize and bring in to us a rebel colonel and captain, who were using considerable force to raise militia in this area." On the fourteenth a British foraging expedition beyond Frankford was used to cover another attack on the local political hierarchy. Some provincial dragoons "who know the country very well, pushed ahead on this occasion and seized several officers and other men who are active in the rebellion, namely a few lawyers and committeemen." On the nineteenth the "new dragoons" captured thirty-four prisoners, including seven officers of undescribed rank or affiliation and "others of distinction."[55]

This offensive was aimed at the local infrastructure of the rebellion. Johann Ewald reported in mid-February that some well-affected residents of "Tulpehocken," near Reading, had "formed themselves into a little republic and have declared for the King." On the sixteenth they brought in their first "offering," which consisted of about fifty prisoners, many badly wounded. The latter included one "Committeeman"—a word that was becoming a British term-of-art for Whig leaders—"a zealous and important rebel." Henry Muhlenberg recorded what he hopefully dismissed as "exaggerated" reports that "about five hundred light cavalrymen and *Tories* are sweeping through the country to capture, dead or alive, any inhabitants who have held offices or posts under the *Independent* government, such as officers of the militia, etc." County "*sublieutenants* who have been directing the militia" were "especially being sought," with large prices on their heads.[56] On February 17, John Benner, a "noted rebel" who specialized in robbing market people, was brought to town and placed into the "dungeon" to await a "trial for his life." By the twentieth, Joseph Kirkbride, a Whig stalwart from Bucks County, had fled to Bordentown, New Jersey, claiming that the "constant alarms" at home in recent days had "put it out of our power to act in the Civil line." Joseph Reed found it inadvisable to sleep at his home at Norriton while serving on the Conference Committee because his "disaffected" neighbors were "laying in wait" for him every night. A Bucks County wagon master warned a superior that his deputies posted "low down in the County . . . dare not act in that department, nor hardly any militia man dare to stay at his own house."[57]

Ironically, this Loyalist offensive not only intimidated Pennsylvania Whigs, but also demoralized some members of Howe's army. When Hovenden's men brought in a herd of oxen captured on its way to the American camp from "Virginia," Captain Ewald of the Hessian jaeger corps noted glumly that he and his comrades "felt like we were dead and forgotten in our quarters." They complained to their superiors and the word soon reached British headquarters. Howe made certain to "sen[d] us his assurance that we should be content," Ewald reported, "because he was allowing us to rest up merely to make better use of us."[58]

Hovenden's possession of the oxen was an ominous sign of the scope of the provincial offensive. Meeting little effective resistance from the Pennsylvania militia or from civil officials, the provincials began stalking more ambitious quarry. On the nineteenth the "new dragoons" broke off from another foraging expedition to attack the fulling mill at Newtown, imprisoning its small Continental guard and seizing several tons of cloth being made into clothing for the army. By the end of February the corps had abandoned the foraging ruse altogether and begun to prey openly on Continental targets. On the twenty-fourth, supported by a detachment of Redcoats, the dragoons attacked a herd of cattle being driven across lower Bucks County on its way from New England to Valley Forge, dispersing its small convoy of weakly armed commissaries and capturing 130 oxen. As a result of the collapse of military force east of the Schuylkill, the main northern supply line was placed into grave jeopardy.[59]

The sudden eruption of British activity north and northwest of Philadelphia stunned Continental commanders and resulted in a rapid reappraisal of American policy toward the area. An aide to Washington castigated John Jameson for the seeming inattention of Continental dragoons to the outbreaks. Washington understood that British dragoons had "ventured rather higher up the country than we supposed," but he was not sure of the import of the movements and could only "conjecture [that] they had some design of which we are entirely ignorant." John Lacey bemoaned his impotence in the face of the attacks. By the nineteenth, he reported, British parties were coming out of the city every night to seize both provisions and local patriots. On receiving the news of the assault on the fulling mill, Lacey rushed his few armed troops toward Newtown, but they arrived too late to rescue the detachment.[60]

From the Continental perspective the worst effects of the British incursions did not stem from the increased flow of supplies into Philadelphia, or even from the political implications of unchecked assaults on Pennsylvania Whigs. John Laurens, whose statements usually reflected Washington's views, implied that the latter development was a "matter of civil cognizance." Washington himself dismissed the kidnapping activities of the self-styled "Royal Refugees" with genuine sympathy for their victims but with no apparent intention to intervene on their behalf. Rather, the seeds of a revised Continental policy toward the area east of the Schuylkill lay in the threat the British thrust now posed to the supply lines of the American army. When they came under attack by British and provincial parties, Washington quickly altered his approach to the distribution of Continental forces. It was no longer enough to lecture the state on the need to fulfill its military obligations. Instead, regular army forces were redeployed, whatever the costs elsewhere in the region, to protect this vital army interest.[61]

The British attacks on the Newtown mill demonstrated how vulnerable the links between the army and the north had become. A convoy of wagons carrying salt provisions from New England was at the mill when the raiders approached and was saved only by the timely action of its guards. The commissaries retreated into New Jersey, proceeded north along the Delaware River, and crossed that river again, following a more difficult route toward the camp through upper Bucks County. The several days' delay entailed by the maneuver, during the depths of the famine at camp, intensified the crisis. The loss of a herd of cattle the next week showed that the threat to the supply line was not the result of random enemy probing; rather, the British outburst had grave implications for the army.[62]

The result was an abrupt bowing of the supply line in a northwesterly direction. Washington sent riders to New Jersey to meet an overdue clothing shipment and direct it to cross the Delaware above Easton. If it had already reached Pennsylvania, he ordered it to "Strike up into the Country and take a circuitous route to Camp." Anthony Wayne, who was convoying cattle from New Jersey, was permitted to take the quicker route through Coryell's Ferry but told to "keep higher up in the Country" once in Pennsylvania and to cross the Schuylkill at Pottsgrove. Washington implored him to maintain a "considerable guard" and to "keep a good look out between you and Philadelphia."

The enemy, he conceded, would have certain intelligence of Wayne's presence from their "friends with which the country abounds."[63] Washington fired off a by now customary letter of tactful reproach to Thomas Wharton to remind him of the critical situation east of the Schuylkill. The "insolence" of disaffected citizens in the area, he observed, had now "risen to a very alarming Height." Placing the civil consequences of this phenomenon squarely in the state's lap, he reminded Wharton that a number of "respectable citizens" had been kidnapped. More important, he noted, members of the army had been captured, and a quantity of clothing—which he pointedly claimed was intended for one of Pennsylvania's regiments—had been seized.[64]

By threatening the American supply lines, the British offensive forced Washington to change his approach to securing the areas along the city's periphery. The new policy represented a modification of tactical emphasis and a reallocation of resources with the security of the army as its continuing focus. The implicit commitment that Washington had made by placing the army in winter quarters at Valley Forge—to try to confine the British as closely as possible in Philadelphia and to protect Pennsylvania's Whig citizens—had been and would continue to be a strictly conditional one. Its performance depended on the cooperation of the state's militia. As long as the army's security could be maintained by a strong and active Continental presence west of the Schuylkill, Washington allowed the state's forces to succeed or fail east of the river according to their own devices. But when the failure of the militia placed the the northern supply line in jeopardy, the security axis of the army shifted dramatically. Where it had previously followed the river it would now cleave to the supply line on both sides. Washington extended Continental responsibility more directly to the east bank. He stated the thrust of the new policy in his orders to one officer sent across the Schuylkill with a mounted company to bolster Continental efforts. That his responsibility included cutting off civil traffic between the city and its hinterland did not need to be mentioned. The real burden of his assignment was to protect the newly vulnerable supply convoys in the area. The officer was directed to keep his patrols "in a position most convenient, for covering any supplies that may be coming to this army." If he met any unescorted convoys he was to "take [them] under your care" and see them safely on their way to camp.[65]

These measures prefaced a thorough reorganization of Continental efforts and resources east of the Schuylkill River. By early March a new set of officers was on duty there, in charge of implementing a broader and more mobile policy of securing the area. Their predecessors became the scapegoats for what had really been an overall failure of policy. One officer removed from duty near Germantown resigned, partly because of "Insinuations . . . thrown out at Head Quarters" about his performance on the lines. John Jameson, who by his own account had his hands full merely maintaining order among his criminally minded subordinates, was quietly reassigned to Virginia to assist in purchasing horses for the cavalry there.[66]

The redistribution of Continental efforts in the region had only a limited effect on the execution of Washington's December commitments to the state leaders. Reinforced patrols east of the Schuylkill might incidentally intimidate market people there, but only at the expense of similar measures on the west side. Until the state could bolster the militia, the overall flow of supplies to city markets would continue undiminished, and the state's citizens would remain vulnerable to selective retaliation from British or refugee patrols. The approach of spring, the return of convalescents, and the arrival of recruits and clothing would eventually permit a more broadly conceived Continental strategy. For now, however, the army was mired in a cycle of strategic retrenchment, and it was focusing its finite energies on survival and reorganization.

The consequences of this cycle were clearest in New Jersey, through the band of small communities stretching along the Delaware River between Trenton and Salem County. The failure of the American cavalry to secure a viable base of operations at Trenton had calamitous consequences for New Jersey. By late January Casimir Pulaski had all but given up on the town as a place to winter and train his troops. The surrounding countryside, he observed, had been "laid waste," while other Continental agencies—such as the navy and the Hospital Department—claimed the "right of first comers." Pulaski still had three companies in the area, but, wanting to train them, he suggested that they be sent to Morristown.[67] Washington was doubtful that the area could be so barren, but he left the decision to Pulaski. Ultimately, the inclination of both men to preserve the cavalry for the 1778 campaign prevailed over their sense that it might serve useful purposes during the winter. The three mounted companies that had been lodged at Pennington and Flemington were sent to Chatham, near Morristown. Pulaski, in nominal command of the whole corps, stayed at Trenton with a picked group of "lanceurs" to provide whatever security he could for that area.[69]

These developments all but guaranteed that both the Pennsylvania and New Jersey militia would be left effectively to their own devices in dealing with recalcitrant civilians as well as any British marauding expeditions they encountered. Joseph Ellis, like his Pennsylvania counterpart John Lacey, was a new and inexperienced commander of the New Jersey troops. He bore few illusions about his ability to accomplish much with the forces at his disposal, whose strength varied continually, he reported, but seldom exceeded five hundred men. With this threadbare contingent he held nominal responsibility for a territory fully as large as that guarded by both the Continental army and militia troops on the Pennsylvania side. He reported that large quantities of provisions were being carried into Philadelphia by the civilians of his state. The most he could do was to patrol the roads sporadically to make spot arrests, and to discourage commerce with the city through occasional demonstrations of token force.[70]

Washington responded with conservative realism, urging the state's leaders to do their best but always keeping Continental interests paramount. By February 2, a regiment of "West Jersey Loyalists" that had organized in Philadelphia carried guerrilla warfare back into their state. A city paper reported that twenty members of this group had crossed the Delaware to "assist some of their friends who had expressed a desire of taking refuge there, to avoid the horrid tyranny and implacable persecution of the rebels." This party clashed with the militia and captured a man named Wilson who was, the paper noted—using the already ubiquitous Loyalist term for local revolutionary leaders—a "committeeman . . . very active in distressing the friends of government."[71]

Before the month was over Daniel Coxe, a wealthy New Jersey Loyalist, sent William Howe a detailed analysis of the strengths and weaknesses of the Continental position in the state, together with a careful proposal for fomenting and supporting a Loyalist uprising against Whig authority throughout its southern and western counties. This plan was never fully implemented, but it foreshadowed in an almost uncanny way the contours of intracommunal violence that engulfed the region during the late winter and early spring of 1778. Nicholas Collin observed that local Loyalists, as Coxe suggested, made the former rebel fortifications at Billingsport into a place of refuge from which to harass their Whig neighbors and to coordinate illicit commerce with the British garrison in Philadelphia. "Everywhere distrust, fear, hatred and abominable selfishness were met with," Collin reported— eerily echoing the observations of his fellow Lutheran pastor, Henry Muhlenberg, across the Delaware River in Pennsylvania:

> Parents and children, brothers and sisters, wife and husband, were enemies to one another. The militia and some regular

troops on one side and refugees with the Englishmen on the
other were constantly roving about in smaller or larger numbers,
plundering and destroying everything in a barbarous manner,
cattle, furniture, clothing and food; they smashed mirrors, tables
and china etc., and plundered women and children of their most
necessary clothing, cut up the bolsters and scattered the feathers
to the winds, burned houses, whipped and imprisoned each
other, and surprised people when they were deep asleep.[72]

The state received its first concerted Continental attention of the winter as a by-product of the mid-February supply crisis. Anthony Wayne
crossed the Delaware on the February 19 to extend Nathanael Greene's
scouring of the region into the communities between Salem and Trenton.
Wayne concluded, as Greene did in Chester County, that most of the state's
residents were either "supine" or "disaffected," and that they had perfected
the art of hiding their property. Like Greene, he concentrated on destroying
whatever goods he could not carry away, with the resigned knowledge that
the British would help themselves to anything left behind. Indeed, Wayne's
expedition had the predictable if ironic and unhappy side effect of drawing a
large detachment of British troops into the area to contest his progress there,
to terrorize area Whigs, and to filter the residue from the troubled waters
that he had roiled. That development, more than any concerted planning by
Daniel Coxe or William Howe, fanned intramural conflicts in the state that
would burn all winter. Finding himself outnumbered by eight to one,
Wayne withdrew, lamenting that the enemy would pass through the countryside "at pleasure" helping themselves to a "prodigious number" of cattle
and a wealth of other goods.[73]

Chapter 9

THE CHAPTER OF EXPERIMENTS

The distress of the army remained palpable even after the supply crisis of February abated. The intermittent torrents of late February yielded seamlessly to an unbroken deluge in early March. As James Varnum observed: "Here there is no distinction of seasons. The weather frequently changes five times in twenty four hours. The coldest I have perceived has been in this month. Snow falls, but falls only to produce mire & dirt. It is cold, [but] braces one only to produce a greater relaxation by the heat. . . . Sometimes the weather is moderate, but that season gives time only to reflect upon gentle breases and cooling zephyrs, that the immediate extremes may excite greater pain." Most soldiers were less poetic in their descriptions. One Pennsylvanian reported a disagreeable journey to camp plagued by such wretched cold that even a nightly bottle of Madiera failed to provide much solace, and a southerner struggling to contain enemy movements near Chestnut Hill complained that the wet weather was "much against" him.[1]

Although the climate remained hostile, a pronounced shift of energy and attention at headquarters suggested that the army would soon be back in the field engaged in a campaign that many hoped would be decisive. As the Conference Committee finished its business at camp, Washington turned his attention to more immediate military concerns. The newly installed officers, Nathanael Greene and Jeremiah Wadsworth, would, he hoped, soon infuse energy into the battered Quartermaster and Commissary departments.

For two weeks after Washington and the Conference Committee assured themselves that he would agree to be quartermaster general, Greene wavered over whether to accept the office. He predicted archly that other members of the army would be "immortallising [themselves] in the golden pages of History" while he was "confin'd to a series of druggery to pave the way for it." His new department had been shattered by Thomas Mifflin's neglect of it, by the ravages of the 1777 campaign, and by the strain of trying to sustain the army in the field during the winter. The debilitating weather that had toppled the old logistical establishment lingered to plague the infancy of its successor. In mid-March one congressman wrote that there had been "no weather fit for any person to travel for two months past." An officer stationed at Lancaster noted that there had been "excessively rainy weather" on the first seventeen days of the month, making personal travel and wagon transport impossible.[2]

In spite of his deep ambivalence, Greene and his deputies moved with alacrity to invigorate the quartermaster's organization. The department was caught in a relentless cycle of retrenchment. Shortages of animal forage threatened to starve the horses the department depended on to move goods, assuring more shortages and still more disruptions. The troops were for the moment adequately supplied with food as a result of the importation of supplies from area magazines in late February. The forage masters were operating on thinner margins. Trying to reap whatever advantages he could from the high water that accompanied the winter rains, Forage Master Clement Biddle assembled an impromptu flotilla of shallow-bottomed transport vessels to move loads of hay and other supplies from Reading and Pottsgrove down the Schuylkill River to the camp.[3]

Greene, meanwhile, brought a healthy sense of economic realism to his new job. Convinced that the conflict would "terminate in a war of funds," in which the "longest purse will be triumphant," he was determined not to let his department be impaled on the narrow spear of fiscal regularity. He presumed that his own financial ruin had been guaranteed by his decision to remain in public service, but he searched for ways to harness the universal passion for private profit to public ends. Caught between the frugality of Congress and the need to recruit competent subordinates, Greene agreed to divide the compensation for his office with his deputies, Charles Pettit and John Cox. He announced the doctrine that would guide his management of the department: "I have no objection to Mr. Butler or any other gentleman belonging to the Department reaping any advantage from their honest industry . . . if the public business is but well executed that will be all that I shall be solicitous about."[4]

Freed of most day-to-day logistical responsibilities, Washington began planning for the coming campaign. He drafted plan that included an ambitious set of alternative scenarios. The first called for carrying the campaign to the enemy, either by a massed assault on the lines north of Philadelphia or by closing the river and starving the British into retreat or submission. The second contemplated the early detachment of 6,000 troops from Pennsylvania to the Hudson River to cooperate with troops already stationed there and with northern militia for an assault on the British headquarters in New York City. The third envisioned the army "lay[ing] quiet in a secure camp" training and disciplining for new operations on the British initiative.[5]

This plan, like the enigmatic "Intended Orders" for a possible Christmas assault on Philadelphia, defies easy analysis. Its more ambitious elements lay at odds with the image of a crippled, half-starved army that considered itself well-off when it could measure the distance between the wolf and the door in terms of weeks rather than days. The plan called for "mature consideration" of each of its alternatives, and it formed the basis for a series of questions that Washington placed before his general officers in April. Its disposition during the six weeks between its drafting and its submission to the generals, however, is uncertain. As with ideas discussed in late December, the plan may have been informally floated among senior commanders in late March to elicit their overall reactions and to stimulate serious thinking about the strategic possibilities of the new year.[6]

The plan's central assumption was that the Continental Army could take the initiative by dictating the direction and preliminary character of the spring campaign. The viability of this assumption depended on strenuous exertions throughout the Continental establishment. Many congressmen were openly doubtful whether their states would fill their regiments early enough to effect any offensive plans. As Jonathan B. Smith of Pennsylvania warned Thomas Wharton: "[The army was] now arriving at an important period. The Campaign will probably open soon. Much depends on its being well reinforced. I hope this state will not fail to exert its utmost influence." Cornelius Harnett of North Carolina feared that "unless the several states exert themselves to compleat their Battalions our Continental Army will cut a poor figure in the spring."[7]

Washington worked feverishly to flog the army's support agencies to prepare for the campaign. He became almost obsessed with the concentration of troops and with the material resources needed to sustain them. He reminded the Board of War that the Philadelphia area was the "place where the Army will rendezvous in the Spring." If the states furnished the quotas of troops that Congress had assigned to them, he added, it would be "a mortifying and discouraging circumstance" to be unable to provide them with weapons and equipment.[8] He urged officers at distant posts, army functionaries, and state leaders to increase their efforts to procure supplies.[9] He pressed Pennsylvania officials to find more wagons and teams for the Quartermaster's Department and touched a sensitive nerve by coolly reminding Thomas Wharton that the "army seems to have a peculiar Claim to the Exertions of the Gentlemen of this State . . . as it was greatly owing to their Apprehensions and Anxieties, expressed in a Memorial to Congress, that the present position was had."[10]

With Nathanael Greene as quartermaster general Washington was able to delegate much of the responsibility for that department's functions, but until Jeremiah Wadsworth assumed the post of commissary general, Washington had to attend personally to the problems of increasing the flow of provisions necessary to support an enlarging army. He implored Henry Champion to "persevere" in sending cattle from New England and to cure salt provisions there to replace the quantities that had been drained from local magazines during the "late want" of mid-February. He interceded with Congress on behalf of Wadsworth and Champion, who complained that price-regulating laws that had been adopted in New England were drying up supplies of meat in that region. He hinted that the army would "experience many advantages" if those laws could be suspended temporarily.[11]

Washington's chief preoccupation, however, remained increasing the size of the army. His plans for attacking Philadelphia or New York required at least 15,000 troops in camp, healthy and fit for duty, no later than early June. Available returns suggest that by late February barely half that number were on duty at Valley Forge. Washington worked to collect Continental troops from the regional pockets to which small numbers had been scattered during the winter. He ordered the companies guarding Continental storehouses in Lancaster to return to camp as soon as possible and demanded the return of a group of North Carolina troops that had been put to work in the row galleys on the Delaware River.[12]

By mid-March, recruits were trickling into camp every day, including southern drafts marching by way of York. As always, the sight of freshly mustered companies stepping smartly through the streets of the capital bolstered spirits in Congress. Cornelius Harnett now wrote that it was "hoped General Washington will be able to open the campaign with some vigorous exertions." Washington continued to express optimism that the offensive options outlined in his plan for the campaign might be implemented. He urged the Board of War to rush artillery from New England to Pennsylvania, observing that it would be "of the greatest use to us . . . if we should take a post below the city," in an attempt to blockade Philadelphia. On March 20 he cut short a review of the hardships the army had faced during the winter with the hopeful observation that "as our prospects begin to brighten, my complaint shall cease."[13]

Even as Washington wrote, however, messengers were racing toward camp with troubling new intelligence. Observers in the Hudson Highlands and in New Jersey reported that large numbers of British troops were embarking on transport ships in New York harbor, bound either for New England or Philadelphia. Transmitting this news to Congress, Washington observed, "our present situation at this advanced season is truely alarming," and he lobbied for a speedy decision on the new "establishment" of the army, which had been proposed by the Conference Committee but not yet passed by the Congress at York.[14] These reports shifted the focus at Valley Forge in late March from formulating offensive plans to preparing for an anticipated enemy blow. Almost daily Washington expressed his growing belief that British reinforcements would allow Howe to attack before his own became numerous enough to repel the assault. By March 29 he was convinced that large numbers of new troops had already reached Philadelphia, and the camp was put on an immediate battle footing. The Commissary Department was ordered to keep hard bread on hand to issue "on any sudden Emergency." Officers were enjoined to lighten their baggage to allow the army to move away quickly. Preparations were hurriedly made to complete the fortification of the camp. Plans were formulated to lay in large stocks of forage along possible escape routes for the army. Washington ordered William Smallwood to be ready to "move at a moment's warning" to evacuate Wilmington and rejoin the army.[15]

By late March it was widely assumed that the British had won the implicit contest between the armies to concentrate their resources and that they would have the luxury of dictating the opening shape of the campaign. Anthony Wayne warned Thomas Wharton that the enemy "will be too powerful for us in the field—unless great and speedy supplies are thrown in." John Laurens predicted that the army could repel a direct assault on its camp only by sacrificing its own huts. John Bannister, a new member of Congress from Virginia, captured the anxieties of his colleagues on "this most critical occasion." He urged that Virginia's recruits be rushed forward to assist "in rescuing a sister state, perhaps an army, from ruin." Washington's message that new enemy troops had reached Philadelphia was referred to the Board of War on April 1. Three days later, Congress authorized Washington to call on Pennsylvania, New Jersey, and Maryland for up to 5,000 militia troops to meet the crisis.[16]

By then, however, Washington had begun to reevaluate the intelligence he had received. On March 31 he told Alexander McDougall that the collection of enemy forces in Philadelphia still left him with a choice between concentrating to oppose them there or trying to take advantage of the withdrawal of troops from New York by attacking that city. Requesting McDougall's advice on the "practicability" of such an assault, he implied that his decision on removing troops from the Hudson Highlands would depend on that advice. On the same day William Smallwood wrote from Wilmington that the fleet allegedly carrying 2,500 British soldiers from New York had actually brought a much smaller number of men. The next day Washington retreated from his assertion that he had "no doubt" about the arrival of enemy reinforcements. The British fleet, he informed Henry Laurens, "is not arrived, supposing they were bound to Philadelphia" in the first place. By early April uncertainty prevailed at camp about the strength and intentions of the enemy, and some staff members had reverted to the high hopes of the first week of March.[17]

Washington resisted drawing any such conclusions. Instead, he seemed to be at a genuine loss to explain the apparent disappearance of the British reinforcements. "I know not certainly where they have gone," he told McDougall on March 31, and by April 10 he admitted that his alarmed reports had been "founded on conjecture, and in some degree misinformation." He thanked Congress for the authority to call out militia reinforcements but chided that body for its mistaken assumption that such a measure had been the "great end" of his appeal. Rather, he noted, it had been to know the fate of the Conference Committee's reorganization proposals, which he testily pointed out would be almost impossible to implement once "any convulsion happen[s] or movement take[s] place." He noted, "My agreement with the [Conference] Cmee. . . . entitled me to expect upwards of Forty thousand Continental troops . . . for the service of the ensuing Campaign . . . instead of these, what are my prospects?"[18]

The acknowledged "freedom" of Washington's message to Congress reflected tensions prevailing both at headquarters and in York about the uncertain circumstances of the approaching campaign. Washington continued to dread the prospect of having to take the field without reinforcements. He told President Laurens that never since the start of the war had he "felt more painful sensations on account of delay than at present." He hesitated to call out militia troops for fear of disrupting state recruiting drives, but he informed the civil authorities of the designated states of his power to do so and reminded Congress that his hesitation should not be construed as a declination of the authority. Instead, he ordered William Smallwood to withdraw the garrison at Wilmington to camp as soon as possible, only to revoke the order a day later after considering the danger into which such a move would cast the Continental stores at Head of Elk.[19]

To understand the sources of this confusion, indecision, and anxiety in American councils, it is necessary to consider developments on the British side. The king's principal field commanders in North America were both waiting to return to England, under varying degrees of implicit censure for their failure to conclude the war in 1777. In London, the British ministry was completing a winter of deep strategic reappraisal. Spurred by Burgoyne's defeat at Saratoga and by the probability of treaties of alliance between France and America, British planners had reluctantly concluded that the military reconquest of the colonies was impossible. In order to meet the threat of an Atlantic war with France, it was now necessary to scale down British political and military objectives in North America. The political result of this conclusion was a decision to offer the Americans a settlement granting everything except an explicit recognition of independence. Peace commissioners would go to America to negotiate an end to the war on this basis. Whether or not they were successful, Britain would have to reduce the number of troops in the colonies to free them for possible use against France in Europe, Canada, and the Caribbean.[20]

The first comprehensive statement of this new strategy came in the ministry's instructions to Henry Clinton, who had been chosen to replace William Howe as commander-in-chief. Framed in early March, these instructions preceded certain knowledge of a French alliance, which had been secretly finalized a month before. They proclaimed the king's hope that his "generous terms" would satisfy the "generality" of his American subjects but acknowledged the need not to "slacken" preparations to continue the war if necessary. Clinton was promised as many reinforcements as the Crown could muster but informed that the war must be "prosecuted upon a different plan" than before. That plan emphasized the need to garrison and protect Canada, Nova Scotia, Newfoundland, and East and West Florida. If Clinton could not bring Washington to a "general and decisive Action" early in the campaign, he was ordered to "relinquish the idea of carrying on Offensive Operations against the Rebels within land." Rather, he should embark as many troops as could be spared from garrison duty on ships to carry on summer raiding against the New England coast to harass the population, damage the maritime economy, and prevent American naval interference with British trade.[21] This would be followed in early fall by a concerted effort to subdue and occupy Georgia and the Carolinas, an operation that would rely heavily on the assistance of Loyalist forces, many of whom were presumed to be ready to "return to their allegiance" with the support of British troops. With the lower south occupied, coastal areas of Virginia and Maryland would be harassed during the winter. The goal of the campaign was the subjugation of all colonies "South of the Susquehanna." The northern provinces could then be "left to their own feelings and distress to bring them back to their duty."[22]

This plan was an interim step in the new British approach to the war. Within days of its formulation, reliable intelligence of France's alliance with America reached London and forced the ministry into a more sweeping strategic review. The king now proclaimed his determination to "resent" the "unprovoked and unjust . . . aggression" implied in the treaties with an "immediate attack" on the French West Indian sugar island of St. Lucia. Clinton was ordered immediately to detach five thousand troops from Philadelphia for an expedition against that island. Three thousand more regulars would be sent to bolster British ground forces at St. Augustine and Pensacola in East and West Florida. Clinton was to withdraw from Philadelphia to New York to await the issue of negotiations that British peace commissioners would offer to Congress. If those negotiations failed, or if New York seemed untenable with his reduced force, he was authorized to transfer the army at his own discretion to Rhode Island or even to Halifax, Nova Scotia. In a matter of weeks the character of the war in North America had changed fundamentally. The Admiralty Board summarized the thrust of the new policy. "The object of the war being now changed," it advised Lord Richard Howe, the admiral commanding British naval forces in American waters, "and the contest in America being a secondary consideration, our principal objects must be distressing France and defending . . . his Majesty's possessions."[23]

These circumstances would shape the 1778 campaign in America, but they do not explain either British military behavior during the early spring or the resulting American confusions. Preliminary indications of the cabinet's reappraisal did not reach Philadelphia until late March, and the formal instructions of March 8 and 21 were not put into Henry Clinton's hands until early May, when he arrived in that city to take command of the army. Rather, British actions in March and April reflected the private views and predicaments of Howe and Clinton as they waited for orders from Whitehall. Clinton, who would be left to execute the ministry's plans, felt that Howe should open the campaign early and in an aggressive fashion. The Americans, he remarked, "are certainly hard pressed. Whether from the little appearance of support from France, or from the great and spirited preparations making by us they are extremely drove to try dangerous experiments." He continued, "Now is the time to press them hard, . . . and offer them terms."[24]

This logic of events did not seem nearly as evident to Howe in Philadelphia as it did to Clinton in New York. By mid-April Howe had received the king's permission to resign his command, and he was in anything but an offensive mood. The Americans, he acknowledged, had been diminished in strength during the winter, yet he felt it would be imprudent for him to try to exploit this fact to close his American service triumphantly: "The want of green forage does not yet permit me to take the Field," he noted, "and [the enemy's] situation is too strong to hazard an attack with a prospect of success which might put an end to the Rebellion." He warned, "A check at this Period . . . would probably counteract his Majesty's intentions of preparing the way for the return of Peace by the Bills proposed." Instead, Howe planned to await Clinton's arrival in Philadelphia, whereupon he would brief him, hand over the army, and embark for England.[25]

Washington's apprehension, then, of an imminent enemy offensive, lay at odds with central British strategic planning and with the intentions of his principle adversary. In reviewing the evidence on which he based his warnings to Congress, it seems clear that he drew conclusions that were not implicit in the information available to him. But this fact cannot explain Washington's understanding of that information or his subsequent actions. Neither he nor anyone on the American side had access to the information cited above to qualify British behavior as they anxiously looked for patterns in that behavior. Washington was simply availing himself of a commander's prerogative of assuming the worst possible consequences from any potentially unfavorable circumstances to protect both his forces and his reputation.[26]

If Washington was exaggerating the significance and apparent consistency of a few disconnected reports of British movements, moreover, he was only following a pattern of indulgence in that prerogative that he had adhered to throughout the winter. This was especially true in his correspondence with political bodies. As early as December 1777, he seems to have concluded that Congress would act expeditiously only under circumstances of genuine alarm. Washington's treatment of the alleged enemy buildup in Philadelphia was an extension of his handling of the provisions crises of December and February. Although his information in all of these situations was partial, he usually had—or could be presumed to have—more and better knowledge than anyone else. Throughout the winter he displayed a consistent inclination to manipulate whatever intelligence he had in support of the broad organizational and strategic goals toward which he was striving to push the Continental establishment.

An even more specific motive underlay Washington's continued indulgence in alarmist tactics during the early spring. The reforms carried out within the logistical departments had been effected with relatively little resistance once the Board of War's ambitious initiatives had been thwarted. There was a broad consensus in Continental circles that the Commissary and Quartermaster departments had to be made more efficient. The deliberations of the committee, however, had spawned other issues and recommendations of much greater political sensitivity. Proposals for quieting the discontent of the officers through a half-pay pension system, which Washington saw as vital to the success of the reorganization effort, collided with deeply rooted fears in Anglo-American political culture about the dangers to liberty inherent in a standing army. Other measures, which looked toward the reorganization and reduction of the regiments, impinged on questions of state and local, as well as Continental, interest and prerogative.[27]

It was congressional resistance to the implementation of these reforms, especially the half-pay proposal, that Washington was trying to overcome by confronting the delegates with the image of the campaign descending on an army caught between an old and a new "establishment." To further the prospects of these measures, Francis Dana and Nathaniel Folsom of the Conference Committee had returned to York in late March to introduce them personally into Congress. Washington's warning about the apparent arrival of enemy troops in Philadelphia and Howe's presumed intention to launch the campaign may have been intended to support their efforts by adding a note of urgency to the deliberations.[28]

The resolutions were referred to a committee of the whole, which debated them during the last week of March, after which Congress voted to postpone a decision indefinitely. Washington continued to lobby for the proposals even after he conceded the chimerical quality of the British reinforcements. Despite his alternately artful and heavy-handed advocacy, Congress remained seriously divided on the question. The debate languished and flared until the middle of May, when Congress resolved the half-pay question. The less controversial but nevertheless contingent proposals for remodeling the state battalions, as well as other elements of the new establishment, were not approved until the end of May. As a result, Washington was forced to undertake what he continued to characterize as folly itself: the hurried preparation of the army for a new campaign without final decisions about the ultimate organization of his force.[29]

The centerpiece of that preparation—the introduction of a new system of field drill and maneuver—began in late March. The task was entrusted to Friedrich Steuben, one of the many foreign "volunteers" who found their way into the American service. Steuben, a veteran of European wars under Frederick the Great, arrived in America in late 1777 and corresponded with Washington in search of a command. Congress, despite a growing aversion to the pretensions of foreigners, voted "cheerfully" to accept his offer of service and directed him to report to Valley Forge. Henry Laurens warned Steuben that while he would receive the best accommodations available in camp, they would "be only tolerable in your soldierly character." Washington, Laurens observed, "lives . . . in a Hut, that is a little temporary cabin such as one inhabited by the poorest Boors."[30] Steuben reached Valley Forge during the provisions crisis in mid-February, carrying a letter of introduction from Henry Laurens. He was cheerfully received at headquarters and accorded several long interviews with John Laurens, who found him "a man profound in the Science of war." Steuben would, Laurens observed, be the "properest" candidate for inspector general. He noted that the newcomer "seems to be perfectly aware of the disadvantages the Army has labored under . . . seems to understand what our Soldiers are capable of, and is not so starch a Systematist as to be averse from adapting established forms to stubborn circumstances."[31]

In spite of Laurens's praise, the exact character of Steuben's service was not immediately determined. The two men exchanged long memoranda on European and American military organizations, and Steuben was sent on a tour of the camp to inspect its fortifications and make recommendations for their completion. By the middle of March he had established enough rapport with Washington to be entrusted with supervising the reform of the army's discipline. Withholding his unease over being asked to suspend his request for a commission until the Conference Committee finished its work, Steuben proclaimed his willingness to serve as a volunteer. He wanted only to "be useful to the United States," he said, "and to participate in the Glory of your Armies. My only ambition is to reap Lawrels in your Fields."[32]

Steuben's service would be much more useful than glorious. Any laurels that it offered, moreover, would initially be won on the parade grounds at camp rather than on the battlefield. Borrowing an idea from his now-disgraced adversary Thomas Conway, Washington decided to introduce a new system of field drill to a small group before trying to impose it on the army as a whole. This model unit consisted of his own Corps of Guards of Virginians, to which were annexed one hundred "chosen men" from the other state lines. A cohort of subinspectors and brigade inspectors was appointed to oversee the introduction of the new system throughout the army.[33] The drilling began on March 24, with each regiment working on its own parade ground at nine in the morning and again in the afternoon between four and five. The maneuvers drew a favorable reaction from the officers almost from the first day. John Laurens attributed this fact to Steuben's own demeanor. The "Baron," he observed, "discovers the greatest zeal and activity which is hardly to be expected at his years . . . he sets . . . an example in descending to the functions of a drill-Sergeant." There seems also to have been a genuine appreciation of the efficacy of the new drills themselves. One colonel found them "more agreeable to the dictates of Reason and common sense than any mode I have before seen . . . we are first taught to march without musick but the time of march is given us. Slow Time is a medium between what was in our service Slow and Quicke Time, Quicke time about as Quicke as a Common Country Dance."[34]

On April 1, John Laurens reported that Steuben was "making a sensible progress with our Soldiers." As he wrote to his father, "It would enchant you to see the enlivened scene of our Campus Martius." By this time some of the exercises had been shifted from the individual brigade grounds to the enormous common parade in the center of the camp. A brigade inspector was designated to "command" the parade, while Steuben gave close attention to the exercises of a different unit every day. Washington supported the exercises with increased emphasis on overall discipline. Noting the irregular arrival of brigades on their parade grounds, he insisted that "greater punctuality . . . be observed in future with respect to time," and he ordered that all watches in camp be regulated "by the Clock at Head Quarters." Greater attention was paid to inspecting the appearance of the troops. Brigade adjutants were reminded of their responsibility for this matter and threatened with arrest for negligence of it. Noncommissioned officers were subjected to reduction in rank for failure to maintain "a conduct and example which ought to distinguish them from privates." The new marching regime was quickly translated from the parade ground to the field. The practice of marching men in single file in small parties was condemned for its "unmilitary appearance." Henceforth, even small groups were to be "march'd by divisions" and officers were enjoined to "see that [their] men march properly."[35]

Steuben continued to show keen sensitivity about his rank. The "Service of Lieut. I am now obliged to make," he told Henry Laurens, "is become Strange Enough to me after forty years," but he would "cheerfully consent" to serve on any terms necessary to accomplish his ends. "Some will enquire," he pointedly warned, "Who is that Man who meddles with our Discipline; on what Authority does he introduce Such or Such thing?" In such cases, Steuben averred, he would leave his "Vindication" to Congress. He reported that he had encountered nothing but good will on the part of the soldiers and most of the officers. President Laurens assured his guileful correspondent that his service would not go unrewarded by Congress. Washington would soon announce his "conditionary appointment," Laurens predicted, and he promised Steuben his own best efforts "consistently with [the honor] of these Infant States."[36]

John Laurens adopted Steuben's metaphor to depict the salutary effect of his work. He is "exerting himself like a Lieutenant anxious for promotion," Laurens wrote his father, "and the good effects of his labours are visible." He surmised that Washington was only waiting to assess the feelings of the brigadiers before recommending an official appointment for Steuben. He wrote that "everyone is convinced of his Zeal and abilities, and thinks him deserving of the Grade which he asks for." Other observers noted approvingly the results of Steuben's exertions. Samuel Ward, a newcomer in camp from Rhode Island, told his wife that the Prussian had "obligingly undertaken to discipline the army and is very indefatigable in his charge." Henry Knox, upon returning to camp after two months in New England, observed that the army was "improving in discipline and increasing in numbers every day." A lieutenant remarked in mid-April that there were no prisoners under arrest and said that this was "a Little unusual but I hope 'tis growing out of fashion as arrests are considered in a more serious Light than heretofore."[37]

Concerted efforts to train and discipline the army coincided with, if they did not precipitate, a gradual improvement in its mood and demeanor as the arrival of spring ended the worst episodes of material deprivation. During Steuben's first weeks in camp the mood remained sullen and contentious in the wake of the dire shortages of mid-February. When supplies were again marginally adequate, soldiers began to voice the discontents they had submerged during the depths of the emergency. As before, those discontents focused on both internal and external targets. Massachusetts troops looked on in amazement as the regiments from other state as were gradually reclothed and asked why their own state did not make similar efforts on their behalf. One officer accused Massachusetts citizens of having "Lost all Bowles of Compassion if they Ever had any" for neglecting the needs of his men. "I would Beg of them to Rouse from there stupedity and Put on some humanity and stir themselves Before it is too late." Enoch Poor notified Governor Weare of New Hampshire that supplies from that state were "very acceptable, though inadequate to our wants." He guessed that state officials had credited reports of the roads being "crowded with teams carrying clothing to the army" but enclosed returns showing that the new supplies provided for only a fraction of the troops, and he observed, "our army still remains in their ragged suffering situation."[38]

While many states felt the sting of their troops' resentment for "not fulfilling their engagements" to the army, the choicest epithets were reserved for Pennsylvania's increasingly maligned inhabitants. After the February famine, Isaac Gibbs registered a familiar disparagement of the local populace: "The country to be sure is good, but the inhabitants are chiefly what we call quakers, & I believe are the far greater part of them. No friends to the Cause we are engaged in but on the Contrary which causes us to suffer much on account of Provisions that sometimes we have been obliged to go out and take their Provisions by force. Thus we suffer for want of the Common Necessaries of Life." James Varnum remained the undisputed laureate of the army's discontent and its occasional bitterness toward its neighbors. "In short," he exclaimed:

> Toryism rules the roost and ugliness, in nameless forms, usurps the Throne of Beauty. But for the virtuous few of the army, I am persuaded that this country must long before this have been destroyed. It is saved for our sakes; & its salvation ought to cause Repentence in us for all our sins, if evil and Misery are the Consequences of Iniquity. For my own part, I believe they are; and

Expect by this Pennance, to emerge into the World, after leaving this place, with all accounts fully ballanced. I shall then take care how I sin again, ever having a retrospect to its Consequences.

Varnum elaborated his purgatorial metaphor for Pennsylvania, calling it both "a heathenish land" and "this Tory Labyrinth." His fellow Rhode Islander, camp neighbor, and sometime mentor, Nathanael Greene, acknowledged that there were "some few [in the states at large] who sympathize with the Army in their distress," but he observed that "we are almost ready to think sometimes that our services are despised and that our Country are determined we shall struggle with cold and hunger without their aid."[39]

Epistles of similarly angry and mournful tenor flowed from the camp, especially from the pens of alienated New Englanders, during the closing weeks of the winter. John Sullivan was so "full of gloomy darkness" that not even an assignment to command American forces in Rhode Island could cheer him up. So unabating did these complaints become that Jedediah Huntington tried to refute rumors circulating in New England that the army had fallen out internally. There was, he claimed, "no Party, as you have heard, in the army." Indeed, he insisted—overstating his case in the wake of Washington's recent controversy with Horatio Gates—that "the General and Subordinate Officers were never better agreed in this or I believe in any Army in the world."[40]

Notwithstanding Huntington's disclaimer, there remained serious pockets of heated disunity within the army. One of these was the division of artillery, a willful, fractious unit of specialists who inhabited their own "park," as they called it, where they refined the arts of contention to an exemplary degree. Isolated by routine and function, as well as location, from the rest of the army, the division squabbled all winter. When Henry Knox left camp in February on a mission to Boston, its officers split along the lines of a preexisting clash among two of his subordinates. The dispute lasted well into the spring, and by late March the principal contestants for day-to-day control of the division, Colonels Thomas Proctor and John Crane, were described by one artilleryman as being "near Daggers points."[41]

In the rest of the army rancor, contention, and grievances were less sharply focused. Almost every day disgruntled soldiers and support department employees resigned, deserted, complained, or lobbied to be transferred. Inevitably, some of this discontent yielded to the increasing tempo of camp life as the army prepared to take the field. The slowly improving climate and the increase of naturally available food tempered some of the material sources of dissatisfaction and made others at least more bearable.[42] The emphasis from headquarters on the enforcement of discipline, and especially Washington's blunt threat to break disorderly noncommissioned officers, raised the threshold of tolerance at the critical organizational interface between field officers and privates.[43] For these reasons and others the prevailing cynical mood began to be alloyed with streaks of optimism as March turned into April. Most soldiers were not caught up in the rapid swings of euphoria and despair that swept through headquarters with the shifting intelligence reports, and they shared only a general perception that the army's metabolism was quickening. Their expectations depended largely on the things they could witness from day to day: the arrival of supplies or reinforcements and the overall strength of the army became the critical yardsticks by which they measured the coming campaign.

Jedediah Huntington declared that he could "hardly wish Gen. Howe in a more convenient situation to attack than he is now in, had we but our compliment of troops." He hoped that "every nerve will be exerted to make our army formidable" and boasted that if every state had "done like Connecticut," Howe would already have shared General Burgoyne's fate. Alexander Scammell wished that the states would "pour in Reinforcements to enable [us] to coope up our bloodthirsty unnatural foes in Philadelphia." Anthony Wayne hoped that Howe's long-rumored recall would not take place "until we have had an opportunity to Burgoyne him." A major from Virginia predicted that the army was "likely to be on a respectable footing before next fall." Although he expected the coming fighting season to "be a very warm one," he thought the army was "50 times in better order this spring than we were last to receive the enemy."[44]

To the optimistic, army life began to wear a more hopeful tint. During April, some letters from the camp were sprinkled with comments that would have seemed ludicrous during the dark days of midwinter. One officer even contrived to find promotions "very rapid in the army at this time." Having been a major for only six months, he learned that there was a vacancy for lieutenant colonel, to which he hoped to be appointed soon. Another sought to persuade a friend at home that the camp "affords much better quarters than you would imagine, if you consider the materials, season, and hurry in which it was built." As the warmer and drier weather repaired some of the ecological havoc that the encampment had wrought on the local landscape, a more benign perception of the region emerged. "The fertile ground which has long laid covered in snow," one officer observed, "seems to be renew'd buy the breases of the south, and the warm shining of the sun." A recent arrival from Rhode Island told his wife that he had taken "two agreeable walks over the Schuylkill this day," and he wrote that "the meadows on each side [of] that beautiful River begin to look charmingly."[45]

Still, a stubborn vein of skepticism continued to manifest itself. Nathanael Greene, a pillar of hope during the crises of midwinter, was by early spring the devil's best advocate. His previously intrepid temper seemed to flag during March as he shouldered the complex problems of the Quartermaster's Department. By April he questioned whether the apparent improvement in the army's circumstances was based on actual gains or wishful thinking. Greene wondered whether the British defeat at Saratoga had made people "too sanguine" about the course of the war and thus reluctant to sacrifice their private interests for the public good. Undoubtedly in closer touch than others with Washington's anxieties about an enemy offensive, Greene continued to worry about the army's strength. Other observers might note the periodic arrival of new troops and pronounce the army "respectable in point of numbers," but Greene held tenaciously to his view that "the Army recruits slow."[46]

Nor was Greene a lonely Jeremiah. William Bradford, the deputy muster master general, whose responsibilities included monitoring the army's size and battle readiness, was also pessimistic about the slow arrival of reinforcements. Bradford shared Greene's view of the effects of Saratoga on public opinion, although he believed that the British were also oddly "content to remain unmolested" in Philadelphia. He thought it "Strange that such powers as Britain and America, contending for such objects as Dominion and Freedom, should have such contemptible armies in the field." Samuel Ward was shocked by the situation he found at Valley Forge. "All our preparations here look rather defensive than offensive," he told his wife, "it would hardly be possible to act in our present situation." Ward, who would soon soften his judgment in reaction to Steuben's work with the troops, stated the conundrum in telling terms: "We are not the strength of the country but much depends upon us. Yet between you and I, much will not be done."[47]

Greene's doubts about the future extended far beyond the slow recruiting effort. He shared Washington's frustration with the divisions in York over the army reform proposals. He believed that "Great jealousies prevail in Congress respecting the army." Its members "think we despise them and are exceedingly vext about it." When he heard that the half-pay question would "end in a reference to the states," he predicted "there it will dye and sink into forgetfulness." He concluded, "We are not yet happy enough to get to the end of the chapter of experiments—the prospect before me looks languid and sickly."[48]

By mid-April, then, the army's mood was delicately balanced between the cautiously growing optimism of many of its members and the persistent skepticism of many others. On April 17, Washington received the first hints of the British policy reappraisal—a draft of the "Conciliation Bills" that the ministry had presented to Parliament in February, which were intended to test the prospects for peace by making broad concessions to the Americans just short of actual independence. He suspected that the bills might be a ruse formulated in Philadelphia but recognized that they might have a "malignant influence" by dividing American Whigs. He therefore asked Congress to investigate the matter carefully.[49]

Within two days Washington was convinced of the authenticity of the bills, and he urged Congress to make a political response. His most immediate responsibility, though, lay in buffering the impact of the proposals on the army itself. Rumors of their contents had already sown some consternation within the camp. The best way to show that the war would not be abandoned lay in vigorous measures to continue prosecuting it. It was thus decided to formally present the alternative plans for opening the campaign, formulated the month before, to the general officers. Washington believed that the enemy would continue with military preparations, but the bills suggested that British policy might be "founded in the despair of [that] Nation succeeding against us." This raised the possibility that Howe would await the American reaction to the peace proposal and yield the short-term military initiative.[50]

The presentation to the generals comprised three options: attacking Philadelphia, transferring the campaign to New York, or "laying quietly in a secure camp" to await events. Washington withheld his own views, leaving it to his field commanders to "fully weigh every circumstance" and give him their views on each option after "mature deliberation." Within five days eleven of them had returned detailed responses. Washington learned, if he did not already know, that his generals were as deeply divided on the question of how the campaign should be opened as they had been five months before on how it should be concluded and on where the army should go next. Four generals recommended an attempt against Philadelphia, four opted for an expedition against New York, and three preferred to keep the army in a secure camp and allow the British to begin the campaign.[51]

A few broad themes emerged from these responses. Nearly all the generals cited the need for at least 25,000 troops to blockade Philadelphia, while many commented favorably on the support that could be expected from New England militias for an expedition against New York. There was a geographic denominator of uncertain significance in the choice between the cities. Of the four generals preferring to move against Philadelphia, three (William Maxwell, Lord Stirling, and Anthony Wayne) were residents of New Jersey or Pennsylvania, while the fourth (John Paterson) came from Massachusetts. Of the four choosing to transfer the campaign to New York, on the other hand, three (James Varnum, Henry Knox, and Enoch Poor) were New Englanders, while the fourth (Peter Muhlenberg) was a Virginian but a native of Pennsylvania. Any effort to interpret these opinions as showing coherent or significant regional blocks should be weighed cautiously. The New Englanders were generally eager to rely on the militias of their native region, who they felt had distinguished themselves at Saratoga, while those from the Middle States had proved unreliable during the Philadelphia campaign. The group preferring Philadelphia displayed less unanimity of viewpoint. It included one New Englander (Paterson) who rejected a New York expedition out of hand, but two of its number (Wayne and Stirling) approved of New York as a second choice.[52]

The choice of remaining in a secure camp elicited a different pattern of response. This option was the least popular of the three alternatives. It was no one's second choice; it was rejected out of hand more frequently than any of the other plans; and, indeed, except for its three advocates, it elicited only one favorable comment. Nathanael Greene, Friedrich Steuben, and Louis Duportail supported this plan, yet they advanced arguments with less convergence of viewpoint than the advocates of the other alternatives. Only Duportail flatly believed that the American army would not soon be a match in the field for its counterpart. Greene and Steuben wanted to use the fortified camp as a base for a transition to one of the other options. Greene believed that it could be used to support a New York expedition, whereas Steuben advocated waiting but looking for a chance to strike a "daring blow" against Philadelphia.[53] These men shared a similarity of role and function in the reorganizing military establishment. All were rising stars in auxiliary parts of that establishment, whose jobs would be facilitated by the adoption of the third alternative but hindered or obviated by the other two.[54]

From Washington's perspective, the division of viewpoints was more important than the reasons behind the preferences. When second choices and off-hand opinions were considered, the plan for transferring the campaign toward New York held a marginal edge over the others. Washington's opinion figured to weigh heavily in any decision. Although he had not voiced it when he submitted the questions to the generals, he gave some indications of his thinking in his "Thoughts Upon a Plan of Operation." The Philadelphia operation was "undoubtedly the most desirable . . . if within the reach of possibility"; the New York effort was "also an important one, if practicable." But the alternative of remaining quiet might "be a means of disgusting our own People by our apparent inactivity."[55]

The solicitation of written opinions from the generals did not constitute a final or formal poll on how the 1778 campaign should be opened. Congress had explicitly authorized Washington to call a Council of War to discuss that question more fully—and had taken the liberty of inviting Horatio Gates and Thomas Mifflin of the Board of War—but the collection of recommendations served a variety of useful functions. It reinforced the sense of momentum Washington had tried to instill into the army since early March. It also served as a useful counterweight to rumors of a negotiated settlement resulting from the British conciliation proposals.[56]

While the energy at Valley Forge slowly shifted from keeping the army intact to preparing it for the new campaign, sporadic conflict continued in the areas between the camp and the city. Military life in the outlying districts was characterized by long periods of tedium, deprivation, and chronic anxiety, punctuated by occasional alarms and brief, violent clashes between British and American forces. Howe continued to encourage partisan violence against Whigs. As Joseph Reed had predicted in February, persons known to have had contact with the American army soon discovered the hazards of traveling unescorted between the camp and their homes.[57] Militia and army patrols believed their movements were watched by inhabitants and reported to the enemy. It was considered imprudent for them to linger more than one night in the same place, while parties operating near the British lines found it advisable to travel after dark and the desertion of a single dragoon was assumed to compromise the security of a piquet post.[58]

Smallwood's garrison at Wilmington played a peripheral role in these activities. The post remained a buffer between Philadelphia and the Head of Elk supply depots, an intelligence station for monitoring river traffic, and a support base for Continental forays into New Jersey. By the middle of March the garrison was suffering from the consequences of the diversion of food from Maryland and Delaware to the main army. Its commissaries, having slaughtered their own scrawny herd, were reduced to scavenging Delaware for small droves of cattle. Smallwood complained that those areas were "intirely drained," and he feared that the army's suppliers would ignore his needs unless they were directed by headquarters to assist him.[59] The garrison became so constrained for food, forage, and wagons that Smallwood had to refuse requests to provide guards and transportation for the movement of goods between the Upper Chesapeake and Valley Forge. Instead he confined his efforts to watching the river for enemy shipping, removing hay from its banks between Wilmington and Chester, and retrieving the cargoes of several British vessels captured in the area. At Congress's request, he detached a party of men to arrest citizens of questionable political allegiance in anticipation of a British invasion of Delaware. In mid-April Hessian Captain Friedrich Muenchhausen proposed to Howe a raid on Dover, to seize two members of Congress and several "topmost rebels" who were reported to be there recruiting militia and helping to mobilize the state's resources in support of the war. Howe demurred at first but then authorized the plan, which ultimately collapsed because of adverse weather and because the prospective American targets "dispersed" unexpectedly.[60]

By early April, Washington began to weigh the utility of these defensive roles against the value of Smallwood's garrison as a reservoir of manpower for the main army. When it appeared that the campaign would open suddenly he decided to recall Smallwood's division to camp and then overruled himself. For the rest of the spring the detachment waited anxiously, poised to march "at a moment's warning." One soldier called its plight "fatiguing, critical, and alarming." Its members had done harder duty during the winter than during the recent campaign, he wrote, and erected more fortifications than the entire army had during its brief stay at Wilmington the previous summer. Until the campaign opened they lay behind those earthworks, exposed to attacks by land and water, dependent for provisions on seizures from Loyalists and market people, anxiously watching for the "visit" from the enemy they had expected all winter.[61]

In Pennsylvania the army struggled to police communications and trade between Philadelphia and its hinterland, but with little success. By early spring the division of the countryside into administrative districts east and west of the Schuylkill River became little more than a politically convenient fiction. After the February supply crisis, Washington found it almost continually necessary to use regular army troops on both sides of the river to secure the army's supply lines and to restrain disaffected civilians. By the end of March he bitterly complained to the state's former militia commander John Armstrong that "instead of relaxation [my troops] have been upon fatigue the whole winter."[62]

Coverage of the area west of the Schuylkill was compromised during February and early March when Captain Henry Lee's corps was sent into Delaware on a foraging mission. On Lee's return to camp the Conference Committee recommended him for promotion to the rank of major and asked him to form a corps of dragoons for independent service in the next campaign. The loss of an experienced skirmisher familiar with the territory hampered efforts to protect this vital region. It ultimately became necessary to rebuild the parties serving in the area virtually from scratch. Reinforcements were drawn from Continental units that had been assigned to guard the military storehouses in Lancaster, who were attached to the small corps stationed at a picquet post near the Radnor Meeting House.[63]

This post supported Continental detachments throughout the district. Its members patrolled the roads, intercepting market people wherever possible, but they were used mainly as a defensive screen for the camp on the west side of the river. The lower part of the district near the city remained effectively out of the zone of American control after Nathanael Greene left it supposedly barren of militarily useful goods in late February. As a result it continued to provide food to the British and recruits for the provincials. The Radnor picquet launched a few preemptive raids into the area. British sources insisted that American troops began "devastating" the countryside and burning the houses and barns of Loyalists in the lower parts of Chester County on about March 20. One officer reported that Washington had "given orders to lay waste the country eighteen miles round this City."[64]

The Americans also intensified their harassment of the market people. Two Hessian officers observed that rebel patrols were "always looking for these people" (or "peasants" as one called them) and that they took their goods or accepted bribes for "safe passage." In early March Washington confessed that he was at a loss to know what to do with the flood of recently captured marketeers. His court martials were trying them as fast as they could be brought to camp under special temporary authority granted by Congress the previous October, but it was hard to get witnesses to come to camp. When their neighbors did testify, he complained, "then they weap."[65] Washington hoped that state would take the accused, either for trial or to exchange them for citizens who had been kidnapped by the Loyalist dragoons. Although the Pennsylvania Assembly passed a law to transfer capital trials from eastern counties where courts were closed to Lancaster, the state was no more anxious than Washington to assume jurisdiction over these difficult categories of opportunistic criminality.[66]

Washington tried to find equitable, effective, and noncorrupting means of controlling the marketing phenomenon. He approved reluctantly the de facto combination of mercenary mercy that one of his patrol leaders devised. Women arrested with incidental quantities of produce and cooked food were released while their "marketing" was kept by the lucky captors. Marginally more culpable profiteers could be flogged on the spot and then turned loose, but the captains were urged to select the "greatest Villains" to be "tried for their lives" at the camp. This system of informal roadside triage offered an incentive to potential captors, kept detached patrols well fed and happy, and spared much record keeping for the beleaguered provost general. But as army commanders had already seen and would continue to learn, it invited abuses on the part of soldiers and blurred the line between martial law and military banditry.[67]

The decreasing number of Continental troops that Washington was able to keep west of the Schuylkill rendered these American missions vulnerable to British reprisals. Having gained relatively uncontested access to the neighborhood, Howe acted aggressively to protect loyal inhabitants who comprised most of its remaining population. Redcoat, Hessian, and provincial parties were sent out "as usual" on the evenings before market days to facilitate what one officer called a "system of smuggling" that involved known hiding places and prearranged signals between country people and British patrols. Captain Meunchhausen led his jaegers across the Schuylkill on March 20 both to support the area's beleaguered Loyalists and also to "earn some credit for the Hessians," who had "not been used on such occasions during the whole winter."[68]

These patrols were made as "systematically as ever" in April. Several captured American skirmishers were "decorated with eggs [and] women's shoes . . . that they had robbed the market people of, and, in that dress, were paraded through the street [of Philadelphia] to prison." British officers were outraged by reports that the Americans engaged in coercive recruiting practices among recalcitrant Pennsylvanians to fill their militia. They were using "much cruelty in every place where the militia is now being raised," one Hessian charged, and "devastating" the property of people who "refuse to go along." Johann Ewald observed that American recruiters resorted to means "such as could be practiced only under a despotic government" by hanging "several fathers in front of their houses for letting their sons escape." On April 17 a party of British dragoons went out to seize Americans who were reportedly "round[ing] up militia."[69]

As circumstances west of the Schuylkill settled into an uneasy stalemate during late winter, the situation on the east side reflected a complete breakdown of American control. John Lacey replied to Washington's latest request that state authorities assume more responsibility for disciplining the marketeers with yet another apology for the weak and badly armed state of his troops. Recognizing the battering that his reputation was taking, he bombarded members of the state's civil and military establishments with poignant descriptions of his plight. The credibility of Lacey's complaint that he had been left "crually off" in a "stupid situation" is undoubtable. There is also evidence, however, to support Thomas Wharton's view of him as a capable officer who was too young to function effectively without close Continental supervision. Although Lacey was a Bucks County native, his limited mobility and his continuing problems controlling many of his men left him ignorant of much of the territory within ten miles of the British lines. He thus found himself dependent on a hostile populace whose members refused to furnish information, as he lamented to Washington, "even [of] the direction of the Roads."[70]

Lacey had also managed to incite a "clammor" against himself among some of his Whig neighbors, who accused him of displaying partiality toward his own friends and relatives. He denied the charges and nothing came of them. The fact that they were circulating among people with influential relations of their own in the state government, however, did not facilitate his mission of pacifying the neighborhood. Lacey had good reason to regard himself as a man adrift on an unfriendly communal sea. He reported that he was being taunted almost daily with threats that the British dragoons or the provincial forces would capture him within a week.[71]

Because of the militia's persistent weakness, Washington reluctantly increased the deployment of Continental troops east of the Schuylkill, but on far too limited a basis to effectively suppress civilian activity there. Instead, he used the regular troops for specific assignments: to control key roads for finite periods of time, to escort shipments of supplies to camp, and to remove militarily useful goods from exposed areas. The newly assigned officers patrolling the roads near the river reported some incidental success in disrupting trade there. Even they, however, were constrained by the size of their parties and by the aggressiveness of enemy patrols in contesting their presence. One officer who had retreated from Chestnut Hill before a superior British force returned the next day to find that the enemy had smashed the doors and windows of houses to discourage their use as lodging for American troops.[72]

The situation might have lapsed into a state of complete anarchy had Howe seen fit to maintain military pressure in the area by a systematic continuation of the provincial raiding he had begun in mid-February. Instead, the British commander redirected much of that pressure in March toward New Jersey, in response to the upheavals that broke out when Anthony Wayne entered the state to forage. The result was a slight relaxation of British presence north and northwest of Philadelphia, which allowed American forces in the area to restore some semblance of public order. For several weeks the British limited their forays into the district to the weekly market days, when they sent out small detachments to protect civilians on their way to town. On those occasions Continental officers reported that the inhabitants had no difficulty eluding them with their goods.[73]

Lacey was quick to claim his share of the credit for the temporary lull in the violence. On March 20 he boasted to Thomas Wharton that for the past three weeks he had "been such a terror to the enemies Light Horse, that they have not Dar'd to shew their heads without their lines." A week later he more modestly claimed that his efforts to prevent British depredations in the area had been "attended with tollerable success," but he conceded that preventing inhabitants' marketing entirely was impossible. Lacey's "terrorism" was more likely effective because it was aimed mostly at the area's civilians. He ordered a subordinate to fire on "villains" taking produce to Philadelphia, and if he was fortunate enough to kill any of them to "leave [them] on the roads and their marketing lying together" as a warning to others.[74]

But even Robert Simcoe, the commander of the Queen's Rangers, admitted that the provincial units had temporarily been "repulsed," and he wrote that they should "recoil" in order to "add to the ascendancy necessary to be maintained in the country." If Lacey "broke into the circle of country which we had hitherto maintained possession of," Simcoe argued, he should be attacked. Intensive British marauding in Philadelphia and Bucks Counties resumed in April after several British units returned from New Jersey. Henry Muhlenberg had never stopped fearing an "attack" in the area, so the renewed outbreak was no surprise to him. But Charles Willson Peale, who left camp in early March for his home in lower Bucks County, had a trau-matic experience. Peale relaxed briefly under Lacey's protection, but when the provincials turned up the heat he "went one night to a poor mans House which was Situated in a Bye Corner—and 2 other Nights I sleep in the Woods," before he decided to return to camp. Reverend William Van Horne, of Bucks County, also spent time at Valley Forge as a volunteer chaplain before returning to his home in early March. By April he was hopeful that Lacey's outmanned troops could protect the vicinity and doubtful that British troops would bother Bucks County, but he was "continually on my guard, and so much from home as to be almost a stranger to it." Like Peale, Van Horne began to have second thoughts about being away from the army, and he finally urged a friend to inquire about the availability of another mil-itary chaplaincy.[75]

Washington tried with mixed success to coordinate the efforts of regu-lar army and militia forces east of the Schuylkill. Anthony Wayne promised to join Lacey in foraging across lower Bucks County on his return from New Jersey in early March. Too often, however, Continental and militia detach-ments failed to connect quickly enough in the sprawling district they were trying to cover to have any good effect. Washington sent small army detach-ments across the river on missions of assigned duration with limited objec-tives. When possible he asked the militia to support these detachments, but his sense of minimal control over the state troops was shown by his request to William Howe that all flags and messengers to Valley Forge be sent by routes on the west side of the river. In this way, he explained, they would avoid any "accidents" with the militia, for which he declined to be held responsible.[76]

This new policy of increased but restricted Continental involvement east of the Schuylkill was underlined by the choice of Lachlan McIntosh to lead one of the detachments into the area. This marked the first time since the army came to Valley Forge that a general officer was sent across that river. McIntosh was not, however, given broad responsibility for military operations in the area. Instead, he was directed to meet a large drove of cattle coming through the district and to fend off a British detachment reportedly on its way to intercept it. He was also ordered to help the militia to disrupt the movements of Quakers traveling to Philadelphia for their Yearly Meet-ing. McIntosh found the cattle, after probing a neighborhood whose people were, he concluded, both aware of and inimically disposed toward his pres-ence there.[77]

In spite of Lacey's threats to fire on Quakers trying to enter the city enough of them eluded his grasp to allow that group to hold their meeting. McIntosh and Lacey met at Newtown on March 23 and developed a plan that testified eloquently to the futility they felt toward their assignment. Lacey urged Washington that the district between the British lines and his own east of the Schuylkill be depopulated, by requiring its inhabitants to "move Back into the Country" for fifteen miles. He had been considering the idea for several weeks and had even ordered his patrols to spread the word that residents would have to leave the area. He was visited by a delegation of angry Quakers who demanded to know his "Reasons for ordering them to Quit their habitations." Caught in a storm of complaint, Lacey sought belated approval from headquarters.[78]

Washington rejected the proposal, but not before deeming it "rather [more] desirable than practicable" and reflecting on "however little consideration the Majority of parties concerned may deserve from us." Ultimately, his unwillingness to consider the "horror of depopulating a whole district" prevailed over his belief that the plan would "undoubtedly put an end to the pernicious illicit Commerce which at present subsists." Instead, Continental and militia officers serving in the area were ordered to continue their laborious mission of roving patrols and selective intimidation. Washington abandoned his earlier efforts to pressure Pennsylvania authorities to keep their agreed quota of troops in the district. He continued to insist, however, that the civil consequences of local criminality be left to the state unless there were pressing Continental interests in the matter. While he retained the temporary authority to do so, he supported military trials and punishment for any "notorious characters" seized by state troops. When that authority lapsed in April, he ordered dangerous offenders sent directly to state authorities and those of known good character or with reputable local friends released with the warning that they would be hung for a second offense. Deprived of the legal authority to punish recalcitrant civilians, Washington advised a county militia lieutenant to begin "shooting some of the most notorious offenders whenever they can be found in flagrante delicto."[79]

Well into the spring the district east of the Schuylkill remained barely within the sphere of American control. As John Lacey struggled to police its inhabitants he had difficulty controlling his own men. Militiamen continued to tread warily near the city. Instead of serving as a visible symbol and enforcer of revolutionary authority they learned to act covertly because the area was so full of disaffected people that movements by large parties were considered certain to be reported to the enemy. While the militia sought security in anonymity, "strolling parties" of furloughed soldiers and would-be brigand civilians readily embraced their identity and in this guise committed "villainous roberys" on unwary travelers.[80] Washington thus continued to require supply convoys approaching his camp from the north to cross the Delaware River at Easton and proceed through the high country to avoid the area altogether.[81]

Lacey's predicament, and Washington's unwillingness or inability to do much to resolve it, reveals many of the difficulties inherent in the dispersed field operations employed by both armies that winter. Some of the finer implications of this issue emerged in southern New Jersey, across the Delaware River from Philadelphia. If Washington was routinely content to treat the district east of the Schuylkill as a zone of secondary consideration, he had been all but compelled to ignore New Jersey. Whigs in Burlington, Gloucester, and Salem counties were just as exposed to British power as those of Bucks, Philadelphia, or Chester counties. But Continental resources simply did not permit even the essentially rhetorical commitment to their security that was extracted from Washington by the Pennsylvania government. As a result, New Jersey's ragged militia forces under Colonel Joseph Ellis endured a winter of hardship and intermittent terror every bit as severe, if much less visible, than that of the Pennsylvania militia under Lacey.

The February provisions crisis, however, generated forces that permanently altered the status of the war in New Jersey. When Anthony Wayne crossed the Delaware on February 19 to forage along the east bank, the effect on New Jersey was like that of a man dragging his flaming coattails into a tinder-dry cornfield. Within days the British landed 4,000 troops in two parties at Billingsport and Cooper's Point to harass Wayne's movements. Almost immediately, he reported that the enemy were in control of the area between Salem and Haddonfield.[82] He received and executed orders to resist this incursion but found himself outnumbered by perhaps eight men to one. His principal mission was to collect as much food as he could and carry it back to Valley Forge as soon as possible. Moving north along the heads of the creeks flowing into the Delaware and sending out foraging and skirmishing detachments, he advanced toward Trenton. Casimir Pulaski had been ordered to bring his dragoons south to support Wayne. Keeping ahead of the British as they moved north, Wayne and Pulaski carried on rear-guard skirmishing maneuvers and forced residents to move goods inland to keep them out of enemy hands. By the middle of March, Wayne had pushed his troops to Burlington and was ready to abandon the state and return to camp.[83]

As Wayne withdrew, Howe sent three more regiments of infantry, Robert Simcoe's dreaded company of Queen's Rangers, and a provincial unit down the Delaware River to Salem County. The ensuing conflagration presented Washington with serious tactical and political problems. Wayne's expedition had ignited a new outbreak of British violence in New Jersey, and the state's authorities were not being unreasonable in expecting Continental assistance in dealing with the problem. Washington found that a regular army presence in the state was required to prevent the complete collapse of its militia. Less than a week after Wayne's withdrawal, he sent Colonel Israel Shreve back across the Delaware with a regiment of New Jersey regulars.[84]

Washington informed Governor Livingston that he hoped the state's militia would "resort to Colo. Shreve with . . . alacrity," and predicted that if they did the British would be "repulsed." Instead, the situation continued to deteriorate, bringing more pressure on Washington to make a decisive response. The presence of regular British troops in the state encouraged its large and increasingly militant Tory population to turn in wrath on their Whig neighbors. Indeed, British military tactics seem to have been explicitly intended to capitalize on this situation. The new detachments from Philadelphia focused their efforts on destroying the structure of the local militia organizations. Several militia companies were overrun by British parties, and, according to their commanders, some of their members were bayoneted after surrendering.[85]

Colonel Charles Mawhood, the commander of the expedition, held the threat of concerted terror over opponents of British supremacy in the area. He circulated a proclamation offering to withdraw from the state if its militia disarmed. "If on the contrary the Militia should be so far deluded and blind to their true interest and Happiness," he announced, "he will put the Arms which he has brought with him into the hands of the Inhabitants well affected called Tories and will attack all such of the Militia as remain in Arms, burn and destroy their houses and other Property and Reduce them, their unfortunate Wives and Children to Beggary and Distress." Mawhood underlined the seriousness of his intentions by attaching a list of seventeen Salem militiamen who would be, he implied, among the "first objects to feel [British] vengeance." The offer was categorically rejected by its targets, who implied that retaliation was "not intirely out of our power," but the bloody acts on which it was premised had immediate effects.[86] Salem and Gloucester County militia crumbled and fled before the prospect of butchery, and their scheduled replacements refused to leave their homes to take up the collective defense. Shreve's arrival offered some hope of relief, but New Jersey authorities—observing that the state's lower counties were "miserably infected with Tories"—urged Washington to increase the Continental commitment to the area. Governor Livingston conceded that the state was partly responsible for the reluctance of the militia to serve because of delays in paying its members, but he asked that the entire New Jersey Continental brigade be returned to the state.[87]

It fell to Washington to handle New Jersey's appeals as diplomatically as he could. He told Livingston that he could not offer the state any more help because the "situation of this Army will not admit the smallest detachment to be made from it." Mawhood's force returned to Philadelphia at the end of March with three hundred tons of hay and many prisoners. Its presence in Salem gave the New Jersey "refugees" or "volunteers" protection behind which to fortify their bastion at Billingsport, to recruit assistance from their Loyalist-minded neighbors, and to protect the market people.[88] The state's Whigs reacted with fury to Mawhood's departure. They began rounding up people who had traded with the British, some of whom belonged to Nicholas Collin's congregation. They held them overnight in the school at the Raccoon Church and then marched them under armed guard into the countryside with orders to shoot them if any British troops appeared. At dawn on April 4 about three hundred refugees and a few British troops surrounded the Whig militia, who scattered into the woods while the raiders burned the school. The militia reappeared and began shooting from the woods at the Loyalists, who returned the fire while Collin and his parishioners huddled in terror in their church.[89]

Shreve gave as much support as he could to local Whigs in this deadly contest. He helped a party of New Jersey militia harass the Loyalists at Billingsport and barely avoided being trapped by a new detachment of British troops from Philadelphia. The "Spirit of Burning," he reported, "prevails still among those Miserable Villons at billingsport." Small parties from that post came at night to Woodbury "in a Skulking Manner and Burnt two Whig houses and ordered other famalys to move out in a few days or they would burn them in them." Finding his force too small to accomplish any objectives by force, and the militia too scattered to protect effectively, Shreve divided his men into scouting parties to patrol the roads and disrupt trade with the enemy. New Jersey's Whigs continued trying to protect themselves. Washington allegedly sent a local officer to the house of the man's own brother near Gloucester Point "whom the English army had carefully protected during its foraging." He burned his brother's crops and warned that if he continued his "friendship" for the English he would return to burn the house itself. On Easter Sunday Collin's service was disrupted by a "terrible cry," and the congregation emerged from church see a parishioner being whipped to death for "profit[ing] by the forbidden trade."[90]

Washington and Livingston reached an uneasy accommodation about the amount of help that the state could realistically expect from the army. Transmitting yet another petition for protection from the inhabitants of his state's lower counties, Livingston asserted that he would understand if Washington found it impracticable to act on it. In disappointing Livingston's hopes for more aid Washington reflected, for one of the few times all winter, on the subtler implications of the problem at hand. Announcing his intention, if reinforcements permitted, eventually to send a second regiment of New Jersey regulars to assist Shreve, he conceded: "A few hundred Continental Troops quiet the minds and give satisfaction to the people of the country, but considered in the true light, they rather do more harm than good. They draw over the attention of the Enemy and not being able to resist them, are obliged to fly and leave the Country at the Mercy of the foe. But as I said before, the people do not view things in the same light, and therefore they must be indulged tho' to their detriment."[91]

Ultimately, Washington may have been able to find a measure of redeeming comfort in this seemingly dismal turn of events in New Jersey. Because of his relatively good working relationship with Governor Livingston, he was able to sustain his decision to limit military aid to that state at minimal political cost. By late March most of the regular British units had returned to Pennsylvania, leaving behind a civil conflagration that would keep Shreve's regiment in New Jersey for the rest of the spring. In April the provincial corps and regular troops were again probing into lower Bucks county to disperse militia patrols and disrupt their recruiting activities. The brief hiatus, however, stabilized matters in the army's backyard while reinforcements trickled into camp, the regiments were drilled, and the recovery of sick and inoculated troops improved Washington's ability to respond to these challenges.

The measure of this limited benefit can be taken primarily from a consideration of what might otherwise have happened. Had British tactics proceeded from a more coherent policy, Howe might have concentrated on aggravating local antipathies in a single location in hopes of igniting a conflict that Washington would be unable to finesse or ignore. Exploiting the havoc wrought in Bucks County during February, he might have increased the pressure there until the maintenance of the Continental supply lines became impossible without a sustained deployment east of the Schuylkill. Instead of merely forcing Lacey's troops to hover pathetically on the fringes of the conflict in Bucks County, he might have used the Pennsylvania provincials to drive the militia higher into the country and encouraged new outbreaks among the restive Loyalists of Northampton County. Such a course of events would have threatened to isolate the American army from the material assistance of the northern states. It might even have forced the "decisive action" with the Americans that Howe's version of British strategy required.

These are speculative considerations but not idle ones. Howe invaded Pennsylvania on the strength of the belief that his army would benefit from operating in the midst of a well-disposed civilian population. Given the physical and social geography of the Delaware Valley, it is hard to imagine where that belief could have been better tested than east of the Schuylkill River. What was lacking was a coherent strategy. Even as British detachments probed for soft spots around Philadelphia, British planners were trying to formulate such a policy and decide where to implement it. For the moment, however, the hope of manipulating civil support in behalf of British war aims was essentially an unarticulated one. Its employment was intermittent, experimental, and unfocused: a few raids in Bucks and Philadelphia counties, then a few more in nearby New Jersey, followed by still a few more back in Pennsylvania.

The result of this activity, from the Continental viewpoint, was a series of annoying situations, attended by internal friction and political embarrassment stemming from the army's inability to respond to the satisfaction of all interested parties. Beyond this, however, the effect was minimal. Too often the British found that the only substantial fruits of their armed forays consisted of the "little plundering" that concluded their visits. At some level Washington must have realized that he would gain by refusing to be drawn more deeply into a regional civil conflict. If he considered the effect Charles Mawhood's terroristic threats would have had if they had been issued from Newtown, Pennsylvania, rather than Salem, New Jersey, he might have decided that the belated commitment of a Continental regiment to the latter state's peace of mind was a cheap form of insurance indeed.[92]

Chapter 10

AS THE FINE SEASON APPROACHES

On May 1 unofficial news of the Treaty of Alliance signed by the United States and France reached camp. Washington withheld a formal announcement to the army until he was notified by Congress, but he was unable to resist "mention[ing] the matter" to several officers who passed through headquarters. The news spread rapidly through the camp, and as Washington observed, "no event was ever received with a more heartfelt joy." Congress rapidly approved the treaty, and Washington requested permission to announce and celebrate the good news. "I will only say," he noted, "that the army are anxious to manifest their joy upon the occasion." The formal announcement appeared in a postscript to general orders for May 5, and ceremonies were planned for the next day.[1]

The news gave the army a timely opportunity to demonstrate the results of its six weeks of training under Steuben. According to the elaborate ceremony Washington prescribed, the troops marched by brigade to the "Grand Parade" in the center of the camp. After forming into two long lines, they performed a *feu de joie* of running musket fire, punctuated by three "huzzas" to "the King of France," "the Friendly European Powers," and "the American States." The event, ripe with the possibility of awkward maneuver and embarrassment for the army, proceeded to the satisfaction of all observers. The day began with the pardoning of two American soldiers under sentences of death, to symbolize Washington's desire to "reclaim [rather] than punish Offenders." The *feu de joie* was performed, John Laurens wrote, "with as much splendor as the short notice would allow," which he attributed to Steuben's "unwearied attention, and to the visible progress which the troops have made under his discipline." The Marquis de Lafayette described the day as "one of the most agreeable I have passed here." Colonel Philip Van Cortlandt called it the "greatest Day Ever yet Experienced in Our Independent World of Liberty."[2]

At a reception that followed for officers, Laurens wrote, "Triumph beamed in every countenance." Most soldiers understood, however, that the day marked only a brief respite from the work of preparing for the new campaign. In his letters to officers at distant posts, congratulating them on the happy news from France, Washington worried that it might result in a fatal relaxation of Continental efforts and initiative. He knew that if American performance on the battlefield disappointed the political expectations on which the treaties were predicated, they would prove at best a temporary palliative for morale and at worst a source of deep disillusionment or even military harm.[3]

There was much hard work to be done before the army would be ready to take the field on anything more than an emergency basis. While the trickle of drafts, recruits, and troops returning from leaves or from army hospitals had increased by early May to a steady stream, there was real concern at headquarters about the army's strength levels. After bottoming out in March at barely more than 7,000 men present and fit for duty—half the number available in late December—the number of "effective" troops at Valley Forge and its nearby satellites in the Delaware Valley reached 13,000 by May 2. Steuben's exercises had born impressive fruit in the *feu de joie*, but that ceremony did not match the dexterity that would be required in complex combat situations. The functioning of the support departments had improved since February under the aegis of new department heads like Nathanael Greene or retainees from the old regime such as Ephraim Blaine, but those officials remained apprehensive about the prospect of having to serve a moving army. Critical questions about the army's structure remained unsettled while Congress wrestled with its ambivalence about such issues as half-pay and the "reduction" of the state battalions.[4]

From Washington's perspective the most important issue was a decision about how to open the campaign. When the British failed to make the first move, it became clear that contingency plans were needed. The opinions collected from the general officers in April showed how deeply divided they were over Washington's suggested alternatives. A Council of War was called to resolve the question. The fact of its sitting would demonstrate to the army that its future depended more on military exertions than on diplomatic or political achievements. The opening of the council awaited only the arrival of Horatio Gates and Thomas Mifflin from the Board of War.[5]

Washington finally convened the council on May 8. In his charge to the group he did not offer specific strategic alternatives. Instead, he presented the best available intelligence of British and American strength and of the state of foreseeable reinforcements on both sides. The enemy, he observed, had about 10,000 troops in Philadelphia, 4,000 in New York, and 2,000 in Rhode Island. He predicted, accurately enough as it turned out, that their reinforcements would "probably not be very large nor very early," whereas American strength would not exceed 20,000 Continental troops. He reported that he had tried to ascertain the Commissary Department's ability to supply provisions without success. With these preliminaries, Washington asked his generals to provide written recommendations "on some general plan, which, considering all circumstances, ought to be adopted for the operations of the next campaign." The council's response is interesting in light of the written opinions that had been collected three weeks before. The group decided unanimously that the army should "remain on the defensive and await events." This decision was consistent in substance, if not specific language, with the alternative that had received the least support in the April canvas.[6]

In trying to understand this reversal it is necessary to consider the overlapping, but not convergent, membership of the groups participating on each occasion. The April solicitation apparently extended to all generals then present in camp. Invitations to the Council of War, in contrast, were restricted to senior military personnel. Members of the second forum were, with two exceptions, all major generals. The others—Henry Knox and Louis Duportail—were brigadiers whose involvement was undoubtedly in consequence of their special responsibilities and expertise as heads, respectively, of the army's artillery and engineering services. Of the dozen men who had divided so evenly on the question of attacking either New York or Philadelphia or of keeping the army in a secure camp, then only six were polled on May 8. Of the latter group, in turn, only Knox, who favored attacking New York, and Lord Stirling, who recommended moving against Philadelphia, represented either of the aggressive options that Washington posed earlier in the spring. But all three proponents of keeping the army on a defensive footing (Greene, Steuben, and Duportail) attended the May council.[7]

There is no evidence that invitations to the council were manipulated to exclude or suppress any existing viewpoints. In his opening statement, Washington did not even refer to his earlier proposals, although the group's recommendation suggests that all three alternatives were considered explicitly. Instead, it is likely that limiting the forum to senior military figures stemmed from broad considerations of army policy and protocol. There can be little doubt, however, that the effective skewing of attendance toward those who advocated the most defensive option influenced the group's final decision. The juxtaposition of the council's decision with the April recommendation does suggest a pattern of division that was not initially apparent: the influence of rank itself. The preference for attacking either Philadelphia or New York in April had been predominantly an enthusiasm among the brigadiers. It appears that the generals were divided along lines of experience and responsibility. When the question was raised in a hypothetical way, a group weighted with brigadiers split more over where, rather than whether, to put the army on the offensive. When a senior group of advisers had to make a concrete decision, however, cooler heads and clearer eyes may have prevailed.[8]

As important as it is to know who from the April group was left out of the council, it is equally important to know who was added. The latter included Horatio Gates and Thomas Mifflin of the Board of War, and General John Armstrong of the Pennsylvania militia. As Pennsylvanians, Mifflin and Armstrong may have been especially sensitive to the security advantages to the state of using the army as a defensive screen against British incursions rather than as a battering ram. By the same token, however, they must also have been aware of the state's interest in seeing the military stalemate broken and Pennsylvania relieved of the increasingly costly burdens of hosting the seat of war. The effect that Gates's differences with Washington—over strategy, politics, and personality—had on the decision are unclear.

That such circumstantial considerations need be entertained at all is a measure of the silence of the documentary record. Washington asked "each member [to] furnish him with his sentiments in writing." Instead, the group responded with a consensus, and the document it produced gives little evidence of a diversity of views over which broad language had to be stretched. The members flatly proclaimed their belief that the army should stay put and use the time until the enemy moved for provisioning and training. Philadelphia, they argued, could neither be taken by storm nor be successfully blockaded with the 20,000 troops Washington estimated might be available. Stripped of the New Englanders who had touted the performance of the "eastern" militia, the group could not see how an outpouring of irregulars from that region would facilitate a successful thrust against New York City.[9] If any new element shaped the council's thinking it was perhaps the impact of the French alliance. The generals agreed that a successful venture against New York would generate great advantages. If it failed, however, it might dislocate the good will of their new European allies. The entry of France into the war could hasten the departure of the British army from the North American mainland. The council observed that by adopting a defensive plan nothing would be risked, and the army would continue to grow in strength and effectiveness for joint operations with the French army and navy.[10]

In the camp, May brought the most frenetic levels of activity since initial construction work ended in early January. Even as the army prepared to abandon its winter ground, the site's facilities had to be expanded to accommodate the growing numbers of men and stocks of material being assembled for the campaign. Fortifying the position continued well into May, work that had been hindered during the winter by frozen ground and by the difficulty of mustering work details from the ranks. By May the fortification crews had to compete with many other departments for the use of wagons, tools, and other resources. With reinforcements streaming into camp in large numbers, more huts had to be built and the facilities for the support departments needed to be expanded.[11]

To accommodate this increase in the army's activity, a longer working day was required. As late as May 5, Samuel Ward, an officer from Rhode Island, could depict for his wife a "specimen" day that was hardly calculated to make his friends back home shudder. "I rise with the sun, after adjusting my Dress, we begin our exercises at 6 O'Clock which last till 8—then we breakfast upon Tea or Coffee—and then I write, read, ride, or play, till Dinner time when we get a piece of good Beef or Pork tho' generally of both—and have as good Bread as I ever eat—the afternoon is also ours till 5 O'Clock when we begin our exercises and leave off with the setting sun . . . so that we live uncommonly well for Camp." By the middle of the month the tempo of life increased markedly. After May 16, the army was required to be under arms and ready for morning exercises by five instead of six o'clock. With all signs pointing toward the early evacuation of Philadelphia, every hour that a regiment spent on the parade ground seemed likely to constitute its last formal training for the season.[12]

For Friedrich Steuben, May brought a series of triumphs and satisfactions as well as responsibilities. Washington finally saw fit to ask Congress to appoint him inspector general to the army with the rank of major general. The celebration of the French alliance was regarded at headquarters as a personal triumph for Steuben and served as a pretext for the announcement of his appointment to the army. Steuben promised to redouble his efforts and congratulated Congress on the cooperation he had received from the troops. It had made possible, he enthused, "a more rapid Progress than any other Army would have made in so Short a time."[13]

The Commissary Department, meanwhile, suffered its third and final general crisis during May. Like the emergencies of December and February, the situation was grounded in continuing organizational deficiencies, but it was triggered by a set of unique circumstances. The December emergency began when supply lines were disrupted by the sudden movement of the army to Valley Forge. The February episode stemmed from cumulative transportation shortages, aggravated by an uninterrupted spell of bad weather. The May crisis loomed when the growth of the army threatened to outstrip the gradual improvement in the Commissary Department's ability to deliver supplies. Although that improvement had been apparent since area roads hardened in March, it had been slow and at best intermittent. When the similarly sporadic influx of reinforcements swelled during April, the commissaries braced for the "next cry" that they had been dreading for three months.[14]

The shortages were confined mainly to supplies of beef, and of the three principal episodes, this was easily the least severe. It was largely a question of anticipation rather than of outright want. Having been caught short twice before, Commissary officials were quick to warn their superiors when they saw the prospect of being straitened again. The sense of urgency was confined mostly within the department itself. Although he was still awaiting Congress's decisions on army reform, Washington found in the episode no useful ammunition for cautionary depictions of a restless or disbanding soldiery. He was nevertheless forced to balance his desire to have the militia of Pennsylvania and adjacent states available on short notice against the realization that the Commissary Department was still not prepared to provision a great outpouring of troops.[15]

The situation was attended by customary flights of rhetorical interplay between the department's harried officials. On May 10 Ephraim Blaine warned his new superior, Jeremiah Wadsworth, that he was once again "kept from hand to Mouth respecting Beef Cattle." They would, he predicted, soon "have a very great army and . . . we will find it difficult to feed them with Meat" without strenuous exertions. The commissaries, asked about their prospects for feeding the army in anticipation of the May 8 Council of War, had been compelled to give "our former answer."[16]

Although Samuel Ward's impression of culinary plenty was probably as idiosyncratic as his account of a typical day in camp, there is no real evidence of hungry soldiers during May. This stemmed from a variety of circumstances, including a lack of opportunities for soldiers to report brief shortages. By late spring the practice of informal local requisitioning, which had supplemented the army's diet the previous fall, had resumed. In early June even the relatively better fed British troops were helping themselves to the first produce of local gardens. Washington set April 21 as a date after which no soldiers could leave camp to buy provisions for themselves. A week later he condemned and forbade the "common practice [of] soldiers to go about the country and make use of [my] name to extort from the inhabitants by way of sale or gift any necessaries they want for themselves or others."[17] There is also evidence that the nutritional balance of power in the countryside was responding to subtle changes in the political climate. One American officer noticed a "great . . . change in this state since the news from France—the Tories all turned Whigs." "They begin," he sneered, "mercenary wretches, to be as eager for continental Money now as they were a few weeks ago for gold." If this observation was accurate, then the new attitude among civilians may have translated into increased attendance at the army's weekly markets and helped to relieve any brief food shortages.[18]

During May there was also conspicuously less evidence of the rancorous acrimony that had infested the camp during the winter. The increasing activity needed to prepare the army for the field undoubtedly relieved the boredom that had permitted isolated grievances to fester into bitter feuds. The improving climate and stabilizing supply flows tempered many of the causes of internal contention. More important, perhaps, disparagement of the local civilian population all but disappeared from the army's discourse during May. Samuel Ward observed that "We have Milk and Sugar in plenty. . . . Our Regiment begins to grow healthy, as the fine season approaches."[19] Ward was not, of course, the army's official spokesman, and pockets of acute deprivation and discontent persisted. Anthony Wayne remained bitterly unreconciled to the poorly clad and sickly condition of his brigade. Admitting that he was "not fond of Danger," Wayne announced that he would "most Chearfully agree to enter into action once every week in place of visiting each hutt in my Encampment—where objects perpetually strike my eye and ear whose wretched condition cannot well be worsted." A colonel from Massachusetts assailed that state's authorities for neglecting its troops' clothing needs. Invoking the covenant ideology that pervaded his region, William Shepard reminded the Massachusetts State Council that "The Gentlemen of this Army, who cannot purchase from his country, what he wants, at Prices as reasonable as the Wages he has consented to receive, will reasonably suppose his obligation to his country, in that way, are at an end."[20]

The very press of activity that allowed some individuals to overlook or defer old grievances in other cases provoked new ones. The Artillery Park remained a focal point for intramural bickering. Disputes over rank were endemic within the camp during the winter and the Corps of Artillery witnessed some of the most bitter of these. Unlike most state brigades, the corps was physically divided, with several of its companies stationed on the Hudson River. Washington and Henry Knox were reluctant to make even interim settlements until the corps was reunited at the beginning of the campaign. Knox tried to mollify his officers with promises of an eventual settlement that would meet the concerns of all parties. One officer remarked that such promises "keep us all Quiet," but another insisted that the "new fangled preposterous Arraingement" had driven a deep wedge between contending claimants to rank.[21]

The most prevalent source of discontent united the officer corps. Congress continued to debate the proposal for the adoption of half-pay pensions during early May. Amendments to define the terms of eligibility were considered, and an attempt to thwart the measure by referring it to the states was defeated. At camp, meanwhile, a "Confused noise" prevailed among the officers, according to one captain, over the likelihood of its passage. "There is a Continual Contrast," he wrote, "some for Resigning, others say you are a D——d fool, it shall take place by g——d." Rumors about the measure occasionally swept through the camp. On May 5 Samuel Ward prematurely announced to his wife that he had "the pleasure of feeling myself in some degree independant," as a result of a report of the settlement of the half-pay issue.[22]

Some officers moved from debate to direct action to make their feelings on the issue known. Earlier in the winter resignation had been the only alternative to patiently waiting for the adoption of the pension scheme. But in late April, Congress inadvertently created a referendum on the issue by linking the pensions to the willingness of the officers to affirm their allegiance to the United States. This raised the possibility of a form of protest that would carry the full implication of soldierly dissatisfaction with political foot-dragging without exposing its participants to being caught out of the army in case a favorable resolution took place.[23] By the time copies of the oath arrived at camp it became clear that some officers would exercise this option. Resistance to the oaths occurred in at least three brigades. The protesters gave many reasons for refusing to sign, including the fear that doing so might compromise their positions in disputes over rank and promotion, and demanded twenty days to consider the matter. Washington and the generals were loathe to use compulsion, but it was clear that the half-pay issue was the sticking point, and they tried to dissuade dissidents from harming their interests.[24]

As this potentially embarrassing situation played itself out at camp, Congress approved a modified pension scheme. The plan limited the half-pay awards to a term of seven years after the conclusion of the war for all eligibles who continued in the Continental service until the war ended. It prohibited recipients from holding offices of profit under the states or the central government and was made contingent on submission to the oaths of allegiance. In deference to objections that the original plan excluded enlisted men, all noncommissioned officers or privates who met the same criteria were promised flat payments of $80 at the conclusion of the war. The passage of the plan was announced to the army on May 18. Washington's hope that it would suppress discontent was at least partially realized: there was a noticeable increase in the incidence of oath-taking.[25]

The resolution of the pension issue neutralized one of the last sources of systematic discontent in the army. Remaining grievances over rank would await the final settlement of the new military "establishment." In the meantime, however, even an inhabitant of the Artillery Park conceded that "joy sparkles in the Eyes of our whole Army" at the prospect of a renewed campaign. Travelers who had visited camp were quoted in newspapers to the effect that the army was now in "grand spirits." The news reached the army's northern outposts on the Hudson River, where one officer who had successfully lobbied to have his regiment transferred north in January recanted his decision.[26]

Washington might have been flattered to learn of a prodigal's desire to return to Valley Forge, but he would have disagreed with the man's prediction that he [Washington] would now be "enabled to unfetter his genius."

From his perspective, the reforms approved by Congress were hardly a sufficient foundation for launching a new campaign, and the broader issue of the
new army establishment still needed to be settled. In fact, in Washington's
view, it was already almost too late. The "moving state," which would make
it difficult to implement any changes Congress might ordain, was at hand.
Throughout the winter he had shown a constant interest in the details of the
reorganization proposals, but his responsibility for preparing the army for
the field now precluded any further direct advocacy on his part.[27]

Soon after the American Council of War decided to keep the army in a
defensive posture, there were strong indications that a British move was
imminent. Henry Clinton arrived in Philadelphia to take command of the
British army on May 7, where he received the king's instructions of March
21, requiring him to make large detachments to the West Indies, Florida,
and Canada, and then to withdraw the rest of the army to New York. After
consulting with Admiral Richard Howe, Clinton concluded that the British
fleet was too dispersed to effect the detachments and the withdrawal simultaneously, so he decided to execute the retreat first and deploy his forces from
New York. In preparation, he ordered the army's baggage to be readied for
loading on ships and the large artillery pieces to be removed from the lines
north of the city and replaced by field guns. To keep the Americans guessing
about British intentions and to forestall panic among civilians, William
Howe ordered large parties to begin extending the town's fortifications.[28]

The ruse achieved neither objective. John Laurens correctly interpreted
the work as proof of the enemy's intention to evacuate the city despite a
"shew . . . of a design to remain."[29] When American intelligence reported
that heavy stores were being moved to the city wharfs, the British decision to
abandon Philadelphia became an open secret. For a month after May 15 the
camp at Valley Forge buzzed with reports that the enemy were about to go.[30]
Washington ordered his staff and department heads to make plans for the
army's movement, and he notified civil and military officials in the various
states of the developments.[31] Incoming intelligence told of houses being prepared in New York for British troops, of boats being readied to transport
those troops across New York Harbor, and of inhabitants leaving Philadelphia with news of the enemy's impending departure.[32] The Commissary and
Quartermaster's departments laid in supplies of provisions and forage along
routes through New Jersey toward the Hudson River.[33] Officers were
reminded to lighten their baggage, and the army was warned to prepare "for
an immediate and sudden Movement."[34]

For the last two weeks of May the army waited expectantly for the signal to move. The "grand fact" of the enemy's intention to evacuate was considered certain at headquarters although doubts prevailed about the timetable for that event. Spies watched ship movements on the Delaware trying to discern whether the withdrawal would be by land or over water. A debate ensued over whether or not to expect a British thrust against Valley Forge. Henry Laurens warned his son that the enemy's behavior might be a "strategem" to lure the army off its guard, and Washington acknowledged that many in the army held similar concerns. An officer from Massachusetts told his wife that he hoped soon to write her from nearer to home, but he foresaw an action in the interim. The enemy, he observed, "seems to be like a wounded Dog, as malicious as ever." Henry Knox expected to inform his brother of "a battle at Valley Forge, for the enemy threaten hard to fight bloodily before they depart."[35]

Washington hesitated to commit himself on either question. He conceded that some signs "justif[y] a report that . . . they will aim a blow at this army before they go off," and he worried about the significance of the continued British fortification work. Elsewhere, however, he dismissed the same evidence as being "merely calculated to deceive and mask their design."[36] Trying to hedge both bets Washington decided to hold his ground at Valley Forge while shifting forces back and forth according to the best available intelligence in order to gain both offensive and defensive advantages. He ordered William Smallwood to withdraw from Wilmington as soon as militia units were able to protect the stores at Head of Elk and to take a post halfway between the Delaware River and the American camp. To bolster the security of the army he briefly ordered three regiments of cavalry to return from New Jersey. Four days later he countermanded the order and instead sent two more regiments of Continental infantry to New Jersey to assist in the harassment of the enemy's expected march through that state.[37]

The awkward situation in which the army found itself stemmed from its decision to allow the enemy's movements to dictate its own, and from the delays that the British were experiencing in putting their plans into motion. However humiliating Henry Clinton found it to be forced to withdraw before a foe whom he considered his inferior, he believed that he had stretched his orders to the limit by postponing the Caribbean detachments until he reached New York. Clinton found the process of disentangling his army from its garrison of eight months to be difficult and time consuming. The process of packing, moving, and loading tons of stores, baggage, and heavy ordnance took many days. The complex and emotionally difficult transfer of military authority between William Howe and Clinton further delayed the business.[38]

An additional obstacle to the British retreat was resistance from the Philadelphia Loyalist community, especially people who had helped the army to govern the city. Rightly fearing that their position would be untenable with a resumption of rebel control, those who had cooperated with the occupation struggled to overturn the decision to withdraw. That decision, made in London on the broadest considerations of the interests of empire, was not reversible, but the field commanders could not overlook entirely the plight of their civilian allies. On the eve of his departure William Howe advised prominent Philadelphia Loyalists to make private arrangements with the rebel leaders. Clinton refused to allow such negotiations for fear of discouraging Loyalists in New York and interfering with the peace negotiations. It was therefore necessary to offer any local Loyalists who felt jeopardized by the army's withdrawal transportation to New York. This expedient greatly complicated the logistical difficulty of the retreat and probably tipped the balance in favor of an overland route across New Jersey.[39]

As was the case throughout the winter, the situation between the lines both reflected and influenced developments at the headquarters of the two armies. The desire of the British to conceal and to prepare for their retreat to New York and the increasing ability of the American army to operate in the field combined to enlarge the scope of contacts between the two sides. As this conflict intensified, the blurring of distinct zones of territorial responsibility that had characterized American tactics all winter continued. This was especially so of the division of Continental and militia spheres along the Schuylkill River. If by April that division had become a convenient fiction, in May even the fiction was all but dispensed with. After a brief respite in March while British raiders focused in New Jersey, April brought renewed pressure north and northwest of Philadelphia. This offensive culminated on May 1 with a devastating predawn attack, spearheaded by Robert Simcoe's corps of Queen's American Rangers, on John Lacey's camp near the Crooked Billet Tavern. The raid sharply revealed the handicaps Lacey had operated under all winter, including inaccurate intelligence, careless sentries, and poorly trained, partially committed troops. It cost him half his meager force and ultimately his command.[40]

Simcoe's attack disabled the Pennsylvania militia for the season. Most of the ambushed party—many of whom had arrived in camp the night before—received their first taste of combat that morning. Even for a partisan war, theirs was an unusually brutal baptism. Accounts from both sides agreed that some victims were burned to death, and American witnesses insisted that wounded men were bayoneted and thrown into heaps of burning straw. Survivors who did not flee were rendered into an even more timid and ineffective force than the state had fielded during the winter. Simcoe boasted that the mission "had its full effect, of intimidating the militia, as they never afterwards appeared, but in small parties, and like robbers."[41]

The attack, which Washington had dreaded all winter, left him with little choice but to continue expanding the scope of Continental responsibility. On May 7 he sent a detachment under Brigadier General William Maxwell across the Schuylkill. This detachment had an open-ended mission and Maxwell had an implicit degree of authority over the militia in the district. He was ordered to see to the security of the main camp; to disrupt communications between Philadelphia and the countryside; to gather intelligence; and to work with the militia to suppress enemy scouting patrols, cover the market people, and harass any British parties that came forward to challenge him. He was also directed to investigate the catastrophe that the militia had suffered, to guard against similar surprises to his own men, and to restrain his troops from abusing civilians.[42]

Washington also worked harder to implement personnel changes designed to prevent the complete collapse of the militia. He urged John Armstrong to resume the command he had resigned the previous fall, but he was pleased enough when General James Potter agreed to take the field. In notifying John Lacey of his replacement Washington acknowledged that his task "must have been fatiguing, considering the smallness of your numbers and the constant motion which you have consequently been obliged to be in." He asked Lacey to remain in the field to reacquaint Potter with the locality and to familiarize him with reliable guides and intelligence sources. He again raised with Pennsylvania authorities the delicate question of their commitment to keep militia troops east of the Schuylkill, an issue he had largely dropped in mid-winter. Yielding to the reality of the state's weak position, he asked it to maintain at least 400 men in the district rather than the 1,000 previously agreed to.[43]

Throughout the winter, any Continental involvement east of the Schuylkill had inevitably reduced the protection of the army on the more vulnerable west side of that river. Washington had thus avoided it as much as possible, even when faced with the dismal performance of the militia.

When it was unavoidable he carefully tailored its scope and duration to the security needs of the army. Troops were kept constantly along roads paralleling the Schuylkill but were sent into the interior only to forage, gather supplies, or protect the northern supply line. This tradeoff remained in place in May, but in diminished degree. The arrival of reinforcements, the improvement in the army's health, and the purchase of new clothing made it possible to keep more troops on detachment. The progress of the fortification work and of Steuben's exercises made the camp a more formidable bastion. The revitalization of the Quartermaster's Department improved the army's ability to retreat before an attacking foe. The geographical ignorance that had made Washington reluctant to disperse his forces had been substantially reduced by winter-long surveying work. The network of small mobile parties operating west of the Schuylkill between the camp and the city kept that area under observation but not pacified. The lower or eastern part of Chester County remained, for Whigs at least, a kind of no man's land. A county militia lieutenant warned the state government that the area's Tories were well armed and were "learning the military exercise." In late May, when it seemed that the British might move against the camp, Washington ordered the Wilmington garrison to move into the area to bolster the defensive screen.[44]

In the meantime, it became clear that the principal area of contention would be north and northwest of Philadelphia. On May 7 a battalion of British light infantry moved by boat up the Delaware to attack state and Continental shipping on both sides of that river between Bristol and Bordentown. General Maxwell was ordered to oppose the raid, but he had no artillery and was unable to offer effective resistance to the intruders. The raiders destroyed forty vessels and burned many houses and storage buildings at Bordentown, but their overall military impact was slight. For the local population the episode merely added another item to the grim catalogue of miseries and alarms that the erratically shifting conflict had imposed during the winter.[45]

The expedition did, however, briefly distort and weaken the distribution of American forces east of the Schuylkill and jeopardize an important detachment of Continental troops. The alarm on the Delaware drew Maxwell's detachment toward the river with some of the parties that had been patrolling the roads near Germantown and Chestnut Hill. The result was a gap in the army's security network near the Schuylkill that the militia, wallowing in the trauma of the Crooked Billet episode, was unable to fill. On May 18 Washington ordered the Marquis de Lafayette to lead between

2,000 and 3,000 troops across the Schuylkill with orders similar to those that Maxwell had carried. He reminded Lafayette that the force he led was a "very valuable one," the loss of which would constitute a "severe blow" to the army. He therefore instructed him to keep the party in motion and always to leave a way open to rejoin the army.[46]

The occasion offered the young general his first independent command of the war and an opportunity to recoup some of the honors that had slipped away when the Canadian "Irruption" was aborted in February. On reaching Barren Hill northwest of Chestnut Hill, however, Lafayette displayed an alarming lack of familiarity with the area and its inhabitants. He wisely called on Allen McLane, the most experienced field officer in the area, for information. He wanted to know whether local residents believed there would be a market in the city the next day, and especially whether people living near the British lines knew that his detachment had entered the area.[47]

If the inhabitants did not know, the British commanders did. To protect the *Meschianza*—an elaborate pageant staged by the officers to bid farewell to the departing William Howe—from American attempts to disrupt it, General Clinton had bolstered his patrols along all roads leading to the city, and American movements were known at the British headquarters. Lafayette also ignored Washington's injunction against taking a stationary position. On reaching Barren Hill he halted his force and sent scouting parties toward the city. On the evening of May 19 Clinton detached between 5,000 and 6,000 troops under Major General James Grant. The party marched north on Old York Road, then turned northwest in an effort to get behind Lafayette's detachment. Early on the twentieth, Howe followed with almost 6,000 more troops, proceeding directly up the Germantown Road with the hope of trapping Lafayette's party.

The surprise foundered mainly because of the difficulty of moving so many troops with any degree of secrecy. Lafayette's scouts spread the alarm before Grant's column could encircle the Americans and well before Howe arrived to contest the American retreat.[48] Lafayette extricated his party by wading it back over the Schuylkill at Matson's Ford. Evaluations of the episode varied predictably according to the source. Americans spoke of a "brilliant," a "glorious," or at least a "timely and handsome" retreat by Lafayette. British observers, in contrast, attributed the outcome to the desertion of several soldiers who warned of the maneuver, to Grant's "overly cautious" movement, to the difficulty of finding roads in the darkness, and finally, in plain frustration, to Washington's "usual good fortune."[49]

After Barren Hill, Washington reverted to his previous policy of limiting the scope of Continental activities beyond the camp to small, mobile parties. William Maxwell remained east of the Schuylkill. His orders, however, reiterated the injunction to keep his troops in motion along the roads leading to Philadelphia and stressed the paramount object of avoiding ambushes. A party of Continental cavalry that had been sent from Trenton to cooperate with Lafayette was ordered to remain there to assist Allen McLane. Although Brigadier General Charles Scott led a small party of regular troops across the Schuylkill, in response to an alarm on May 23 warning of yet another British excursion, Lafayette's aborted mission was the last significant Continental venture into the treacherous district east of the Schuylkill before the army's departure from Valley Forge.[50]

Whereas Continental involvement east of the Schuylkill was intermittent and hesitating, in New Jersey it ballooned rapidly after May 1. The British army turned its attention back toward Pennsylvania after its April forays into New Jersey, but it left behind intensifying civil conflict. Howe sent frequent detachments across the Delaware to seize supplies or to terrorize Whigs. The result was an increase in Tory violence and new calls for Continental protection. When two British regiments landed at Cooper's Ferry, Colonel Israel Shreve, already on detachment with a regiment of New Jersey regulars, found his forces outmatched and asked Washington for assistance. Washington ordered another regiment of New Jersey Continentals to cross the Delaware and promised the state's militia commander more assistance as soon as possible.[51]

Thereafter, the Continental and militia forces in New Jersey for the most part held their own against scattered outbreaks of British violence and sometimes even drove back enemy thrusts. From several points along the Delaware they monitored the British preparations to evacuate Philadelphia. Washington reinforced the Continental regiments there by letting Shreve annex recruits from West Jersey passing through the area on their way to camp. By late May Shreve reported that the situation was substantially under control. The British had ceased night patrols and withdrawn their piquets toward their redoubts at Cooper's Ferry. In response to this tactical retreat, Tories near Billingsport were again submitting to local civil authority, and trade with the city, which had begun to slacken earlier in the month, nearly ceased altogether.[52]

By this time Washington viewed the presence of a strong Continental force in New Jersey as a valuable impediment to the impending enemy retreat. He regretted his inability to send more troops from camp to that state. When he was convinced that Clinton would take an overland route to New York, Washington ordered William Maxwell to take two regiments from Bucks County join Shreve. Maxwell was directed to take command of all Continental forces in New Jersey and to rally the militia to retard the enemy's retreat by "hanging on their flanks and rear, breaking down Bridges over the Creeks in their route, blocking up the roads by falling trees and by every other method that can be devised."[53]

Thus the desire of New Jersey's civil authorities to have the state's entire brigade of Continental troops devoted to its own defense was belatedly fulfilled. This disparate sequence of troop movements and countermovements converged into a coherent strategic pattern. It was never articulated in the records of the event, however, and becomes visible only by reference to the earlier deployment of forces. The crescent-shaped configuration of American troops in the region remained intact until the eve of the British march from Philadelphia. The movements depicted above comprised a stuttering rotation of that configuration around an axis centered in Philadelphia. The left wing of the crescent, which in January hinged to the Delaware River at Trenton, was by late May anchored by Shreve's regiment and Maxwell's brigade between Mount Holly and Haddonfield, New Jersey. Its center was roughly described by the camp at Valley Forge and by its shifting areas of operations on either side of the Schuylkill.

The ultimate effect of this rotation was to tear the crescent loose from its southern anchor. As early as May 17 Washington considered recalling the Maryland division from Wilmington. The return of these troops would give him a "large compact body or regulars" and offset the increasing numbers of regiments being sent to New Jersey.[54] The sticking point remained the security of the army's stores at Head of Elk. When Maryland Governor Thomas Johnson responded with a favorable estimate of the state's ability to protect the stores, Washington ordered Smallwood to fall back into the countryside and be ready to make a hurried march to Valley Forge. Two days later he directed that one brigade be sent directly to camp while Smallwood took the second to Chads Ford, from which point he could cover Head of Elk or rejoin the army within a day.[55] With this decision the army's anchor on the Delaware River below Philadelphia was severed and the rotation of the Continental defensive configuration was nearly complete. Smallwood delayed his departure for several days in order to finish removing stores and to observe British ship movements on the Delaware. By May 29 he had moved his division to

Pennsbury Township in Chester County, near Chads Ford, on the supply line to Valley Forge from Head of Elk and approximately equidistant from both places.[56]

Thus poised, the army waited for more than two weeks for the signal to march. The departure was regularly reported to be imminent, often on an "hourly" basis. Despite Washington's well-known prohibition of gaming in the ranks, a series of pools and wagers sprung up, with large sums of money and many fine "Beaver Hatts" hanging on the date of the British departure.[57] This informal lottery reflected the more serious dialogue that continued at headquarters over the enemy's real intentions. The debate revolved around the question of whether or not to expect a British attack before they abandoned Pennsylvania.[58] Some members of Congress supported Henry Laurens's view that "flimsy assurances" of a British retreat should not be relied upon. Washington was increasingly inclined to believe that Clinton would march his army overland to New York City without a fight. As late as June 15, however, he acknowledged that the contrary opinion was "worthy of attention."[59]

American anxieties about the mode of the British withdrawal and the possible threat it posed were basically groundless. The main reason for the delay was the arrival in Philadelphia on June 6 of the peace commissioners who had come to offer Congress the "Conciliation Bills" passed by Parliament in February. Despite Henry Clinton's dismay at having to retreat before an enemy he considered inferior, he intended to obey his orders. He decided to go by land because he believed it necessary to ensure the security of New York. Although he expected to meet American resistance in New Jersey, Clinton estimated he could reach New York within ten days, whereas a sea route might delay the army indefinitely.[60]

The delay, though irritating and anxiety producing, was not an untimely occurrence for the Americans. Preparations continued at a frantic pace, all of them more easily performed from a stationary camp than along the road. It was not even certain that each soldier would have a musket until a shipment of 2,000 arms arrived from New England on June 6, after which there were still severe shortages of ammunition canisters. As late as June 18 the clothiers were scrambling to find enough shoes to furnish all of the regiments. Each day brought more recruits and drafts to fill understrength units. Although Washington remained unhappy with the pace of reinforcement, the influx of troops strained the ability of the support departments to supply them. One commissary officer, struggling to find enough beef, exclaimed that he wished the "Devil had blown [the enemy] to California rather than New Jersey."[61]

The June 9 arrival of the first brigade of Maryland troops from Wilmington effectively burst the boundaries of the camp at Valley Forge. The growth of the army and the cumulative environmental damage from six months of intensive occupation spurred a decision to abandon the ground and to move the troops into tents nearby. In addition to safeguarding the army's precariously restored health, the move provided for a graduated transition from a stationary to a field deployment. It was accomplished with relatively little difficulty on June 10, with the troops marching across Sullivan's Bridge and setting up tents approximately one mile northeast of the Schuylkill River in Providence Township. Work parties were sent back to the old camp to clean the area and to bury debris, while functionaries, such as the paymaster and the auditor, were ordered to move their offices from local houses into abandoned huts in order to remain convenient to the troops.[62]

The most important result of the delayed British departure was that it gave Washington an opportunity to address the problems presented by Congress's last-minute approval of resolves about the army's new "establishment" or organizational structure. After approving half-pay pensions on May 15, the delegates at York moved with reasonable alacrity to finish work on the establishment. The resolutions—passed between May 27 and June 2— regularized the size and structure of infantry, artillery, and cavalry units; provided rules for the selection of individuals for staff department positions; and attacked the longstanding problem of officers' rations. They constituted an important first step toward standardizing the conditions of army service. Washington reserved the right to recommend further regulations, but he was happy to get any definitive response from Congress. His chief problem lay in the lack of time to implement the measures before the the campaign began. His repeated warnings that little could be done once the army returned to the field would soon be tested by events.[63]

The resolves were published verbatim in general orders on June 7, and army members were enjoined to become familiar with their provisions and to govern their behavior accordingly. Saying so, alas, would not make it so. Congress tried to mitigate the problem by sending Joseph Reed and Francis Dana of the Conference Committee back to camp to advise and assist Washington in implementing the reforms. As a practical matter, however, little could be done other than to improvise solutions as specific problems arose.[64]

The troublesome consequences of this approach soon became apparent. Having received neither Congress's approval nor disapproval of his request that three lieutenant generals be appointed, Washington designated his three most senior major generals to act in that capacity during marches or in battle. In all other situations the army's regular divisional structure would be maintained.

This arrangement, made in response to "misunderstandings" among the major generals, brought an aggrieved remonstrance from newly restored division commander Charles Lee, who objected to the practice of shifting commands as contrary to good military order. This allowed Washington to articulate his own frustration at the difficulty of implementing piecemeal reforms. Agreeing with Lee in principal, Washington testily observed that "Heaven and my own Letters to Congress can Witness, on the one hand, how ardently I have laboured to effect these points during the past Winter and Spring. The Army on the other, bear witness to the effect. Suspended between the old and new establishment, I could govern myself by neither, with propriety." Washington concluded with the cool assertion that the expedient, which he had adopted as a "kind of medium course," would remain in effect pending instructions from Congress.[65]

A more serious problem arising from the delayed approval of the new establishment was that of defining the role of Friedrich Steuben in a fighting rather than a wintering army. Steuben's reception into the army was a remarkably amicable one, considering the disposition of his fellow officers to assert their own prerogatives and to resent rivals suspected of intruding on them. This was partly a result of the clear need for training the troops and the lack of anyone else with the skills and temperament for this exacting responsibility. As the spring progressed and Steuben's star ascended in the army hierarchy, however, signs of jealousy began to emerge.[66] There was no serious doubt about the efficacy of Steuben's work with the regiments. Two observers who were in camp during the winter but absent for much of the spring commented approvingly on their return in June on the newly "respectable" appearance they discerned in the troops' discipline. Rather, it was a question of the role the new inspector general and major general would play in the field. Trying to head off jealousies that he could see were "too apparently . . . arising" among the generals, Washington issued a complex directive that sought to delineate the powers of the inspectorship from those of the field officers. This brought a strong protest from Steuben himself, complaining of untoward restrictions on his authority.[67]

Treating Steuben more warmly than he had Lee, Washington allowed him to go to York to confer with Congress on the matter. The case raised delicate political and military questions that Washington was prudent enough to defer to public authorities. After uniting in opposition to the pretensions of Thomas Conway and in implicit support of their beleaguered commander-in-chief, the general officers had constituted a relative bedrock of stability throughout the winter, on which the fragile unity of the rest of the army had been delicately erected. The Steuben and Lee episodes suggested, on the threshold of the campaign, however, the beginnings of fine lines of fracture in that stability. Had those lines widened into open breaches, the costs of reform would have rapidly begun to outweigh the benefits.[68]

As Washington worked to devise interim solutions to unpredictable problems, Congress turned its attention to the British peace terms. Their rejection would signal the beginning of the campaign and close the season for military reforms. Before the arrival of the peace commissioners, Henry Clinton tried to proceed with the formality of offering the ministry's terms to Congress. His request to send an officer to Valley Forge for a pass to York with the proposals was refused as unnecessary and improper. These maneuvers were more a matter of protocol than of substance. Congress had received reliable printed copies of the Conciliation Bills in April, and its only debate was over how to reject them. Bowing to American unwillingness to give even the appearance of entering face-to-face negotiations, the commissioners sent Washington a packet with the bills and a letter to Congress. The issue dragged on to its foregone conclusion on June 17, when the delegates unanimously adopted a reply calling the proposals "inadmissable . . . [and] derogatory to the honor of an independent nation" and affirmed that only an "explicit acknowledgement" of independence or a withdrawal of enemy troops could bring peace.[69]

The commissioners did not wait in Philadelphia for the formal rejection of their efforts. Both armies used the delay to make final preparations for taking the field. Every night wagonloads of baggage and supplies were loaded on flat-bottomed boats and ferried across the Delaware to Cooper's Point in New Jersey. By day, various regiments were also embarked and shipped across the river. The British army made a final excursion into the countryside on June 11, when a detachment set out on an almost-ceremonial procession to Germantown. By the sixteenth, Clinton reported that only the rear guard of his "noble little army" remained in the city. Its sentries were sent to the redoubts for the final time, with the injunction not to "look upon the city any longer as their cantonment."[70]

On the American side of the lines, an increasingly buoyant if somewhat chaotic tone marked the occasion. State and Continental officials descended on Valley Forge in anticipation of an early opportunity to reenter the city. They found themselves in the company of large numbers of displaced Philadelphians who had begun "hovering around the camp" with similar hopes. The latter group, in turn, mixed uneasily with swarms of "Country Refugees" who had remained in or fled to Philadelphia during the winter. These individuals— whose actions had marked them as politically suspect in most patriot eyes— had come out, notwithstanding Henry Clinton's prohibition, to sue privately for terms of peace. In many ways, during the army's last week at Valley Forge, then, the neighborhood of the camp came to resemble—if only in symbolic microcosm—the diverse and heterogeneous Pennsylvania community disrupted and dispersed just ten months before as war moved into the state.[71]

This diverse multitude of solicitors did not provide ideal conditions for the army's preparations. It did, however, underline the fact that although the army would soon leave Pennsylvania, it would play a transitional role in restoring civilian authority to the area. In late May, the state government called Washington's attention to the danger of disorders in Philadelphia after Continental forces reentered the city. Washington promised to try to ensure order, and he directed officers commanding detachments to forbid their men to set foot in the town, but he also urged state authorities to reestablish control as rapidly as possible.[72]

Once begun, both the British evacuation of Philadelphia and the American march from Valley Forge proceeded rapidly. On June 16, Washington issued orders for the army's march toward the Hudson River. Three divisions would cross the Delaware at Coryell's Ferry, one slightly higher at Sherard's Ferry, and the last one at Easton. Washington convened a final Council of War. Summarizing the situation of both armies, he observed that the enemy might still move toward New York by land or sea and acknowledged the possibility of an attack before they left. He offered a series of options, including an immediate attack on Philadelphia, a movement either toward that city or the Delaware, further detachments to New Jersey, and an attempt to overtake and attack the enemy if they marched through that state. The council offered a wide variety of opinions, but strong majorities formed in favor of both allowing the enemy to move first and offering only cautious annoyance to their march through New Jersey.[73]

On June 18 Washington received intelligence that the British had completed their evacuation. He ordered the first two divisions, consisting of six brigades, to march toward the Delaware River that afternoon. The rest of the army would follow the next day. Benedict Arnold, who had recently rejoined the army after recovering from wounds received during his heroic service at Saratoga, was directed to proceed to Philadelphia to take command of the small Continental occupying force. These troops consisted mainly of men who had performed detached duty along the lines around the city during the spring. Washington warned Arnold of his responsibility to preserve order until civil authority was restored. Support department officials were ordered to send agents into the town to seize abandoned enemy supplies and establish public stores. As the Pennsylvania summer began, the long Valley Forge winter lurched toward its ambiguous conclusion and into the pages of myth and history.[74]

Chapter 11

THE SEATED WAR

For both armies, the road to myth and history ran straight across New Jersey. Clinton sent his heaviest military equipment with most of the German troops and perhaps 3,000 evacuating Delaware Valley Loyalists to New York with the British fleet. His main force of about 10,000 men, with their 1,500-wagon baggage train, formed a column that extended up to twelve miles along two parallel roads. The path of the British retreat lay north along the Delaware River to Allentown, near Trenton, and then across the waist of New Jersey to New Brunswick, Staten Island, and Manhattan. The less heavily encumbered Americans reached the Delaware in four days, whereas the British needed six days to march to Allentown.[1]

By June 24, the American columns had converged at Hopewell, northwest of Princeton. Washington called another Council of War, which revealed deep divisions among his generals about how aggressively the British withdrawal should be resisted. A majority, coalescing around Charles Lee, advised against attacking the enemy. A smaller group, led by Nathanael Greene and Anthony Wayne, argued for more vigorous interference. Washington, who still felt the sting of criticisms of his military performance in 1777 and whose own instincts lay with Greene and Wayne, adopted a middle course. He decided to close steadily but cautiously with the Redcoats, while looking for opportunities to strike at their vulnerable rearguard units.[2]

Clinton felt pressured by this shadowy escort. At Allentown he turned northeast toward Sandy Hook, from there his troops could be ferried safely to Manhattan by the British fleet. His column lengthened even more as the two parallel roads merged into one. General Knyphausen led 4,000 men in the front, followed by the wagons, and then by Clinton with his best 6,000 troops. The pace quickened and temperatures rose into the nineties on June 25 and 26 when the British arrived at Monmouth Court House. The terrain also flattened as the road moved onto the sandy coastal plateau. The broken landscape of scrub pine thickets and open clearings cut by swampy brooks and dry ravines hampered infantry units that tried to travel away from the main roads but favored the mounted troops on which British security relied.[3]

Both armies rested on June 27, exhausted from marching and from the heat. That day Washington decided to attempt an attack. The Americans were moving due east toward the coast, through Princeton, Cranbury, and Englishtown, homing on the enemy's left rear flank. Charles Lee at first refused the command of a vanguard of about 1,500 troops that Washington ordered forward to probe for weak spots on the British flank. When Washington increased the detachment to between 4,000 and 5,000 men, however, Lee claimed the assignment as a prerogative of his rank as the senior major general. Washington assented and ordered Lee to engage the enemy the next day. But neither general developed a specific plan of battle or made any concerted effort to scout the complex terrain over which the assault would be made.[4]

Clinton sensed the threat and ordered Knyphausen to march off with the baggage early on the morning of June 28. He posted General Cornwallis and a rear guard at Monmouth Court House and slowed his own march to be able to support those troops. Washington trailed Lee's detachment with the main part of the American army by several miles but promised to bring them up to support any action. After sunrise on the twenty-eighth, Lee moved toward Cornwallis's position and notified Washington that he expected to be able to cut off the British rear guard. His approach crossed three ravines carrying branches of the Wemrock Brook. Generals Wayne, Scott, Lafayette, and Maxwell, leading American advanced units, engaged the British troops. Clinton turned his force of 6,000 veteran troops around and raced back toward Monmouth to reinforce Cornwallis. They attacked the right wing of the poorly formed American line, which quickly began to be enveloped and to retreat. Lee ordered his troops to withdraw behind the first brook for fear that his detachment would be trapped in the ravines.[5]

Washington approached the scene of action, unaware that it involved more than a limited skirmish. As he had at Brandywine, he initially discounted reports from junior officers and civilians that the situation was deteriorating. When he reached the first ravine he saw that the American attack had unraveled. Lee was trying to form a defensible position, and he and Washington exchanged angry words over the debacle. Washington used his charismatic presence and keen battlefield sense to stop the retreat, adding his reserve force to the new defensive line.[6]

Now it was Clinton's turn to attack aggressively over tricky ground. The armies fought intermittently through the afternoon, with the British making four separate thrusts in an effort to break the ranks of the main body of the American army. The Continentals stood bravely against the more experienced Redcoats, as they had done after their near-rout at Brandywine. American artillery positions on hills flanking the British line raked the attackers and contributed substantially to driving them back. Both armies camped on the battlefield that night, and Washington hoped to resume the action the next day. Before dawn, however, Clinton marched his army toward New York. The British troops reached Sandy Hook on July 1, and for the next week they were transported across New York Harbor and back into their garrison quarters.[7]

Both sides claimed at least a partial victory at Monmouth, and the unusually complex and confusing engagement rapidly became one of the most heatedly politicized military episodes of the war. By most contemporary standards of analysis, both sides could stake their claims on plausible evidence. They temporarily shared possession of the ground disputed in the fight, and their casualty figures were roughly comparable. If Washington had the satisfaction of knowing that he had gotten in a few good licks and reminded Clinton that his army was still dangerous, Clinton could honestly inform London that he had safely executed a withdrawal to New York.[8]

The battle ended Charles Lee's military career. Still smarting over his angry exchange with Washington on the twenty-eighth, Lee reopened their dispute several days later in a series of sharp letters to the commander-in-chief. He demanded a court martial on Washington's bitter charges that he had failed to follow orders to attack the enemy; that he had conducted a "disorderly" and even a "shameful" retreat; and that he had later treated Washington disrespectfully. As John Shy has suggested, Lee was clearly innocent of the first two charges, but guilty of the third. Washington and the Congress needed an unambiguous victory at Monmouth. Lee's obvious tactical difficulties on June 28, and the fact of the dispute itself, put that objective at risk.[9]

Washington's close-knit group of young aides-de-camp, especially John Laurens and Alexander Hamilton, worked hard to interpret the engagement as a triumph for their chief's leadership marred by Lee's tactical errors. The court martial was staffed by Washington's appointees, drawn from an officer corps that had rallied around him during the previous winter. Most saw criticisms of him as being bound up with intrigues surrounding the Conway affair, and thus as representing civil and political misunderstanding of military culture at best, or of contempt for the army at worst. The court convicted Lee on all three charges and sentenced him to be suspended from the army for a year. The Congress, badly divided on partisan grounds, debated for months before voting narrowly to confirm a modified verdict and the sentence.[10]

These circumstances make it especially difficult to use the battle as a retrospective lens into the army's experience at Valley Forge. In popular lore and even some scholarly accounts, Monmouth provides the "proof of the forge"; a test under harsh field conditions of how three months of careful drilling by Steuben—combined with the American soldier's raw courage and resilience—transformed a human horde into a real army.[11] The battle simply was not sustained enough to carry such an evidentiary burden. Most of the fighting before Washington met Lee behind the first ravine was of the desperate and improvisational kind that had typified the army's experience since late 1776. Continentals showed the same virtues as before: they were not afraid to attack their enemies boldly under a variety of ambiguous circumstances, and they fought back stubbornly even when they were being mauled by a stronger force.

After Washington formed a defensible line and the British became the attacking party, splayed across ravined terrain, the Americans had somewhat the better of the action. During the afternoon they may have employed some of the formal lessons that Steuben had taught them. Alexander Hamilton observed that before Monmouth, he had never "known or conceived the value of military discipline," but Hamilton's role as one of Washington's main apologists puts his reliability into a problematic light. Although Steuben played little direct part in those aspects of the battle that set Washington and Lee at odds, his role in the army itself was critical to Washington's vision of a conventional European fighting machine. Lee, by contrast, had advocated turning the Americans into a partisan force based in the interior.[12]

Even if we accept, for argument's sake, that American late-day momentum and the British retreat under cover of dark tipped the balance of honors in favor of the former, we might credit that outcome as much to terrain as to training. There has also been little explicit attention given to the effect of American flanking artillery fire on the British charges, which was perhaps the determining element at day's end. If so, we should recall that the artillerists—a group of fractious, individualistic technocrats—may have spent less time on the Grand Parade at Valley Forge after Steuben arrived than any troops in the army. In the final analysis, it is not entirely clear that the men who extracted themselves from the jaws of destruction at Brandywine in 1777, and then went back for more at Germantown three weeks later, would have fared much worse at Monmouth if Steuben had spurned Congress's commission and returned to Europe. What is clear is that the general officers—beginning prominently with Washington himself—still had at least as much to learn about how to effectively use their increasingly complex military machine as Continental privates did about how to maneuver around on the field of battle.

More important, for our purposes, is the fact that Monmouth was effectively the last general engagement between the two sides in the north. Henry Clinton went to ground on Manhattan in mid-1778. By the end of the year he made detachments for service in the Caribbean and in the lower south. The effect of the changes in British strategy was to drain energy from the northern front. After Monmouth Washington marched his troops back to the Hudson Valley and established his headquarters at White Plains, noting with irony that nearly two years of campaigning had left both sides virtually where they had begun.

Clinton often considered sallying forth against Washington, and he launched a few coastal raids in Connecticut and modest probes into New Jersey and the lower Hudson Valley. But the ministry's inability to supply him with more troops kept these initiatives limited. Washington likewise often longed to meet his adversary in open battle, and several times he drew up plans for an assault on New York City. But he could never establish the required degrees of trust in, or levels of rapport with, the French commanders and admirals who cruised the North American coast between the West Indies and New England, whose cooperation he needed to translate those designs into a concrete strategy. Like Clinton, Washington had either to make small detachments to the south or, more often, to forego potential reinforcements so that new armies could be raised for service in that region. Some of his most trusted generals, especially Nathanael Greene in 1781, were sent to the southern states to manage campaigns there.[13]

Although the long-term dynamics of the war may have deprived the army of a chance to prove its mettle in conventional combat situations, we can still try to assess the military effects of Valley Forge. Washington's wry observation in July 1778 that he was back on the same ground he had occupied in October 1776 was a rhetorical commonplace, based on a literal reading of geography. In reality, his "new" army of early 1777 was returning to its mountainous New Jersey birthplace, tempered by its trials on the rich alluvial plains (and in the chaotic political cauldron) of southeastern Pennsylvania. American forces now perched around yet another occupied city, in another awkward, misshapen crescent, this one at least twice as long in circumference as the one they had maintained along the Delaware.

The comparative anatomy of those deployments is ungainly to envision, but it will still be useful to try to imagine it. The regional backbone after 1778 was not the scrawny Schuylkill River, but instead the lordly Hudson, more than a mile wide in some places and navigable by British warships as far north as the rugged Highlands. Southwestern Connecticut and lower Westchester County replaced Bucks County as the left wing of the Continental crescent. Connecticut was, like Bucks, at best a middling granary, but more important, a major supplier of beef cattle and garden crops to the American troops. Also like Bucks, Connecticut was of necessity left largely to the protection of its own militia. That force was, by longstanding historical and cultural circumstances, considerably more energetic and engaged with the war than its fledgling Pennsylvania counterpart had been, but it was equally hard pressed to keep enough troops in the field and vulnerable to regular British forces whenever they came out. Westchester was, like the lower parts of Bucks County, a haven for armed Loyalist militias and a no-man's-land for rebels.[14] The right wing of the Continental position around New York was anchored at the mouth of the Raritan River near Perth Amboy. Washington could not afford to permanently garrison that site, as he had Wilmington, but it served much the same role by monitoring British naval traffic into and out of New York Harbor. Long Island, meanwhile, became an oddly contorted counterpart to southern New Jersey in 1777–78—cut off from effective Continental succor behind the British stronghold in New York City and a place where Whigs were usually left to their own devices.[15]

The hearth of the main army was in the rugged terrain of the Appalachian foothills, from the Hudson Highlands above West Point through the Ramapo Mountains to the old cantonments at Morristown. The

regiments shifted along this arc—through the middle third of the crescent—between 1778 and 1783, according to strategic needs. They did much
soldiering but relatively little real fighting, and almost none of the kind that
specifically required the skills practiced on their brigade or parade grounds
at Valley Forge. By fall 1778, Washington learned how to better utilize
whatever militia troops he could extract from regional civilian authorities
and his own forces in effective support of each other. A continuous, low-
grade partisan war, largely pitting American militia detachments against
armed Loyalist units, infested the near-hinterland of New York City,
between the British garrison and Washington's camps. Its dynamics resem-
bled those of the Valley Forge winter, but the army was less intensely
engaged than it had been in 1778. Washington used small Continental
detachments in support of the state troops whenever it seemed both feasible
and useful, but he tried to keep his own men out of harm's way as much as
possible.[16]

The relatively equal division of civil authority among three different
state governments might have complicated the politics of these decisions,
but in practice that circumstance probably helped to diffuse them. Washington had good relationships with Governors William Livingston of New Jersey, George Clinton of New York, and Jonathan Trumbull of Connecticut.
He was never tempted to use the army as a surrogate for civil legitimacy
around New York, as he had reluctantly done at Philadelphia, and he was
under little pressure to do so. Whatever protection Washington could afford
these states was paid for by the militia cooperation that they now competed
to offer him. New Jersey and Connecticut had fairly stable internal politics,
with regimes reasonably continuous from before the war. New York had
experienced an internal revolution only somewhat less turbulent than the
one raging in Pennsylvania. Its Whig government operated in similar exile
from its traditional seat of power at Manhattan, but its political institutions
and geography had been so fully disarranged by the war, and by the presence
at its heart of the British headquarters force, that few held unrealistic hopes
that they might be restored with a little more help from the army.[17]

The main threat to Continental security around New York thus came
neither from war nor from revolution—nor, as in Pennsylvania, from the vir-
ulent combination of the two phenomena—but in many ways from just the
opposite circumstance. It was the absence of manifest war and the ambiguous or almost suspended status of the Revolution that challenged Continental soldiers. The army had to be kept intact and maintained at moderate

levels of vigilance to keep violence in check in the region. Its absence might tempt the British to ravage the hinterland or send reinforcements southward. But its reduced activity levels militated against preparedness. Apathy, war weariness, corruption, and resignation defined the public mood as the war shifted south and toward the sea. No comprehensive account of this "dull period" in the north has been written, but its highlights are familiar. Attention has been paid to the civil and social costs of British coastal raiding in Connecticut; to the impact on revolutionary morale of Benedict Arnold's 1780 treason; to abortive mutinies in the Continental line; and to the demobilization crises of 1783. But the specific ways in which these complex phenomena interacted in the popular imagination, and their effects on public policy, are more obscure.[18]

We can at least speculate about how the army weathered these and related storms, many of them internal to its own structure and culture but others enmeshed with the surrounding society. The years after 1778 flattened most of the presumed operational distinctions between active campaigning and winter encampments. The summer months surely quickened the organizational metabolism of army life, just as the cold season reduced military activity levels, but to a much smaller degree than had been foreseen when the long-term force was being assembled in 1777. As Washington and his generals envisioned the situation during that year, when they debated the army's winter "disposition," soldiers might be either quiescent and retired in the off-season, or else more actively engaged with the enemy and local civilians. These were the very poles they invoked when they chose between "recruiting" the army and "covering the country" as tactical goals. But whichever option they preferred, they expected the spring to bring much higher levels of military activity. Decisions taken in London the next winter, however, orphaned these premises for the northern states, where the main armies stayed as the war went south. This put Washington's broad military reform agenda and Steuben's careful work with the troops on the parade ground to very different kinds of tests from those that their authors had anticipated.

The winter of 1777–78 forged a temporal—and especially a spatial—template for the rest of the war in the north. Although it offers few compelling anecdotal materials for morality tales to inspire school children, the army's experience at Valley Forge (including its drilling by Steuben) schooled its members less for withstanding bayonet charges or countering enemy flanking attacks than for the timeless imperatives of military life embodied in the private's cynical aphorism about his orders to "hurry up and wait." At Morristown and Middle Brook in New Jersey; at West Point and New Windsor in New York; at Reading in Connecticut, and at other, smaller, temporary bivouacs, soldiers became increasingly adept in the life-ways of what may be called ramshackle village living. Some became better hut builders, as bitter and milder winters alternated during the late 1770s and early 1780s. Others continued to refine and elaborate on Steuben's drills, both for their operational utility in case the British ever came out of New York or Washington decided to invade that city, and also perhaps for the sheer enjoyment of the exercise itself. When camp life became too much with them, some troops took self-granted leaves to enjoy the liberty of the neighborhood; others tried to spend as much time as possible on detach-ment. By learning to be competent in one aspect of their profession—even if they had few actual occasions to practice it—soldiers began to tolerate, if not always to enjoy, military routines that could not be dispensed with and that kept the army itself in existence.[19]

If his soldiers learned to embrace discipline—or its less glamorous concomitant, routine—Washington grew more realistic about how tightly the strings of either phenomenon could be drawn. Indeed, one important effect of the army's drilling on the parade ground at Valley Forge may have been to redefine his rhetorical linkages between the terms "dissolve" and "disperse." As the war went on and the national economy weakened, the army's ability to recruit or retain members declined. Its size peaked as troops either had to be shifted to the southern states or else new ones raised there at the expense of the main army. Divisions were thinly stretched around a much longer operational perimeter than in Pennsylvania. Occasional bouts of near starvation added ecological imperatives (as they had in 1777–78) to the tac-tical reasons for widely distributing the remaining troops across the New York region.[20]

The result was weakly nucleated, loosely jointed disposition that kept soldiers in close and unsupervised contact with civilians in ways that were sometimes more benign but often no more salubrious than they had been at Valley Forge. As the war ebbed in the north, citizens tired of what little there was of it, and the soldiers enjoyed less tacit esteem from members of the middling or better "sorts" in the civilian population than had accompa-nied the *rage militaire* of 1775–76. But the large amounts of time on the troops' hands, the porous membrane between their camps and their regional host communities, and the diminishing intensity or lethality of the contest, promoted various kinds of subterranean intercourse. Much of this traffic was commercial, sexual, or political, as well as purely military. Soldiers found sweethearts among the army's neighbors or boarded with farmers and exchanged labor for goods and services to supplement their meager salaries. Civilian camp followers—who had been strictly regulated earlier in the war, when the armies were regularly engaged and public morale or regard for the army's reputation seemed more critical and more redeemable—became more brazenly visible.[21]

As the army became a more alien presence on the American landscape to many citizens, it also emerged, in the evocative words of one historian, as "one of America's great spectacles, which people went out of their way to see." Charles Royster has persuasively documented the psychological and political rift between the army and its sustaining society, which opened at Valley Forge and widened steadily during the rest of the war. After the American victory at Yorktown in 1781, while statesmen negotiated treaties that most citizens perceived as ratifying the impending triumph of independence, many Continental officers and some politically articulate civilians wrangled publicly not just over material issues like military pensions, but also over the question of who deserved credit for the outcome of the war itself.[22]

This division was a very real and a crucially important one on both an institutional and an ideological level, but to isolate it obscures important social dynamics of the end of the Revolution. Some of the most bitter of the American officers contemplated taking the Revolution itself hostage in 1783, by refusing to disband or by threatening to lead the army into the mountainous interior. This shocking step might at the very least have invited the British to remain in America after the fighting ended, punishing American civilians both for opposing military pensions and for begrudging the army credit for the American victory. The scheme failed unequivocally because officers were divided and ambivalent about it, because Washington strongly resisted it, and ultimately, because the Continental privates would have refused to take part in it. That refusal stemmed not just from their understandable desire to return to their homes and get on with their lives, as Royster rightly suggests, but also from the fact that many of them had already begun to be reabsorbed into civil society—by their fraternization with some of the least of its members—during the last years of the war.[23]

Somewhat more complicated, because of the breadth of the subject and the indefinite temporal frame within by it might be addressed, is the question of the broader impacts of the Valley Forge episode on the Delaware Valley civilians and communities who hosted two armies. These may be best understood in different categories, by their immediacy, scope of effects, and transient or durable character. The *immediate* impacts of the occupation at the individual level should be apparent, expressed in terms of the hundreds of civilians killed or wounded; the thousands of families who had property seized, damaged, or destroyed by one or both of the invading armies; or the many thousands more who were watched, pursued, detained, searched, or fired upon on the lonely highways of the Philadelphia hinterland. Occupied Pennsylvania was a dangerous and demoralizing place to be for many civilians and an exhilarating one for others. By the same token, it is unrealistic to expect that an episode of only nine months' duration—however dramatic or traumatic—would have deep, long-term, social-structural or macroeconomic effects. The onset of industrialization was not delayed, deflected, or advanced in the Delaware Valley by even half a decade by the occupation, nor did farmers begin planting new kinds of crops, nor did changes in the patterns of birth, death, marriage, or inheritance appear because of this episode.

It is rather at the *intermediate* level of impact—between the individually tangible and the societally transformative—that we can attempt to measure the Valley Forge experience. The Continental Army, by mid-1778, could claim at least some credit for helping to stabilize the internal revolution in Pennsylvania. It may seem self-evident that if the army had been decisively crushed at Brandywine, the radical government that seized power the year before might have been driven from office. But any of an array of other plausible scenarios might also have sent the locality in very different directions. If Washington had pounced on the dazed and sea-weary British troops as they struggled ashore at Head of Elk in late August 1777, and by a fortunate Trenton-style stroke persuaded the cautious and fickle William Howe to retreat to New York to assist General Burgoyne's march toward Albany, the Continental Army would have quickly retraced its steps into New Jersey. The resulting reprise of the transient civilian panic of late 1776—followed by another interval of precarious and illusory security— might have provoked Pennsylvania's moderate and radical Whig factions to clash violently over their constitution. If the army had retired toward the Susquehanna Valley in late 1777, as a majority of its general officers desired, it could still have protected the state and Continental governments but probably only at the cost of alienating the region's backcountry citizens. And, as the prevailing dissenters in Washington's straw poll of early December warned, British forces would have had more time and opportunities to organize their followers and to abuse patriot citizens in eastern Pennsylvania. If Washington had executed his "Intended Orders" for a Christmas attack on Philadelphia, he might have gratified his critics in Lancaster and induced timid Whigs to rise up against their foes, only to abandon them when that adventure almost certainly failed.

These counterfactual scenarios would have had disparate, specific effects on the revolutionary dynamic, but they all would have intensified the adverse impacts of the conjunction of war and revolution on Pennsylvanians. Such scenarios might be multiplied and juxtaposed indefinitely. They require us to rearrange more of the obdurate historical record than seems justifiable, even in a speculative concluding survey. But they all suggest the degree to which decisions that major institutional actors make in the course of events of this magnitude, complexity, and duration fundamentally matter; albeit often in ways that their principle figures can only barely discern.

Measured by their own goals and intentions, the choices that American revolutionary agents made in Pennsylvania in 1777–78 were probably for the most part appropriate ones. Washington was correct to override his reservations about keeping his army in the field during the winter, but he was also wise to revert quickly to cautious form by refusing to be swept along by his political concessions to Pennsylvania toward their logical tactical ends. By taking an awkward position in the "middle foreground" between Philadelphia and the vital organs of revolutionary government, and making earnest but pragmatically limited—and often little more than symbolic—efforts to uphold revolutionary order there, he slowly fixed on his foes the burdens of apparent ascendancy. Unable to rapidly shatter Howe's vision of the Delaware Valley as an ideal place to rally "well-affected" colonials and end the rebellion, Washington contrived gradually to smother that dream. This slow and in some ways almost fortuitous outcome had effects on Pennsylvania and its diverse inhabitants different from those that any of the above contingencies would have produced. During the winter it was the king's wary friends in the community—not the rebels—who were regularly tempted to risk disclosing their allegiance by behaviorally committing themselves to the enemy. When the British fleet sailed down the Delaware River in June 1778, it withdrew from the polity several thousand of its most alienated members. Many of them abandoned large amounts of property and took away vast stores of practical political experience. The exigencies of the Revolution in Pennsylvania before 1777 had effectively precluded most of them from using either of those resources, but they were still members of the polity, and their presence in it always had important shaping effects on revolutionary politics.

The removal from Pennsylvania of its strictest pacifists and active Loyalists created more political space for varieties of Whigs. Radicals and moderates were now freed from the pressing need to protect each other to avoid catastrophe, but they were also able to oppose each other in more complex and less categorical ways. Philadelphia's politics were immediately radicalized in the wake of the British retreat. The worst ravages of the occupation had occurred there, and both the rapid return of leading Pennsylvania radicals and the presence there of Continental Army officers like Benedict Arnold, who saw their roles as including intervention in domestic politics, quickly made the city a cockpit of internal conflict. Property confiscation began in the city almost as soon as the British left. A series of treason trials during fall 1778 resulted in the acquittal or pardoning of a large number of accused collaborators—often after only token punishments—but also in the controversial hanging of two respected Quakers.[24]

The Pennsylvania polity as a whole, however, swung slightly to the right in the six months after the British occupation ended. Moderates increased their strength in the Assembly, while the death of President Thomas Wharton in May 1778 and his replacement by George Bryan solidified the hold of radicals on the executive branch. Revolutionaries of both persuasions came to see the existing machinery of government as being temporarily legitimate, or at least as being preferable to armed occupation. In November 1778 both sides agreed to a compromise that moderated the punitive "Test Act" passed by the radicals that April. They also agreed to a statewide referendum in March 1779 to decide whether a new constitutional convention should be held. Diehard radicals killed both compromises—by flooding the Assembly with petitions in February 1779 demanding that the convention not be held, and then by voting to reimpose the stringent oaths. But to an important degree both sides were now, however grudgingly or temporarily, bringing their conflicts within a known framework of existing rules.[25]

In the early winter of 1779, both radicals and moderates began to rationalize and then to institutionalize their internal political organization to operate effectively within that arena. In February the moderates created the "Republican Society," using that name both to coopt many prevailing ideological symbols of the revolutionary generation and to brand their foes as being beyond the pale of respectable political thought. The radicals responded by forming the "Constitutional Society," by which name they tried implicitly to monopolize not merely an abstract body of salient political ideas, but rather all of the legitimate governing space then available in Pennsylvania. This indulgence in name games continued the totalizing approach to revolutionary politics that most Whig leaders had practiced since the overthrow of the old Assembly. But in spite of their rhetorical strategies, many Pennsylvania Whigs were now retrofitting their political behavior onto vestigial traditions in their native state of limited-but-legitimate public competition for power. These were in fact the same customs that had developed in the colony two generations before, when the Quakers realized that in order to hold power as a minority of the population they would have to seek it, to exercise it, and sometimes even to share it through popularly acceptable institutional structures and procedures.[26]

The fluctuating battle for control of Pennsylvania's government in the 1780s involved an implicit contest by both sides to appropriate the moral legacy and the methodological regime of the old "quakerized" provincial political system. The radicals (now called "Constitutionalists") won the first part of this contest and emerged as the heirs to the founding generation of Pennsylvania Quakers as embattled-but-effective visionaries. They projected their support for the reform of the electoral machinery, proportional representation in the Assembly, and the inclusion of all loyal white men in the institutions of power as the moral face of the Revolution in Pennsylvania. Moreover, they protected their constitution with surprising effectiveness under sustained resistance for most of the decade after the war.[27] But the moderates (now called "Republicans") seized the mantle of second and third generation Quakers, those who had worked pragmatically but relentlessly to build effective popular coalitions. Starting with a narrow Assembly majority in 1780, they shed the Constitutionalist epithet of crypto-Tory "aristocrats" who were indifferent to the welfare of their fellow citizens and persuaded many Pennsylvania voters that they stood for the common good. The parties battled back and forth in the mid-1780s—each winning about as many electoral seats—and shared power alternately in the Assembly. But the Republicans began to make significant inroads with the radical constituency in the artisan community of Philadelphia and its surrounding counties, whose members slowly concluded that they would better protect their entrepreneurial interests. The Constitutional party was gradually stripped down to its original, and by now apparently irreducible, membership in the rural Scots-Irish Presbyterian community, especially in the western parts of the state.

The British acknowledgment of independence in 1783 nullified the obstacle of allegiance to the Crown for Quakers and pietistic Germans and obviated the pacifist issue, allowing some members of both groups to promise their loyalty. Most returning voters supported the opponents of the 1776 constitution. After 1785 the Republicans mounted effective attacks against the Test Acts, which seemed like shabby political relics as the war slipped into the past. Each bill weakening those acts added voters to their rolls, until the Republicans forced the creation of a more conservative state constitution in 1790, ending the internal revolution in Pennsylvania.[28]

The Republicans overcame their Constitutional rivals in much the same way that the Continental Army had outlasted its opponent in Pennsylvania: by accepting the de facto ascendancy of an adversary in the contest—or at least their temporary ability to dictate the shape of that contest—and then wearing them down patiently on their own terms. Besides preventing the British from ravaging the Delaware Valley from late 1776 until mid-1778, and serving as a stabilizing agent while public institutions solidified there, however, the Continental Army played no real part in the political processes just described. Some of its members, particularly high-ranking officers like Anthony Wayne, who were natives of the state, participated vigorously and often effectively in those contests after they left the army, usually on the Republican side. And they surely brought to the task social and political perspectives formed at Valley Forge.

But many Pennsylvanians would probably have not, by 1785, either recalled or perceived any close or direct links between the traumas of the occupation year and the political struggle by which their state was being reconstructed. Revolutionary memory was, for them, more of an episodic, idiosyncratic, and personal phenomenon. Sometimes they displayed little or no articulated memory at all. Elizabeth Drinker, for example, paid more attention to the progress of the war and the Revolution after it receded from her neighborhood than we would expect her to have done. She took occasional notice of the ebb and flow of campaigns—especially the outcome of battles in the south—or of Benedict Arnold's treason in New York in 1780. But except for her perfunctory acknowledgment on September 26, 1778—at the end of a long and otherwise pedestrian entry on the comings and goings of friends—that it was "a year this day since the British Troops enterd" the city, she ignored both painful and happy anniversaries in an almost studied way.[29]

Henry Muhlenberg also let the past remain in the past, while clearly being influenced by his harsh experiences with it. Probably because one of his sons, Peter, was a general in the Continental Army and because his house at Trappe remained for the rest of the Revolution a public accommodation for soldiers, militiamen, commissaries, and military wagoneers, he paid more attention to the contours of war than Drinker did. He followed with particular interest the turbulent course of the contest in the Carolinas, but he also recorded rumors about a proposed duel between the disgraced general Charles Lee and his former commander-in-chief, the shocked reactions of his neighbors to Arnold's plan to sacrifice West Point, and the 1781 mutinies of the Pennsylvania and New Jersey troops at Morristown. Regularly, between autumn 1778 and the surrender of Cornwallis's army at Yorktown three years later, Muhlenberg heard stories that the British would return and lay waste to eastern Pennsylvania.

As he had during the crisis of 1776, Muhlenberg took solace from his belief that whatever happened was the will of the Lord. But he showed surprisingly little inclination to recall, much less to think about, specific episodes related to his experiences in the winter of 1777–78. On Christmas Day 1778, during an early spell of bitter cold, he acknowledged "God's gracious Providence" when he received a supply of firewood from a ten-acre woodlot that the American militia had somehow failed to strip the year before. During the winter of 1781, news from Philadelphia that 300 discharged American soldiers had menaced the house of Joseph Reed, the president of the Supreme Executive Council, set him off on an odd reverie about the refusal of a Quaker farmer to sell beef to some hungry American soldiers in 1778. But to an overwhelming degree, Muhlenberg's consciousness was fixed on issues of family welfare, ecclesiastical politics, and his own growing sense of being "near the borders of Eternity."[30]

Christopher Marshall likewise moved on after 1778 with little difficulty. As soon as the British army left Philadelphia he visited his old homestead to survey the damage, which "struck [him] with horror and detestation of the promoters and executors of such horrid deeds." He and his wife decided to remain in Lancaster for the time being despite the inadequate social life in that town. Like Drinker and Muhlenberg, Marshall regularly recorded news of the war, including wildly inaccurate accounts of a battle in White Plains in July 1778, in which the British left 3,000 men dead and wounded on the battlefield, and a bizarre but ultimately a prescient rumor in 1779 that Benedict Arnold had defected to the British side.[31]

While he hardly eschewed politics after the occupation, Marshall seemed more interested in domestic concerns and personal health matters.

Then in early 1779 he hurried to Philadelphia where he joined the Constitutional Society and was elected to chair its meeting and to serve on price-fixing committees. He returned to Lancaster to continue these activities on a local level and seemed briefly reenergized.[32] But by 1781, the war-weariness that was gripping the rest of the region had drained the energy from Marshall too. On July 4 he was in Philadelphia, but he could not bring himself to attend the celebration of independence at the State House. That September the movement of the British fleet down the Atlantic Coast to rescue Cornwallis's army at Yorktown, and the march of the American and French troops to trap that army, led Pennsylvanians to conclude that they would be ravaged again. In August, Marshall heard that the English would land at the Head of Elk, as they had four years earlier, to "pay Lancaster a visit." On September 21 he recorded a rumor that Henry Clinton's force, which was too late to raise the siege at Yorktown, would attack Philadelphia instead. But none of these alarms occasioned any recollections about, or comparisons with, the region's experience in 1777–78.[33]

Other survivors were more deeply scarred by the occupation. On July 8, 1778, three weeks after the British left the area, Nicholas Collin, the Swedish minister from Salem County, New Jersey, wrote to his bishop in Uppsala, "solicit[ing] in pressing terms for my recall." Alone among the civilians who left articulate evidence, Collin frequently described the events of 1777–78 as "a Civil War," and he made it clear that he wanted no more part in it. But "after the seat of war had been removed from the Delaware," he recalled, "I obtained at least more tranquillity; and therefore resolved to wait for my recall." He spent 1778 and the early months of 1779 lobbying local authorities for the release of several of his parishioners who had been imprisoned for cooperating with the enemy. As late as 1780, some members of Collin's flock boycotted his services in anger over each other's (and his own) misconduct two years before. Even when they came to church the services "at times broke out in quarrels and fights." In 1783 he received permission to return to Sweden, but the plight of his parish moved him to stay. In 1785, he was offered the rectorship of the Swedish churches at Wicacoa, Kingsessing, and Upper Merion, in Pennsylvania, from where he informally tended the spiritual needs of Lutherans in both states.[34]

Elizabeth Farmer's calculated gamble in December 1777, in staying at Kensington to "share the dangers" with her husband and daughter, paid off. Her family survived the occupation and even preserved their house intact— albeit in a shambles—while the abandoned dwellings of their neighbors were all but destroyed. But she long remembered the details of their hardships by heart: of the cold days when British foragers took their last load of firewood; of rising early in the morning to ride through the deserted countryside in search of market provisions; of American Light Horse patrols riding down from the hinterland to exchange fire across their property with British units coming out of town; or of learning to live without domestic help when the Farmers' servant man enlisted and no young women would come to live in the country.

She admitted that they were "well of[f] in comparison with most" of their neighbors, who had been "stripped of all turned out and their houses burned before their eyes." But her memories were so fresh that she could pour them out in an emotional torrent during the fall of 1783, shortly after the British army left America for good, in response to a nephew's innocent note of congratulations that the Farmers had "got through these troublesome times." Although her family was apparently of Quaker affiliation, and while she gratefully accepted the protection of the Queen's Rangers when they were stationed near her house in the spring of 1778, Farmer closed the war by wishing that the Revolution had "ended more to the honour of England, for they have behaved here wors than savages in their behaviour to the inhabitants and prisoners."[35]

For many younger members of the civilian community, the mere act of recording their experiences regularly during the occupation may itself have been sufficient to stabilize their understandings of that event. Robert Morton apparently gave up the effort with the new year in 1778, while Sarah Wister made only intermittent and largely self-absorbed entries in her journal after her family returned to Philadelphia in July of that year. Joseph Townsend stayed on his family's farm in Chester County until the war came to an end in 1782, when he married and removed to Maryland. By 1783 he was in Baltimore, where he prospered in the insurance business and held many public and civic offices. He lived until he was eighty-five years old, in 1841, and fathered twenty-three children by three wives. He made no effort to record his experiences with the war until well into his adult life, and it is not known when or why he wrote the engrossing memoir that he titled "Some Account of . . . the Battle of Brandywine."[36]

For many civilians, reminders of the winter of Valley Forge arrived suddenly and jarringly out of historical context. As Mary Frazer sparred with Captain De West during the sacking of her house after Brandywine, his men took fifty bushels of threshed wheat from the barn and threw them onto the ground nearby. In spring 1778, before the armies even left Pennsylvania, new wheat came up where the British horses had fed on it, a reminder of the vulnerability of citizens to military havoc mockingly wrapped in evidence of the renewal of life itself. Decades later the daughter of a tenant family on the Frazer farm saw a gleaming object in the beak of her pet crow. She retrieved a "gold sleeve button" and brought it to the house. Sarah Frazer, by now the widowed matriarch of her clan, recognized it as "one of a pair she had thrown with some other things among the vines in the garden, the day the British plundered the house."[37]

The episode added to the stock of Frazer family lore about the war, but the Revolution remained a private subject among Pennsylvanians a generation after the armies left the state. The button had moved a quarter of a mile from its place of loss, and America had traveled a quarter of a century from its birth. The War of 1812 affirmed a sense of nationalism, partly by blurring the Revolution as a unique agent of American destiny. Continental veterans had not begun dying in large enough numbers for their survivors to become celebrated, nor had the panic of 1819 impoverished enough of them to embarrass the nation into funding military pensions. Pennsylvanians were not ready—as New Englanders had been since the Boston Massacre—to infuse places with revolutionary memory. Valley Forge was kept by the army through 1779 as a field hospital. Prisoners from John Burgoyne's "Convention Army" of Saratoga found shelter in surviving huts in December 1778 on their march from Boston to Virginia. Then local farmers reinscribed on the terrain the marks and landforms of Middle Atlantic grain and cattle culture.[38]

The first tourists to visit Valley Forge were Revolutionary War veterans, often in discrete or even furtive ways, unlike the spectacular ceremonial returns of the members of the Grand Army of the Republic to Civil War battlegrounds three generations later. On July 30, 1787, during a recess in the Constitutional Convention (and a decade to the day after he led the Continental Army into Pennsylvania), George Washington and Gouverneur Morris came out from Philadelphia to catch trout in Valley Creek. Washington apparently tired of the sport, however, and while his companion fished he "rid over the old Cantonment of the American [army] of the Winter 1777 & 8. Visited all the works, wch. were in Ruins; and the Incampments in woods where the ground had not been cultivated." The general—who hoped to return to his Virginia plantation when his work with the convention was done—spent most of the afternoon in conversation with local farmers about their crops, planting methods, and harvest yields.[39]

Washington was not the first soldier to come back for a look. In 1782 three privates from North Carolina, mustering out in the Hudson Valley, decided to detour by the "old cantonment" as they rode through Pennsylvania on their way home. They wanted to see what had become of the place, of course, but they also needed clothing and a place to rest. Edward Woodman had befriended Abijah Stephens, a Quaker farmer in the area in 1777, and his recommendation got them clean clothes, warm beds, and home-cooked meals. They were persuaded to stay for two weeks so that they could carry letters from local Friends to Quakers in western North Carolina. Woodman took sick before his mates could resume their journey. He was nursed back to health and found work in the area, before marrying Sarah Stephens, the daughter of his host, in 1789.[40]

Woodman's father-in-law gave the couple a small farm next to his own, partly within the former campground. Having been orphaned as a child, and after spending much of his youth drifting from the eastern shore of Maryland to uninhabited islands in the Caribbean to the Carolina frontier, Woodman found his new clothing and his adoptive community much to his liking. According to his granddaughter, he always dressed "plain . . . in cut and color, went regularly to meeting on First Days, was particular to pay meeting rates, and to discharge a full share of the necessary work" of the community. He died after a fall in his barn in 1820 and was escorted to the burying ground at the Valley Meetinghouse by a procession of neighbors and relatives more than a mile long. He never formally joined the Friends because he could not bring himself to renounce either the practice of war itself or his own decision to fight when the Revolution came. But his life course gives concrete social meaning to the analytical term "quakerized," and it testifies to the resiliency of the communities that shared the seat of war with two armies.[41]

Woodman was not one of the locals who talked with Washington in 1787, but in later life he insisted to his children that he had indeed met his old chief at Valley Forge a decade later. Washington was called back into public life, of course, long before he could profitably use any of the agricultural advice he received that day, but after eight years as president he again hoped to return to the land. In late summer 1796, Woodman was plowing a field near the front lines of the old camp. A dignified and well-dressed elderly gentleman rode up, he recalled, and asked him about the planting practices that he used, taking careful notes. Woodman identified himself as a Continental Army veteran who was neither bred to farming nor even a native of the area. His visitor introduced himself as one of the same, and said that he had come for a last look at the place before returning forever to Virginia the next spring. Woodman apologized for failing to recognize his former commander and current president, and the men reminisced briefly, before the stranger rode back to Philadelphia to see about some pressing business.[42]

Notes

INTRODUCTION

1. The Continental Army spent the winter of 1776–77 near Morristown, and—after wintering at Valley Forge in 1777–78—large parts of the force returned to the Morristown area in 1779–80 and 1780–81. It is generally agreed that the latter two winters were colder and snowier than the Valley Forge winter and that supply shortages were as bad if not worse at Morristown. Several brief but dramatic mutinies interrupted the winter of 1779–80.

2. "Valley Forge Encampment: Separating Fact from Fancy," *Wilmington (Del.) Morning News,* August 30, 1978; "Study Chops Down 'Myths' of Washington, Valley Forge," *Philadelphia Bulletin,* November 6, 1978; "Valley Forge History Probed," *North Penn (Pa.) Reporter,* November 6, 1978; "Valley Forge: Fact or Myth?" *Vincennes (Ind.) Sun-Commercial,* November 8, 1978; "Cold Water Thrown on Frozen Army Myth," *Los Angeles Times,* November 8, 1978; "Like Cherry Tree, Myths About Valley Forge Axed," *Muskegon (Mich.) Chronicle,* November 8, 1978; "History: I Cannot Tell a Lie, It's All Baloney," *Philadelphia Inquirer,* November 13, 1978; "Standing Tall at Valley Forge," *Philadelphia Bulletin,* November 14, 1978. Harlan D. Unrau, *Administrative History, Valley Forge National Historical Park* (Denver: Denver Service Center, National Park Service, United States Department of the Interior, 1984), 617–19; Lorett Treese, *Valley Forge: Making and Remaking a National Symbol* (University Park: The Pennsylvania State University Press, 1995), 208–13.

3. For analyses of the cultural dynamics of the mythology of Valley Forge, see Barbara MacDonald Powell, "The Most Celebrated Encampment: Valley Forge in American Culture, 1777–1983," Ph.D diss., Cornell University, 1983, and Treese, *Valley Forge.*

4. Harry Emerson Wildes, *Valley Forge* (New York: Macmillan, 1938), 1; Alfred Hoyt Bill, *Valley Forge: The Making of an Army* (New York: Harper & Row, 1952), 99, 191; Donald Barr Chidsey, *Valley Forge* (New York: Crown, 1959), 18–19, 138.

5. No evidence has been produced that this episode happened, and it is doubtful that any shad would have been in the river until long after the army's last severe food shortage in February.

6. Christopher Ward, *The War of the Revolution,* 2 vols. (New York: MacMillan, 1952) 2: 550; Lynn Montross, *The Reluctant Rebels: The Story of the Continental Congress* (New York: Harper, 1950), 238;

7. John R. Alden, *The American Revolution, 1775–1783* (New York: Harper Brothers, 1954), 199–202; Howard H. Peckham, *The War for Independence* (Chicago: University of Chicago Press, 1958), 84–96 (quote on 84); Piers Mackesy, *The War for America, 1775–1783* (Cambridge: Harvard University Press, 1964), 215; Don Higginbotham, *The War of American Independence: Military Attitudes, Policies, and Practice, 1763–1789* (New York: MacMillan, 1971), 213, 222, 247.

8. Robert Middlekauf, *The Glorious Cause: The American Revolution, 1763–1789* (New York: Oxford University Press, 1982), 411, 413; "Valley Forge, 1777–1778: Diary of Surgeon Albigence Waldo, of the Connecticut Line," *Pennsylvania Magazine of History and Biography* (hereafter *PMHB*) 21 (1897), 299–323.

9. Higginbotham, *War of American Independence,* 213; Alden, *American Revolution,* 197–98; Mackesy, *War for America,* 212–13.

10. Powell, "Most Celebrated Encampment," 223; Theodore H. White, *In Search of History: A Personal Adventure* (New York: Harper and Row, 1978), 196.

11. Paul F. Paskoff, *Industrial Evolution: Organization, Structure, and Growth of the Pennsylvania Iron Industry, 1750–1860* (Baltimore: Johns Hopkins University Press, 1983), 44–46; Lester J. Cappon et al., eds., *Atlas of Early American History: The Revolutionary Era, 1760–1790* (Princeton: Princeton University Press, 1976), 29.

12. Arthur Cecil Bining, *Pennsylvania Iron Manufacture in the Eighteenth Century,* 2d ed., (Harrisburg, Pa.: Pennsylvania Historical and Museum Commission, 1973), 21, 34, 42, 111, 125, 171, 173; Jacqueline Thibaut, *In the True Rustic Order: Material Aspects of the Valley Forge Encampment,* in Wayne K. Bodle and Jacqueline Thibaut, *Valley Forge Historical Research Project,* 3 vols. (Washington, D.C.: National Park Service, 1980), 3: 92–94.

13. James T. Lemon, *The Best Poor Man's Country: A Geographical Study of Early Southwestern Pennsylvania,* (Baltimore: Johns Hopkins University Press, 1972), 46–47, 79; Rosemary S. Warden, "Chester County," in John B. Frantz and William Pencak, eds., *Beyond Philadelphia: The American Revolution in the Pennsylvania Hinterland* (University Park: Penn State University Press, 1998), 1–22.

14. Lemon, *Best Poor Man's Country,* 88–93.

15. Ibid., 193–97.

16. Ibid., 160–66; Joan M. Jensen, *Loosening the Bonds: Mid-Atlantic Farm Women, 1750–1850* (New Haven: Yale University Press, 1986), 79–82.

17. Lemon, *Best Poor Man's Country,* 73–76, esp. n. 4, and 91–92.

18. Ibid., 76, see also 93. For population growth figures, see p. 23, table 7.

19. James T. Lemon and Gary B. Nash, "The Distribution of Wealth in Eighteenth-Century America: A Century of Change in Chester County, Pennsylvania, 1693–1802," *Journal of Social History* 2 (1968): 1–24.

20. Lucy Simler, "Tenancy in Colonial Pennsylvania: The Case of Chester County," *William and Mary Quarterly* (hereafter *WMQ*), 3d ser., 43 (1986): 542–69.

21. Ibid., esp. 556–59.

22. Ibid., esp. 567–69.

23. Paul G. E. Clemens and Lucy Simler, "Rural Labor and the Farm Household in Chester County, Pennsylvania, 1750–1820," in Stephen Innes, ed., *Work and Labor in Early America* (Chapel Hill: University of North Carolina Press, 1988), 106–43; Lucy Simler, "The Landless Worker: An Index of Economic and Social Change in Chester County, Pennsylvania, 1750–1820," *PMHB* 114 (1990): 163–99.

24. Stella H. Sutherland, *Population Distribution in Colonial America* (New York, AMS Press, 1966), 129.

25. Owen S. Ireland, "Bucks County," in Frantz and Pencak, eds., *Beyond Philadelphia,* 23–45.

26. Peter O. Wacker, *Land and People: A Cultural Geography of Preindustrial New Jersey, Origins and Settlement Patterns* (New Brunswick: Rutgers University Press, 1975), Larry R. Gerlach, *Prologue to Independence: New Jersey in the Coming of the American Revolution* (New Brunswick: Rutgers University Press, 1976), 7–13 (population figures, p. 389, n. 26).

27. John A. Munroe, *Colonial Delaware: A History* (Millwood, N.Y.: KTO Press, 1978), 161–67 (population, 167), 197–99.

28. Paul G. E. Clemens, *The Atlantic Economy and Colonial Maryland's Eastern Shore: From Tobacco to Grain* (Ithaca: Cornell University Press, 1980), chap. 6 and "Conclusion."

29. Major General Charles Gray to ?, November 28, 1777, Andre deCoppet Collection, Princeton University Library.

30. Lemon, *Best Poor Man's Country*, 98–106, 118–31.

31. Eugene R. Slaski, "The Lehigh Valley," and Karen Guenther, "Berks County," in Frantz and Pencak, eds., *Beyond Philadelphia*, 46–66 and 67–84; Francis S. Fox, *Sweet Land of Liberty: The Ordeal of the American Revolution in Northampton County, Pennsylvania* (University Park: The Pennsylvania State University Press, 2000), "Introduction."

32. Lemon, *Best Poor Man's Country*, 94.

33. Paul E. Doutrich, "York County," in Frantz and Pencak, eds., *Beyond Philadelphia*, 85–106; Lemon, *Best Poor Man's Country*, 34–35.

CHAPTER 1   The Seat of War

1. Charles A. Royster, *A Revolutionary People at War: The Continental Army and American Character, 1775–1782* (Chapel Hill: University of North Carolina Press, 1979), chap. 1; Piers Mackesy, *The War for America, 1775–1783* (Cambridge: Harvard University Press, 1964), chap. 1; Robert L. Brunhouse, *The Counter-Revolution in Pennsylvania, 1776–1790* (Harrisburg: Pennsylvania Historical and Museum Commission, 1942, 1971), 10–13; David Freeman Hawke, *In the Midst of a Revolution* (Philadelphia: University of Pennsylvania Press, 1961); Richard Alan Ryerson, *The Revolution Is Now Begun: The Radical Committees of Philadelphia, 1765–1776* (Philadelphia: University of Pennsylvania Press, 1978), chap. 9.

2. Mackesy, *War for America*, 87–93.

3. Ira D. Gruber, *The Howe Brothers and the American Revolution* (New York: Atheneum, 1972), 145–50; William M. Dwyer, *The Day Is Ours! November 1776–January 1777: An Inside View of the Battles of Trenton and Princeton* (New York: Viking Press, 1983), 3–114.

4. *Journals of the Continental Congress* (hereafter *JCC*), 34 vols., ed. Worthington C. Ford et al. (Washington, D.C.: United States Government Printing Office, 1904–37), 6: 1027; Washington to John Augustine Washington, December 18, 1776, John W. Fitzpatrick, ed., *The Writings of George Washington* (hereafter *WGW*), 37 vols., (Washington, D.C.: U.S. Government Printing Office, 1931–40), 6: 396–99.

5. Stephen Rosswurm, *Arms, Country, and Class: The Philadelphia Militia and the ""Lower Sort" During the American Revolution, 1775–1783* (New Brunswick: Rutgers University Press, 1987), 125–34. Elizabeth Farmer to "Dear Madam," October 25, 1783; Elizabeth Farmer to "Dear Nephew," December 4, 1783, Elizabeth Farmer Letterbook, Historical Society of Pennsylvania (hereafter HSP) (partly reprinted in *PMHB* 40 [1916]: 205–7).

6. Theodore G. Tappert and John W. Doberstein, eds., *The Journals of Henry Melchior Muhlenberg*, 3 vols. (Philadelphia: Evangelical Lutheran Ministerium, 1945) (hereafter Muhlenberg, *Diary*), 2: 762, 763, 765. Trappe is on the Perkiomen Creek, five miles above the Schuylkill River at Valley Forge. There, two major roads from Philadelphia converged and ran northwest toward Reading. Elizabeth Farmer and her daughter almost certainly passed by Muhlenberg's door on December 13. Elizabeth Farmer to "Dear Madam," October 25, 1783, Elizabeth Farmer Letterbook, HSP.

7. Muhlenberg, *Diary*, 2: 761–64.

8. Nicholas B. Wainwright, ed., "'A Diary of Trifling Occurrences': Philadelphia, 1776–1778," [Sarah Logan Fisher Diary] *PMHB* 82 (October 1958): 415–18; "John Hunt's Diary," *Proceedings of the New Jersey Historical Society* 52 (1934): 192–93.

9. Wainwright, ed., "Diary of Trifling Occurrences," 417; Muhlenberg, *Diary*, 2: 764–65.

10. John Henderson, John Boyd, and Samuel Quimby to Captain Richard Lockhard, December 10, 1776, RG-27, 11: 429, Pennsylvania Historical and Museum Commission, Harrisburg (hereafter PHMC).

11. Loyalist memorial of John Johnson, Records of the British Loyalist Commission, Audit Office, series 12, bundle 42, pp. 57–64, and loyalist memorial of Peter Partier, A.O.

12/40/295–300, Great Britain, Public Record Office, Kew; Washington to Brigadier General William Maxwell, December 8, 1776, Fitzpatrick, ed., *WGW*, 6: 337–38.

12. Northampton Committee to Committee of Safety, December 14, 1776; Colonel Henry Geigy [Geiger] to the Council of Safety, December 23, 1776, RG-27, 11: 474, 579, PHMC.

13. James Thomas Flexner, *George Washington in the American Revolution, 1775–1783* (Boston: Little, Brown, 1967, 1978), 171–90; Gruber, *Howe Brothers*, 153–57; Dwyer, *Day Is Ours*.

14. On Washington's military orientation see Don Higginbotham, *George Washington and the American Military Tradition* (Athens: University of Georgia Press, 1985), esp. 12–16. For evidence of previous British familiarity with partisan conflict in both Europe and America, see Peter E. Russell, "Redcoats in the Wilderness: British Officers and Irregular Warfare in Europe and America, 1740–1760," *WMQ*, 3d ser., 35 (1978): 629–52.

15. Gruber, *Howe Brothers*, 148–51; Northampton Committee to the Pennsylvania Committee of Safety, December 14, 1777, RG-27, 11: 474, PHMC; Charles Leonard Lundin, *The Cockpit of the Revolution: The War for Independence in New Jersey* (Princeton: Princeton University Press, 1940), chap. 5.

16. Wainwright, ed., "Diary of Trifling Occurrences," 419; Muhlenberg, *Diary*, 2: 768, 770–71.

17. Elizabeth Farmer to "Dear Madam," October 25, 1783, Elizabeth Farmer Letterbook, HSP; Muhlenberg, *Diary*, 2: 768, 770–71.

18. See Adrian C. Leiby, *The Revolutionary War in the Hackensack Valley: The Jersey Dutch and the Neutral Ground, 1775–1783* (New Brunswick: Rutgers University Press, 1962), chap. 7; Mark V. Kwasny, *Washington's Partisan War, 1775–1783* (Kent, Ohio: Kent State University Press, 1996), for accounts of this intracommunal violence.

19. Gruber, *Howe Brothers*, 157. John Pancake, *1777: Year of the Hangman* (University: University of Alabama Press, 1977), 65.

20. Robert A. Gross, *The Minutemen and Their World* (New York: Hill and Wang, 1976), chaps. 6–7; Richard Buel, *Dear Liberty: Connecticut's Mobilization for the Revolutionary War* (Middletown, Conn.: Wesleyan University Press, 1980).

21. John Adams to Thomas Jefferson, August 24, 1815; John Adams to Hezekiah Niles, February 13, 1818, in Charles Francis Adams, ed., *The Works of John Adams* (Boston, 1856), 10: 172, 282 (emphasis added). John Shy, *A People Numerous and Armed: Reflections on the Military Struggle for American Independence* (New York: Oxford University Press, 1976), 197, and "Introduction," xi.

22. For New England, e.g., see Donald Weber, *Rhetoric and History in Revolutionary New England* (New York: Oxford University Press, 1988); Alice M. Baldwin, *The New England Clergy and the American Revolution* (New York: Frederick Ungar, 1928, 1958); Nathan Hatch, *The Sacred Cause of Liberty* (New Haven: Yale University Press, 1977); Christopher M. Jedrey, *The World of John Cleaveland: Family and Community in Eighteenth Century New England* (New York: W. W. Norton, 1979), esp. chaps. 4–5; For Virginia, see, T. H. Breen, *Tobacco Culture: The Mentality of the Great Tidewater Planters on the Eve of Revolution* (Princeton: Princeton University Press, 1985), esp. 90–93, 167–68, 196–98; Edmund S. Morgan, *American Slavery, American Freedom: The Ordeal of Colonial Virginia* (New York: W. W. Norton, 1975); Emory Evans, "Planter Indebtedness and the Coming of the Revolution in Virginia," *WMQ*, 3d ser., 19 (October 1962): 511–33; For the evolution of allegiance in the Middle Atlantic region, see Joseph Tiedemann, "Response to Revolution: Queens County, New York, During the Era of the American Revolution," Ph.D. diss., City University of New York, 1977; "Communities in the Midst of the American Revolution: Queens County, New York, 1774–1775," *Journal of Social History* 18 (fall 1984): 57–78; "A Revolution Foiled: Queens County, New York, 1775–1776," *Journal of American History* 75 (September 1988): 417–44; and "Patriots by Default: Queens County, New York, and the British Army, 1776–1783" *WMQ*, 3d ser., 43 (January 1986): 35–65; Jonathan Clark, "The Problem of Allegiance in Revolutionary Poughkeepsie," in David D. Hall et al., eds., *Saints and Strangers: Essays on Early American History* (New York: W. W. Norton, 1984), 285–317; Milton M. Klein, "Why Did the British Fail to Win the Hearts and Minds of New Yorkers," *New York History* 64 (October 1983): 357–75; Sung Bok Kim, "The Limits of Politicization in the American Revolution: The Experience of Westchester County, New York," *Journal of American History* 80 (December 1993): 868–89.

23. Allen French, *The Day of Lexington and Concord: The Nineteenth of April, 1775* (Boston: Little, Brown, 1925); Allen French, *The First Year of the American Revolution* (New York: Houghton, Mifflin, 1934); Gross, *Minutemen and Their World*, esp. chap. 5; David Hackett Fischer, *Paul Revere's Ride* (New York: Oxford University Press, 1994); Fred Anderson, *A People's Army: Massachusetts Soldiers and Society During the Seven Years' War* (Chapel Hill: University of North Carolina Press, 1984), esp. pt. 1; Harold E. Selesky, *War and Society in Colonial Connecticut* (New Haven: Yale University Press, 1990, esp. chap. 6; Stanley M. Pargellis, "The Four Independent Companies of New York," in *Essays in Colonial History Presented to Charles McLean Andrews* (New Haven: Yale University Press, 1931), 96–123; Robert Middlekauf, *The Glorious Cause: The American Revolution, 1763–1789* (New York: Oxford University Press, 1982), 340–43; Ronald Hoffman, Thad W. Tate, and Peter J. Albert, eds., *An Uncivil War: The Southern Backcountry During the American Revolution* (Charlottesville: University of Virginia Press, 1985).

24. Gary B. Nash, *Quakers and Politics, 1681–1726* (Princeton: Princeton University Press, 1968); Alan Tully, *Forming American Politics: Ideas, Interests, and Institutions in Colonial New York and Pennsylvania* (Baltimore: Johns Hopkins University Press, 1994); Benjamin H. Newcomb, *Political Partisanship in the American Middle Colonies, 1700–1776* (Baton Rouge: Louisiana State University Press, 1995); Wayne Bodle, "Themes and Directions in Middle Colonies Historiography, 1980–1994," *WMQ*, 3d ser., 51 (July 1994): 360–64.

25. Tully, *Forming American Politics*, 148–58, 290–99; Alan Tully, "Quaker Party and Proprietary Policies: The Dynamics of Politics in Pre-Revolutionary Pennsylvania, 1730–1775," in Bruce C. Daniels, ed., *Power and Status: Officeholding in Colonial America* (Middletown, Conn.: Wesleyan University Press 1986), 75–105; Alan Tully, "Ethnicity, Religion and Politics in Early America," *PMHB* 107 (1983): 491–536; A. G. Roeber, "The Origin of Whatever Is Not English Among Us: The Dutch-Speaking and German-Speaking Peoples of Colonial British America," in Bernard Bailyn and Philip D. Morgan, eds., *Strangers Within the Realm: Cultural Margins of the First British Empire* (Chapel Hill: University of North Carolina Press, 1991), 220–83; Marianne Wokeck, *Trade in Strangers: The Beginnings of Mass Migration to North America* (University Park: The Pennsylvania State University Press, 1999); Sally Schwartz, *A "Mixed Multitude": The Struggle for Toleration in Pennsylvania, 1681–1776* (New York: New York University Press, 1991); Aaron Fogleman, *Hopeful Journeys: German Immigration, Settlement, and Political Culture in Colonial America, 1717–1775* (Philadelphia: University of Pennsylvania Press, 1996).

26. Tully, *Forming American Politics*, 126, 146, 157, 184–90; Maldwyn A. Jones, "The Scotch-Irish in British America," in Bailyn and Morgan, eds., *Strangers Within the Realm*, 284–313; Patrick Griffin, *The People with No Name: Ireland's Ulster Scots, America's Scots Irish, and the Creation of a British Atlantic World, 1689–1764* (Princeton: Princeton University Press, 2001).

27. See Robert L. D. Davidson, *War Comes to Quaker Pennsylvania, 1682–1756* (New York: Columbia University Press, 1957), chaps. 9–10, for the traditional view. The gradual but steady erosion of this interpretation in the scholarly literature can be followed in William S. Hanna, *Benjamin Franklin and Pennsylvania Politics* (Stanford: Stanford University Press, 1964) chaps. 3–6; James H. Hutson, *Pennsylvania Politics 1746–1770: The Movement for Royal Government and Its Consequences* (Princeton: Princeton University Press, 1972), chap. 1; Joseph E. Illick, *Colonial Pennsylvania* (New York: Charles Scribner's Sons, 1976), chap. 8. Tully, *Forming American Politics*, esp. 285–303, traces the growth of a political culture characterized by an ideological discourse that he calls "civil Quakerism" between the late 1730s and the 1760s.

28. Hutson, *Pennsylvania Politics*, chaps. 3–5; Hanna, *Franklin and Pennsylvania Politics*, chaps. 10–11; Benjamin H. Newcomb, *Franklin and Galloway: A Political Partnership* (New Haven: Yale University Press, 1972).

29. Richard Alan Ryerson, "Republican Theory and Partisan Reality in Revolutionary Pennsylvania: Towards a New View of the Constitutionalist Party," in Ronald Hoffman and Peter J. Albert, eds., *Sovereign States in an Age of Uncertainty* (Charlottesville: University Press of Virginia, 1981), 95–133; J. Paul Selsam, *The Pennsylvania Constitution of 1776: A Study in Revolutionary Democracy* (Harrisburg: Pennsylvania Historical Commission 1936 [1971]); Brunhouse, *The Counter-Revolution in Pennsylvania*, chaps. 1–2; Theodore Thayer, *Pennsylvania Politics and the Growth of Democracy, 1740–1776* (Harrisburg: Pennsylvania Historical and Museum Commission, 1953), chap. 8; Douglas

McNeil Arnold, *A Republican Revolution: Ideology and Politics in Pennsylvania* (New York: Garland, 1989); Rosswurm, *Arms, Country, and Class,* chaps. 2–3; Eric Foner, *Tom Paine and Revolutionary America* (New York: Oxford University Press, 1976), chap. 4.

30. James Kirby Martin, *Men in Rebellion: Higher Government Leaders and the Coming of the American Revolution* (New Brunswick: Rutgers University Press, 1973), esp. chap. 2, and charts 2.1 and 2.2 on pp. 45 and 51.

31. Charles H. Lincoln, *The Revolutionary Movement in Pennsylvania, 1760–1776* (Philadelphia: University of Pennsylvania Press, 1901). See also Carl L. Becker, *The History of Political Parties in the Colony of New York, 1760–1776* (Madison: University of Wisconsin Press, 1909, 1960), and Robert Gough, "Charles H. Lincoln, Carl Becker, and the Origins of the Dual Revolution Thesis," *WMQ,* 3d ser., 39 (January 1981): 97–109.

32. Anne M. Ousterhout, *A State Divided: Opposition in Pennsylvania to the American Revolution* (Westport, Conn.: Greenwood Press, 1987), esp. chap. 8; Robert M. Calhoon, *The Loyalists in Revolutionary America, 1760–1781* (New York: Harcourt, Brace, Jovanovich, 1973), 170–74, 387–98; Wallace Brown, *The King's Friends: The Composition and Motives of the American Loyalist Claimants* (Providence: Brown University Press, 1965), 142–43; Arthur J. Mekeel, *The Quakers and the American Revolution* (Washington, D.C., 1979; York, Eng.: Sessions Book Trust, 1996), esp. chaps. 8–9; William C. Kashatus III, *Conflict of Convictions: A Reappraisal of Quaker Involvement in the American Revolution* (Lanham, Md.: University Press of America, 1990), esp. chap. 3; Stephen Brobeck, "Revolutionary Change in Colonial Philadelphia: The Brief Life of the Proprietary Gentry," *WMQ,* 3d ser., 33 (July 1976): 410–34.

33. Wayne L. Bockelman and Owen S. Ireland, "The Internal Revolution in Pennsylvania: An Ethnic-Religious Interpretation," *Pennsylvania History* 41 (April 1974): 125–59; Owen S. Ireland, "The Ethnic-Religious Dimension of Pennsylvania Politics, 1778–1779," *WMQ,* 3d ser., 30 (July 1973): 422–48; O. S. Ireland, "The Crux of Politics: Religion and Party in Pennsylvania, 1778–1789," *WMQ,* 3d ser., 42 (October 1985): 453–75.

34. Ousterhout, *State Divided;* Brown, *King's Friends,* 129–53; Ryerson, *Revolution Is Now Begun,* chap. 9; Charles S. Olton, *Artisans for Independence: Philadelphia Mechanics and the American Revolution* (Syracuse: Syracuse University Press, 1975); John K. Alexander, *Render Them Submissive: Responses to Poverty in Philadelphia, 1760–1800* (Amherst: University of Massachusetts Press, 1980); Billy G. Smith, *The "Lower Sort": Philadelphia's Laboring People, 1750–1800* (Ithaca: Cornell University Press, 1990); Gregory Palmer, *Biographical Sketches of Loyalists of the American Revolution* (Westport, Conn.: Meckler, 1984).

35. Ryerson, *Revolution Is Now Begun,* 211–13; David Freeman Hawke, *In the Midst of a Revolution* (Philadelphia: University of Pennsylvania Press, 1961), 156–57.

36. Brunhouse, *Counter-Revolution in Pennsylvania,* chap. 2; Ryerson, "Republican Theory and Partisan Reality," 109–10.

37. Elizabeth Farmer to "Dear Nephew," December 11, 1777, Elizabeth Farmer Letterbook, HSP.

38. For an account of the "redefinition of Philadelphia's 'radicals'" see Ryerson, *Revolution Is Now Begun,* 207, and esp. n. 2. The state's embryonic militia, which was effectively organized only in Philadelphia's artisan community, was deeply politicized and provided a source of power for the committed radicals. See Rosswurm, *Arms, Country, and Class,* 39–48.

39. Shy, *People Numerous and Armed,* 133.

40. Washington to Lund Washington, August 20, 1775, Fitzpatrick, ed., *WGW,* 3: 433; Flexner, *George Washington in the American Revolution,* chap. 4.

CHAPTER 2 The Campaign for Pennsylvania

1. Harry Emerson Wildes, *Valley Forge* (New York, Macmillan: 1938), 1; Donald Barr Chidsey, *Valley Forge* (New York: Crown, 1959), 8; Eric Robson, review of Alfred Hoyt Bill, *Valley Forge: The Making of an Army* in *American Historical Review* 58 (1952–53): 390–91; Hugh F. Rankin, review of Bill, *Valley Forge, WMQ,* 3d ser., 9 (1952): 566–67; George F. Scheer and Hugh F. Rankin, *Rebels*

and Redcoats (Cleveland: World Publishing, 1957), 305. See also Wayne Bodle, "The Vortex of Small Fortunes: The Continental Army at Valley Forge," Ph.D. diss., University of Pennsylvania, 1987, chap. 1.

2. Mackesy, in *War for America*, 121, writes that although the army "virtually disbanded" at the end of 1776, "the *cadre* survived on which to build afresh." Don Higginbotham, *The War of American Independence: Military Attitudes, Policies, and Practice, 1763–1789* (New York: Macmillan, 1971), 170, observes that a "*core* of regulars . . . endured [the] winter" of 1777 at Morristown. Mark Edward Lender, "The Enlisted Line: The Continental Soldiers of New Jersey," Ph.D. diss., Rutgers University, 1975, 71, argues that a "*core* of regulars *eventually* reinlisted" in that state's regiments for the 1777 campaign, but he implies that most of them first went home. John Richard Alden, *The American Revolution, 1775–1783* (New York: Harper and Brothers, 1954), 119–20, writes that "fewer than a thousand of the Continentals *promptly reenlisted*," pursuant to Congress's adoption of long-term enlistments and bounties, and that "something like a thousand Continentals *clung faithfully*" to Washington during the winter of 1776–77. Robert K. Wright, *The Continental Army* (Washington, D.C.: Center of Military History, 1983), 109, 119, notes that each unit of the new army began the 1777 campaign "with an experienced *core*" and ended it with "sizable veteran *cadres*," which were "retained through reenlistment," but he does not make clear whether these were soldiers who had remained in the field all winter after Trenton. (Italics added in all quotations.)

3. Charles H. Lesser, ed., *The Sinews of Independence: Monthly Strength Reports of the Continental Army* (Chicago: University of Chicago Press, 1976), 43–44. These consolidated armywide returns are nowhere more fragmentary during the war than for the months of January to May 1777. This reflected the disarray in the army at this time. The adjutant general, Joseph Reed, resigned in December 1776 and he was not replaced until June 1777. Washington complained of his inability to get reliable accounts of the effective number of troops available to him. Dwyer, *Day Is Ours,* 227–29, 292–95; Washington to the President of Congress, January, 19, 1777; Washington to Jonathan Trumbull, March 6, 1777; Washington to the President of Congress, March 14, 1777, Fitzpatrick, ed., *WGW,* 8: 29–30, 254, 288.

4. Lawrence Delbert Cress, *Citizens in Arms: The Army and the Militia in American Society to the War of 1812* (Chapel Hill: University of North Carolina Press, 1982); John Todd White, "Standing Armies in Time of War: Republican Theory and Military Practice During the American Revolution," Ph.D. diss., George Washington University, 1978; Anderson, *People's Army,* esp. pt. 1. The memoir of Sergeant Joseph White of Charlestown, Massachusetts, published as "The Good Soldier White," in *American Heritage* 4 (June 1956): 74–79.

5. Washington to Edmund Pendleton, April 12, 1777 ("mere handful"); Washington to Landon Carter, April 15, 1777 ("mere nothing"), Fitzpatrick, ed., *WGW,* 7: 394, 413 (italics added). For examples of his lobbying with Congress for longer enlistments and less reliance on the militia, see Washington to the President of Congress, September 2, 1776, September 20, 1776, Ibid., 6: 4–6, 85–86. On September 16, Congress authorized the formation of eighty-eight new battalions, apportioned among the states, with men enlisted to serve "during the war." *JCC,* 5: 762–63. On December 27 it voted to allow Washington to raise sixteen "additional" regiments from the states at large. *JCC,* 5: 1045–1046. These units would have theoretically comprised approximately 75,000 men.

6. Joseph Plumb Martin left the Continental service on the Hudson River at Christmas to return to his family's home in Connecticut, and in April 1777 he hesitantly agreed to reenlist. James Kirby Martin, ed., *Ordinary Courage: The Revolutionary War Adventures of Joseph Plumb Martin* (St. James, N.Y.: Brandywine Press, 1993), 35–39. It is important to our understanding of this point to know how many "Martins" and how many "Whites" there were in the army in 1776–77.

7. Washington to Robert Morris, March 2, 1777; Washington to Horatio Gates, March 4, 1777; Washington to Governor Jonathan Trumbull, March 6, 1777, Fitzpatrick, ed., *WGW,* 7: 223–24, 245, 255.

8. Washington to the President of Congress, January 19, 1777; Washington to the Pennsylvania Council of Safety, January 19, 1777; Washington to Philemon Dickenson, January 21, 1777; Washington to General Philip Schuyler, January 27, 1777; Washington to Horatio Gates, February 5, 1777; Washington to the President of Congress, February 14, 1777; Washington to William Maxwell, February 18, 1777; Washington to Horatio Gates, February 20, 1777; Washington to

Alexander McDougall, February 20, 1777; Washington to John Augustus Washington, February 24, 1777; Washington to Robert Morris et al., February 27, 1777; Washington to Robert Morris, March 2, 1777; Washington to Horatio Gates, March 4, 1777; Washington to Jonathan Trumbull, March 6, 1777; Washington to the President of Congress, May 21, 1777, Fitzpatrick, ed., *WGW,* 7: 29, 34–36, 45–46, 69, 110, 146, 158, 176, 179, 198, 203–4, 222–23, 244–45, 253–54, *WGW,* 8: 99. Hugh Ledlie, a Connecticut officer hoping to raise a Continental regiment, visited Morristown in late February 1777, and on his way back home he told William Smith, Jr., a prominent Loyalist New Yorker under house arrest on Livingston Manor, that Washington did not *know* how many men he had. They were, in any case, Ledlie said, *"all . . . Militia,* and come and go all Day long." William H. W. Sabine, ed., *Historical Memoirs from 12 July 1776 to 25 July 1778 of William Smith* (New York, 1958), 87. Washington wrote to John Hancock, the president of Congress, on March 14, 1777, to complain that his forces amounted to "but a handful," and he promised to enclose an army return. But before he sent the letter he admitted that he could not "make [one] out with precision." His best "estimate" was that there were fewer than 3,000 American troops in New Jersey, all but 981 of them militia. This estimate contradicted the written return—dated the next day—that did not go with the letter, which put the number of Continental troops at 2,500. The editors of Washington's papers conjecture that this return was hand delivered to Congress by General Nathanael Greene, who Washington sent to confer with that body, but there is no hard evidence for this view. The significance of these facts for the reliability of the return is undeterminable, but is not advisable to give much weight to it in considering the size and makeup of Washington's forces in early 1777. Ledlie, a Yankee with militia experience dating to the Seven Years' War, presumably knew militiamen when he saw them, and Washington continued to emphasize the absence of the new Continental levies—and his reliance on militia substitutes—well into April. Washington to John Hancock, March 14, 1777; "Return of the American Forces in New Jersey" (March 15, 1777); Washington to Nathanael Greene, March 18, 1777; Washington to John Hancock, March 18, 1777, in Frank Grizzard et al., eds., *The Papers of George Washington, Revolutionary Series* (Charlottesville: University Press of Virginia, 1998), 8: 570–72, 576, 596–97.

9. Mackesy, *War for America,* 121; Douglas Southall Freeman, *George Washington* (New York: Charles Scribner's Sons, 1951) 4: 384n. Washington to the President of Congress, January 26, 1777, Fitzpatrick, ed., *WGW,* 7: 66; Washington to John A. Washington, February 24, 1777; Washington to Robert Morris et al., February 27, 1777; Washington to Robert Morris, March 2, 1777; Washington to Jonathan Trumbull, March 6, 1777; Washington to Samuel Holden Parsons, March 6, 1777; Washington to John A. Washington, April 12, 1777, Ibid., 198, 204, 223, 255, 259–60, 395.

10. Lesser, *Sinews of Independence,* 45–47; Washington to General John Sullivan, May 23, 1777; Washington to General Alexander McDougall, May 23, 1777; Washington to General William Smallwood, May 26, 1777, Fitzpatrick, ed., *WGW,* 8: 106–8, 127–29; Washington, General Orders, May 22, 29, 30, 31, June 1, 1777, Ibid., 99–101, 141–44, 152–56.

11. Washington to William Smallwood, May 26, 1777, Fitzpatrick, ed., *WGW,* 8: 128 (emphasis added).

12. Washington to General Adam Stephen, April 20, 1777, Fitzpatrick, ed., *WGW,* 7: 443–44.

13. Lender, "Enlisted Line," 110–39 ; Edward Papenfuse and Gregory Stiverson, "General Smallwood's Recruits: The Peacetime Career of the Revolutionary War Private," *WMQ,* 3d ser., 30 (1973): 117–32; James Kirby Martin and Mark E. Lender, *A Respectable Army: The Military Origins of the Republic, 1763–1789* (Arlington Heights, Ill., Harlan Davidson, 1982), 87–97; John R. Sellers, "The Common Soldier in the American Revolution," in Stanley J. Underdal, ed., *Military History of the American Revolution: Proceedings of the Sixth Military History Symposium, United States Air Force Academy* (Washington, D.C.: Office of Air Force History, 1976), 151–61; Gross, *Minutemen and Their World,* 146–53.

14. Martin and Lender, *Respectable Army,* 78–79; Washington to Patrick Henry, May 17, 1777, Fitzpatrick, ed., *WGW,* 8: 77; Smith, *"Lower Sort"*; Alexander, *Render Them Submissive;* Robert E. Cray, *Paupers and Poor Relief in New York City and Its Rural Environs, 1700–1830* (Philadelphia: Temple University Press, 1988), chap. 3; Lemon, *Best Poor Man's Country,* 85–97; Simler, "Tenancy in Colonial Pennsylvania," 542–69; Simler, "The Landless Worker"; Douglas Lamar Jones, "The Strolling Poor: Transiency in Eighteenth Century Massachusetts," *Journal of Social History* 8 (spring

1975): 28–54; Ruth Wallis Herndon, *Unwelcome Americans: Living on the Margins in Early New England* (Philadelphia, University of Pennsylvania Press, 2001), esp. 10–15.

15. Gary B. Nash, *The Urban Crucible: Social Change, Political Consciousness, and the Origins of the American Revolution* (Cambridge: Harvard University Press, 1979); Martin and Lender, *Respectable Army*, 76–79; Charles Neimeyer, *America Goes to War: A Social History of the Continental Army* (New York: New York University Press, 1996), 15–26; Lender, "Enlisted Line," 71.

16. This view has been vigorously criticized by historians who argue that subtle human motivations about military or political behavior cannot be directly linked to or inferred from objective conditions of social structure. See Royster, *Revolutionary People at War*, 373–78; Robert Middlekauf, "Why Men Fought in the American Revolution," *Huntington Library Quarterly* 42 (1980): 135–48.

17. John B. B. Trussell, *Birthplace of an Army: A Study of the Valley Forge Encampment* (Harrisburg: Pennsylvania Historical and Museum Commission, 1976); John F. Reed, *Valley Forge: Crucible of Victory* (Monmouth Beach, N.J.: Philip Freneau Press, 1969).

18. Scholars' estimates of the number of troops that Howe took to Pennsylvania range from 13,000 to 19,000. See John F. Reed, *Campaign to Valley Forge: July 1 to December 19, 1777* (Philadelphia, University of Pennsylvania Press, 1963), 20; Middlekauf, *Glorious Cause*, 384; Don Higginbotham, *The War of American Independence: Military Attitudes, Policies, and Practices, 1763–1789* (New York: MacMillan, 1971), 183; John R. Alden, *A History of the American Revolution* (New York: Alfred A. Knopf, 1976) 121; Christopher Ward, *The War of the American Revolution*, 2 vols., ed. John R. Alden (New York: MacMillan, 1952), 1: 329; Pancake, *1777*, 163; Howard H. Peckham, *The War for Independence: A Military History* (Chicago: University of Chicago Press, 1958), 69. This study adopts Piers Mackesy's estimate of "nearly 14,000 rank-and-file." See his *War for America*, 125

19. Bodle, "Vortex of Small Fortunes," chap. 2; Reed, *Campaign to Valley Forge*, chaps. 2, 3, 4; Mackesy, *War for America*, 137. One French observer of the parade through Philadelphia said that the Americans, "gave an appearance of health and vigor that one would scarcely expect to see in sick and exhausted troops." See "The American Revolutionary Army: A French Estimate in 1777," ed. Durand Echeverria and Orville T. Murphy," *Military Affairs* 27 (spring 1963): 2.

20. Mackesy, *War for America*, chap. 5; Pancake, *1777*, chap. 6. The plan was formulated mainly by Burgoyne, who returned to London during the winter and sold the idea to the American Secretary, Lord George Germain.

21. Mackesy, *War for America*, 123–26; Reed, *Campaign to Valley Forge*.

22. Reed, *Campaign to Valley Forge*, 77–116; Nathanael Greene to Catharine Greene, September 10, 1777, in Richard K. Showman, ed., *The Papers of General Nathanael Greene*, 7 vols. (Chapel Hill: University of North Carolina Press, 1980–94), 2: 154–56.

23. Reed, *Campaign to Valley Forge*, 112–13, 117–28; Mackesy, *War for America*, 128–29. For reports of civilians trying to warn Washington, see [Sarah Frazer], "The Battle of Brandywine, September 11, 1777," in *General Persifor Frazer, A Memoir* (Philadelphia, 1907), 155–56.

24. Reed, *Campaign to Valley Forge*, 128, 134–36. Reed cites—but gives no source for—Cornwallis's remark.

25. Reed, *Campaign to Valley Forge*, 138–40; Howard H. Peckham, *The Toll of Independence: Engagements and Battle Casualties of the American Revolution* (Chicago, University of Chicago Press, 1974), 40

26. Mackesy, *War for America*, 129 (quotation); Reed, *Campaign to Valley Forge*, 139–43.

27. Higginbotham, *War of American Independence*, 186; Reed, *Campaign to Valley Forge*, 147–58, 160–62, 168–76; Thomas J. McGuire, *The Battle of Paoli* (Mechanicsburg, Pa.: Stackpole Books, 2000); Peckham, *Toll of Independence*, 41, writes that 200 Americans were killed, 100 wounded, and 71 captured at Paoli; *JCC*, 8: 754. Revolutionary folklore dubbed the clash on September 16 the "Battle of the Clouds" and the assault on Wayne's camp the "Paoli Massacre." On the "Virginia Exiles," see Robert F. Oaks, "Philadelphians in Exile: The Problem of Loyalty During the American Revolution," *PMHB* (July 1972): 298–325; Thomas Gilpin, *Exiles in Virginia, With Observations on the Conduct of the Society of Friends During the Revolutionary War* (Philadelphia, privately printed, 1848).

28. Bodle, "Vortex of Small Fortunes," 53; Reed, *Campaign to Valley Forge*, 188. See Stephanie Grauman Wolf, *Urban Village: Population, Community, and Family Structure in Germantown, Pennsylvania, 1683–1800* (Princeton: Princeton University Press, 1976), for a description of that community.

29. R. Arthur Bowler, *Logistics and the Failure of the British Army in America, 1775–1783* (Princeton: Princeton University Press, 1975), 70–72; Daniel Weir to John Robinson, Esq., October 25, 1777, Daniel Weir Letterbook, HSP, p. 45; Ward, *War of the Revolution,* chap. 34, esp. map; John W. Jackson, *The Pennsylvania Navy, 1775–1781: The Defense of the Delaware* (New Brunswick: Rutgers University Press, 1974), esp. chap. 9; John W. Jackson, *Fort Mifflin: Valiant Defender of the Delaware* (Philadelphia: Old Fort Mifflin Historical Society, 1986), chap. 2.

30. Council of War, September 28, 1777, Fitzpatrick, ed., *WGW,* 9: 277–79; Reed, *Campaign to Valley Forge,* 206–7; Bernhard A. Uhlendorf, trans. and ed., *Revolution in America: Confidential Letters and Journals, 1776–1784, of Adjutant General Major Baurmeister of the Hessian Forces* (hereafter Baurmeister, *Journal*) (New Brunswick: Rutgers University Press, 1957), 118.

31. Washington, General Orders, October 3, 1777, Fitzpatrick, ed., *WGW,* 9: 307–8.

32. Bodle, "Vortex of Small Fortunes," 60–62; Thomas J. McGuire, *The Surprise of Germantown, or the Battle of Cliveden, October 4, 1777* (Philadelphia: Thomas Publications, 1994).

33. John Armstrong to Thomas Wharton, October 5, 1777, Gratz Collection, case 4, box 11, HSP; John Keegan, *The Face of Battle: A Study of Agincourt, Waterloo, and the Somme* (New York: Viking, 1976).

34. George Weedon to ?, October 4, 1777, Weedon Papers, Chicago Historical Society (hereafter ChiHS); Lord Stirling to ?, October 5, 1777, Dealer's Catalogue, American Art Association, 1926; Benjamin Tallmadge to Jeremiah Wadsworth, October 5, 1777, Jeremiah Wadsworth Papers, Connecticut Historical Society (hereafter CHS); William Beatty to his father, October 6, 1777, RG-15, M-804, roll 1561, National Archives (hereafter NA); Jonathan Todd to his father, October 6, 1777, RG-15, M-804, roll 1561 [NA].

35. Charles Stewart to Samuel Gray, October 7, 1777, Samuel Gray Collection, vol. 2, CHS; Eliphalet Dyer to Joseph Trumbull, October 8, 1777, Paul H. Smith, ed., *Letters of Delegates to Congress,* 24 vols. (Washington, D.C.: Library of Congress, 1976–2000) (hereafter *LDC*), 8: 75–76.

36. George Weedon to ?, October 8, 1777, Weedon Papers, ChiHS; Mordecai Gist to John McClure, October 10, 1777, Gist Family Papers, Maryland Hall of Records, Annapolis.

37. Jedediah Huntington to Joseph Trumbull, October 12, 1777, and Henry Knox to Joseph Trumbull, October 19, 1777, Joseph Trumbull Letters, CHS; Thomas McKean to Caesar Rodney, October 15, 1777, John Reed Collection, Valley Forge National Historical Park (hereafter VFNHP); John Armstrong to Wharton, October 14, 1777, Gratz Collection, HSP; Thomas Wharton to Robert Morris, October 18, 1777, Gratz Collection, HSP.

38. Washington to the President of Congress, October 16, 1777, Fitzpatrick, ed., *WGW,* 9: 382; Jedediah Huntington to Andrew Huntington, October 12–18, 1777, Jedediah Huntington Letters, CHS; Jeremiah Talbot to his wife, October 12–18, 1777, Manuscript Division, Princeton University Library (hereafter PUL); Reed, *Campaign to Valley Forge,* 249–53, 262–63.

39. Charles Stewart to Samuel Gray, October 7, 1777, Samuel Gray Papers, CHS; Washington to Governor George Clinton, October 15, 1777, Fitzpatrick, ed., *WGW,* 9: 372–74. For fuller accounts of Burgoyne's campaign, see Pancake, *1777,* chaps. 10, 12; Rupert Furneaux, *The Battle of Saratoga* (New York: Stein and Day, 1971); Max M. Mintz, *The Generals of Saratoga: John Burgoyne and Horatio Gates* (New Haven: Yale University Press, 1990).

40. Washington to the President of Congress, October 16, 1777, Fitzpatrick, ed., *WGW,* 9: 381–83; Jeremiah Talbot to his wife, October 12–18, 1777, Manuscript Division, PUL.

41. William Howe to Henry Clinton, October 8, 1777, Clinton Papers, William L. Clements Library, Ann Arbor, Mich. (hereafter WLC); John Montressor, "Journals of Captain John Montressor, 1777–1778," *Collections of the New-York Historical Society* (New York, 1881), 129.

42. Washington, "Circular Letter to the General Officers," October 26, 1777; Council of War, October 29, 1777; Council of War, November 8, 1777, Fitzpatrick, ed., *WGW,* 9: 441–42, 461–64; X, 23–24; Nathanael Greene to Catharine Greene, November 20, 1777, Showman, ed., *Greene Papers,* 2: 189–90

43. John Armstrong to Thomas Wharton, October 14, 1777, Gratz Collection, HSP; William Howe to Lord George Germain, October 23, 1777, Germain Papers, WLC; Reed, *Campaign to Valley Forge,* 242–43; Ward, *War of the Revolution,* 369–70.

44. See Jacqueline Thibaut, *This Fatal Crisis: Logistics, Supply, and the Continental Army at Valley Forge* (Washington, D.C.: National Park Service, 1980), esp. 96–109. See also E. Wayne Carp,

To Starve the Army at Pleasure: Continental Army Administration and American Political Culture, 1775–1783 (Chapel Hill: University of North Carolina Press, 1984), esp. 35–45.

45. Thomas Jones to Charles Stewart, October 6, 1777, Charles Stewart Collection, NYSHA.

46. *JCC,* 9: 799; John Hancock, Circular Letter to the States, October 17, 1777, PCC, RG 93, M-247, roll 23, NA; Board of War to Thomas Wharton, October 18, 1777, RG-27, 12: 1264–5, PHMC; Thomas Jones to Charles Stewart, October 10, 22, 1777; Robert Dill to Charles Stewart, October 12, 1777, Charles Stewart Collection, NYSHA.

47. Washington to James Potter, October 18, 20, 21, 1777, Fitzpatrick, ed., *WGW,* 9: 391–92, 405–6, 408–9; Supreme Executive Council to the militia lieutenants of Chester County, October 23, 1777, RG-27, 12: 1274–1280, PHMC.

48. Reed, *Campaign to Valley Forge,* 312–19. See John W. Jackson, *Whitemarsh 1777: Impregnable Stronghold* (Norristown, Pa.: Historical Society of Fort Washington, 1984). Jedediah Huntington to his father, October 12, 1777, John Reed Collection, VFNHP; Washington to James M. Varnum, October 28, 1777, Fitzpatrick, ed., *WGW,* 9: 455–57. See Washington to James Potter, October 31, 1777, Fitzpatrick, ed., *WGW,* 9: 474–75; Jedediah Huntington to Jeremiah Wadsworth, November 9, 1777, Jeremiah Wadsworth Papers, LC.

49. Jackson, *Pennsylvania Navy,* chaps. 9–10; Reed, *Campaign to Valley Forge,* chaps. 18–20; Peckham, *Toll of Independence,* 44.

50. George Weedon to John Page, October 31, 1777, Weedon Papers, ChiHS; Matthew Irwin to Colonel Trumbull, October 28, 1777, Joseph Trumbull Collection, CHS; Jedediah Huntington to Colonel Trumbull, October 27, 1777, CHS; John Eccleston to Major Joseph Richardson, October/November 1777, Department of Special Collections, Rutgers University Library, New Brunswick, N.J. (hereafter RUL); Thomas Jones to Charles Stewart, October 29, 1777, Charles Stewart Collection, NYSHA.

51. See Reed, *Campaign to Valley Forge,* 320–50; Jackson, *Pennsylvania Navy,* 225–81; Letterbook of Samuel Smith, September-November, 1777, Maryland Historical Society, Baltimore (hereafter MdHS); Benjamin Tallmadge to Jeremiah Wadsworth, November 12, 1777, John Reed Collection, VFNHP.

52. Clement Biddle to President Thomas Wharton, November 3, 1777, frame 15, reel 13, PHMC; Jedediah Huntington to Jabez Huntington, Jedediah Huntington Letters, CHS; Ephraim Blaine to Colonel John Patton, November 3, 1777, Society Collection, HSP. "Sutlers" were small private retailers of produce and especially liquor who served the army by license on the fringe of its camps. See Holly Mayer, *Belonging to the Army: Camp Followers and the American Revolution* (Columbia: University of South Carolina Press, 1996), chap. 3.

53. Thomas Jones to Charles Stewart, November 16, 1777, Charles Stewart Collection, NYSHA.

54. Daniel Brodhead to Benedict Arnold, November 7, 1777, MS 3305-B, Western Reserve Historical Society, Cleveland, Ohio; Joseph Ward to James Bowdoin, November 12, 1777, Bowdoin-Temple Papers, Massachusetts Historical Society, Boston (hereafter MHS); Jedediah Huntington to his father, November 11, 1777, Jedediah Huntington Letters, CHS.

55. John Armstrong to Thomas Wharton, October 14, 1777, Gratz Collection, HSP; Samuel Hay to William Irvine, November 14, 1777, Draper MSS, series AA, Irvine Papers, State Historical Society of Wisconsin, Madison (hereafter SHSW); Mordecai Gist to "John," November 19, 1777, Force Transcripts, series 7-E, LC. For a more balanced assessment see Rosswurm *Arms, Country, Class,* 140–47.

56. Supreme Executive Council to Congress, November 3, 1777; Board of War to Supreme Executive Council, November 7, 1777, RG-27, reel 13: 008, 013, PHMC (emphasis in original).

57. Arthur St. Clair to Robert Morris, November 13, 1777, Arthur St. Clair Papers, in "The Papers of Thirteen Early Ohio Political Leaders," roll 1, Ohio Historical Society, Columbus (hereafter OHS); Samuel Hay to William Irvine, November 14, 1777, Draper MSS, series AA, Irvine Papers, SHSW; Anthony Wayne to Thomas Wharton, November 22, 1777, Dreer Collection, Generals of the American Revolution, HSP.

58. Henry Laurens to William Palfrey, November 14, 1777, Papers of the Continental Congress, RG-93, M-247, roll 23, NA; Thomas Jones to John Magee, November 23, 1777, RG-27, reel 13: 0142, PHMC.

278 **NOTES TO PAGES 51–54**

59. Reed, *Campaign to Valley Forge,* 320–46; Jackson, *Pennsylvania Navy,* 225–81; Charles Scott to "Frankey," November 15, 1777, John Reed Collection, VFNHP.

60. This is not to suggest that Pennsylvania forces assumed exclusive responsibility for keeping the river closed. Most troops stationed in the twin garrisons, at Fort Mifflin and Fort Mercer, were Continentals after early October. But militia forces were indispensable for supporting the forts and also for upholding a blockade of the roads running along the river. And Pennsylvania also contributed the bulk of the small vessels and crews that were used to obstruct and harass British warships and transports on the river below the *chevaux de frise.* See Jackson, *Pennsylvania Navy,* esp. 215–16, 220–21, 244–45, 250–52, 256–58.

61. The newcomers were already rendering their recently defeated nemesis into a folkloric verb form that must have maddened the Middle Atlantic and southern troops who dominated the main army. Early in 1778, only two months after joining Washington's troops in Pennsylvania, Major Samuel Armstrong of Massachusetts dismissed a Continental skirmish that captured a British vessel on the Delaware River by recording it in his diary with the laconic entry that it was *"something like Burgoining."* See "From Saratoga to Valley Forge: The Diary of Lt. Samuel Armstrong," ed. Joseph Lee Boyle, *PMHB* 121 (1997): 261 (italics added).

62. Anderson, *People's Army,* esp. chaps. 1–2; Kenneth A. Lockridge, *Literacy in Colonial New England: An Enquiry into the Social Context of Literacy in the Early West* (New York: W. W. Norton, 1974), esp. chap. 2.

63. Philip Greven, *Four Generations: Population, Land, and Family in Colonial Andover, Massachusetts* (Ithaca: Cornell University Press, 1970), chaps. 7–8; Jones, "Strolling Poor," and "Poverty and Vagabondage: The Process of Survival in Eighteenth Century Massachusetts," *New England Historical and Genealogical Register* 133 (October 1979): 243–54; Douglas Lamar Jones, *Village and Seaport: Migration and Society in Eighteenth Century Massachusetts* (Hanover, N.H.: University Press of New England, 1981); Daniel F. Vickers, *Farmers and Fishermen: Two Centuries of Work in Essex County, Massachusetts, 1630–1850* (Chapel Hill: University of North Carolina Press, 1994), esp. 143–203, 263–73; Nash, *Urban Crucible,* 313–15; Herndon, *Unwelcome Americans;* Sharon Salinger and Cornelia Dayton, "Mapping Migration into Pre-Revolutionary Boston: An Analysis of Robert Love's Warning Out Book," unpub. paper given at the seminar of the McNeil Center for Early American Studies, Philadelphia, September 10, 1999, and at a workshop at the University of California, Riverside, March 4, 2000.

64. Lemon, *Best Poor Man's Country,* esp. chaps. 1, 8; Thomas M. Doerflinger, *A Vigorous Spirit of Enterprise: Merchants and Economic Development in Revolutionary Philadelphia* (Chapel Hill: University of North Carolina Press, 1986), esp. chaps. 1–3; Nash, *Urban Crucible,* chap. 12; Boyle, ed., "From Saratoga to Valley Forge."

65. Lemon, *Best Poor Man's Country,* on farm sizes, 88–93. Farm sizes were shrinking near Philadelphia, too, but see the introduction, above, for a discussion of the buffering contexts of this phenomenon. See Jackson, *Pennsylvania Navy,* chap. 12, for the row-galley fleet, esp. 259–69.

66. Washington to Generals St. Clair, DeKalb, and Knox, November 17, 1777; Washington to John Glover or [the] Officer Commanding his Brigade, November 19, 1777; Washington to James M. Varnum, November 19, 1777; Washington to Nathanael Greene, November 22, 1777 (two letters), November 24, 1777, Fitzpatrick, ed., *WGW,* 10: 77–78, 83–85, 95–96, 103; John Armstrong to Thomas Wharton, November 23, 29, 1777, Gratz Collection, HSP.

67. Nathanael Greene to Catharine Greene, November 21, 1777, Showman, ed., *Greene Papers,* 2: 200; Elias Boudinot to his wife, November 30, 1777, Division of Special Collection, PUL; Washington to Greene, November 25, 1777, Fitzpatrick, ed., *WGW,* 10: 104–5.

68. Major General Charles Gray to ?, November 28, 1777, Andre deCoppet Collection, PUL; Samuel Hay to William Irvine, November 14, 1777, Draper MSS, series AA, Irvine Papers, SHSW; John Eccleston to Major Joseph Richardson, November 15, 1777, Special Collections, RUL; Joseph Ward to James Bowdoin, November 12, 1777, Bowdoin-Temple Papers, MHS; Thomas Conway to Robert Morris, August 9, 1777, Sol Feinstone Collection, David Library of the American Revolution, Washington Crossing, Pa., doc. no. 199 (microfilm).

69. Louis Lebeque Duportail to St. Germaine, November 12, 1777, (copy) Andre deCoppet Collection, PUL.

CHAPTER 3   Doing What We Can

1. Supreme Executive Council to Congress, November 28, 1777, frame 0140, reel 13, PHMC; Jedediah Huntington to his father, November 11, 1777, Jedediah Huntington Letters, CHS; Elias Boudinot to Joshua Mersereau, December 14, 1777, Elias Boudinot Letterbook, SHSW. For some of these "canvasses," see Washington, Circular to the General Officers, October 26, 1777; Council of War, October 29, 1777, Fitzpatrick, ed., *WGW,* 9: 441–42, 461–64.

2. Supreme Executive Council, "Remonstrance of Council and Assembly to Congress, 1777," in Samuel Hazard, ed., *Pennsylvania Archives,* ser. 1 (Philadelphia, 1953), vol. 6, 104–5; Ousterhout, *State Divided,* chap. 5. Brunhouse, *Counter-Revolution in Pennsylvania,* chap. 2; Hawke, *In the Midst of a Revolution;* Arnold, *Republican Revolution,* 58–148.

3. See also, Wayne Bodle, "This Tory Labyrinth: Community, Conflict, and Military Strategy During the Valley Forge Winter," in Michael Zuckerman, ed., *Friends and Neighbors: Group Life in America's First Plural Society* (Philadelphia: Temple University Press, 1982), 222–50.

4. See H. James Henderson, *Party Politics in the Continental Congress* (New York: McGraw-Hill, 1974), esp. chaps. 5, 6, and 7. Henderson emphasizes the regional and, secondarily, the ideological bases of division, and he consciously characterizes these patterns as illustrative of loosely organized "parties." For a contrary view, denying the existence of parties, see Jack N. Rakove, *The Beginnings of National Politics: An Interpretive History of the Continental Congress* (New York: Alfred A. Knopf, 1979), esp. chaps 7–10. Both books offer valuable insights into Continental politics and are used here wherever they seem appropriate. This study suggests that there were important alignments in Congress along the lines traced by Henderson, but that during 1777–78 they were not automatically triggered in predictable ways by every issue facing the delegates. See also Calvin Jillson and Rick K. Wilson, *Congressional Dynamics: Structure, Coordination, and Choice in the First American Congress, 1774–1789* (Stanford: Stanford University Press, 1994), chaps. 6–7.

5. Rakove, *Beginnings,* 116–17 and chap. 7, esp. 176–82; Henderson, *Party Politics,* chap. 6, esp. 146–52. These articles were not finally ratified by the states until 1781.

6. During summer 1777, for example, Congress joined in a dispute over the command of the northern army in the Hudson Valley, thereby exacerbating factional tensions between New Englanders, on the one hand, and New Yorkers and southerners, on the other. That episode bore happy fruit in the October 1777 victory at Saratoga, but it caused bitter resentments within the military establishment and these ultimately penetrated the command hierarchy around Washington. Jonathan Gregory Rossie, *The Politics of Command in the American Revolution* (Syracuse: Syracuse University Press, 1975), chaps 8–11; Pancake, *1777,* 146–50.

7. William Ellery to Nicholas Cooke, November 30, 1777; Cornelius Harnett to William Wilkinson, November 30, 1777; William Duer to James Wilson, November 30, 1777; Henry Laurens to John Rutledge, December 1, 1777, in Smith, ed., *LDC,* 8: 345, 347–48, 359; *JCC,* 9: 972. The delegates were Robert Morris of Pennsylvania, a conservative who usually sided with the Southern bloc, Elbridge Gerry of Massachusetts, a strong member of the New England party, and Joseph Jones of Virginia, a moderate conservative.

8. Washington to Joseph Reed, December 2, 1777, Fitzpatrick, ed., *WGW,* 10:, 133.

9. Ibid. "Embarrassed" should be understood here in its secondary eighteenth-century meaning of "perplexed" or "confused." See the *Compact Oxford English Dictionary,* 2d ed. (Oxford: Oxford University Press, 1991) (hereafter *Compact OED*), 509.

10. These opinions are found in series 4 (microfilm), George Washington Papers, Library of Congress (hereafter GWP, LC). "Recruiting" clearly included the process of raising the army's numerical strength, but it also seems to have connoted the eighteenth-century medical meaning: to "recover vigor or health" or to "refresh and reinvigorate." See *Compact OED,* 1530.

11. Opinions of Generals Henry Knox, Peter Muhlenberg, and George Weedon (quoted); and those of Generals Johan De Kalb, William Maxwell, Enoch Poor, John Sullivan, James Varnum, and William Woodford, all December 1, 1777, in GWP, LC.

12. Muhlenberg, Poor, Weedon, and Woodford were the Virginians. Henry Knox came from Massachusetts, John Sullivan from New Hampshire, and James Varnum from Rhode Island. Johan De Kalb was a Bavarian volunteer, while William Maxwell lived in New Jersey.

13. Opinions of Nathanael Greene and the Marquis de Lafayette, December 1, 1777, GWP, LC.

14. Opinions of Generals John Armstrong, Anthony Wayne, and Louis Lebeque Duportail, December 1, 1777, GWP, LC (emphasis added). General William Smallwood of Maryland also voted for Wilmington, as did Charles Scott of Virginia.

15. Opinions of Lord Stirling and James Irvine, December 1, 1777, GWP, LC.

16. Washington to Joseph Reed, December 2, 1777; Washington to Horatio Gates, December 2, 1777, Fitzpatrick, ed., *WGW*, 10: 133. See Benjamin Newcomb, "Washington's Generals and the Decision to Quarter at Valley Forge," *PMHB* 117 (October 1993): 309–29, esp. 321, for the insightful suggestion that Washington's preference was at least implied, if not signaled, by his manner of stating the results of the poll.

17. Washington, Circular to the General Officers, December 3, 1777, Fitzpatrick, ed., *WGW*, 10: 135. The divisions on the second question were Generals John Cadwallader, John Armstrong, James Irvine, James Potter, and Anthony Wayne in favor of a winter campaign, and Nathanael Greene, Henry Knox, Lord Stirling, James Varnum, William Maxwell, Peter Muhlenberg, John Paterson, Richard Poor, Charles Scott, William Smallwood, James Sullivan, George Weedon, and William Woodford opposed in varying degrees of intensity. Louis Duportail and the Marquis de Lafayette withheld their sentiments on the question, while Johan De Kalb qualified his opinion carefully. The opinions are all dated December 3 or December 4, 1777, GWP, LC.

18. Opinions of Generals Armstrong, Cadwallader, Irvine, Potter, and Wayne, Ibid.

19. Robert Morris to President Wharton, November 30, 1777, Smith, ed., *LDC*, 8: 352–53; "In Council of Safety," November 28, 1777, *Minutes of the Supreme Executive Council of Pennsylvania* (Harrisburg, 1852), 11: 350–51. The identity and background of "James Young, Esq." are obscure. The Council of Safety met between sittings of the Assembly and had broad, if vaguely specified, authority to act under the latter body's many constitutional powers. *JCC*, 9: 976.

20. John Laurens to Henry Laurens, December 3, 1777, David R. Chesnutt, ed., *The Papers of Henry Laurens*, 12: 129–30. Laurens, of course, loaded the question by his description of the alternatives.

21. Elbridge Gerry to John Adams, December 3, 1777, Smith, ed., *LDC*, 8: 373.

22. Colonel John Bayard to President Wharton, December 4, 1777, *Pennsylvania Archives*, ser. 1, vol. 6, 61–62.

23. "Robert Morris' Committee Notes" (c. December 4, 1777); Committee at Headquarters to Henry Laurens, December 6, 1777; Elbridge Gerry to James Warren, December 12, 1777, Smith, ed., *LDC*, 8: 377–78, 380–81, 404; Reed, *Campaign to Valley Forge*, 371–73; Mackesy, *War for America*, 130.

24. See John Armstrong to Thomas Wharton, December 7–9, 1777 (typescript), Society Collection, HSP; William Howe to Henry Clinton, December 12, 1777, Clinton Papers, WLC; William Howe to Lord George Germain, December 13, 1777, Germain Papers, WLC; Benjamin Tallmadge to Jeremiah Wadsworth, December 9, 1777, Jeremiah Wadsworth Papers, Correspondence, CHS.

25. Jedediah Huntington to Joshua Huntington, December 9, 1777, Jedediah Huntington Letters, CHS; Jedediah Huntington to Joseph Trumbull, December 10, 1777, Joseph Trumbull Papers, CHS; John Steel Tyler to ?, December 10, 1777, John Reed Collection, VFNHP; Benjamin Tallmadge to Jeremiah Wadsworth, December 9, 1777, Jeremiah Wadsworth Papers, Correspondence, CHS.

26. Elbridge Gerry to John Adams, December 8, 1777, Smith, ed., *LDC*, 8: 388.

27. Cornelius Harnett to Thomas Burke, December 8, 1777, Ibid., 389; John Armstrong to Supreme Executive Council, December 7/9 1777, *Pennsylvania Archives*, ser. 1, vol. 6, 71; Elias Boudinot to Thomas Wharton, December 9, 1777, and Joseph Reed to [Thomas Wharton], December 10, 1777, Joseph Reed Papers, reel 2, New-York Historical Society (hereafter NYHS).

28. James Young left camp for Easton by December 8 to investigate the collection of clothing there, the stated point of his and Bayard's visit. See James Young to Thomas Wharton, December 8, 1777, RG-27, 13: 200–201, PHMC. But Bayard's oblique remark about staying at Whitemarsh until the army's disposition was settled suggests the continued involvement of the state's emissaries in the larger question of winter quarters and tactics.

29. Committee at Headquarters to Washington, December 10, 1777, Smith, ed., *LDC,* 8: 399. John Armstrong, who was summoned to meet with the conferees that day, "suppose[d] our next movement is the subject & perhaps the much heavier point—a dispossission of this Army for the Winter." He called the latter "a point . . . of the utmost importance to Pennsylva[ni]a, and to which I have paid & shall pay every degree of attention in my power." John Armstrong to Thomas Wharton, December 7/[9], 1777, *Pennsylvania Archives,* ser. 1 vol. 6, 71–72.

30. Joseph Reed to Thomas Wharton, December 10, 1777, Joseph Reed Papers, NYHS, reel 2.

31. Joseph Reed to Thomas Wharton, December 13, 1777, Ibid; "Order of March from Whitemarsh" (December 10, 1777), in Showman, ed., *Papers of Nathanael Greene,* 2: 238–41. For New Jersey's pleas, see William Maxwell to Washington, December 9, 1777, GWP, LC.

32. Reed, *Campaign to Valley Forge,* 384–87. The orders specified that on "the first day's march, the head of the Column [would] reach the Lancaster Road." Such a movement would have carried the army beyond Valley Forge. "Order of March from Whitemarsh" (December 10, 1777), Showman, ed., *Greene Papers,* 2: 239. This suggests that while an agreement in principal had been struck on the ninth to keep the army near Philadelphia, the exact site of its winter quarters was not settled by the eleventh. Circumstantial evidence, and the renewed debate discussed below, suggest that Washington may have presumed that the December 9 agreement left the army free to move to the generals' "second choice" site at Wilmington, and that he may have intended to take it there.

33. Joseph Reed to Thomas Wharton, December 13, 1777, Joseph Reed Papers, NYHS, reel 2; "Order of March from Whitemarsh" (December 10, 1777), Showman, ed., *Greene Papers,* 2: 239. Reed lamented that now "Whig inhabitants [west of the Schuylkill] must fly." He may have misconstrued Greene's phrase "to serve as a covering party" to mean that the brigade in question would "cover" the Pennsylvania countryside rather than the army's movement across the river.

34. Elias Boudinot to Thomas Wharton, December 9, 1777, Joseph Reed Papers, NYHS, reel 2; Jedediah Huntington to Andrew Huntington, December 9, 1777, Jedediah Huntington Papers, CHS; Jedediah Huntington to Col. Joseph Trumbull, December 10, 1777, Joseph Trumbull Papers, CHS.

35. James Potter to President Thomas Wharton, December 11, 1777; John Armstrong to President Thomas Wharton, December 14, 1777, *Pennsylvania Archives,* ser. 1, vol. 6, 83, 90–91.

36. Thomas Wharton to Elias Boudinot, December 13, 1777, *Pennsylvania Archives,* ser. 1, vol. 6, 89; *Minutes of the Supreme Executive Council,* 11: 386; "Remonstrance of Council and Assembly to Congress" (December 1777), *Pennsylvania Archives,* ser. 1, vol. 6, 104–5. The remonstrance is undated but was probably drawn up on December 15, and no later than the seventeenth.

37. John Laurens to Henry Laurens, December 15, 1777, in Chesnutt, ed., *Papers of Henry Laurens,* 12: 157–58; John Armstrong to Thomas Wharton, December 16, 1777, *Pennsylvania Archives,* ser. 1, vol. 6, 101. The precise moment when Valley Forge was chosen as the army's winter campsite remains unclear, but December 16 stands out as the likeliest day.

38. Washington, General Orders, December 17, 1777, Fitzpatrick, ed., *WGW,* 10: 167–68.

39. These proceedings can be followed in *JCC,* 9: 1029–36. Jonathan Bayard Smith to George Bryan, December 19, 1777 (two letters); Abraham Clark to William Alexander, December 20, 1777, Smith, ed., *LDC,* 8: 442–44.

40. Henderson, *Party Politics in the Continental Congress,* chaps. 5–7; Rossie, *Politics of Command,* chaps. 10–11; Gerry to Adams, and Harnett to Burke, December 8, 1777, Smith, ed., *LDC,* 8: 388–89.

41. Brunhouse, *Counter-Revolution in Pennsylvania,* chaps. 2–3. *JCC,* 9: 976–78 (November 28, 1777); Joseph S. Foster, *In Pursuit of Equal Liberty: George Bryan and the Revolution in Pennsylvania* (University Park: The Pennsylvania State University Press, 1994).

42. John F. Roche, *Joseph Reed: A Moderate in the American Revolution* (New York: Columbia University Press, 1957), 76–83, 114–25; Ryerson, *Revolution Is Now Begun,* 156–62, 169, 172n, 219–20; Hawke, *In the Midst of a Revolution,* 140.

43. Ryerson, *Revolution Is Now Begun,* 132, 191, 205n, 210, 214, 237, 242–43; Hawke, *Midst of a Revolution,* 100; Thayer, *Pennsylvania Politics,* 187–88; Brunhouse, *Counter-Revolution in Pennsylvania,* 18–19; Selsam, *Pennsylvania Constitution of 1776,* 226–27; Arnold, *Republican Revolution,* 70; Brunhouse, *Counter-Revolution in Pennsylvania,* 76.

44. Milton E. Flower, *John Dickinson, Conservative Revolutionary* (Charlottesville: University Press of Virginia, 1983), 87; Ryerson, *Revolution Is Now Begun,* 214, 227; Hawke, *In the Midst of a Revolution,* 135–36, 195–96; Rosswurm, *Arms, Country, and Class,* 99–100; John Cadwallader to Joseph Reed, December 10, 1777, Joseph Reed Papers, NYHS, reel 2.

45. Cornelius Harnett to William Wilkinson, December 8, 1777, Smith, ed., *LDC,* 8: 390–91. For the view that the decision was so forced, see Reed, *Campaign to Valley Forge,* 393–94. Reed and other historians who see a political dimension to the decision about the army's winter placement rely entirely for evidence on the Pennsylvania "Remonstrance," which did not reach the army until after it was at Valley Forge. For a critique of the political interpretation, which differs from the arguments presented here, see Newcomb, "Washington's Generals," 309–11.

46. John C. Miller, *The Triumph of Freedom: 1775–1783* (Boston: Little, Brown, 1948), 221; Thomas Jones to Thomas Wharton, December 19, 1777, RG-27, 13: 302, PHMC.

47. Washington to the President of Congress, December 23, 1777, Fitzpatrick, ed., *WGW,* 10: 192.

48. The "Diary of Albigence Waldo," *PMHB* 21 (1897): 299–323, is by far the most often-quoted source of these disorderly behaviors by Continental troops at the beginning of the encampment.

49. Joseph Ward to Samuel Adams, December 17, 1777 (typescript), Chicago Historical Society (original in New York Public Library). For Congress's proclamation of December 18 as a "day of prayer and thanksgiving" for the American victory at Saratoga, see *JCC,* 9: 851, 854–55.

CHAPTER 4   Learning to Live with War

1. Brigadier General James M. Varnum to (Mrs.?) William Greene, March 7, 1778, John Reed Collection, VFNHP; Major General Charles Gray to ?, November 28, 1777, Andre deCoppet Collection, PUL.

2. Colonel Stuart to Lord Bute, August 21, 1777, in Violet Stuart Wortley, ed., *A Prime Minister and His Son: From the Correspondence of the 3rd Earl of Bute and of Lt.-General The Hon. Sir Charles Stuart, K.B.* (New York: E. P. Dutton, 1925), 114–15.

3. Ibid., August 31, 1777, 116; "Journal of General von Heister, 1776–1778," August 28, 1777, Lidgerwood Collection, Morristown National Historical Park, Hessian Documents of the American Revolution, microfiche 45; "The Services of Lieut-Colonel Francis Downman, R.A.," *Minutes of Proceedings of the Royal Artillery Institution,* 25 (Woolwich, Eng., 1898), 154. See also Edward H. Tatum, Jr., ed., *The American Journal of Ambrose Serle, Secretary to Lord Howe, 1776–1778* (San Marino, Calif.: Huntington Library, 1940) (hereafter Serle, *Journal*), 246; Captain Johan Ewald, *Diary of the American War: A Hessian Journal,* trans. and ed. by Joseph P. Tustin (New Haven: Yale University Press, 1979), 75–76.

4. Colonel Stuart to Lord Bute, August 31, 1777, in Wortley, ed., *Prime Minister and His Son,* 115; "Services of Francis Downman," 155; Journal of a British officer, "Campaign of 1777," Sol Feinstone Collection, David Library of the American Revolution," doc. no. 409 (September 8, 1777); Robert Francis Seybolt, ed., "A Contemporary British Account of General Sir William Howe's Military Operations in 1777," *Proceedings of the American Antiquarian Society,* n.s. 40 (1930): 77.

5. "Journal of General von Heister" (September 6–7, 1777).

6. Ewald, *Diary,* 81, 87–88.

7. "Narrative of Sarah Frazer, daughter of Gen. Frazer" (September 11, 1840?), in *General Persifor Frazer, A Memoir,* 155. This is a complex text, integrating the narratives of several of Frazer's descendants from various times between 1800 and 1850, which are later combined in ways difficult for us to recover today. The "voices" in question are sometimes ambiguous, but the text, if handled cautiously, offers valuable perspectives on the events of 1777–78.

8. Ibid., 155–56. Linda K. Kerber, *Women of the Republic: Intellect and Ideology in Revolutionary America* (Chapel Hill: University of North Carolina Press, 1980), esp. chaps. 2 and 3; Mary Beth Norton, *Liberty's Daughters: The Revolutionary Experience of American Women, 1750–1800* (Boston: Little, Brown, 1980), esp. chap. 7.

9. Joseph Townsend, *The Battle of Brandywine* (Philadelphia, 1846; rpt. New York: New York Times and Arno Press, 1969), 18–19. See chap. 1, supra, esp. 16–21.

10. Townsend, *Battle of Brandywine,* 20–21.

11. Ibid., 21–22 (emphasis added in Sarah Boake quotation).

12. Ibid., 22–23.

13. Ibid., 23–25.

14. Ibid., 26.

15. Ibid., 26–27.

16. Ibid., 28.

17. Ibid., 28–29

18. *General Persifor Frazer, A Memoir,* 157.

19. Ibid., 157–59. On Anglo-Scottish relations, see Linda Colley, *Britons: Forging the Nation, 1707–1837* (New Haven: Yale University Press, 1992), esp. 113–32.

20. *General Persifor Frazer, A Memoir,* 158–60.

21. Ibid., 161. On Grant's ethnicity, see Paul David Nelson, *General James Grant: Scottish Soldier and Royal Governor of East Florida* (Gainesville: University Press of Florida, 1993), 4.

22. "Some Extracts from the Papers of General Persifor Frazer," *PMHB* 31 (1907): 129–44, 311–19, 447–51.

23. See chap. 3, above.

24. Thomas Livezey to Joseph Reed and John Cadwallader, October 29, 1777, Cadwallader Collection, General John Cadwallader Papers, box 15, folder 18, HSP. Galloway, the former speaker of the Pennsylvania Assembly and a leading opponent of independence, fled to the British army in New York in late 1776 and returned with them when they invaded the state the next year. In December 1777 General Howe named him to oversee the civilian constabulary in Philadelphia.

25. Thomas Livezey to Joseph Reed and John Cadwallader, October 29, 1777, Cadwallader Collection, General John Cadwallader Papers, HSP.

26. Kathryn Zabelle Derounian, ed., *The Journal and Occasional Writings of Sarah Wister* (Rutherfurd, N.J.: Fairleigh Dickinson University Press, 1987), 13–16.

27. Ibid., 41–43.

28. Ibid., 44, 50.

29. Ibid.

30. Ibid., 46–47 (October 20, 21, 27, 1777).

31. Ibid., 48–50 (October 31, November 1, 3, 1777).

32. Ibid., 50–52 (December 5, 7, 1777).

33. Ibid., 43, 52–53 (September 5, December 7, 11, 1777).

34. Ibid., 53.

35. Ibid., 54–57 (December 12–14, 19, 20, 1777).

36. Amandus Johnson, ed., *The Journal and Biography of Nicholas Collin, 1746–1831* (Philadelphia: New Jersey Society of Pennsylvania, 1936), 241.

37. Ibid., 240–49 (quotations on pp. 240–41).

38. Muhlenberg, *Diary,* 3: 73–105. Sixteen reports of firing in sixty entries amount to 26 percent. Quotations on pp. 73–74, 76.

39. Ibid., 79, 81–82, 84.

40. Ibid., 85–91.

41. Ibid., 95, 97–105 (November 3, 5, 14, 1777).

42. Ibid., 74–75, 77, 79 (September 10, 13, 14, 15, 19, 22, 1777). Emphasis in original.

43. Ibid., 76–77.

44. Ibid., 78, 79, 80, 82, 84 (September 23, 25, 26, October 9, 1777).

45. Ibid., 77–78 (September 17–21, 1777). See chap. 1, passim.

46. Ibid.

47. Ibid., 81, 87 (September 28, October 15, 1777).

48. Ibid., 88 (October 19, 1777).

49. Ibid., 92 (October 24, 1777).

50. Ibid., 106, 109 (November 21, December 1, 1777), 67–71.

51. Ibid., 112, 114 (December 11, 17, 1777).

52. William F. Duane, ed., *Extracts from the Diary of Christopher Marshall During the American Revolution, 1774–1781,* (Albany, N.Y.: J. Munsell, 1877), 128–38 (September 19 and October 22–23, 1777). For Marshall, see Ryerson, *Revolution Is Now Begun,* 240–41.

53. Duane, ed., *Marshall Diary,* 140–41, (October 30, November 2, November 22, 1777); Marshall to his sons, November 22, 1777, Marshall Letterbook, HSP.

54. Duane, ed., *Marshall Diary,* 149 (December 13, 1777, emphasis added).

55. Elaine Forman Crane et al., eds., *The Diary of Elizabeth Drinker,* 3 vols. (Boston: Northeastern University Press, 1992), 1: 236–38 (September 27, 29, 30, October 2, 1777).

56. Ibid., 240, 243 (October 4, 14, 16, 1777).

57. Ibid., 240–41, 246 (October 6, 7, 20, 1777).

58. Ibid., 246 (October 18, 19, 1777).

59. Ibid., 238, 250 (October 2, November 1, 1777).

60. Ibid., 251 (November 7, 1777), 261 (December 9, 1777).

61. Ibid., 254–58.

62. Ibid., 258, 266 (November 25, December 19, 1777); 261–63 (December 1, 4, 8, 13 1777). The use of such an explicitly military term as "countermanded" by a Quaker woman, again, suggests the increasingly complex entanglement of civil and military worlds as the occupation proceeded.

63. Ibid., 262, 266, 267, 271 (December 9, 18, 19, 20, 29, 31, 1777). For the military and civilian uses of the term "family," see *OED,* 4: 55 [1 ©, and 2 (a)].

64. "The Diary of Robert Morton, Kept in Philadelphia While That City Was Occupied by the British Army in 1777," *PMHB* 1 (1877): 4, 8, 10 (September 19, 26, 30, 1777).

65. See the 1777 William Faden map of Philadelphia (London, 1778) for most of these geographical referents, and the maps in John W. Jackson, *With the British Army in Philadelphia, 1777–1778* (San Rafael, Calif.: Presidio Press, 1979), 166–67, for some depiction of the militarization of these features after the occupation began.

66. "Morton Diary," 13–15. (October 4, 5, 1777).

67. Ibid., 15–18 (October 6, 7, 8, 11, 12, 1777).

68. Ibid., 17–19 (October 11, 13, 15, 18, 1777).

69. Ibid., 19 (October 16, 1777).

70. Ibid., 20 (October 19, 1777).

71. Ibid., 22–23.

72. Ibid., 23 (October 24, 1777).

73. Ibid., 25–26, 28 (November 15, 1777).

74. Ibid., 32–33. (c. November 30, December 1, 2, 3, 1777).

75. E. James Ferguson, *The Power of the Purse: A History of American Public Finance, 1776–1790* (Chapel Hill: University of North Carolina Press, 1961), pt. 1, esp. chap. 2; William Graham Sumner, *The Financier and the Finances of the American Revolution* (New York: Burt Franklin, 1970; orig. pub. 1891), chaps. 2–4; Albert S. Bolles, *The Financial History of the United States from 1774 to 1789* (New York: D. Appleton, 1879; rpt. New York, August M. Kelley, 1969), 3 vols., 1: chaps. 1–5; Charles J. Bullock, *The Finances of the United States from 1775 to 1789, With Especial Reference to the Budget* (Madison, Wis., 1895: rpt. Philadelphia: Porcupine Press, 1979); William G. Anderson, *The Price of Liberty: The Public Debt of the American Revolution* (Charlottesville: University Press of Virginia, 1983), pt. 1.

76. "Morton Diary," 32–33 (c. December 1–3, 1777).

77. Mary M. Schweitzer, *Custom and Contract: Household, Government, and the Economy in Colonial Pennsylvania* (New York: Columbia University Press, 1987), esp. chaps. 4–5; Tully, "Quaker Party and Proprietary Policies," 84–85.

78. I am grateful to John Shy for making this perceptive suggestion about the real meaning of the winter-long struggle between the armies over the area's foodstuffs—the geopolitical implications of which I was far too long in fully comprehending—many years ago.

79. See Bodle, "This Tory Labyrinth," 236–44, for a fuller discussion of these points, and Shy, *People Numerous and Armed,* 195–224, for a somewhat different point of view; "Morton Diary," 37.

80. "Morton Diary," 39 (December 30, 1777).

CHAPTER 5   Starve, Dissolve, or Disperse

1. Thomas Jones to President Thomas Wharton, December 19, 1777, RG-27, frame 0302, reel 13, PHMC.

2. John Armstrong to Washington, December 19, 1777, GWP, LC. The question of how many men Pennsylvania would keep in the field was the subject of much correspondence between Washington and state leaders. Eventually they agreed to place 1,000 east of the Schuylkill, but the state actually fielded far fewer men for most of the winter. See John Armstrong to Washington, December 29 and 30, 1777, GWP, LC; Washington to Thomas Wharton, January 1, 1778, Fitzpatrick, ed., *WGW*, 10: 246–47; Wharton to Washington, January 3, 1778, GWP, LC; James Potter to Wharton, December 28, 1777, Gratz Collection, HSP.

3. Washington to James Potter, December 21, 1777, Fitzpatrick, ed., *WGW*, 10: 182; Lord Stirling to Washington, December 23, 1777, GWP, LC.

4. Washington, General Orders, December 20, 1777, Fitzpatrick, ed., *WGW*, 10: 180–81; Jedediah Huntington to Joseph Trumbull, December 10, 1777, Joseph Trumbull Collection, CHS; Mordecai Gist to John McClure (typescript), December 16, 1777, Gist Family Papers, folder 23, Maryland Hall of Records, Annapolis. For a definitive account of the design and construction of the Valley Forge camp see Thibaut, *In the True Rustic Order.*

5. Thomas Paine to Benjamin Franklin, May 16, 1778, in William B. Willcox et al., eds., *The Papers of Benjamin Franklin* (New Haven: Yale University Press, 1959–), vol. 26, 487; Washington to William Smallwood, December 19, 1777; Washington to Governor George Read of Delaware, December 19, 1777, Fitzpatrick, ed., *WGW*, 10: 171–72, 174–75. Smallwood took about 1,800 Maryland and Delaware troops, only two-thirds of them fit for duty, to Wilmington. See Lesser, *Sinews of Independence,* 54.

6. Washington, General Orders, December 20, 1777, Fitzpatrick, ed., *WGW*, 10: 181; Anthony Wayne to Washington, December 26, 1777, GWP, LC.

7. Wayne to Washington, December 26, 1777; John Clark to Washington, December 30, 1777, GWP, LC.

8. Benjamin Tallmadge to Jeremiah Wadsworth, December 30, 1777, Jeremiah Wadsworth Papers, Correspondence, CHS; Washington, General Orders, December 20, 26, 27, 28, Fitzpatrick, ed., *WGW*, 10: 180–81, 205–7, 214–15.

9. John Armstrong to Washington, December 19, 23, 1777, GWP, LC.

10. Washington to Major John Jameson, December 24, 1777; Washington to President Thomas Wharton, January 1, 1778, Fitzpatrick, ed., *WGW*, 10: 199, 246–47; Jameson to Washington, December 31, 1777, GWP, LC; Lord Stirling to Washington, December 26, 1777, GWP, LC.

11. John Clark to Washington, December 19, 20, 1777, GWP, LC.

12. Clark to Washington, December 19, 1777, GWP, LC; Bowler, *Logistics and the Failure of the British Army,* 113–19, 265–67, "Appendix: British Army Food Reserves, 1775–1783." The Delaware islands below the city had historically furnished salt grass hay and provided for the considerable grazing needs of Philadelphians. See Lemon, *Best Poor Man's Country,* 175.

13. Washington to Potter, December 21, 1777, Fitzpatrick, ed., *WGW*, 10: 182; Tench Tilghman to Major Clark, December 21, 1777; Clark to Washington, December 21, 1777, GWP, LC.

14. Jedediah Huntington to Timothy Pickering, December 22, 1777; James Varnum to Washington, December 22, 1777, GWP, LC.

15. Washington to the President of Congress, December 22, 1777, Fitzpatrick, ed., *WGW*, 10: 183.

16. Ibid. ("3 O'Clock P.M.").

17. Ernst Kipping and Samuel Stelle Smith, trans. and eds., *At General Howe's Side, 1776–1778: The Diary of General William Howe's Aide-de-Camp, Captain Friedrich von Muenchhausen* (Monmouth Beach, N.J.: Philip Freneau Press, 1974), 46 (hereafter Muenchhausen, *Diary*). Montressor, "Journal," 480. John Clark to Washington (two letters), December 22, 1777; James Potter to Washington (four letters), December 23, 1777, GWP, LC.

18. Washington, After Orders, December 22, 1777, Fitzpatrick, ed., *WGW*, 10: 192. See Washington to the President of Congress, December 23, 1777, Ibid., 195, for this estimate of the

number disabled by clothing shortages. In *Sinews of War,* 55, Lesser writes that 958 men lacked "shoes, etc.," but 2,000 more were listed as being "sick present." Based on the sixteen brigades present in camp, these detachments would have comprised (with officers) approximately 950 men.

19. Daniel Morgan to Washington, December 23, 1777; James Potter to Washington, December 23, 1777, GWP, LC.

20. James Potter to Washington, December 23, 1777, GWP, LC; Muenchhausen, *Diary,* 46.

21. Daniel Morgan to Washington, December 23, 24, 1777; Henry Lee to Washington, December 23, 1777; Lord Stirling to Washington, December 24, 1777; James Potter to Washington, December 24, 1777, GWP, LC; Muenchhausen, *Diary,* 46.

22. John Armstrong to Washington (two letters), December 23, 1777, GWP, LC; Lord Stirling to Washington, December 23, 24, 1777; Morgan to Washington, December 24, 1777; William Smallwood to Washington, December 25, 1777, GWP, LC.

23. Stirling to Washington, December 24, 1777, GWP, LC.

24. Washington, General Orders, December 25, 1777, Fitzpatrick, ed., *WGW,* 10: 205; Tench Tilghman to Lord Stirling, December 25, 1777, GWP, LC.

25. Clark to Washington, December 25, 26 1777; Stirling to Washington, December 25, 1777, GWP, LC; Muenchhausen, *Diary,* 46.

26. John Clark to Washington, December 26, 28, 1777; Lord Stirling to Washington, December 26, 1777 (7 P.M.), GWP, LC; Muenchhausen, *Diary,* 46; Montressor, "Journal," December 28, 1777, 480; *Pennsylvania Evening Post,* January 3, 1777.

27. Washington to Lord Stirling, December 28, 1777, Autograph Letters of George Washington, Pierpont Morgan Library, New York; James Potter to Thomas Wharton, December 28, 1777, Gratz Collection, HSP; John Clark to Washington, December 28, 30, 1777, GWP, LC.

28. Washington to the President of Congress, December 23, 1777, Fitzpatrick, ed., *WGW,* 10: 192–93.

29. Ibid.

30. Ibid., 194. Washington's published correspondence renders this claim doubtful. See Fitzpatrick, ed., *WGW,* 7: 160–61, 182–83, 189, 304, 325–26; *WGW,* 8: 25, 54–55, 130, 135–36, 176, 280, 373–74.

31. Washington to President of Congress, December 23, 1777, Fitzpatrick, ed., *WGW,* 10: 195–98. (quotation on p. 196)

32. See, e.g., Bill, *Valley Forge,* 98–99; Busch, *Winter Quarters,* 59–62; Flexner, *Washington in the American Revolution,* 261–62; Douglas Southall Freeman, *George Washington: Leader of the Revolution* (New York: Charles Scribner's Sons, 1951), 568; Reed, *Valley Forge,* 11–12; Trussell, *Birthplace of an Army,* 17.

33. Lord Stirling to Washington, December 23, 1777, GWP, LC; John Armstrong to Washington, December 23, 1777 (two letters) GWP, LC.

34. Washington to the President of Congress, December 23, 1777, Fitzpatrick, ed., *WGW,* 10: 193.

35. "Diary of Surgeon Albigence Waldo," *PMHB* 21 (1897): 299–323, esp. 308–15; Boyle, ed., "From Saratoga to Valley Forge," 258–59. The diary of Colonel Israel Angell, of Rhode Island, acknowledges a somewhat straitened situation with respect to officially issued provisions during and just after the march to Valley Forge, but it offers no evidence to support images of a heavily distressed, much less an incipiently mutinous, soldiery. See "The Israel Angell Diary, 1 October 1777–28 February 1778," ed. Joseph Lee Boyle, *Rhode Island History* 58 (2000): 120–22.

36. Washington to the President of Congress, December 22, 23, 1777, Fitzpatrick, ed., *WGW,* 10: 187, 197–98.

37. Washington to Elbridge Gerry, December 25, 1777; Washington to Governor Richard Caswell of North Carolina, December 25, 1777; Washington to Governor Patrick Henry of Virginia, December 27, 1777, Fitzpatrick, ed., *WGW,* 10: 200–201. 201–2, 208–10.

38. "Orders for a Move That was Intended Against Philadelphia By Way of Surprize," December 25, 1777, Fitzpatrick, ed., *WGW,* 10: 202–5. This document was written in Washington's handwriting. See GWP, LC.

39. Ibid.

40. Ibid.

41. John Sullivan to Washington, December 26, 27, 1777, GWP, LC

42. Ibid. This statement again suggests the degree to which political pressure from the army's host state was affecting military decision making, even if only in a hypothetical way.

43. Baurmeister, *Journal,* 149; Muenchhausen, *Diary,* 46.

44. John Bull to Thomas Wharton, December 25, 1777, RG-27, 13: 0358, PA, PHMC.

CHAPTER 6   Trublesum Times for Us All

1. Daniel Roberdeau to Thomas Wharton, December 26, 1777, Smith, ed., *LDC,* 8: 482–83.

2. *JCC,* 9: 1052–54, 1065. In addition to the members of the Board of War, the panel consisted of Elbridge Gerry of Massachusetts, Cornelius Harnett of North Carolina, and Abraham Clark of New Jersey; See Daniel Roberdeau to George Bryan, December 29, 1777, Smith, ed., *LDC,* 8: 498. In late 1777, Congress reorganized the Board of War from a standing committee of its own members into an administrative group of external appointees. General Horatio Gates, the hero of Saratoga, was named chairman. Other members included Thomas Mifflin, Washington's recently resigned quartermaster general; Timothy Pickering, then serving on Washington's staff as adjutant general; and the former commissary general, Joseph Trumbull of Connecticut (who declined to serve). See Jillson and Wilson, *Congressional Dynamics,* 106–8. The new Board of War was not fully operational until late January 1778, so in November, Congress ordered the old board to continue working until the new one was organized.

3. Francis Lightfoot Lee to Thomas Wharton, December 30, 1777, Smith, ed., *LDC,* 8: 499, 501n.

4. *JCC,* 9: 1067–68, 1073.

5. "Returns" are unit-by-unit lists of the personnel strength and disposition of the army, prepared for the commander's information. Washington, Circular to the States, December 29, 1777, Fitzpatrick, ed., *WGW,* 10: 221–25; John Johnson to Washington, December 30, 1777, GWP, LC. For the memoranda from the officers, see, Theodoric Bland to Washington (December 1777); Henry Lutterloh to Washington, December 25, 1777; Thomas Conway to Washington, December 29, 1777; Casimir Pulaski to Washington, December 29, 1777; George Weedon to Washington, December 29, 1777; Daniel Brodhead to Washington, December 30, 1777; Jedediah Huntington to Washington, January 1, 1778; Henry Knox to Washington, January 3, 1778; James Varnum to Washington, January 3, 1778; Arthur St. Clair to Washington, January 5, 1778; and Charles Scott to Washington, January 14, 1778, all in GWP, LC.

6. Washington, "Instructions to Count Pulaski," December 31, 1777, Fitzpatrick, ed., *WGW,* 10: 219–20, 234–36. The cavalry consisted of four companies, with three hundred privates present and fit for duty at Valley Forge, and a total strength of just over five hundred men and officers. Lesser, *Sinews of War,* 55.

7. Jedediah Huntington to Washington, December 27, 1777, GWP, LC; Richard Platt to Alexander McDougall, December 29, 1777, Philip S. and A. S. W. Rosenbach Foundation, Philadelphia; George Weedon to Patrick Henry, January 4, 1778, Weedon Papers, Anne Marie Brown Library, Brown University; Jedediah Huntington to his father, December 29, 1777, Jedediah Huntington Letters, CHS.

8. Washington to John Armstrong, December 28, 1777; Washington to Richard Caswell, December 25, 1777; Washington to Henry Lutterloh, December 27, 1777; Washington to Clement Biddle, December 28, 1777; Washington to William Buchanan, December 28, 1777; Washington to the Board of War, December 30, 1777; Washington to Major Samuel Blagden, December 30, 1777, and Washington to Nicholas Cooke, December 31, 1777, Fitzpatrick, ed., *WGW,* 10: 215–17, 201–2, 213–14, 217 and note, 226, 229–30, 234; Nathanael Greene to Washington, December 29, 1777, GWP, LC; Lachlan McIntosh to Henry Laurens, January 8, 1778, Chesnutt, ed., *Papers of Henry Laurens,* 12: 278–79.

9. Washington to the President of Congress, January 1, 1778, Fitzpatrick, ed., *WGW,* 10: 243–46.

10. Henry Laurens to William Livingston, December 30, 1777; Henry Laurens to Washington, January 1, 1778, Smith, ed., *LDC,* 8: 505–6, 512–13.

11. Jedediah Huntington to Matthew Irwin, January 20, 1778, Society Collection, HSP.

12. Richard Platt to Alexander McDougall, December 29, 1777, Rosenbach Foundation, Philadelphia; John Armstong to Washington, December 23, 24, 26, 1777; Lord Stirling to Washington, December 26, 1777; John Jameson to Washington, December 30, 1777, GWP, LC.

13. Jedediah Huntington to his father, January 7, 1778, John Reed Collection, VFNHP; Huntington to Governor Trumbull, January 13, 1778, Trumbull Papers, vol. 8, no. 45, Connecticut State Library, Hartford (hereafter CSL); John Brooks to ?, January 5, 1777, Miscellaneous Collection, Massachusetts Historical Society, Boston (hereafter MHS); John Buss to his parents, January 2, 1778, Knollenberg Collection, Yale University Library, New Haven (hereafter YUL).

14. Washington to the President of Congress, December 23, 1777, Fitzpatrick, ed., *WGW,* 10: 192–93.

15. Washington to the Board of War, January 2–3, 1778, Fitzpatrick, ed., *WGW,* 10: 250–54. Available returns are fragmentary, but the number of officers and troops at Valley Forge declined from about 15,000 on December 31, 1777, to perhaps 13,500 a month later. The number of troops listed as sick, either at camp or in nearby field hospitals, fell from about 7,000 to about 5,000 during January, but the number disabled by clothing shortages swelled rapidly from fewer than 1,000 to almost 4,000. See Lesser, *Sinews of Independence,* 54–58.

16. The "Conway Cabal" is a staple episode in the Valley Forge story. Conway was a man of abrasive personality with a flair for self-promotion. The success of the northern army under Horatio Gates at Saratoga in October 1777 became an item of invidious comparison with the more modest progress of the main army in Pennsylvania. An overheard remark critical of Washington was attributed by a third party to a November letter from Conway to Gates and sent to the commander-in-chief as if it was a direct quotation. Washington believed there was a conspiracy in Continental circles to embarrass him, if not to replace him with Gates. He confronted Conway with his knowledge of the letter, and he and his allies used the episode to intimidate his critics. Conway soon left the army, while Washington and Gates barely papered over their differences. Most historians today rightly doubt the existence of any conspiracy, but Washington's belief in it seems undeniable, and the mere fact of the dispute underlines the political tensions within the army command and between military and civilian authority. For judicious assessments of the episode, see Higginbotham, *War of American Independence,* 216–22; Paul David Nelson, *General Horatio Gates: A Biography* (Baton Rouge: Louisiana State University Press, 1976), chap. 6; John E. Ferling, *The First of Men: A Life of George Washington* (Knoxville: University of Tennessee Press, 1988), 225–30. For an alternative model examining Washington's and Gates's *institutional* struggle over military functions and prerogatives, which better explains the army's situation at this point, see chap. 7, below.

17. Nathanael Greene to Washington, January 1, 1778, GWP, LC; Washington, General Orders, January 1, 1778, Fitzpatrick, ed., *WGW,* 10: 242–43.

18. William Gifford to Benjamin Holme, January 24, 1778, Revolutionary Era Documents, no. 50, New Jersey Historical Society (hereafter NJHS).

19. John McDowell to Colonel David Grier, January 16, 1778, Toner Collection, box 257 LC; Jedediah Huntington to his father, January 7, 1778, John Reed Collection, VFNHP; George Fleming to Major Sebastian Bauman, January 21, 1778, Sebastian Bauman Papers, NYHS; Henry B. Livingston to Washington, January 12, 1778, GWP, LC.

20. John Brooks to ?, January 5, 1778, Miscellaneous Collections, MHS.

21. Anonymous officer, January 7, 1778, Joseph Reed Papers, reel 2, NYHS.

22. For evidence of soldiers' unfamiliarity with Pennsylvania's pluralistic religious landscape, see especially A. Chapman to Theodore Woodbridge, February 1, 1778, Woodbridge Papers, CHS; Isaac Gibbs to his brother, March 5, 1778, photostat copy on file at VFNHP. The Friends were peculiarly equipped to retaliate for the incursions of the war on their communal life. Members of one local meeting extracted a measure of passive literary revenge for the seizures of goods and food that they suffered by cataloguing their losses under the mocking rubric "taken . . . by the Army under George Washington, Commonly Called the American Army." See "Sufferings of Friends," in the "Minutes of the Radnor Monthly Meeting, 1777–1778," Friends Historical Library, Swarthmore College, Swarthmore, Pa.

23. Jedediah Huntington to his father, January 7, 1778, John Reed Collection, VFNHP; John Clark to Nathanael Greene, January 10, 1778, Nathanael Greene Papers, WLC; John Brooks to ?, January 5, 1778, Miscellaneous Collection, MHS.

24. Richard Butler to Colonel James Wilson, January 22, 1778, Gratz Collection, case 4, box 11, HSP; William Gifford to Benjamin Holme, January 24, 1778, Revolutionary Era Documents, no. 50, NJHS; John Brooks to ?, January 5, 1778, Miscellaneous Collection, MHS. States clothed their own regiments through the administrative care of a Continental clothier general, whereas feeding the army was mainly a Continental function. Thibaut, *This Fatal Crisis*, 245–335.

25. Enoch Poor to Mesech Weare, January 21, 1778, Force MSS, series 7-E, New Hampshire Council, LC.

26. Ibid.; Jedediah Huntington to his brother, January 19–20, 1778, Jedediah Huntington Letters, CHS. Fred Anderson, *People's Army*, explores the social circumstances and rhetorical traditions binding New England soldiers to the colonies that had recruited them. These formed a "contractual" ideology—based on Puritan "covenant" doctrines—on which Poor, Huntington, and other New Englanders still drew a generation later in their appeals to their home states for aid.

27. Ichabod Ward to Abraham Pierson, January 19, 1778, Pierson and Sargeant Family Papers, CSL.

28. Ibid.

29. Elias Boudinot to Thomas Peters, March 2, 1778, Elias Boudinot Letterbook, SHSW; William Palfrey to Washington, January 14, 1778, GWP, LC.

30. Jedediah Huntington to Governor Jonathan Trumbull, January 13, 1778, Trumbull Papers, vol. 8, no. 45, CSL; Richard Butler to Colonel James Wilson, January 22, 1778, Gratz Collection, case 4, box 11, HSP; John Brooks to ?, January 5, 1778, Miscellaneous Collection, MHS; John Laurens to Henry Laurens, January 23, 1778, in Chesnutt, ed., *Laurens Papers*, 12: 331.

31. Thomas Conway to Washington, December 29, 1777, GWP, LC; Washington to Thomas Conway, December 30, 1777, Fitzpatrick, ed., *WGW*, 10: 226–28; Conway to Washington, December 31, 1777, GWP, LC. A similar idea had at least one field trial at Valley Forge before Steuben's arrival. See Richard Platt to Alexander McDougall, January 24, 1778, Manuscript Collection, Rosenbach Foundation, Philadelphia. Washington described Conway as his "enemy" in early January. See Washington to Henry Laurens, January 2, 1778, Fitzpatrick, ed., *WGW*, 10: 249.

32. George Weedon to John Page, January 25, 1778, document no. 22954a, Virginia State Library, Richmond (hereafter VSL).

33. John Eccleston to Major Richardson, January 20, 1778, Revolutionary War Letters, RUL.

34. See Thibaut, *In the True Rustic Order*, Map Pocket, map #3.

35. William Smallwood to Washington, December 27, 29, 1777, January 1, 1778, GWP, LC.

36. Henry Lee to Washington, January 4, 9, 1778, GWP, LC; Richard Kidder Meade to Lee, January 9, 1778, GWP, LC.

37. Lord Stirling to Washington, December 26, 1777; John Jameson to Washington, December 31, 1777; Henry Lee to Washington, January 4, 1777, GWP, LC. See also, Charles Royster, *Light-Horse Harry Lee and the Legacy of the American Revolution* (New York: Alfred A. Knopf, 1981), esp. chap. 1, 24–28.

38. Anonymous, memorandum specifying criteria for honoring civilian claims for the seizure of provisions by American soldiers, January, 1778, GWP, LC.

39. John Lesher to the Supreme Executive Council, January 9, 1778, RG-27, 13: 294–95, PHMC; Muhlenberg, *Diary*, 3: 122, 127 (January 14, 23, 1778).

40. Other officers, however, reached opposite conclusions about prices. Compare Ewald, *Diary*, 117, with Baurmeister, *Journal*, 149–51; Muenchhausen, *Diary*, 47; Johann Conrad Dohla, *A Hessian Diary of the American Revolution*, ed. Bruce E. Burgoyne (Norman: University of Oklahoma Press, 1990) (hereafter Dohla, *Diary*), 65, 67–69; "Services of Francis Downman," 216–17.

41. Ewald, *Diary*, 117–18.

42. Loyalist claim of Jacob James, December 19, 1783, A.O. 13/102/549, Great Britain, Public Record Office, Kew; Nathanael Greene to Washington, February 16, 18, 1778, Showman, ed., *Greene Papers*, 2: 286–87, 290–92.

43. See John Lacey to Thomas Wharton, January 24, 1778, Gratz Collection, case 4, box 12, HSP; Supreme Executive Council to the Militia Lieutenants of Bucks and Philadelphia Counties, January 9, 1778, RG-27, 13: 485, PHMC; Thomas Wharton to James Potter, January 9, 1778, ibid., 13: 487; Thomas Wharton to John Lacey, January 9, 1778, ibid., 13: 493.

44. Richard Kidder Meade to John Jameson, January 1, 1778, GWP, LC.

45. Walter Stewart to Washington, January 18, 1778, GWP, LC.

46. Washington to Walter Stewart, January 22, 1778, Fitzpatrick, ed., *WGW,* 10: 336–37; James Potter to Washington, January 11, 1778, GWP, LC.

47. John Fitzgerald to John Jameson, January 12, 1778; Charles Craig to Washington, January 15, 1778, GWP, LC; John Graves Simcoe, *A Journal of the Operations of the Queens Rangers* (Exeter, Eng.: privately printed, n.d.; New York: Bartlett and Welford, 1844), 36.

48. Charles Craig to Washington, January 15, 1778, GWP, LC.

49. "Memoirs of Brigadier-General John Lacey, of Pennsylvania," *PMHB* 25 (1901): 510–15; 26 (1902): 101.

50. Ibid., 26 (1902): 103–11, 265–69. Lacey was thus an adherent of the radical Whig coalition that had overthrown the proprietary government in 1776 and an adversary of the "anticonstitutionalist" Whigs symbolized by his nemesis Wayne.

51. Ibid., 267–68; John Lacey to Washington, January 21, 1778, GWP, LC; John Lacey to Thomas Wharton, January 24, 1778, Gratz Collection, case 4, box 12, HSP.

52. Lacey to Washington, January 21, 1778, GWP, LC; [John Miller], "A Journal of Sundry Matters happening during the Stay of the Enemy at Germantown, Philadelphia, taken by an Inhabitant of the Former," July 2, 1778, Joseph Reed Papers, reel 2, NYHS; Simcoe, *Journal of the Queen's Rangers,* 36–37.

53. Washington to James Potter, January 12, 1778; Washington to John Lacey, January 23, 1778, Fitzpatrick, ed., *WGW,* 10: 295–96, 340; John Fitzgerald to John Jameson, January 12, 1778; John Fitzgerald to Walter Stewart, January 29, 1778, GWP, LC.

54. Washington to the President of Congress, December 23, 1777; Washington to Israel Putnam, January 22, 1778, Fitzpatrick, ed., *WGW,* 10: 195, 334. See also Lesser, *Sinews of War,* 58.

55. *JCC,* 9: 1036; Henry Laurens to Washington, December 20, 1777, in Smith, ed., *LDC,* 8: 449; See John Armstrong to Washington, December 19, 1777, GWP, LC.

56. William Clayton et al., to Washington, January 1, 1778, GWP, LC; Charles Pettit to Elias Boudinot, January 1, 1778, Manuscript Division, PUL.

57. Washington to William Clayton et al., January 6, 1778, Fitzpatrick, ed., *WGW,* 10: 270–71.

58. Casimir Pulaski to Washington, January 9, 1778; Benjamin Tallmadge to Washington, January 12, 1778, GWP, LC.

59. Washington to Casimir Pulaski, January 14, 1778, Fitzpatrick, ed., *WGW,* 10: 303–4; Casimir Pulaski to Washington, January 20, 1778, GWP, LC. The modern place names for the towns in question are Flemington in Hunterdon County, and Pennington in Mercer County.

60. Benjamin Tallmadge to Washington, January 12, 1778, GWP, LC. See William Livingston to Washington, January 9, 12, 14, 15, 1778 GWP, LC.

61. Washington to Joseph Ellis, January 18, 1778; Washington to John Lacey, January 23, 1778, Fitzpatrick, ed., *WGW,* 10: 315–16, 340–41.

CHAPTER 7   The Stone Which the Builders Have Rejected

1. *JCC,* 10: 40–41, 67. Among the congressional delegates, Carroll was replaced by Harvie before the committee left York for unknown reasons.

2. See Washington to Horatio Gates, January 4 and February 9, 1778, Fitzpatrick, ed., *WGW,* 10: 263–65, 437–41; Horatio Gates to Washington, January 23, 1778, Gates Papers, NYHS.

3. James Lovell to Samuel Adams, January 22, 1778, Smith, ed., *LDC,* 8: 638; Richard Peters to Robert Morris, January 21, 1778, in Edmund C. Burnet, ed., *Letters of Members of the Continental*

Congress, 8 vols. (Washington, D.C.: Carnegie Institute of Washington, 1921–36), 3: 45, n. 6; Jedediah Huntington to Joseph Trumbull, January 31, 1778, Joseph Trumbull Collection, CHS.

4. James Lovell to Samuel Adams, January 13, 1778; Henry Laurens to William Livingston, December 30, 1777; Laurens to Nicholas Cooke, January 3, 1778; Laurens to William Heath, January 5, 1778; Laurens to Washington, January 5, 1778; Laurens to George Clinton, January 14, 1778, Smith, ed., *LDC,* 8: 506, 520, 532, 535, 581, 587–88.

5. John Henry to Thomas Johnson, January 27, 1778; Abraham Clark to William Alexander, January 15, 1778; Daniel Roberdeau to Thomas Wharton, January 16, 1778; James Lovell to Samuel Adams, January 20, 1778; Henry Laurens to the Marquis de Lafayette, January 22, 1778, Smith, ed., *LDC,* 8: 661, 598, 607, 618, 634.

6. John Witherspoon to William Churchill Houston, January 27, 1778, Ibid., 669–72; Henry Laurens to John Rutledge, January 30, 1778, Ibid., 694.

7. Henry Laurens to the Marquis de Lafayette, January 12, 1778, Ibid., 572.

8. Washington to the President of Congress, January 31, 1778, Fitzpatrick, ed., *WGW,* 10: 411. For these memoranda, see above, chap. 6, n. 5; Washington, "To the Committee of Congress with the Army," January 29, 1778, Fitzpatrick, ed., *WGW,* 10: 362–403; Committee of Conference, Minutes (January 29, 1778), Smith, ed., *LDC,* 8: 673.

9. Washington, "To the Committee of Congress," Fitzpatrick, ed., *WGW,* 10: 362.

10. Ibid., 363–65; Henderson, *Party Politics,* 120–24; Edmund C. Burnett, *The Continental Congress* (New York: MacMillan, 1941), 311. This plan was discussed by Washington and the congressional committee at Whitemarsh in December 1777. See *JCC,* 10: 18–21. Jillson and Wilson, *Congressional Dynamics,* 213–15.

11. Fitzpatrick, ed., *WGW,* 10: 366–77, passim.

12. Ibid., 377–99, passim.

13. Committee at Camp, Minutes of Proceedings (January 28–31, 1778), Smith, ed., *LDC,* 8: 673; Committee at Camp to Henry Laurens, January 28, 1778, Ibid., 676. Nathaniel Folsom's objection to Schuyler was the only dissent recorded in the committee's minutes.

14. Committee at Camp, Minutes of Proceedings, January 28–29, 1778, Smith, ed., *LDC,* 8: 673.

15. Committee at Camp, Minutes of Proceedings, January 30, 1778, Smith, ed., *LDC,* 8: 673. From the brevity of their consideration of the matter it seems likely that the members accepted Washington's broad views on the size of the army, although they finally proposed an "establishment" of eighty-eight battalions rather than the eighty Washington considered adequate. Committee at Camp to Henry Laurens, February 5, 1778, Ibid., 9: 23–25.

16. *JCC,* 10: 40.

17. Henry Laurens to William Livingston, December 30, 1777; Laurens to Washington, January 5, 1778; Committee at Camp, Minutes of Proceedings, January 31, 1778, Smith, ed., *LCD,* 8: 505–7, 535, 673.

18. Committee at Camp, Minutes of Proceedings, January 31, 1778, Smith, ed., *LDC,* 8: 673.

19. Gouverneur Morris to John Jay, February 1, 1778, Smith, ed., *LDC,* 9: 3–4; For a similar account the temper of the committee at this time see Joseph Reed to Thomas Wharton, Ibid. 4–6.

20. Committee at Camp, Minutes of Proceedings, February 3, 5, 7, 13, 1778, Smith, ed., *LDC,* 9: 7, 50.

21. Committee at Camp to Henry Laurens, February 6, 1778, Ibid., 36–38.

22. Committee at Camp, Minutes of Proceedings, February 14, 1778, Ibid.; Committee at Camp to William Livingston, February 13, 1778; Committee at Camp to Thomas Johnson, February 16, 1777, Ibid., 50–51, 87–89, 107. Committee at Camp to George Clinton, February 17, 1778, Ibid., 112–13; Gouverneur Morris to George Clinton, February 17, 1778, Emmet Collection #4190, New York Public Library.

23. Committee at Camp to Thomas Johnson, February 16, 1778, Smith, ed., *LDC,* 9: 107.

24. Committee at Camp, Minutes of Proceedings, February 2, 3, 4, 6, 10, 19, 1778; Committee at Camp to Henry Laurens, February 3, 11, 20, 1777, Smith, ed., *LDC,* 9: 7, 13–15, 50, 72–75, 105, 143–46; Washington to the Committee of Congress, January 29, 1778, Fitzpatrick, ed., *WGW,* 10: 400.

25. Committee at Camp to Henry Laurens, February 12, 1778, Smith, ed., *LDC,* 9: 79.

26. Committee of Congress to Henry Laurens, January 28, 1778; Committee at Camp, Minutes of Proceedings, January 28, 1778, Ibid., 673, 676. See Martin H. Bush, *Revolutionary Enigma: A Reappraisal of General Philip Schuyler of New York* (Port Washington, N.Y.: I. J. Friedman, 1969), 135–37; *JCC,* 10: 103.

27. *JCC,* 10: 102 (January 30, 1778).

28. Ibid., 103–4, 126.

29. Ibid., 53–56, 84–85. Thibaut, *This Fatal Crisis,* 139–43, and Carp, *To Starve the Army at Pleasure,* 111–12.

30. See Laurens's letters at the turn of the new year to William Livingston, Nicholas Cooke, William Heath, and to Washington, December 30, 1777, January 3 to January 5, 1778, Smith, ed., *LDC,* 8: 505–6, 520–21, 531–32, 535.

31. Washington to the President of Congress, December 22, 23, 1777, Fitzpatrick, ed., *WGW,* 10: 183–88, 192–98.

32. *JCC,* 10: 102–3; Thibaut, *This Fatal Crisis,* 4–7; Carp, *To Starve the Army at Pleasure,* 35–43.

33. *JCC,* 10: 138; John Fitzgerald to Washington, February 16, 1778, GWP, LC; James Forbes to Thomas Johnson, February 13, 1778, Smith, ed., *LDC,* 9: 90.

34. Committee at Camp to Washington, February 11, 1778; Committee at Camp, Minutes of Proceedings, February 12, 13, 1778. Smith, ed., *LDC,* 9: 50, 75–77; Jedediah Huntington to Lord Stirling, February 12, 1778; James Varnum to Nathanael Green, February 12, 1778, GWP, LC; Washington to Nathanael Greene, February 12, 1778, Fitzpatrick, ed., *WGW,* 10: 454–55.

35. Committee at Camp to Henry Laurens, February 12, 1778, Smith, ed., *LDC,* 9: 79–82.

36. Committee at Camp to Henry Laurens, February 14, 1778, Ibid., 95. Laurens's letter of the seventh was potentially explosive. It is not clear that Washington would have stayed at the head of the army if his enemies controlled such a key part of its apparatus as the Quartermaster's Department. See Henry Laurens to Francis Dana, February 7, 1778, Smith, ed., *LDC,* 9: 47.

37. Committee at Camp, Minutes of Proceedings, February 17, 18, 1778, Smith, ed., *LDC,* 9: 105.

38. *JCC,* 10: 184, 185. The committee was now empowered not merely to recommend agents but to fill the offices themselves, presumably still subject to Congress's retroactive approval. It had thus been restored to the mandate it had originally brought to camp in January.

39. Committee at Camp to Henry Laurens, February 20, 24, 1778, Smith, ed., *LDC,* 9: 143–44, 163–64; Nathanael Greene to Henry Knox, February 26, 1778; Nathanael Greene to William Greene, March 7, 1778; Nathanael Greene to Joseph Reed, March 9, 1778, Showman, ed., *Greene Papers,* 2: 293–94, 303, 307.

40. Committee of Congress to Henry Laurens, February 25, 1778, Smith, ed., *LDC,* 9: 168–74 (quotation on p. 169).

41. Ibid.

42. *JCC,* 10: 210–11.

43. Supreme Executive Council to the Pennsylvania Delegates to Congress, February 7, 1778, RG-27, 13: 694, PHMC; Thibaut, *This Fatal Crisis,* 146–48, 184–88; *JCC,* 10: 176–77; Marquis de Lafayette to Robert Morris, February 23, 1778, Lafayette Papers, LC; *JCC,* 10: 216–17.

44. Nathanael Greene to William Greene, Esq., March 7, 1778, Showman, ed., *Greene Papers,* 2: 303. Washington was recorded as "not present" at the committee's sessions on seven of the fifteen days after the organization of the Quartermaster's Department was finalized on February 25. His attendance was noted affirmatively only three times. See Committee at Camp, Minutes of Proceedings, Smith, ed., *LDC,* 9: 158–59, 184, 240.

45. John Harvie left camp on February 19 and was in York by the twenty-sixth. (Committee at Camp, Minutes of Proceedings, February 19, 1778, Smith, ed., *LDC,* 9: 105). The committee's minutes do not extend beyond March 12. Dana was present in York for a recorded vote on March 24 (*JCC,* 10: 283). Folsom was appointed to another committee on March 26 (*JCC,* 10: 285, 289). Reed and Morris were still in camp as late as April 4 (see David Brearly to John Ellis, April 4, 1778, Israel Shreve Papers, RUL).

46. In general, Congress settled questions in roughly the order that they might be expected to affect the army's operations. The plan for drafts from state militias and Washington's desire to recruit a force of Indians, which related to the enhancement of army strength, were acted on before the Conference Committee returned to York from Valley Forge. See *JCC,* 10: 199–200 (drafts, February 26), 220–21 (Indians, March 4). The "regulation," or "arrangement," of the regiments was passed in time for transmission to Washington in early June, before the army took the field. *JCC,* 11: 507, 514–15, 538–43; 550, 570 (May 18–June 4, 1778). The clarification of the system of rank and promotion was settled by late May (*JCC,* 12: 1154–60). The half-pay pension scheme, about which there were real ideological differences in Congress, was debated furiously in April and May and passed as pensions limited to seven years (not life) on May 15 (*JCC,* 10: 255, 289, 299, 357, 398; 11: 482, 502–3). But a still-divided and by now largely bankrupt Congress was raising questions about whether it would honor these commitments during the early 1780s. The Clothier's Department was investigated during the spring and summer, and Congress was still trying to settle its arrangement on November 30. (*JCC,* 10: 366; 11: 768, 812; 12: 972–73, 995–96, 1176).

47. There was a fairly rapid attrition from Congress among the committee members. Only Folsom, Morris, and Dana were reelected for 1779, and Dana did not attend Congress that year. By 1780 only Folsom was still active, and after that year none of the members sat in Congress until Dana and Reed returned in 1784.

CHAPTER 8 The Lord's Time to Work

1. Thomas Bradford to Elias Boudinot, January 28, 1778, Elias Boudinot Papers, LC; George Weedon to John Page, January 25, 1778, doc. no. 22954a, Virginia State Library, Richmond (hereafter VSL); Gustavus B. Wallace to Captain Michael Wallace, January 27, 1778, MS 38–150, University of Virginia Library, Charlottesville (hereafter UVL); James Varnum to Governor Nicholas Cooke, February 6, 1778, Letters, vol. 12, Rhode Island State Archives, Providence (hereafter RISA); Richard Fitzpatrick to his brother, January 31, 1778, Richard Fitzpatrick Papers, LC (quotations).

2. For inflation and the economics of wartime Pennsylvania, see Ann Bezanson, *Prices and Inflation During the American Revolution: Pennsylvania, 1770–1790* (Philadelphia: University of Pennsylvania Press, 1951), esp. 10–23, 31–39. Bezanson finds the inflation rate for early 1778 to have been "gradual." This is in comparison, however, with later upward spirals and does not account for local fluctuations or for brief price spurts for scarce and militarily crucial goods.

3. For the various emergency powers that Congress granted to Washington during late autumn 1777, see *JCC,* 8: 752; 9: 784, 905, 1014–15, 1068.

4. Washington, "Proclamation to the Inhabitants of the States of Pennsylvania, New Jersey, and Delaware" (copy), January 30, 1778, Theodore Woodbridge Papers, CHS.

5. Ibid.

6. *Pennsylvania Packet,* February 14, 1778; Washington to Nathanael Greene, February 12, 1778, Fitzpatrick, *WGW,* 10: 454–55.

7. Tench Tilghman to Robert Morris, February 2, 1778, John Reed Collection, VFNHP; Washington to John Glover, February 18, 1778, Fitzpatrick, *WGW,* 10: 477–78; Jedediah Huntington to Joseph Trumbull, January 31, 1778, Joseph Trumbull Collection, CSL.

8. Enoch Poor and John Patterson to Henry Laurens, February 2, 1778, Papers of the Continental Congress, RG 93, M-247, roll 180, item 163, p. 518, National Archives. The abandonment of Fort Ticonderoga on Lake Champlain in July 1777 had facilitated Burgoyne's advance toward Albany. See Bush, *Revolutionary Enigma,* chap. 9; Lachlan McIntosh to Henry Laurens, February 4, 1778, Chesnutt, ed., *Laurens Papers,* 12: 400–403.

9. Officers of Artillery to Washington, February 10, 1778; George Slaughter to Washington, February 1, 1778; Henry B. Livingston to Washington, February 10, 1778; Henry Lutterloh to Washington, January 30, 1778; John Taylor [et al.] to Washington, January 25, 1778; H. Russell [et al.] to Washington, February 24, 1778, all GWP, LC.

10. See Washington to the Board of Artillery Officers, March 2, 1778, Fitzpatrick, *WGW,* 11: 15–18; William Smallwood to Washington, January 25, 1778, GWP, LC.; James Varnum to

Nathanael Greene, February 1, 1778; James Varnum to Governor Nicholas Cooke, February 6, 1778, Letters, vol. 12, RISA.

11. Washington to Henry Laurens, February 3, 1778, Fitzpatrick, ed., *WGW,* 10: 411–12; See Eliphalet Dyer to ? Williams, February 17, 1778, Force Collection, series 7-E, LC; George Weedon to William Palfrey, January 31, 1778, John Reed Collection, VFNHP.

12. Jedediah Huntington to Joseph Trumbull, January 31, 1778, Joseph Trumbull Collection, CSL; Washington to the President of Congress, February 3, 1778, Fitzpatrick, ed., *WGW,* 10: 418; Thomas Smythe to Washington, January 25, 1778, GWP, LC.

13. A. Emerick to Henry Clinton, January 31, 1778, Clinton Papers, WLC; Samuel Carlton to William Heath, January 28, 1778, Governor and Council Letters, Massachusetts State Archives, Boston (hereafter MSA); Jedediah Huntington to Joseph Trumbull, January 31, 17787, Joseph Trumbull Collection, CSL; Jedediah Huntington to Jabez Huntington, February 20, 1778, Jedediah Huntington Papers, CHS; James Varnum to Alexander McDougall, February 7, 1778, McDougall Papers, NYHS. Comparative desertion rates are hard to calculate. The monthly strength reports for February show 247 desertions at Valley Forge and Wilmington, slightly below the average of 259 per month for the first half of 1778 (January not reported). Lesser, *Sinews of Independence,* 54–70.

14. For a comprehensive account of this crisis, concentrating on its organizational causes and consequences, see Thibaut, *This Fatal Crisis,* 162–91. For the weather, see Charles Marshall to Christopher Marshall, February 7, 1778, Andre deCoppet Collection, PUL; Cornelius Harnett to William Wilkinson, February 10, 1778, Smith, ed., *LDC,* 9: 68; Committee at Camp to Washington, February 11, 1778, Smith, ed., *LDC,* 9: 75; Ephraim Blaine to Thomas Wharton, February 12, 1778, RG-27, 13: 723, PHMC; John Fitzgerald to Washington, February 16, 1778, GWP, LC; Thomas Semour to the Board of War, February 19, 1778, Peters Papers, HSP; Tench Tilghman to Washington, February 19, 1778, GWP, LC; Elias Boudinot to Hugh Ferguson, March 2, 1778, Elias Boudinot Letterbook, SHSW; Muenchhausen, *Diary,* 47; Washington to Casimir Pulaski, February 6, 1778, GWP, LC.

15. Committee at Camp to Henry Laurens, February 6, 1778, Smith, ed., *LDC,* 9: 36–38; Washington to William Buchanan, February 7, 1778; Washington to Henry Champion, February 7, 1778, Fitzpatrick, ed., *WGW,* 10: 425–28.

16. Washington to Benjamin Lincoln, February 9, 1778, Fitzpatrick, ed., *WGW,* 10: 441–42.

17. Jedediah Huntington to Lord Stirling, February 12, 1778, GWP, LC; James Varnum to Nathanael Greene, February 12, 1778, in Showman, ed., *Greene Papers,* 2: 280.

18. Washington to Nathanael Greene, February 12, 1778, Fitzpatrick, ed., *WGW,* 10: 454–55; Ephraim Blaine to John Ladd Howell, February 10, 1778, Andre deCoppet Collection, PUL. The army's returns dated February 29 show about 4,100 privates fit for duty at Valley Forge. See Lesser, *Sinews of Independence,* 59. There were 3,000 more men sick at camp, while almost 4,000 were "sick absent," and 3,000 were effectively disabled by their lack of shoes or clothing.

19. Washington to William Livingston, February 14, 1778; Washington to Robert L. Hooper, Nathaniel Falconer, and Robert Mifflin, February 15, 1778, Fitzpatrick, ed., *WGW,* 10: 459–60, 463–64. See Thomas Jones to Charles Stewart, February 15, 16, 1778; Ephraim Blaine to Charles Stewart, February 15, 1778, Charles Stewart Collection, NYSHA for corroborating testimony.

20. Washington to Henry Lee, February 16, 1778, Fitzpatrick, ed., *WGW,* 10: 467–68.

21. Washington to William Smallwood, February 16, 25, 1778; Washington to William Livingston, February 16, 1778, Fitzpatrick, ed., *WGW,* 10: 467, 471, 511–12; Tench Tilghman to Washington, February 19, 1778, GWP, LC.

22. Jasper Yeates to James Burd, February 15, 1778, Shippen Family Papers, HSP; *JCC,* 10: 36, 58; John Laurens to Henry Laurens, February 17, 1778, Chesnutt, ed., *Laurens Papers,* 12: 457.

23. Thomas Jones to Charles Stewart, February 18, 21 1778; Ephraim Blaine to Charles Stewart, February 18, 21, 1778, Charles Stewart Collection, NYSHA; Jedediah Huntington to Governor Trumbull, February 20, 1778, Trumbull Papers, vol. 6, CSL; Washington to George Gibson, February 21, 1778, Fitzpatrick, ed., *WGW,* 10: 494–96 (italics added).

24. Washington, "Address to the Inhabitants of New Jersey, Pennsylvania, Maryland, and Virginia," February 18, 1778, Fitzpatrick, ed., *WGW,* 10: 480–81; Jedediah Huntington to Jabez Huntington, February 20, 1778, Jedediah Huntington Papers, CHS.

25. Washington to the President of Congress, December 23, 1777, Fitzpatrick, ed., *WGW,* 10: 193

26. Thomas Jones to Charles Stewart, February 15, 16, 18, 1778; Ephraim Blaine to Charles Stewart, February 16, 18, 21, 1778, Charles Stewart Collection, NYSHA.

27. Francis Dana to Elbridge Gerry, February 16, 1778, Smith, ed., *LDC,* 9: 108; John Laurens to Henry Laurens, February 17, 1778, Chesnutt, ed., *Laurens Papers,* 12: 457.

28. Nathanael Greene to Henry Knox, February 26, 1778, Showman, ed., *Greene Papers,* 2: 293.

29. Anthony Wayne to Thomas Wharton, February 10, 1778, Wayne Papers, WLC (emphasis in original); John Paterson to Colonel Marshall, February 23, 1778, Ely Collection, NJHS.

30. Josiah Stoddard to Jeremiah Wadsworth, February 21, 1778, Wadsworth Family Papers, YUL; Officers of the Virginia Line, February 22, 1778, Emmett Collection, no. 5904, NYPL.

31. William Smallwood to Washington, January 26, 1778; Thomas Smythe to Washington, January 25, 1778; John Taylor to Washington, January 26, 1778; George Read to Washington, February 5, 1778, GWP, LC; William Smallwood to Allen McLane, February 11, 1778, McLane Papers, NYHS; Smallwood to Washington, February 21, 1778, GWP, LC; Washington to William Smallwood, February 25, 1778, Fitzpatrick, ed., *WGW,* 10: 511–13.

32. William Gray et al., Oath of the Officers Employed in Surveying the Roads, February 27, 1778, Society Miscellaneous Collection, HSP.

33. "Jacob Piatt Orderly Book" (January 14–February 18, 1778), NJHS, MG #226 (entry for February 2, 1778). Washington let these tribunals run their awkward course, probably as a way of venting soldierly wrath at civilian collaborators, but then he intervened to confirm the corporal punishments while overruling the other sentences.

34. Joseph Reed to Thomas Wharton, February 1, 1778, Smith, ed., *LDC,* 9: 3–6.

35. Nathanael Greene to Washington, February 15, 16, 18, 1778, Showman, ed., *Greene Papers,* 2: 285–87, 290–92.

36. Washington to Nathanael Greene, February 12, 1778, Fitzpatrick, ed., *WGW,* 10: 454–55.

37. Nathanael Greene to Washington, February 15, 1778, Showman, ed., *Greene Papers,* 2: 285.

38. Greene to Washington, February 16, 17, 18, 20, 1778, Ibid., 286–92; Washington to Greene, February 16, 1778, Fitzpatrick, ed., *WGW,* 10: 466; Henry Lutterloh to ?, February 20, 1778, RG-27, 13: 0821, PHMC.

39. Nathanael Greene to Washington, February 16, 17, 1778, Ibid., 286–88; Frank H. Stewart, "Foraging for Valley Forge by General Anthony Wayne in Salem and Gloucester Counties, New Jersey, with Associated Happenings" (pamphlet, Woodbury, N.J., 1929), 3–29.

40. Nathanael Greene to Washington, February 17, 1778, Showman, ed., *Greene Papers,* 2: 289.

41. Nathanael Greene to Washington, February 17, 20, 1778, Ibid., 289–90.

42. Greene to Washington, February 17, 18, 1778, Ibid., 289–91; Anthony Wayne to Washington, February 26, 1778, GWP, LC.

43. Nathanael Greene to Washington, February 20, 1778, Showman, ed., *Greene Papers,* 2: 289–91.

44. Washington to Thomas Wharton, February 23, 1778, Fitzpatrick, ed., *WGW,* 10: 503–5.

45. Joseph Reed to Thomas Wharton, February 1, 1778, Smith, ed., *LDC,* 9: 5.

46. Washington to John Jameson, February 1, 1778; Washington to Israel Angell, February 1, 1778, Fitzpatrick, ed., *WGW,* 10: 412–13.

47. Walter Stewart to Washington, January 29, 1778; John Jameson to Washington, February 2, 1778; John Fitzgerald (aide-de-camp) to Colonel Stewart, January 29, 1778, GWP, LC.

48. John Jameson to Washington, February 1, 1778, GWP, LC.

49. John Fitzgerald to Colonel Stewart, January 29, 1778; John Jameson to Washington, February 2, 1778; Casimir Pulaski to Washington, January 29, 1778, GWP, LC; Washington to William Livingston, February 2, 1778, Fitzgerald, ed., *WGW,* 10: 420.

50. Washington to Thomas Wharton, February 12, 1778, Fitzpatrick, ed., *WGW,* 10: 452–53; John Lacey to Thomas Wharton, February 2, 1778, Gratz Collection, HSP; John Lacey to Washington, February 11, 1778, GWP, LC; John Lacey to Thomas Wharton, February 15, 1778, Lacey Papers, NYHS.

51. John Lacey to Colonel Joseph Hart, Esquire, February 11, 1778, Lacey Papers, NYHS; John Lacey Orderly Book (February 9, 1778), manuscript group 164, folder 139, Bucks County (Pa.) Historical Society, Doylestown (hereafter BCHS).

52. Major Francis Murray to Washington, February 13, 1778, GWP, LC.

53. Washington to John Lacey, February 18, 21, 1778, Fitzpatrick, ed., *WGW*, 10: 478–79, 492–93.

54. John Lacey to Thomas Wharton, February 15, 1778, Lacey Papers, NYHS; John Lacey to Washington, February 19, 1778, GWP, LC.

55. Muenchhausen, *Diary*, 47–48. William Coats, the Philadelphia County Lieutenant, and several other militia officers, were reportedly seized in their beds on February 3, "by the invidious arts of the enemy and their emmissaries." *New Jersey Gazette*, February 11, 1778.

56. Ewald, *Diary*, 119–20; Muhlenberg, *Diary*, 3: 128–33, (February 2, 18, 25, 26). Muhlenberg began February by noting that the "*sub-lieutenants* of the *Independent* government" were holding "appellate courts" at which shirkers of militia duty could plead for indulgence. He ended the month fearing that the British cavalry was "coming nearer and nearer, and is taking captive former officers of the American militia," and that they were hoping to capture him.

57. Extract from *Towne's Evening Post;* Joseph Kirkbride to Thomas Wharton, February 20, 1778; John Thompson to Clement Biddle, February 26, 1778, RG-27, 13: 784, 815–16, 893, PHMC; Elizabeth Reed to Mrs. Cox, February 23, 1778, Joseph Reed Papers, reel 2, NYHS. The targeted nature of the raids is supported by a report that enemy patrols were "in Search of Major [John] Jameson." See Lillian B. Miller, ed., *The Selected Papers of Charles Willson Peale and His Family*, 3 vols. (New Haven: Yale University Press, 1983), 1: 265–66.

58. Ewald, *Diary*, 121.

59. Ibid.; John Lacey to Washington, February 19, 1778, GWP, LC; Joseph Kirkbride to Thomas Wharton, February 20, 1778, RG-27, 13: 0815, PHMC; Lachlan McIntosh to Henry Laurens, February 26, 1778, Smith, ed., *LDC*, 8; Muenchhausen, *Diary*, 48. These were undoubtedly the animals that Ewald mistakenly identified as having come from "Virginia."

60. Richard Kidder Meade to John Jameson, February 15, 1778, GWP, LC; John Lacey to Washington, February 19, 1778, Lacey Papers, NYHS.

61. John Laurens to Henry Laurens, February 17, 1778, Chesnutt, ed., *Laurens Papers*, 12: 459; Washington to Nathanael Greene, February 18, 1778, Fitzpatrick, ed., *WGW*, 10: 476–77.

62. J. Paxton to Charles Stewart, February 20, 1778, Charles Stewart Collection, NYSHA; Lachlan McIntosh to Henry Laurens, February 26, 1778, Chesnutt, ed., *Laurens Papers*, 12: 482; John Lacey to Washington, February 27, 1778, GWP, LC; Muenchhausen, *Diary*, 48.

63. Washington to John Sullivan, February 26, 1778; Washington to Anthony Wayne, February 28, 1778, Fitzpatrick, ed., *WGW*, 10: 516–17, 524–25.

64. Washington to Thomas Wharton, February 23, 1778, Fitzpatrick, ed., *WGW*, 10: 503–5.

65. Ibid. Washington to Thomas Wharton, February 13, 1778; Washington to Captain Stephen Chambers, February 27, 1778, Fitzpatrick, ed., *WGW*, 10: 504–5, 522–23.

66. Charles Craig to Washington, March 5, 1778, GWP, LC; Washington to John Jameson, March 7, 1778, Fitzpatrick, ed., *WGW*, 11: 37.

67. Casimir Pulaski to Washington, January 26, 1778, GWP, LC.

69. Casimir Pulaski to Washington, February 4, 1778; Benjamin Tallmadge to Washington, February 9, 1778, GWP, LC; Washington to Casimir Pulaski, January 26, 1778; Washington to Benjamin Tallmadge, February 20, 1778, Fitzpatrick, ed., *WGW*, 10: 352–53, 486.

70. Joseph Ellis to Washington, February 8, 1778, GWP, LC.

71. *Pennsylvania Evening Post*, February 3, 1778; *New York Weekly Mercury*, February 23, 1778.

72. "Rough Plan of Arming the Refugees from Jersey, taking Post at Billingsport, and Insurrection in West Jersey, Sent in to Sir. Wm. Howe in February 1778 by D[aniel] C[oxe]," A.O. 13/137/768–769, Great Britain, Public Record Office, Kew; See also, "Services of Francis Downman," 217 (February 25, 1778); *Journal of Nicholas Collin*, 245; Muhlenberg, *Diary*, 3: 79 (September 23, 1777).

73. See Anthony Wayne to ?, February 20, 1778; Joseph Ellis to Anthony Wayne, February 21, 1778; Anthony Wayne to Lt. Col. Sherman, February 22, 1778; Anthony Wayne to Theodore

Woodbridge, February 23, 1778; Anthony Wayne to Washington, February 25, 26, 1778, all GWP, LC; Anthony Wayne to Theodore Woodbridge, February 22, 1778, Woodbridge Papers, CHS; Washington to Anthony Wayne, February 28, 1778, Fitzpatrick, ed., *WGW*, 10: 524–26; Stewart, "Foraging for Valley Forge by General Anthony Wayne."

CHAPTER 9   The Chapter of Experiments

1. James Varnum to [Mrs.?] William Greene, March 7, 1778, John Reed Collection, VFNHP; James Bradford to Captain Thomas Wooster, March 4, 1778, John Reed Collection, VFNHP; Colonel George Nagel to Washington, March 4, 1778, GWP, LC. Lieutenant Samuel Armstrong concurred with Varnum: "one day will be like mayday and the Next so cold there will be no . . . living in our Hutts with good fires and the next perhaps snow or rain" (March 1, 1778), in Boyle, ed., "From Saratoga to Valley Forge," 266.

2. Nathanael Greene to William Greene, March 7, 1778; Nathanael Greene to Joseph Reed, March 9, 1778; Nathanael Greene to James Abeel, March 11 and 16, 1778; Nathanael Greene to William Smallwood, March 16, 1778; Nathanael Greene to Alexander McDougall, March 28, 1778, Showman, ed., *Greene Papers*, 2: 300–304, 307, 313–16, 326. Cornelius Harnett to William Wilkinson, March 18, 1778, Smith, ed., *LDC*, 9: 308; George Gibson to Washington, March 19, 1778, GWP, LC; Charles Blagden to Joseph Banks, March 26, 1778, *New York Public Library Bulletin* 7 (1903): 418–19.

3. Clement Biddle to Washington March 5, 1778, GWP, LC; Washington to John Cadwallader, March 20, 1778, Fitzpatrick, ed., *WGW*, 11: 117.

4. Nathanael Greene to William Greene, March 7, 1778; Nathanael Greene to Joseph Reed, March 9, 1778; Nathanael Greene to James Abeel, March 16, 1778; Nathanael Greene to William Smallwood, March 16, 1778, Showman, ed., *Greene Papers*, 2: 300–304, 307, 315–16.

5. Washington, "Thoughts Upon a Plan of Operation for Campaign 1778" (March 1778), Fitzpatrick, ed., *WGW*, 11: 185–94.

6. Washington to the General Officers, April 20, 1778, Fitzpatrick, ed., *WGW*, 11: 282–83.

7. Jonathan B. Smith to Thomas Wharton, March 1, 1778, Gratz Collection, case 1, box 21, HSP; Cornelius Harnett to William Wilkinson, March 3, 1778; Eliphalet Dyer to Jeremiah Wadsworth, March 10, 1778; John Henry to Governor Thomas Johnson, March 10, 1778; Thomas Burke to Governor Richard Caswell, March 12, 1778; Virginia Delegates to Governor Patrick Henry, March 23, 1778, Smith, ed., *LDC*, 9: 208, 255, 258, 274–75, 325.

8. Washington to Henry Knox, March 5, 1778; Washington to Samuel H. Parsons, March 5, 1778; Washington to the Board of War, March 6, 1778, Fitzpatrick, ed., *WGW*, 11: 24–27, 33–34.

9. Washington to Francis Hopkinson and John Wharton, March 1, 1778; Washington to the Pennsylvania Navy Board, March 2, 1778, Fitzpatrick, ed., *WGW*, 11: 7–8, 12–13; William Bradford to the Supreme Executive Council, March 5, 1778; Thomas Wharton to Washington, March 11, 1778; William Bradford to Washington, March 14, 1778, GWP, LC; Washington to William Bradford, March 15, 1778, Fitzpatrick, ed., *WGW*, 11: 88–89; Washington to George Baylor, March 4, 1778; Washington to John Jameson, March 7, 1778, Fitzpatrick, ed., *WGW*, 11: 22–23, 37.

10. Washington to Thomas Wharton, March 7, 1778, Fitzpatrick, ed., *WGW*, 11: 45–48. See also Supreme Executive Council to Henry Laurens, March 6, 1778 (copy), GWP, LC; Thomas Wharton to Washington, March 10, 1778, GWP, LC.

11. Washington to Henry Champion, March 9, 1778; Washington to Governor Thomas Johnson, March 21, 1778, Fitzpatrick, ed., *WGW*, 11: 54–55, 123–24; Washington to the President of Congress, March 12, 1778, Fitzpatrick, ed., *WGW*, 11: 72–73. For the January 1778 convention at which delegates from the New England and Middle Atlantic states adopted schedules of prices for domestic commodities, see Simeon E. Baldwin, "The New Haven Convention of 1778," *Papers of the New Haven Colony Historical Society* (New Haven, privately printed, 1882), 3: 33–62. For Congress's ambivalence about price controls, see *JCC*, 9: 956–57, and 11: 569–70.

12. Washington, "Thoughts Upon a Plan of Operation," 185–94. Lesser, *Sinews of Independence,* 59, shows that there were about 7,500 men fit for duty at Valley Forge and Wilmington on February 29. Washington to George Gibson, March 11, 1778; Washington to William Stephens Smith, March 14, 1778; Washington to William Bradford, March 18, 1778, Fitzpatrick, ed., *WGW,* 11: 64–65, 79, 105; William Smith to Washington, March 19, 1778; John Hazlewood to Washington, February 4, 1778, GWP, LC.

13. John Chaloner to Henry Champion, March 17, 1778, MS 69472, CHS; Washington to the Board of War, March 20, 1778, Fitzpatrick, ed., *WGW,* 11: 111–13; Cornelius Harnett to William Wilkinson, March 18, 1778, Smith, ed., *LDC,* 9: 308; Washington to John Cadwallader, March 20, 1778, Fitzpatrick, ed., *WGW,* 11: 117–18.

14. Samuel H. Parsons to Washington, March 20, 1778; Sylvanus Seely to Washington, March 20, 1778, GWP, LC; Washington to the President of Congress, March 24, 1778, Fitzpatrick, ed., *WGW,* 11: 137–40.

15. Washington to William Heath, March 25, 1778; Washington to William Livingston, March 25, 1778; Washington to Alexander McDougall, March 25, 1778; Washington to John Armstrong, March 27, 1778; Washington to Governor Richard Caswell, March 28, 1778; Washington to President James Bowdoin, March 31, 1778; Washington to Governor Jonathan Trumbull, March 31, 1778, Fitzpatrick, ed., *WGW,* 11: 144–46, 149–50, 157–59, 166–67, 169–70, 180–84. Washington to the President of Congress, March 29, 1778; Washington, General Orders, March 24, 28, 1778; Washington to William Smallwood, March 28, 1778, Fitzpatrick, ed., *WGW,* 11: 171–72, 140–42, 161–62, 166–67; John Laurens to Henry Laurens, March 28, 1778, Chesnutt, ed., *Laurens Papers,* 13: 51; Nathanael Greene to Clement Biddle, March 30, 1778, Showman, ed., *Greene Papers,* 2: 327–28.

16. Anthony Wayne to Thomas Wharton, March 27, 1778, Manuscript Division, PUL; John Laurens to Henry Laurens, March 28, 1778, Chesnutt, ed., *Laurens Papers,* 13: 51; John Bannister to Patrick Henry, March 27, 1778, Smith, ed., *LDC,* 9: 340 (emphasis in original); *JCC,* 10: 300, 305, 309–10.

17. Washington to Alexander McDougall, March 31, 1778, Fitzpatrick, ed., *WGW,* 11: 178–79; William Smallwood to Washington, March 31, 1778, GWP, LC; Washington to the President of Congress, April 1, 1778, Fitzpatrick, ed., *WGW,* 11: 195–96; John Laurens to Henry Laurens, April 1, 1778, Chesnutt, ed., *Laurens Papers,* 13: 67–68; Alexander Scammell to Dr. Samuel Scammell, April 8, 1778, Society Collection, HSP.

18. Washington to Alexander McDougall, March 31, 1778; Washington to the President of Congress, April 10, 1778, Fitzpatrick, ed., *WGW,* 11: 227–28, 235–41 (quotations on 236, 240).

19. Washington to the President of Congress, April 10, 1778, Fitzpatrick, ed., *WGW,* 11: 235–41 (quote on 239); Washington to William Livingston, April 11, 1778; Washington to Thomas Wharton, April 11, 1778; Washington to the President of Congress, April 18, 1778, Fitzpatrick, ed., *WGW,* 11: 247–48, 276–78; Washington to William Smallwood, April 12, 13, 1778, Fitzpatrick, ed., *WGW,* 11: 250–51, 254–55.

20. The discussion in the following paragraphs draws heavily on Troyer S. Anderson, *The Command of the Howe Brothers in the American Revolution* (New York: Oxford University Press, 1936), 303–7; Gerald S. Brown, *The American Secretary: The Colonial Policy of Lord George Germain, 1775–1778* (Ann Arbor: University of Michigan Press, 1963), 139–55; Weldon A. Brown, *Empire or Independence: A Study in the Failure of Reconciliation, 1774–1783* (Baton Rouge: Louisiana State University Press, 1941; rev. ed., Port Washington, N.Y.: Kennikat Press, 1966), chap 9; Ira D. Gruber, *The Howe Brothers in the American Revolution* (New York: Atheneum, 1972), 268–86; Mackesy, *War for America,* 180–89.

21. Brown, *American Secretary,* 152–53; Lord George Germain to Sir Henry Clinton, March 8, 1778, Secret Dispatch Book, Germain Papers, WLC.

22. Germain to Clinton, March 8, 1778, Secret Dispatch Book, Germain Papers, WLC.

23. George III, "Secret Instructions for our Trusty and Welbeloved Sir Henry Clinton, K.B. and General & Commander in Chief of Our Forces in North America or the Commander in Chief of Our Forces for the time being," March 21, 1778, Clinton Papers, WLC; Germain to Sir Henry Clinton, March 21, 1778, Clinton Papers, WLC; Admiralty Board to Lord Richard Howe, March 22, 1778, quoted in Mackesy, *War for America,* 186.

24. Sir Henry Clinton to the Duke of Newcastle, March 22, 1778, Newcastle MSS, Nottingham University Library. Howe received Germain's sketchy instructions of February 19 on March 27. See William Howe to Lord George Germain, April 19, 1778, Germain Papers, WLC; Mackesy, *War for America,* 213–14.

25. William Howe to Lord George Germain (extract), April 19, 1778, Germain Papers, WLC.

26. For the chain of information leading to Washington's March 29 assertion to Congress that he had "no doubt" about the arrival of British reinforcements in Philadelphia, see Samuel H. Parsons to Washington, March 20, 1778; Sylvanus Seely to Washington, March 20, 1778; William Smallwood to Washington, March 20, 28, 1778; James Lovell to Washington, March 24, 1778, GWP, LC; Washington to William Smallwood, March 21, 1778; Washington to the President of Congress, March 24, 1778; Washington to William Heath, March 25, 1778; Washington to John Armstrong, March 27, 1778; Washington to the President of Congress, March 29, 1778, Fitzpatrick, ed., *WGW,* 11: 120, 137–40, 144–46, 157–59, 171–72.

27. On republican fears of a standing army in Anglo-American political culture, see Cress, *Citizens in Arms,* pt. 2, esp. 67–73; White, "Standing Armies in Time of War," esp. chap. 6.

28. *JCC,* 10: 285–86; Elbridge Gerry to the Massachusetts Council, March 28, 1778, Smith, ed., *LDC,* 9: 347.

29. *JCC,* 10: 285–86, 289, 292–93, 298–302. See Henderson, *Party Politics in the Continental Congress,* 122; Jillson and Wilson, *Congressional Dynamics,* 215–18; William Ellery to Governor Nicholas Cooke, April 5, 1778; Gouverneur Morris to Washington, April 18, 1778, Smith, ed., *LDC,* 9: 371, 439–40; Washington to the President of Congress, April 10, 1778; Washington to John Bannister, April 21, 1778, Fitzpatrick, ed., *WGW,* 11: 235–41, 284–93.

30. *JCC,* 10: 50. Henry Laurens to Baron von Steuben, January 14, 1778, Smith, ed., *LDC,* 8: 594. This was not true, of course. After the hut-building project was underway in late December, Washington moved into the snug—but otherwise quite comfortable—stone house in Valley Forge village, belonging to the iron master Isaac Potts and rented to Deborah Hewes. See Thibaut, *In the True Rustic Order,* 77–80.

31. Henry Laurens to John Laurens, February 18, 1778; John Laurens to Henry Laurens, February 28, 1778, Chesnutt, ed., *Laurens Papers,* 12: 462, 483–84.

32. John Laurens, "Reponses aus Questions de Monsieur de Baron Steuben (de) l'ordre de Battaille et deux liques, Avec un Corps," February 1778, Steuben Papers, ChiHS; Steuben, memorandum, March 1778, ibid; Steuben, "A Few Observations Made on My Reconnoitring the Camp," March 5, 1778, ibid.

33. Thomas Conway to Washington, December 29, 31, 1777, GWP, LC; Washington, General Orders, March 17, 21, 22, 1778, Fitzpatrick, ed., *WGW,* 11: 98, 119, 132; Isaac Sherman, "Regimental Orders, March 17, 1778," Isaac Sherman Orderly Book, American Revolution, Journals and Orderly Books, box 3, CHS; Richard Platt to Alexander McDougall, January 24, 1778, Rosenbach Foundation.

34. Washington, General Orders, March 24, 1778, Fitzpatrick, ed., *WGW,* 11: 142–43; John Laurens to Henry Laurens, March 25, 1778, Chesnutt, ed., *Laurens Papers,* 13: 434–37; Henry B. Livingston to Robert R. Livingston, March 25, 1778, Robert R. Livingston Papers, NYHS; Isaac Sherman, "Regimental Orders, March 28, 30. 1778," Isaac Sherman Orderly Book, CHS.

35. John Laurens to Henry Laurens, April 1, 1778, Chesnutt, ed., *Laurens Papers,* 13: 67–68; Washington, General Orders, April 1, 2, 8, 9, 10, 1778, Fitzpatrick, ed., *WGW,* 11: 194–95, 199–201, 228–29, 231, 233.

36. Friedrich Steuben to Henry Laurens, April 2, 1778; Henry Laurens to Friedrich Steuben, April 4, 1778, Chesnutt, ed., *Laurens Papers* 13: 69, 71.

37. John Laurens to Henry Laurens, April 18, 1778, Chesnutt, ed., *Laurens Papers,* 13: 140; Samuel Ward to Phoebe Ward, April 28, 1778, Ward Papers, RIHS; Henry Knox to William Knox, April 29, 1778, Knox Papers, MHS; Lieutenant B. Howe to Major Sebastian Bauman, April 12, 1778, Sebastian Bauman Papers, NYHS.

38. Edward Mitchell to the Massachusetts General Court, March 2, 1778, Governor and Council Letters, MSA; Joseph Hodgkins to Sarah Hodgkins, February 22, 1778, in Herbert T. Wade

and Robert A. Lively, *This Glorious Cause: The Adventures of Two Company Officers in General Washington's Army* (Princeton: Princeton University Press, 1958), 235–36; Enoch Poor to Governor Mesech Weare, March 4, 1778, Force MSS, series 7-E, New Hampshire Miscellaneous, LC.

39. Isaac Gibbs to his brother, March 5, 1778, photostat copy on file at VFNHP; James Varnum to (Mrs.) William Greene, March 7, 1778, John Reed Collection, VFNHP; James Varnum to Colonel Nathan Miller, March 7, 1778, Harvard University Library (hereafter HUL); Nathanael Greene to William Greene, March 7, 1778, Showman, ed., *Greene Papers,* 2: 301.

40. John Sullivan to William Palfrey, March 11, 1778, Sol Feinstone Collection, David Library of the American Revolution, doc. no. 1339; Jedediah Huntington to Jeremiah Wadsworth, March 5, 1778, Jedediah Wadsworth Papers, Correspondence, CHS.

41. George Fleming to Sebastian Bauman, March 26, 1778, Sebastian Bauman Papers, NYHS.

42. One of the more colorful Valley Forge traditions concerns the allegedly fortuitous arrival of a large and providentially early run of shad in the Schuylkill River, which at least one writer has credited with having terminated the army's winter of famine. See Busch, *Winter Quarters,* 88–89; Chidsey, *Valley Forge,* 128–29. This episode is undocumented and chronologically implausible. The worst period of the army's hunger ended in late February, long before the shad run could have begun. The British did try to obstruct the mouth of the Schuylkill at Philadelphia to block the shad run. See Jackson, *With the British Army in Philadelphia,* 229–30.

43. James Bradford to Thomas Wooster, March 4, 1778, John Reed Collection, VFNHP; John Else to Samuel Gray, March 4, 1778, Samuel Gray Papers, CHS; Jonathan Flagg to Jeremiah Wadsworth, March 4, 1778, Jeremiah Wadsworth Papers, Correspondence, CHS; Washington, General Orders, Fitzpatrick, ed., *WGW,* April 9, 1778, 11: 231; Gouverneur Morris to Governor George Clinton, February 17, 1778, Smith, ed., *LDC,* 9: 117–18.

44. Jedediah Huntington to Jabez Huntington, March 13, 1778, Jedediah Huntington Papers, CHS; Alexander Scammell to Dr. Scammell, April 8, 1778, Society Collection, HSP; Anthony Wayne to Thomas Wharton, April 10, 1778, Wayne Papers, WLC; Dr. S. Tenny to Dr. Peter S. Turner, March 22, 1778, Dr. Peter Turner Papers, LC; Ebenezer Crosby to Norton Quincy, April 14, 1778, HUL; Gustavus B. Wallace to Michael Wallace, March 28, 1778, UVL; Israel Angell to the Governor and Council of Rhode Island, March 28, 1778, Letters, vol. 12, RISA; Samuel Ward to Phoebe Ward, April 28, 1778, Ward Papers, RIHS. The number of soldiers "sick-absent" at field hospitals or at home on medical furloughs fell from about 5,000 in December to just over 3,500 in January and February to under 3,000 by late March. See Lesser, *Sinews of Independence,* 55, 58–60. (These figures include the troops at Wilmington and on detachment.)

45. Gustavus B. Wallace to Michael Wallace, March 28, 1778, UVL; Ebenezer Crosby to Norton Quincy, April 14, 1778, HUL; Lieutenant B. Howe to Major Sebastian Bauman, April 23, 1778, Sebastian Bauman Papers, NYHS; Samuel Ward to Phoebe Ward, April 17, 1778, Ward Papers, RIHS. For weather observations, see Jonathan Clark diary, April 1 to July 1, 1778, VSL.

46. Nathanael Greene to William Smallwood, March 16, 1778; Nathanael Greene to George Weedon, April 27, 1778, Showman, ed., *Greene Papers,* 2: 315–16, 364; Nathanael Greene to Alexander McDougall, April 16, 1778, McDougall Papers, NYHS; Lieutenant B. Howe to Sebastian Bauman, April 23, 1778, Sebastian Bauman Papers, NYHS; Samuel Ward to Phoebe Ward, April 28, 1778, Ward Papers, RIHS.

47. William Bradford to Richard Varick, April 16, 1778, Miscellaneous Collection, MHS; Samuel Ward to Phoebe Ward, April 19, 1778, Ward Papers, RIHS.

48. Nathanael Greene to Alexander McDougall, April 16, 1778, McDougall Papers, NYHS.

49. Washington to the President of Congress, April 18, 1778, Fitzpatrick, ed., *WGW,* 11: 276–77.

50. Washington to the President of Congress, April 20, 23, 25, 27, 1778; Washington to William Livingston, April 22, 1778; Washington to John Bannister, April 22, 1778, Fitzpatrick, ed., *WGW,* 11: 281–82, 287–88, 295–97, 300–302, 313–14; John Laurens to Henry Laurens, April 18, 1778, Chesnutt, ed., *Laurens Papers,* 13: 139; Samuel Ward to Phoebe Ward, April 19, 1778, Ward Papers, RIHS; Elias Boudinot to his wife, April 20, 1778, Boudinot Papers, PUL; Henry Knox to his brother, April 21, 1778, Knox Papers, MHS.

51. Washington to the General Officers, April 20, 1778, Fitzpatrick, ed., *WGW,* 11: 282–83; Louis Duportail to Washington, April 23, 1778; Henry Knox to Washington, April 23, 1778; William Maxwell to Washington, April 23, 1778; Peter Muhlenberg to Washington, April 23, 1778; Enoch Poor to Washington, April 23, 1778; Lord Stirling to Washington, April 23, 1778; James Varnum to Washington, April 23, 1778; Anthony Wayne to Washington, April 23, 1778; Nathanael Greene to Washington, April 25, 1778; Marquis de Lafayette to Washington, April 25, 1778; William Maxwell to Washington, April 25, 1778, all in GWP, LC.

52. Ibid.

53. See Louis Lebeque Duportail to St. Germaine, November 12, 1777, Andre deCoppet Collection, PUL; Duportail to Washington, April 23, 1778; Nathanael Greene to Washington, April 25, 1778; Friedrich Steuben to Washington, April 25, 1778, GWP, LC.

54. Nathanael Greene to Colonel Clement Biddle, March 30, 1778, Nathanael Greene to James Abeel, April 17, 1778, Showman, ed., *Greene Papers,* 2: 327–28, 344; Charles Pettit to Moore Furman, March 18, April 16, 1778, Moore Furman Papers, New Jersey Bureau of Archives and History (hereafter NJBAH). For Greene, the job of rebuilding the Quartermaster's Department would be difficult if the army stayed put and almost impossible if it moved. Steuben's and Duportail's recommendations may have been prefigured by the very wording of the third alternative. Given Steuben's responsibility for training the army and Duportail's role in overseeing its engineering functions, their support for "remaining quiet, in a secure, *fortified* camp, *disciplining* and arranging the army" was almost a foregone conclusion.

55. Washington, "Thoughts Upon a Plan of Operation," 185–94, quotes on 185.

56. *JCC,* X: 364.

57. Muenchhausen, *Diary,* 48–51; Baurmeister, *Journal,* 154–63; Joseph Reed to Thomas Wharton, February 1, 1778; William Ellery to William Whipple March 2, 1778, Smith, ed., *LDC,* 9: 4–6, 203; Gunning Bedford to Washington, March 7, 1778, GWP, LC.

58. John Lacey to Washington, March 9, 1778; Stephen Chambers to Washington, March 23, 1778, GWP, LC; Washington, General Orders, March 26, 1778, Fitzpatrick, ed., *WGW,* 11: 155; John Laurens to Cornet George White, April 16, 1778, GWP, LC.

59. William Shannon to Henry Hollingsworth, March 15, 1778, Sol Feinstone Collection, David Library of the American Revolution, doc. no. 1259; William Smallwood to Washington, March 16, 1778, GWP, LC.

60. William Smallwood to Henry Hollingsworth, March 31, 1778, Western Reserve Historical Society, Cleveland, Ohio; William Smallwood to Henry Hollingsworth, April 5, 1778, Sol Feinstone Collection, David Library of the American Revolution, doc. no. 1273; William Smallwood to Washington, March 31, 1778, GWP, LC; *JCC,* 10: 285; William Smallwood to Caesar Rodney, March 31, 1778, MS 1875, MdHS; Muenchhausen, *Diary,* 51 (April 21–24, 1778).

61. Washington to William Smallwood, March 28, 1778; April 12, 13, 1778, Fitzpatrick, ed., *WGW,* 11: 167, 250–51, 254–55; Anonymous, April 17, 1778, Andre deCoppet Collection, PUL.

62. Washington to John Armstrong, March 27, 1778, Fitzpatrick, ed., *WGW,* 11: 157–59.

63. Joseph Reed to Washington, March 30, 1778, GWP, LC; Henry Lee to Washington, March 31, 1778, GWP, LC; Washington to Henry Lee, April 1, 1778; Washington to the President of Congress, April 3, 1778, Fitzpatrick, ed., *WGW,* 11: 198, 205–6; *JCC,* 10: 315; Alexander Hamilton to ?, March 29, 1778, Gratz Collection, HSP; Washington to George Gibson, March 11, 1778; Washington to the Board of War, March 29, 1778, Fitzpatrick, ed., *WGW,* 11: 64–65, 112; William Smith to Washington, March 18, 1778; George Gibson to Washington, March 19, 1778; ? to Colonel Bigelow, March 1, 1778; John Laurens to Cornet White, April 16, 1778, all in GWP, LC; Baurmeister, *Journal,* 157.

64. Baurmeister, *Journal,* 157; Muenchhausen, *Diary,* 49; Ewald, *Diary,* 121; "Services of Francis Downman," 218; Charles Blagden to Joseph Banks, March 26, 1778, *Bulletin of the New York Public Library* 7 (1903): 419.

65. Baurmeister, *Journal,* 157 (March 17, 1778); Muenchhausen, *Diary,* 49 (March 18, 1778); Washington to John Lacey, March 2, 1778, Fitzpatrick *WGW,* 11: 14; *JCC,* IX: 784.

66. Washington, General Orders, March 1, 1778; Washington to Lacey, March 2, 1778, Fitzpatrick, ed., *WGW,* 11: 11–12, 14; "An Act for Better Securing and Punishing Persons Guilty of

Crimes and Offences," March 13, 1778, James T. Mitchell and Henry Flanders, *The Statutes at Large of Pennsylvania from 1681 to 1801,* 18 vols. (Harrisburg: 1896–1915), 9: 220–21; Thomas Wharton to John Lacey, March 27, 1777, RG-27, 13: 1069, PHMC.

67. See Stephen Chambers to Washington, March 12, 1778, GWP, LC; Alexander Scammell [to Stephen Chambers?], March 18, 1778, William Henry MSS, vol. 1, p. 24a, HSP.

68. Muenchhausen, *Diary,* 49; Baurmeister, *Journal,* 157; Johann Heinrichs to his brother, April 14, 1778, "Extracts from the Letter-Book of Captain Johann Heinrichs of the Hessian Jager Corps, 1778–1780," *PMHB* 22 (1898): 142.

69. Simcoe, *Journal of the Queen's Rangers,* 54; Baurmeister, *Journal,* 165; Ewald, *Diary,* 122; Muenchhausen, *Diary,* 50–51.

70. John Lacey to Washington, March 3, 9, 1778, GWP, LC; John Lacey to General John Armstrong, March 4, 1778; John Lacey to James Potter, March 4, 1778; John Lacey to Thomas Wharton, March 4, 1778, Lacey Papers, NYHS; Thomas Wharton to Washington, March 2, 1778, GWP, LC. See also John Lacey Orderly Book, March 1, 1778, BCHS.

71. John Lacey to Joseph Kirkbride, March 10, 1778; Joseph Kirkbride to John Lacey, March 14, 1778, Lacey Papers, NYHS. Kirkbride had heard the allegations from the father-in-law of Colonel John Bayard, the speaker of the Pennsylvania Assembly. See also John Lacey to Robert Levers, Esq., April 3, 1778, Lacey Papers, NYHS.

72. George Nagel to Washington, March 3, 1778; Stephen Chambers to Washington, March 12, 1778, GWP, LC.

73. Ibid.; Baurmeister, *Journal,* 157.

74. John Lacey to Thomas Wharton, March 20, 1778, Lacey Papers, NYHS; John Lacey to Thomas Wharton, March 26, 1778, Society Collection, HSP; John Lacey to Lt. Robert Van Horne, in "Crooked Billet Papers," folder 1, BCHS, printed in W. W. H. Davis, *History of the Battle of Crooket Billet* (Doylestown, Pa., 1860), 5.

75. Simcoe, *Journal of the Queen's Rangers,* 55–56; Muhlenberg, *Diary,* 134, 138–40 (March 2, 25, 29, April 5, 1778); Peale, "Diary," March 4-April 20, 1778, in Miller, ed., *Selected Papers,* 1: 268–71; William Van Horne to Colonel Joseph Hart, March 4, 1778 and April 2, 1778, in William E. Van Horne, ed. "Revolutionary War Letters of The Reverend William Van Horne" *Western Pennsylvania Historical Magazine* 53 (1970): 108–11.

76. Anthony Wayne to John Lacey, March 4, 1778, Sol Feinstone Collection, David Library of the American Revolution, doc. no. 1653; John Lacey to Washington, March 11, 1778, Lacey Papers, NYHS; John Lacey to Captain [Stephen] Chambers, March 19, 1778, William Henry MSS, 1: 24(a), HSP.

77. Washington to John Lacey, March 20, 1778; Washington to Lachlan McIntosh, March 21, 1778, Fitzpatrick, ed., *WGW,* 11: 114, 120–21; Lachlan McIntosh to Washington, March 23, 25, 1778, GWP, LC; John Laurens to Henry Laurens, March 25, 28, 1778, Chesnutt, ed., *Laurens Papers,* 13: 34, 49.

78. John Lacey to Washington, March 9, 21, 29, 1778; Lachlan McIntosh to Washington, March 23, 1778, GWP, LC; Nicholas Waln, "Epistle from the General Spring Meeting," March 21–24, 1778, John Reed Collection, VFNHP; Phineas Pemberton to James Pemberton, March 24, 1778, and George Churchman to John Pemberton, March 28, 1778, Pemberton Papers, 32: 7, 9, HSP; Drinker, *Diary,* 1: 291 (March 25, 1778).

79. Washington to John Lacey, March 31, 1778; Washington to John Lacey, April 11, 1778; Washington to Joseph Kirkbride, April 20, 1778, Fitzpatrick, ed., *WGW,* 11: 179, 243–44, 283–84.

80. George Emlen to John Lacey, April 3, 1778, Lacey Papers, NYHS; Baurmeister, *Journal,* 166; John Lacey to Nathanael Greene, April 27, 1778, Lacey Papers, NYHS.

81. John Chaloner to Henry Champion, April 2, 1778, MS 69494, CHS; Muhlenberg, *Diary,* 136 (March 15, 1778); John Wetzel to John Lacey, March 31, 1778, Western Reserve Historical Society, Cleveland, Ohio.

82. Anthony Wayne to Washington, February 26, 1778, GWP, LC.

83. Anthony Wayne to Washington, February 20, March 5, 14, 1778; Anthony Wayne to Lt. Colonel Sherman, February 22, 1778, GWP, LC; Anthony Wayne to Theodore Woodbridge, February

23, 1778, Woodbridge Papers, CHS; Washington to Casimir Pulaski, March 1, 1778, Washington to Anthony Wayne, March 2, 1778, Fitzpatrick, ed., *WGW,* 11: 6–7, 13–14.

84. Muenchhausen, *Diary,* 48; Baurmeister, *Journal,* 155–56; Washington to Israel Shreve, March 19, 1778, Fitzpatrick, ed., *WGW,* 11: 109–10.

85. Washington to William Livingston, March 19, 1778, Fitzpatrick, ed., *WGW,* 11: 110–11; Elijah Hand to Colonel Charles Mawhood, March 22, 1778, GWP, LC.

86. Colonel Charles Mawhood, "Proclamation to the New Jersey Militia," undated copy enclosed in Elijah Hand and Benjamin Holme to William Livingston, March 21, 1778, GWP, LC; "Proposals of Col. Charles Mawhood to the Salem Militia" (with a Reply by Col. Hand, March 22, 1778)," *Proceedings of the New Jersey Historical Society,* ser. 1, 8 (1858): 99–101.

87. William Livingston to Washington, March 21, 23, 1778, GWP, LC; Civil and Military Officers of Cumberland Country, petition to Governor William Livingston, March 28, 1778; Resolution of New Jersey State Assembly to Congress (copy), April 3, 1778, GWP, LC.

88. Washington to William Livingston, March 25, 1778, Fitzpatrick, ed., *WGW,* 11: 149–50; Baurmeister, *Journal,* 160; Muenchhausen, *Diary,* 49; "Services of Francis Downman," 218; Major Gabriel D. Vebber to Daniel Coxe, Esq., March 24 and March 31, 1778, A.O. 13/137/770–773, Great Britain, Public Record Office, Kew.; Andrew Snape Hammond to Captain Ferguson, April 7, 1778, Andrew Snape Hammond Papers, UVL.

89. *Journal of Nicholas Collin,* 245–46.

90. Israel Shreve to Washington, April 4, 6, 7, 10, 1778, GWP, LC. Muenchhausen, *Diary,* 50; Baurmeister, *Journal,* 162; "Services of Francis Downman," 219; Montressor, "Journal," 484; Ewald, *Diary,* 126–27; *Journal of Nicholas Collin,* 246.

91. William Livingston to Washington, April 9, 1778, GWP, LC; Washington to William Livingston, April 14, 1778, Fitzpatrick, ed., *WGW,* 11: 256–57.

92. Baurmeister, *Journal,* 166 ("a little plundering").

CHAPTER 10   As the Fine Season Approaches

1. Washington to Alexander McDougall, May 1, 1778; Washington to the President of Congress, May 1, 4, 1778; Washington, General Orders, May 5, 1778, Fitzpatrick, ed., *WGW,* 11: 332, 335, 348, 354–56; *JCC,* 11: 457.

2. Washington, General Orders, May 5, 1778, Fitzpatrick, ed., *WGW,* 11: 332, 335, 348, 354–56; John Laurens to Henry Laurens, May 7, 1777, Chesnutt, ed., *Laurens Papers,* 13: 265; Marquis de Lafayette to ?, May 7, 1778, John Reed Collection, VFNHP; Philip Van Cortlandt to Pierre Van Cortlandt, May 7, 1778, in Jacob Judd, ed., *The Revolutionary War Memoir and Selected Letters of Philip Van Cortlandt* (Tarrytown, N.Y.: Sleepy Hollow Restorations, 1976), 124–26.

3. John Laurens to Henry Laurens, May 7, 1778, Chesnutt, ed., *Laurens Papers,* 13: 265; Washington to Israel Putnam; Washington to William Heath; Washington to Nathanael Greene; Washington to Alexander McDougall, all May 5, 1778, Fitzpatrick, ed., *WGW,* 11: 348–53.

4. Lesser, *Sinews of Independence,* 64–66.

5. Washington to Horatio Gates, April 24, 1778, Fitzpatrick, ed., *WGW,* 11: 303–4.

6. Washington, Council of War, May 8, 1778, Fitzpatrick, ed., *WGW,* 11: 363–66; Ephraim Blaine to Jeremiah Wadsworth, May 10, 1778, Jeremiah Wadsworth Papers, Correspondence, CHS; John Armstrong et al., Summary of Opinions of the Council of War, May 8, 1778, GWP, LC.

7. Armstrong et al., Summary of Opinions.

8. Ibid.

9. Washington, Council of War, May 8, 1778, Fitzpatrick, ed., *WGW,* 11: 366; Armstrong et al., Summary of Opinions, May 8, 1778, GWP, LC.

10. Ibid.

11. Thibaut, *In the True Rustic Order,* 45–60; Caleb North to Lord Stirling, May 2, 1778, Mrs. Archibald Crossley Autograph Collection, LC; Peter Muhlenberg to Nathanael Greene, May 8, 1778, Greene Papers, HSP; Charles Pettit to Davis Bevan, May 12, 1778, Weiss Papers, RG 15, M-804, roll

2523, NA; Robert C. Bray and Paul E. Bushnell, eds., *Diary of a Common Soldier in the American Revolution, 1775–1783: An Annotated Edition of the Journal of Jeremiah Greenman* (DeKalb: Northern Illinois University Press, 1978), 119.

12. Samuel Ward to Phoebe Ward, May 5, 1778, Ward Papers, RIHS; Washington, General Orders, May 16, 1778, Fitzpatrick, ed., *WGW,* 11: 399.

13. Washington to the President of Congress, May 1, 1778; Washington, General Orders, May 7, 9, 1778, Fitzpatrick, ed., *WGW,* 11: 328–31, 362–63, 366; *JCC,* 11: 465; Friedrich Steuben to Henry Laurens, May 15, 1778, Chesnutt, ed., *Laurens Papers,* 13: 307.

14. See Thomas Jones to Charles Stewart, February 21, 1778, Charles Stewart Collection, NYSHA.

15. Ephraim Blaine to Governor Thomas Johnson, May 7, 1778, Red Book, no. 4587–11, Maryland Hall of Records; Washington to Thomas Wharton, May 11, 1778; Washington to Thomas Johnson, May 11, 1778; Washington to William Livingston, May 12, 1778, Fitzpatrick, ed. *WGW,* 11: 369–71, 377–79.

16. Ephraim Blaine to Jeremiah Wadsworth, May 10, 1778, Jeremiah Wadsworth Papers, Correspondence, CHS; John Chaloner to Charles Stewart, May 23, 1778, Charles Stewart Papers, NYSHA; Thibaut, *This Fatal Crisis,* 219–27.

17. John Miller, "A Journal of Sundry Matters," June 3, 1778, Joseph Reed Papers, NYHS; Baurmeister, *Journal,* 162; "Orderly Book of the Second Pennsylvania Continental Line," *PMHB* 36 (1913): 33, 45 (April 17, 26, 1778).

18. George Fleming to Sebastian Bauman, May 14, 1778, Sebastian Bauman Papers, NYHS; George Thomas to Richard Thomas, June 14, 1778, MS 1487, Chester County (Pa.) Historical Society.

19. Samuel Ward to Phoebe Ward, May 5, 1778, Ward Papers, RIHS.

20. Anthony Wayne to Richard Peters, May 13, 1778, Wayne Papers, HSP; Colonel William Shepard to the Massachusetts Council, May 18, 1778, Governor and Council Letters, MSA.

21. George Fleming to Sebastian Bauman, May 14, 1778; Lieutenant B. Howe to Sebastian Bauman, May 16, 1778, Sebastian Bauman Papers, NYHS.

22. *JCC,* 11: 482–83, 485, 491, 495–96, 502–3; Abraham Tuckerman to Jeremiah Wadsworth, May 8, 1778, Jeremiah Wadsworth Papers, Correspondence, CHS; Samuel Ward to Phoebe Ward, May 5, 1778, Ward Papers, RIHS.

23. Henry Laurens to Washington, April 27, 1778, Smith, ed., *LDC,* 9: 506; *JCC,* 10: 114–18, 394–97.

24. Washington to the Marquis de Lafayette, May 17, 1778, Fitzpatrick, ed., *WGW,* 11: 410–11; Johan De Kalb to Henry Laurens, May 17, 1778, Laurens Papers, South Carolina Historical Society.

25. *JCC,* 11: 502–3 (May 15, 1778); Washington, General Orders, May 18, 1778; Washington to the President of Congress, May 18, 1778, Fitzpatrick, ed., *WGW,* 11: 412–13, 415–17; Johan De Kalb to Henry Laurens, May 19, 1778, Laurens Papers (typescript), Brooklyn Historical Society.

26. George Fleming to Sebastian Bauman, May 14, 1778, Sebastian Bauman Papers, NYHS; *Massachusetts Independent Chronicle,* May 21, 1778. A Hessian officer noticed a marked decline in the incidence of American desertion after the announcement of the French alliance. See Muenchhausen, *Diary,* 52; John Taylor to William Woodford, May 22, 1778, John Taylor Miscellaneous Manuscripts, LC.

27. John Taylor to William Woodford, May 22, 1778, John Taylor Miscellaneous Manuscripts, LC; Washington to Gouverneur Morris, May 18, 1778, Fitzpatrick, ed., *WGW,* 11: 413–14.

28. Sir Henry Clinton to Lord George Germain, May 10, 1778, summarized in Clinton to Germain, May 24, 1778; Henry Clinton, Memorandum on Evacuating Philadelphia (May 1778); William Howe, Orders, May 11, 1778, all in Henry Clinton Papers, WLC. See also Muenchhausen, *Diary,* 52; Baurmeister, *Journal,* 173; Jackson, *With the British Army in Philadelphia,* 232, 255–56.

29. John Laurens to Henry Laurens, May 12, 1778, Chesnutt, ed., *Laurens Papers,* 13: 295.

30. Eleazer Oswald to John Lamb, May 15, 1778, Lamb Papers, NYHS; Gustavus B. Wallace to his brother, Wallace Papers, May 16, 1778, UVL; Lieutenant B. Howe to Sebastian Bauman, May 16, 1778, Sebastian Bauman Papers, NYHS; Lord Stirling to Gouverneur Morris, May 16, 1778, Manuscript Collection, Rosenbach Foundation; Clement Biddle to Moore Furman, May 17, 1778, Moore Furman Papers, NJBAH; John Chaloner to Jeremiah Wadsworth, May 17, 1778, Jere-

miah Wadsworth Papers, Correspondence, CHS; Alexander Breckenridge to ?, May 17, 1778, Draper MSS, Preston Papers, series QQ, SHSW.

31. Washington to Nathanael Greene, May 16, 1778; Washington to Ephraim Blaine; Washington to Henry Knox; Washington to William Smallwood; Washington to Alexander McDougall; Washington to Horatio Gates, all May 17, 1778; Washington to Horatio Gates; Washington to the President of Congress, May 18, 1778; Washington to President Jeremiah Powell, May 19, 1778; Washington to John Sullivan, May 20, 1778, Fitzpatrick, ed., *WGW*, 11: 397–98, 401–2, 405–8, 415–18, 423–25, 428–29.

32. Israel Shreve to Washington, May 18, 1778; Philemon Dickenson to Washington, May 19, 1778, GWP, LC.

33. Clement Biddle to Moore Furman, May 17, 18, 1778, NJBAH; John Chaloner to Jeremiah Wadsworth, May 17, 1778, Jeremiah Wadsworth Papers, Correspondence, CHS; John Chaloner to Charles Stewart, Charles Stewart Collection, NYSHA.

34. Washington, General Orders, May 16, 18, 23, 28, 29 May, 1778, Fitzpatrick, ed., *WGW*, 11: 399, 412–13, 441–42, 463–67.

35. John Laurens to Allen McLane, May 26, 1778, Hamilton-McLane Papers, LC; John Laurens to Henry Laurens, May 27, 1778, Chesnutt, ed., *Laurens Papers,* 13: 351–53; Philemon Dickinson to Washington, May 27, 1778, GWP, LC; Washington to Philemon Dickinson, May 28, 1778; Washington to the President of Congress, May 28, 1778; Washington to George Clinton, May 29, 1778, Fitzpatrick, ed., *WGW*, 11: 468–69, 471–74; Henry Laurens to John Laurens, May 31, 1778, Chesnutt, ed., *Laurens Papers,* 13: 376; Dudley Colman to his wife, May 30, 1778, Dudley Colman Papers, MHS; Henry Knox to William Knox, May 27, 1778, Knox Papers, MHS.

36. Washington to Richard Henry Lee, May 25, 1778; Washington to Horatio Gates, May 25, 1778; Washington to Philemon Dickinson, May 28, 1778; Washington to the President of Congress, May 28, 1778, Fitzpatrick, ed., *WGW*, 11: 447, 450–52, 469, 471–72.

37. Washington to William Smallwood, May 22, 23, 25, 1778; Washington to Stephen Moylan, May 24, 28, 1778; Washington to William Maxwell, May 25, 1778, Fitzpatrick, ed., *WGW*, 11: 434–36, 446, 448–50, 469–70.

38. Henry Clinton to the Duke of Newcastle, May 23, 1778, Newcastle MSS, Nottingham University Library; Henry Clinton to ?, June 6, 1778, Clinton Papers, WLC.

39. Serle, *Journal,* 287–89, 292, 295–97; Muenchhausen, *Diary,* 173–74; Jackson, *With the British Army,* 232–33, 251–52; Henry Clinton, minutes of conversations with Lord Howe and Joseph Galloway (May 1778), Clinton Papers, WLC.

40. See John Lacey to Washington, May 2, 1778; Lacey to Thomas Wharton, May 4, 1778, Lacey Papers, NYHS; For British accounts see Simcoe, *Journal of the Queen's Rangers,* 656–60; Baurmeister, *Journal,* 164–69; Muenchhausen, *Diary,* 50–51. This camp was on the York Road near the northern end of the modern town of Hatboro, in Philadelphia County. Lacey's reported casualties included twenty-six men killed, nine wounded, and thirty captured.

41. Simcoe, *Journal of the Queen's Rangers,* 60; John Lacey to Washington, May 2, 1778, Lacey Papers, NYHS; William Stayner, deposition, May 14, 1778; F. Watts and Samuel Henry, deposition, May 14, 1778; Thomas Craven, deposition, May 15, 1778; Samuel Irwin, deposition, May 15, 1778, GWP, LC.

42. Washington to William Maxwell, May 7, 1778, Fitzpatrick, ed., *WGW*, 11: 357–58.

43. Washington to John Armstrong, March 27, 1778; Washington to John Lacey, May 11, 1778, Fitzpatrick, ed., *WGW*, 11: 157–59, 374; Washington to Thomas Wharton, May 11, 1778, Fitzpatrick, ed., *WGW*, 11: 369–70; Supreme Executive Council to Washington, May 5, 1778, RG-27, 13: 1301, PHMC.

44. Richard Peters to Washington, May 6–9, 1778, GWP, LC; Washington to the Board of War, May 9, 1778; Washington to William Smallwood, May 25, 1778, Fitzpatrick, ed., *WGW*, 11; 267–368, 449–50; Andrew Boyd to Timothy Matlack, May 7, 1778, RG-27, 13: 1317, PHMC.

45. Baurmeister, *Journal,* 174; Muenchhausen, *Diary,* 52; Stephen Moylan to Washington, May 7–9, 1778; Philemon Dickenson to Washington, May 9, 1778; Alexander Hamilton to William Maxwell, May 10, 1778, GWP, LC; Washington to William Maxwell, May 7, 1778, Fitzpatrick, ed., *WGW*, 11: 357–58; Eleazer Oswald to John Lamb, May 15, 1778, Lamb Papers, NYHS.

46. Washington to the Marquis de Lafayette, May 18, 1778, Fitzpatrick, ed., *WGW*, 11: 418–20.

47. Marquis de Lafayette to Allen McLane, May 18, 1778, McLane Papers, NYHS.

48. Baurmeister, *Journal*, 175–76; Muenchhausen, *Diary*, 52–54; Jackson, *With the British Army in Philadelphia*, 227–28.

49. Dudley Colman to his wife, May 22, 1778, Dudley Colman Papers, MHS; John Laurens to Henry Laurens, May 27, 1778, Chesnutt, ed., *Laurens Papers*, 13: 350; Alexander Scammell to Allen McLane, May 20, 1778, McLane Papers, NYHS; Washington to the President of Congress, May 24, 1778, Fitzpatrick, ed., *WGW*, 11: 443; Muenchhausen, *Diary*, 54; Baurmeister, *Journal*, 176; Simcoe, *Journal of the Queen's Rangers*, 60–61; Serle, *Journal*, 294–95.

50. Richard K. Meade to Allen McLane, May 23, 1778, McLane Papers, NYHS; John Fitzpatrick to Allen McLane, May 24, 1778, McLane Papers, NYHS; John Laurens to Allen McLane, May 26, 1778, Hamilton-McLane Papers, LC; Washington to Allen McLane, May 27, 1778, GWP, LC; Alexander Scammell to Allen McLane, May 28, 1778, McLane Papers, NYHS; Tench Tilghman to William Maxwell, May 13, 1778, GWP, LC; Robert H. Harrison to Stephen Moylan, May 17, 1778; Allen McLane to Alexander Clough, May 23, 1778, GWP, LC; Charles Scott to Allen McLane, May 23, 1778, McLane Papers, NYHS; Allen McLane to Alexander Clough, May 23, 1778, GWP, LC; Alexander Clough to Washington, May 23, 1778, GWP, LC.

51. Israel Shreve to Washington, May 3, 4, 1778; Stephen Moylan to Washington, May 7, 1778; Philemon Dickinson to Washington, May 9, 1778, GWP, LC; Muenchhausen, *Diary*, 51–52; Baurmeister, *Journal*, 169–70; Washington to Israel Shreve, May 7, 1778; Washington to Philemon Dickinson, May 13, 1778, Fitzpatrick, ed., *WGW*, 11: 358–59, 383–84; Alexander Hamilton to Lieutenant Colonel De Hart, May 7, 1778, GWP, LC.

52. Baurmeister, *Journal*, 170; Muenchhausen, *Diary*, 52; Philemon Dickenson to Washington, May 17, 1778; Israel Shreve to Washington, May 4, 18, 25, 1778, GWP, LC; Washington to Israel Shreve, May 23, 1778, Fitzpatrick, ed., *WGW*, 11: 436–37.

53. Washington to Richard Henry Lee, May 25, 1778; Washington to Philemon Dickinson, May 28, 1778; Washington to William Maxwell, May 25, May 29 (two letters) 1778, Fitzpatrick, ed., *WGW*, 11: 448–52, 468–69, 478–79.

54. Washington to Governor Thomas Johnson, May 17, 1778, Fitzpatrick, ed., *WGW*, 11: 404–5.

55. Washington to William Smallwood, May 17, 22–23, 25, 1778, Fitzpatrick, ed., *WGW*, 11: 406–7, 434–36, 449–50; Thomas Johnson to Washington, May 20, 1778; William Smallwood to Washington, May 22, 1778, GWP, LC.

56. William Smallwood to Washington, May 26 (two letters), 28, 1778, GWP, LC.

57. Henry Knox to John Lamb, June 2, 1778, Lamb Papers, NYHS; Henry Knox to William Knox, June 3, 1778, Knox Papers, MHS; Dudley Colman to his wife, June 5, 1778, Dudley Colman Papers, MHS; Henry Knox to ?, June 6, 1778, Knox Papers, MHS; Eleazer Oswald to John Lamb, June 7, 1778, Lamb Papers, NYHS; Richard Mount to "Dear Bill," June 7, 1778, NYHS; Peter Grubb to Allen McLane, June 10 (misdated May 10), 1778, McLane Papers, NYHS; John Laurens to Henry Laurens, June 15, 1778, Chesnutt, ed., *Laurens Papers*, 13: 461.

58. Jedediah Huntington to Andrew Huntington, June 2, 1778, Huntington Papers, CHS; Henry Knox to William Knox, June 3, 1778, Knox Papers, MHS; Eleazer Oswald to John Lamb, June 7, 1778, Lamb Papers, NYHS; John Laurens to Henry Laurens, June 9, 16, 1778, Chesnutt, ed., *Laurens Papers*, 13: 430, 470; John Chaloner to Charles Stewart, June 9, 1778, Charles Stewart Papers, NYSHA; John Eccleston to ?, June 15, 1778, Revolutionary War Letters, 1778, RUL; Elias Boudinot to his wife, June 11, 1778, Boudinot Papers, PUL; Clement Biddle to ?, June 15, 1778, NJBAH.

59. Henry Laurens to John Laurens, June 5, 7, 1778, Chesnutt, ed., *Laurens Papers*, 13: 408–9, 414; Abraham Clark to Elias Dayton, June 8, 1778, Louis Bamberger Autograph Collection, NJHS; Washington to Horatio Gates, June 2, 1778; Washington to Charles Lee, June 15, 1778, Fitzpatrick, ed., *WGW*, 12: 9–10, 60–63; Washington to the President of Congress, June 18, 1778, Fitzpatrick, ed., *WGW*, 12: 82–83.

60. Baurmeister, *Journal*, 179; Sir Henry Clinton to Lord George Germain, June 5, 13, 1778; Sir Henry Clinton to ?, June 6, 1778, Clinton Papers, WLC; Sir Henry Clinton to the Duke of Newcastle, June 16, 1778, Newcastle MSS, Nottingham University Library.

61. Washington to the Board of War, June 6, 1778; Washington to Jonathan Lawrence, June 6, 1778; Washington to John A. Washington, June 10, 1778; Washington to Lachlan McIntosh, June 10, 1778; Washington to John Sullivan, June 10, 1778; Richard K. Meade to Daniel Kemper, June 18, 1778, Fitzpatrick, ed., *WGW,* 12: 25–26, 41–45, 81; John Cox to James Abeel, June 4, 1778, John Cox Correspondence, NJHS; Jedediah Huntington to Andrew Huntington, June 5, 1778, CHS; John Chaloner to Charles Stewart, June 10, 1778; Thomas Jones to Charles Stewart, June 10, 1778; Ephraim Blaine to Charles Stewart, June 10, 1778, Charles Stewart Collection, NYSHA

62. Washington to Nathanael Greene (two letters), June 8, 1778; Washington, General Orders, June 9, 13, 1778; Washington to William Palfrey, June 13, 1778, Fitzpatrick, ed., *WGW,* 12: 35–36, 40, 53–54, 57; Dudley Colman to his wife, June 12, 1778, Dudley Colman Papers, MHS. Local tradition has usually placed the site of the new encampment on the west side of the Schuylkill River, somewhere in front of the outer line entrenchments. The most specific pieces of contemporary evidence, however, all suggest that it was on the east side. See Bray and Bushnell, eds., *Diary of a Common Soldier in the American Revolution,* 120; George F. Scheer, ed., *Private Yankee Doodle: A Narrative of Some of the Adventures, Dangers, and Sufferings of a Revolutionary Soldier. Joseph Plumb Martin* (Salem, N.H.: Ayer, 1985), 122; Edward A. Holt, ed., "A Revolutionary Diary of Captain Paul Brigham: November 19, 1777–September 4, 1778," *Vermont History* 34 (January 1966): 24.

63. *JCC,* 11: 502, 538–66; Washington to the President of Congress, June 7, 1778, Fitzpatrick, ed., *WGW,* 12: 27–28.

64. *JCC,* 11: 570; Washington, General Orders, June 7, 1778; Washington to Francis Dana, June 9, 1778, Fitzpatrick, ed., *WGW,* 12: 29–35, 38; Joseph Reed to his wife, June 9, 1778, Reed Papers, NYHS.

65. Washington, General Orders, June 11, 1778; Washington to Charles Lee, June 15, 1778, Fitzpatrick, ed., *WGW,* 12: 46–47, 61; Charles Lee to Washington, June 15, 1778, GWP, LC. Lee arrived at Valley Forge after a long imprisonment in New York in April and then went to York and home to Virginia before returning to the army at the end of the spring. For an assessment of Lee and his difficult relationship with Washington, see Shy, "American Strategy: Charles Lee and the Radical Alternative," in *People Numerous and Armed,* esp. 154–60.

66. As early as the beginning of May caustic references to the "prussand general" circulated along the camp rumor mills. See James Varnum to Washington, May 5, 1778, GWP, LC.

67. Joseph Reed to his wife, June 9, 1778, Joseph Reed Papers, NYHS; Jedediah Huntington to Jabez Huntington, June 10, 1778, Huntington Papers, CHS; Washington, General Orders, June 15, 1778, Fitzpatrick, ed., *WGW,* 12: 66–68. Steuben's letter is not found in Washington's papers, but it can be inferred from Washington to Steuben, June 18, 1778, Ibid., 78–79.

68. Washington to Friedrich Steuben, June 18, 1778, Fitzpatrick, ed., *WGW,* 12: 78–79.

69. Washington to Sir Henry Clinton, May 31, 1778, Fitzpatrick, ed., *WGW,* 12: 496–97; *JCC,* 11: 583–84, 605–6, 609–11, 614–15; Henry Laurens to George Johnstone, June 14, 1778, Smith, ed., *LDC,* 10: 91–92.

70. Montressor, "Journal," 497–99; [John Miller] "Journal of Sundry Matters . . . at Germantown," Joseph Reed Papers, NYHS; Sir Henry Clinton to the Duke of Newcastle, June 16, 1778, Newcastle MSS, Nottingham University Library.

71. John Bayard to George Bryan, June 5, 1778; Joseph Reed to his wife, June 9, 1778, Joseph Reed Papers, NYHS; Supreme Executive Council to Washington, May 27, 1778, RG-27, 14: 0134, PHMC.

72. Supreme Executive Council to Washington, May 27, 1778, RG-27, 14: 0134, PHMC; Washington to George Bryan, May 28, 1778, Fitzpatrick, ed., *WGW,* 11: 467–68.

73. Washington, Order of March and Route of the Army from Valley Forge, June 17, 1778, Fitzpatrick, ed., *WGW,* 12: 74–75; Washington, Council of War, June 17, 1778, Ibid., 75–78, and esp. n. 38, p. 75.

74. Washington to the President of Congress, June 18, 1778; Washington, Order of March . . . from Valley Forge," June 17, 1778; Washington to Benedict Arnold, June 19, 1778; Washington to Jeremiah Wadsworth, June 18, 1778; Washington to James Mease, June 18, 1778, Fitzpatrick, ed., *WGW,* 12: 74–75, 88–89, 94–95.

CHAPTER 11　The Seated War

1. My account of the British withdrawal and American pursuit to Monmouth draws mainly on Middlekauf, *Glorious Cause,* 420–23.

2. Ibid.; John R. Alden, *A History of the American Revolution* (New York: Alfred A. Knopf, 1976), 391–92.

3. Middlekauf, *Glorious Cause,* 422.

4. Ibid., 423–24.

5. Ibid., 426–27.

6. Ibid., 427; Ward, *War of the American Revolution,* 580.

7. Middlekauf, *Glorious Cause,* 427–28.

8. Casualty figures are harder to verify for Monmouth than for most Revolutionary-era battles. Some bodies were dragged away by the British while others were found scattered in the woods. Official accounts put American losses at 106 killed, 161 wounded, and 95 missing. Henry Clinton acknowledged 177 killed, 170 wounded, and 64 missing, although his figures were almost surely higher than this. See Peckham, *Toll of Independence,* 52; Alden, *History of the American Revolution,* 392. Washington claimed to have buried 249 British soldiers in the field. Some scholars have suggested much higher British casualties by using calculating formulae that may be considered at best relatively indirect. See, e.g., Mark Lender, "What Kind of Victory? Washington, the Army, and Monmouth Reconsidered," in *An Account of the Action. From Brandywine to Monmouth: A Seminar on the Impact of the Revolutionary War on the Delaware Valley* (Philadelphia: Council of American Revolutionary Sites, 1997), 65–68.

9. Lender, "What Kind of Victory?" 69–70; Shy, "American Strategy," esp. 159.

10. Lender, "What Kind of Victory?" 63–82, esp. 71–72, 76–78. Lee rejected the sentence, and Congress removed him from duty. He died in impoverished obscurity in Philadelphia in 1782.

11. Bill, *Valley Forge,* 187; Ward, *War of the Revolution,* 550–55, 582; and the sources discussed in Bodle, "Vortex of Small Fortunes," chap. 1.

12. Quoted in Ward, *War of the Revolution,* 582; William S. Stryker, *The Battle of Monmouth* (Port Washington, N.Y.: Kennikat Press, 1970; orig. pub. 1927), 209; See also Higginbotham, *War of American Independence,* 247; Shy, "Lee and the Radical Alternative."

13. Mark V. Kwasny, *Washington's Partisan War, 1775–1783* (Kent, Ohio: Kent State University Press, 1996), chaps 8–11, esp. 306–8; Middlekauf, *Glorious Cause,* 429–31, 560–63.

14. Joy Day Buel and Richard Buel, *The Way of Duty: A Woman and Her Family in Revolutionary America* (New York, W. W. Norton, 1984), chap. 6; Kwasny, *Washington's Partisan War,* chaps 8–11, passim; Harold E. Selesky, *War and Society in Colonial Connecticut* (New Haven: Yale University Press, 1990), esp. 228–43; Edward Countryman, *A People in Revolution,* 109–10, 150–51; Robert A. East and Jacob Judd, *The Loyalist Americans: A Focus on Greater New York* (Tarrytown, N.Y.: Sleepy Hollow Restorations, 1975).

15. Leonard A. Lundin, *Cockpit of the Revolution: The War for Independence in New Jersey* (Princeton: Princeton University Press, 1940), chap. 13; Joseph E. Tiedemann, "Response to Revolution: Queens County, New York During the Era of the American Revolution," Ph.D. diss., City University of New York, 1977.

16. Kwasny, *Washington's Partisan War,* chaps. 7–11. See John Lewis Seidel, "The Archaeology of the American Revolution: A Reappraisal and Case Study of the Continental Artillery Cantonment of 1778–1779, Pluckemin, New Jersey," Ph.D. diss., University of Pennsylvania, 1987, 137–52, for a description and analysis of the Continental winter deployments in New Jersey in late 1778, which largely adumbrated those of the rest of the war in the north.

17. Countryman, *People in Revolution,* esp. chap. 10; Joseph E. Tiedemann, *Reluctant Revolutionaries: New York City and the Road to Independence* (Ithaca: Cornell University Press, 1997); Judith Van Buskirk, *Generous Enemies: Patriots and Loyalists in Revolutionary New York* (Philadelphia: University of Pennsylvania Press, 2002).

18. Buel and Buel, *Way of Duty,* 154–56; Richard Buel, *Dear Liberty: Connecticut's Mobilization for the Revolutionary War* (Middletown, Conn.: Wesleyan University Press, 1980), 190–95, 272–75; James Kirby Martin, *Benedict Arnold, Revolutionary Hero: An American Warrior Reconsidered*

(New York: New York University Press, 1997); Carl Van Doren, *Mutiny in January,* (New York: Viking Press, 1943); Richard H. Kohn, "The Inside History of the Newburgh Conspiracy: America and the Coup d'Etat," *WMQ,* 3d ser., 27 (April 1970): 187–220; Paul David Nelson, "Horatio Gates at Newburgh, 1783: A Misunderstood Role (with a rebuttal by Richard H. Kohn)," *WMQ,* 3d ser., 29 (January 1972): 143–58; Higginbotham, *War of American Independence,* 250. The phrase "dull period" is taken from the latter work.

19. This is not to deny or minimize the significance of the continued incidence of what James Kirby Martin has called "protest and defiance" in the ranks, including the mutinies of 1779–81. It is, rather, to acknowledge that in the end most members of the army continued to do their jobs, choosing either to place their grievances and resentment over the neglect of civil society in a broader context of self-interest, or else simply to make sacrifices for the collective good. The mutinies ran their course with relatively little harm to the army's operational integrity precisely because most soldiers did not join them, and some showed a readiness to help suppress them. See James Kirby Martin, "A 'Most Undisciplined, Profligate Crew': Protest and Defiance in the Continental Ranks, 1776–1783," in Hoffman and Albert, eds., *Arms and Independence,* 119–40.

20. The average number of troops present and fit for service with Washington's main army between July and December 1778 was 21,586. During 1779 this number fell to 18,860; then to 12,284 in 1780; and to 5,379 during the first seven months of 1781. After the Continental victory at Yorktown in fall 1781 the number of troops in the north rose again to an average of 8,525 in 1782. The average fell again in the first half of 1783 to 7,388, due to the final demobilization of the army. These figures comprise only a rough approximation of the army's actual strength in the north. They reflect the presence of troops as far west as Fort Pitt and north into the Albany-Mohawk region, as well as along the Continental "crescent" around New York City. See Lesser, *Sinews of War,* 76–255, passim.

21. John Shy, ed., *Winding Down: The Revolutionary War Letters of Benjamin Gilbert of Massachusetts 1780–1783* (Ann Arbor: University of Michigan Press, 1989), and Rebecca D. Symmes, ed., *A Citizen-Soldier in the American Revolution: The Diary of Benjamin Gilbert in Massachusetts and New York* (Cooperstown, N.Y.: New York State Historical Association, 1980) illustrate these phenomena through a company officer's eyes. The Revolutionary War pension application of Sarah (Osborn) Benjamin, in the National Archives, microfilm publication M804, file W 4558, and summarized in John C. Dann, *The Revolution Remembered: Eyewitness Accounts of the War for Independence* (Chicago: University of Chicago Press, 1980), 240–50, captures both the restless mobility of low-level soldiers and the increasing porosity of the boundaries between civil and military cultures late in the war. Mayer, *Belonging to the Army.*

22. Royster, *Revolutionary People at War,* chap. 8 (quotation on p. 242).

23. Ibid., 335–36; Kohn, "Inside History of the Newburgh Conspiracy," and Nelson, "Horatio Gates at Newburgh."

24. Ousterhout, *State Divided,* 184–95, 210–12; Rosswurm, *Arms, Country, and Class,* 152–62; Bradley Chapin, *The American Law of Treason: Revolutionary and Early National Origins* (Seattle: University of Washington Press, 1964), 57–59, 67–69; Peter C. Messer, "A Species of Treason and Not the Least Dangerous Kind: The Treason Trials of Abraham Carlisle and John Roberts," *PMHB* 123 (1999): 303–32.

25. Foster, *In Pursuit of Equal Liberty,* 92–93. The Test Act imposed fines and double taxes on any Pennsylvanians who refused to sign oaths pledging to uphold the constitution. Ireland, "Ethnic-Religious Dimension of Pennsylvania Politics, 1778–1779," 432–33.

26. Rosswurm, *Arms, Country, and Class,* 176–77; Tully, *Forming American Politics,* "Conclusion," esp. 426–30.

27. Richard Alan Ryerson, "Republican Theory and Partisan Reality in Revolutionary Pennsylvania: Toward a New View of the Constitutionalist Party," in Hoffman and Albert, eds., *Sovereign States,* 95–133, esp. 130–33.

28. See Owen S. Ireland, *Religion, Ethnicity, and Politics: Ratifying the Constitution in Pennsylvania* (University Park: The Pennsylvania State University Press, 1995), chap. 7, and conclusion for this "quiet counterrevolution." Ireland, "Crux of Politics," and "Ethnic-Religious Dimension"; Bockelman and Ireland, *"Internal Revolution in Pennsylvania";* Jackson Turner Main, *Political Parties Before the Constitution* (Chapel Hill: University of North Carolina Press, 1973), chap. 7.

29. These included the anniversary dates of such benchmark episodes as her husband Henry's arrest (September 2) and exile to Virginia (September 11), and her hard-won reunion with him (April 25). See Crane, *Drinker Diary* 1, 312–450, passim (quotation on 332).

30. Muhlenberg, *Diary*, 3: 170–75, passim, and esp. 192, 210, 229, 324–26, 355, 387, 398 (quotations on 208, 561). Wolfgang Splitter, *Pastors People Politics: German Lutherans in Pennsylvania, 1740–1790* (Trier: Wissenschafter Verlag, 1998), 190–201.

31. Marshall, *Diary*, 189–284, and esp. 189, 195, 211.

32. Ibid., 217–21.

33. Ibid., 277, 279, 284.

34. *Journal of Nicholas Collin,* 250–53; Collin, "A Brief Account of the Swedish Mission, From its Commencement, and Cessation in Racoon and Pensneck," (December 12, 1791), in Amandus Johnson, ed., *The Records of the Swedish Lutheran Churches at Raccoon and Penns Neck, 1713–1786* (Elizabeth, N.J.: Colby and McGowan, for the Federal Writers' Project), 216–22.

35. Elizabeth Farmer to "Dear Madame," October 25, 1783 (quotation); Elizabeth Farmer to "Dear Nephew," December 4, 1783, Elizabeth Farmer Letterbook, (Am. 061), HSP.

36. "Diary of Robert Morton"; *Journal of Sarah Wister;* Joseph Townsend, "The Battle of Brandywine."

37. *General Persifor Frazer, A Memoir,* 159, 167.

38. John Resch, *Suffering Soldiers: Revolutionary War Veterans, Moral Sentiment, and Political Culture in the Early Republic* (Amherst: University of Massachusetts Press, 1999); Thibaut, *In the True Rustic Order,* 32–34; William L. Stone, trans., *Memoirs, Letters, and Journals of Major General Riedesel* (New York: Arno Press, 1969); Alfred F. Young, *The Shoemaker and the Tea Party: Memory and the American Revolution* (Boston: Beacon Press, 1999), 92–98.

39. Donald Jackson and Dorothy Twohig, eds., *Diaries of George Washington,* vol. 5 (Charlottesville: University of Virginia Press, 1979); entry for July 30, 1787, p. 178–79. Three weeks later Washington visited the site of what he called "my old Incampment" at Whitemarsh, where he "Contemplated on the dangers which threatnd the American Army at that place," Washington *Diaries,* 5: 181.

40. Mary S. Woodman, "Appendix: Edward Woodman, Father of the Historian," in Henry Woodman, *The History of Valley Forge: With a Biography of the Author and the Author's Father Who Was a Soldier With Washington at Valley Forge During the Winters of 1777 and 1778* (1850; rpt. Oaks, Pa.: John U. Francis, Sr., 1922), 157–64, esp. 163.

41. Ibid., 164. For the terms "Quakerized" and "civil quakerism" as political concepts, see Tully, *Forming American Politics,* 157, 285–303.

42. Henry Woodman, *History of Valley Forge,* 126–27. There is no way of verifying this story. Washington's diaries for 1796 end in June. He spent twenty-nine days in Philadelphia that summer (August 22–September 19), a time that correlates with Woodman's memory of the meeting as having been in the late summer. But Woodman may, like George Roberts Twelves Hewes, have incorporated into his memory images that acquired an iconic significance during the nineteenth-century consolidation of Revolutionary memory. See John Alexander Carroll and Mary Wells Ashworth, *George Washington: First in Peace* (completing the seven-volume biography of Washington by Douglas Southall Freeman) (New York: Charles Scribner's Sons, 1957). William Spohn Baker, *Washington After the Revolution, 1784–1799* (Philadelphia, J. B. Lippincott, 1898), accounts for Washington's presence during only five days (August 25 and 30, and September 5, 11, and 17) of this period. Young, *Shoemaker and the Tea Party.*

Bibliography

Manuscripts

Brooklyn Historical Society, Brooklyn, N.Y.
    Laurens Papers (typescripts)
Anne Marie Brown Library, Brown University, Providence, R.I.
    Weedon Papers
Bucks County Historical Society, Doylestown, Pa.
    John Lacey Orderly Book
Chicago Historical Society, Chicago, Ill.
    Steuben Papers
    Weedon Papers
William L. Clements Library, Ann Arbor, Mich.
    Clinton Papers
    Nathanael Greene Papers
    Sackville-Germain Papers
    Anthony Wayne Papers
Connecticut Historical Society, Hartford
    Samuel Gray Collection
    Jedediah Huntington Letters
    Isaac Sherman Orderly Book
    Joseph Trumbull Letters
    Jeremiah Wadsworth Papers
    Theodore Woodbridge Papers
Connecticut State Library, Hartford
    Pierson and Sargeant Family Papers
    Trumbull Papers
David Library of the American Revolution, Washington Crossing, Pa.
    Sol Feinstone Collection
Friends Historical Library, Swarthmore College, Swarthmore, Pa.
    Minutes of the Radnor Monthly Meeting. "Sufferings of Friends, 1778."

Great Britain, Public Record Office, Kew, Surrey
  Records of the British Loyalist Commission, Audit Office, series 12 and 13 (microfilm, 186 reels)
  British Headquarters Papers (Sir Guy Carleton Papers)
  "British Headquarters Papers," WO 28/2–10, roll 3A, #877
Historical Society of Pennsylvania, Philadelphia
  General John Cadwallader Papers, Cadwallader Collection
  Ferdinand Dreer Collection
  Elizabeth Farmer Letterbook
  Gratz Collection
  William Henry Manuscripts
  Christopher Marshall Letterbook
  Pemberton Papers
  Peters Papers
  Robert Proud Papers
  Shippen Family Papers
  Society Collection
  Anthony Wayne Papers
  Daniel Weir Letterbook
Library of Congress, Department of Special Collections, Washington, D.C.
  Elias Boudinot Papers
  Mrs. Archibald Crossley Autograph Collection
  Richard Fitzpatrick Papers
  Force Transcripts
  Hamilton-McLane Papers
  Lafayette Papers
  John Taylor Miscellaneous Manuscripts
  Toner Collection
  Dr. Peter Turner Papers
  Jeremiah Wadsworth Papers
  George Washington Papers, series 4 (microfilm, 124 reels): reels 43–50 (July 23, 1777–July 23, 1778)
Maryland Hall of Records, Annapolis
  Gist Family Papers
  Red Books
Maryland Historical Society, Baltimore
  Samuel Smith Letterbook, September-November 1777.
Massachusetts Historical Society, Boston
  Bowdoin-Temple Papers
  Dudley Colman Papers
  Henry Knox Papers
  Miscellaneous Manuscript Collection
Massachusetts State Archives, Boston
  Governor and Council Letters
Morristown National Historical Park, Morristown, N.J.
  Lidgerwood Collection, Hessian Documents of the American Revolution (microfiche)
National Archives, Washington, D.C.
  Record Group 15 (Military Pension files)
  Record Group 93 (Papers of the Continental Congress)
  Weiss Papers

New Jersey Bureau of Archives and History, Trenton
 Moore Furman Papers
New Jersey Historical Society, Newark
 Louis Bamberger Autograph Collection
 John Cox Correspondence
 Ely Collection
 Jacob Piatt Orderly Book
 Revolutionary Era Documents
New-York Historical Society, New York, N.Y.
 Sebastian Bauman Papers
 Lacey Papers
 Lamb Papers
 Robert R. Livingston Papers
 McDougall Papers
 McLane Papers
 Joseph Reed Papers
New York Public Library, New York, N.Y.
 Emmett Collection
New York State Historical Association, Cooperstown
 Charles Stewart Collection
Nottingham University Library, Nottingham, U.K.
 Newcastle Manuscripts
Ohio Historical Society, Columbus
 Arthur St. Clair Papers
Pennsylvania Historical and Museum Commission, Division of Archives and Manu-
 scripts, Harrisburg
 Record Group 27, Records of Pennsylvania's Revolutionary Governments, 1775–90
 (microfilm, 54 reels)
Pierpont Morgan Library, New York, N.Y.
 Autograph Letters of George Washington
Princeton University Library, Department of Special Collections, Princeton, N.J.
 Boudinot Papers
 Andre deCoppet Collection
 Miscellaneous Manuscripts
Rhode Island State Library, Providence
 Miscellaneous Manuscripts
 Samuel Ward Papers
Philip S. and A. S. W. Rosenbach Foundation, Philadelphia, Pa.
 Miscellaneous Manuscripts
Royal Artillery Institution Library, Woolwich, London
 Orderly Book of General James Pattison (Microform Publications, East Ardsley,
 Yorkshire, n.d.) reel 1
Rutgers University Library, New Brunswick, N.J.
 Miscellaneous Manuscripts
 Revolutionary War Letters Collection
 Israel Shreve Papers
South Carolina Historical Society, Columbia
 Laurens Papers

State Historical Society of Wisconsin, Madison
    Elias Boudinot Letterbook
    Theodore Draper MSS, series AA: Irvine Papers
    Theodore Draper MSS, series QQ: Preston Papers
Valley Forge National Historical Park, Valley Forge, Pa.
    John Reed Collection
University of Virginia Library, Charlottesville
    Miscellaneous Manuscripts
    Andrew Snape Hammond Papers
Virginia State Library, Richmond
    Jonathan Clark Diary
    Miscellaneous Manuscripts
Western Reserve Historical Society, Cleveland, Ohio
    Miscellaneous MSS Collections
Yale University Library, New Haven, Conn.
    Knollenberg Collection
    Wadsworth Family Papers

Published Primary Sources

Adams, Charles Francis, ed. *The Works of John Adams.* 10 vols. Boston: Little, Brown, 1856.

[Anonymous]. "Letters of a French Officer, Written at Easton, Penna., in 1777–1778," *Pennsylvania Magazine of History and Biography*, 35 (1911), 90–102.

Bray, Robert C., and Paul E. Bushnell, eds. *Diary of a Common Soldier in the American Revolution, 1775–1783: An Annotated Edition of the Journal of Jeremiah Greenman.* DeKalb: Northern Illinois University Press, 1978.

Burnett, Edmund C., ed. *Letters of Members of the Continental Congress.* 8 vols. Washington, D.C.: Carnegie Institute of Washington, 1921–36.

Continental Congress. *Journals of the Continental Congress, 1774–1789,* ed. Worthington C. Ford et al. 34 vols. Washington D.C.: 1904–37.

Crane, Elaine Forman, ed. *The Diary of Elizabeth Drinker.* 3 vols. Boston: Northeastern University Press, 1992.

Derounian, Kathryn Zabelle, ed. *The Journal and Occasional Writings of Sarah Wister.* Rutherfurd, N.J.: Fairleigh Dickinson University Press, 1987.

"The Diary of Robert Morton" (September 16 to December 30, 1777), *Pennsylvania Magazine of History and Biography* 1 (1877): 1–39.

Dohla, Johann Conrad. *A Hessian Diary of the American Revolution,* ed. Bruce E. Burgoyne. Norman: University of Oklahoma Press, 1990.

Duane, William, ed. *Extracts from the Diary of Christopher Marshall During the American Revolution, 1774–1781.* Albany, N.Y.: 1877.

Ewald, Captain Johann. *Diary of the American War: A Hessian Journal.* Trans. and ed. by Joseph P. Tustin. New Haven: Yale University Press, 1979.

"Extracts from the Letter-Book of Captain Johann Heinrichs of the Hessian Jager Corps, 1777–1780." *Pennsylvania Magazine of History and Biography* 22 (1898): 137–70.

Fitzpatrick, John W., ed. *The Writings of George Washington.* 37 vols. Washington, D.C.: 1931–40.

[Ganot, Louis de Recicourt de?]. "The American Revolutionary Army: A French Estimate in 1777," ed. Durand Echeverria and Orville T. Murphy. *Military Affairs* 27 (spring 1963): 1–7, and (winter 1963–64): 153–62.

Holt, Edward A., ed. "A Revolutionary Diary of Captain Paul Brigham: November 19, 1777–September 4, 1778." *Vermont History* 34 (January 1966): 3–30.

"John Hunt's Diary," *Proceedings of the New Jersey Historical Society* 52 (July and October 1934): 177–93, 223–39.

Johnson, Amandus, ed. *The Journal and Biography of Nicholas Collin, 1746–1831.* Philadelphia: New Jersey Society of Pennsylvania, 1936.

"Journal of John Charles Von Krafft" (January 1–June 26, 1778), *Collections of the New-York Historical Society for the Year 1882.* New York, 1883.

Judd, Jacob, ed. *The Revolutionary War Memoir and Selected Letters of Philip van Cortlandt.* Tarrytown, N.Y.: Sleepy Hollow Restorations, 1976.

Kipping, Ernst, and Samuel Stelle Smith, trans. and eds. *At General Howe's Side, 1776–1778: The Diary of General William Howe's Aide-de-Camp, Captain Friedrich von Muenchhausen.* Monmouth Beach, N.J.: Philip Freneau Press, 1974.

"Letters from Sir Charles Blagden to Sir Joseph Banks, on American National History and Politics, 1776–1780." *Bulletin of the New York Public Library* 7 (1903): 407–46.

Martin, James Kirby, ed. *Ordinary Courage: The Revolutionary War Adventures of Joseph Plumb Martin.* St. James, N.Y.: Brandywine Press, 1993.

"Memoirs of Brigadier-General John Lacey, of Pennsylvania," *Pennsylvania Magazine of History and Biography* 25 (1901), 26 (1902).

Miller, Lillian B., et al., eds. *The Selected Papers of Charles Willson Peale and His Family.* 3 vols. New Haven: Yale University Press, 1983.

Mitchell, James T., and Henry Flanders. *The Statutes at Large of Pennsylvania from 1681 to 1801.* 18 vols. Harrisburg, 1896–1915.

Montressor, John. "Journals of Captain John Montressor, 1777–1778." *Collections of the New-York Historical Society.* New York, 1881.

"Orderly Book of the Second Pennsylvania Continental Line." *Pennsylvania Magazine of History and Biography* 36 (1913).

"Proposals of Col. Charles Mawhood to the Salem Militia" (with a Reply by Col. Elijah Hand, March 22, 1778), *Proceedings of the New Jersey Historical Society,* ser. 1, 8 (1858), 99–101.

Robson, Eric, ed. *Letters from America, 1773–1780: Being the Letters of a Scots Officer, Sir James Murray, to His Home During the War of American Independence.* New York: Barnes and Noble, 1951.

Scheer, George F., ed. *Private Yankee Doodle: A Narrative of Some of the Adventures, Dangers, and Sufferings of a Revolutionary Soldier. Joseph Plumb Martin.* Salem, N.H.: Ayer, 1985.

"The Services of Lieut-Colonel Francis Downman, R.A.," *Minutes of Proceedings of the Royal Artillery Institution* 25 (Woolwich, Eng., 1898).

Seybolt, Robert Francis, ed. "A Contemporary British Account of General Sir William Howe's Military Operations in 1777," *Proceedings of the American Antiquarian Society,* n.s. 40 (April-October 1930): 69–92.

Showman, Richard K., ed. *The Papers of General Nathanael Greene.* 7 vols. Chapel Hill: University of North Carolina Press, 1976–.

Simcoe, John Graves. *A Journal of the Operations of the Queens Rangers.* Exeter, n.d.; New York: Bartlett and Welford, 1844.

Smith, Paul H., ed. *Letters of Delegates to Congress.* 24 vols., Washington, D.C.: Library of Congress, 1976–2000.

[Tallmadge, Benjamin]. *The Memoir of Colonel Benjamin Tallmadge.* New York, 1858; rpt. New York: New York Times and Arno Press, 1968.

Tappert, Theodore G., and John W. Doberstein, eds. *The Journals of Henry Melchior Muhlenberg.* 3 vols. Philadelphia: Philadelphia Evangelical Lutheran Ministerium and Muhlenberg Press, 1945.

Tatum, Edward H., ed. *The American Journal of Ambrose Serle, Secretary to Lord Howe, 1776–1778.* San Marino, Calif.: Huntington Library, 1940.

Townsend, Joseph. *The Battle of Brandywine.* Philadelphia, 1846; rpt. New York: *New York Times* and Arno Press, 1969.

Uhlendorf, Bernhard A., trans. and ed. *Revolution in America: Confidential Letters and Journals, 1776–1784, of Adjutant General Major Baurmeister of the Hessian Forces.* New Brunswick: Rutgers University Press, 1957.

"Valley Forge, 1777–1778: Diary of Surgeon Albigence Waldo, of the Connecticut Line." *Pennsylvania Magazine of History and Biography* 21 (1897): 299–323.

Van Horne, William E., ed. "Revolutionary War Letters of the Reverend William Van Horne." *Western Pennsylvania Historical Magazine* 53 (April 1970): 105–38.

Wainwright, Nicholas B., ed. "'A Diary of Trifling Occurrences': Philadelphia, 1776–1778," *Pennsylvania Magazine of History and Biography* 82 (October 1958): 411–65.

Willcox, William B. et al., eds. *The Papers of Benjamin Franklin.* 32 vols., New Haven: Yale University Press, 1959–.

Wortley, Mrs. E. Stuart, ed. *A Prime Minister and His Son: From the Correspondence of the 3rd Earl of Bute and of Lt.-General The Hon. Sir Charles Stuart, K.B.* New York: E. P. Dutton, 1925.

Articles

Baldwin, Simeon E. "The New Haven Convention of 1778." *Papers of the New Haven Colony Historical Society* (New Haven, privately printed, 1882), 3: 33–62.

Bockelman, Wayne L., and Owen S. Ireland. "The Internal Revolution in Pennsylvania: An Ethnic-Religious Interpretation." *Pennsylvania History* 41 (April 1974): 125–59.

Bodle, Wayne. "Themes and Directions in Middle Colonies Historiography, 1980–1994." *William and Mary Quarterly,* 3d ser., 51 (July 1994): 355–88.

———. "Generals and 'Gentlemen': Pennsylvania Politics and the Decision for Valley Forge." *Pennsylvania History* 62 (winter 1995): 59–89.

Brobeck, Stephen. "Revolutionary Change in Colonial Philadelphia: The Brief Life of the Proprietary Gentry." *William and Mary Quarterly* 33 (July 1776): 410–34.

Conway, Stephen. "British Army Officers and the American War for Independence." *William and Mary Quarterly,* 3d ser., 42 (April 1984): 265–76.

———. "To Subdue America: British Army Officers and the Conduct of the Revolutionary War." *William and Mary Quarterly,* 3d ser., 44 (July 1986): 381–407.

———. "'The Great Mischief Complained of': Reflections on the Misconduct of British Soldiers in the Revolutionary War." *William and Mary Quarterly,* 3d ser., 47 (July 1990): 370–90.

Evans, Emory. "Planter Indebtedness and the Coming of the Revolution in Virginia." *William and Mary Quarterly,* 3d ser., 19 (October 1962): 511–33.

Gough, Robert. "Charles H. Lincoln, Carl Becker, and the Origins of the Dual-Revolution Thesis." *William and Mary Quarterly,* 3d ser., 39 (January 1981): 97–109.

Higginbotham, Don. "The Early American Way of War: Reconnaissance and Appraisal." *William and Mary Quarterly,* 3d ser., 44 (April 1987): 230–73.

Ireland, Owen S. "The Ethnic-Religious Dimension of Pennsylvania Politics, 1778–1779." *William and Mary Quarterly,* 3d ser., 30 (July 1973): 422–48.

———. "The Crux of Politics: Religion and Party in Pennsylvania, 1778–1789." *William and Mary Quarterly,* 3d ser., 42 (October 1985): 453–75.

Jones, Douglas Lamar. "The Strolling Poor: Transiency in Eighteenth Century Massachusetts." *Journal of Social History* 8 (spring 1975): 28–54.

———. "Poverty and Vagabondage: The Process of Survival in Eighteenth-Century Massachusetts." *New England Historical and Genealogical Register* 133 (1979): 243–54.

Kaplan, Roger. "The Hidden War: British Intelligence Operations During the American Revolution." *William and Mary Quarterly,* 3d ser., 47 (January 1990): 115–38.

Kim, Sung Bok. "The Limits of Politicization in the American Revolution: The Experience of Westchester County, New York." *Journal of American History* 80 (December 1993): 868–89.

Klein, Milton M. "Why Did the British Fail to Win the Hearts and Minds of New Yorkers." *New York History* 64 (October 1983): 357–75.

Knight, Betsy. "Prisoner Exchange and Parole in the American Revolution." *William and Mary Quarterly,* 3d ser., 48 (April 1991): 201–22.

Newcomb, Benjamin. "Washington's Generals and the Decision to Quarter at Valley Forge." *Pennsylvania Magazine of History and Biography* 117 (October 1993): 309–29.

Oaks, Robert F. "Philadelphians in Exile: The Problem of Loyalty During the American Revolution." *Pennsylvania Magazine of History and Biography* 96 (July 1972): 298–325.

Papenfuse, Edward C., and Gregory A. Stiverson. "General Smallwood's Recruits: The Peacetime Career of the Revolutionary War Private." *William and Mary Quarterly,* 3d ser., 30 (January 1973), 117–32.

Pargellis, Stanley M. "The Four Independent Companies of New York," in *Essays in Colonial History Presented to Charles McLean Andrews.* New Haven: Yale University Press, 1931. 96–123.

Russell, Peter E. "Redcoats in the Wilderness: British Officers and Irregular Warfare in Europe and America, 1740–1760." *William and Mary Quarterly,* 3d ser., 35 (October 1978): 629–52.

Salinger, Sharon V. "Artisans, Journeymen, and the Transformation of Labor in Late Eighteenth Century Philadelphia," *William and Mary Quarterly,* 3d ser., 41 (January 1983): 61–84.

Sellers, John R. "The Common Soldier in the American Revolution," in Stanley J. Underdal, ed., *Military History of the American Revolution: Proceedings of the Sixth Military History Symposium, United States Air Force Academy.* Washington, D.C.: United States Air Force Academy, 1976. 151–61.

Sheldon, Richard N. "Editing a Historical Manuscript: Jared Sparks, Douglas Southall Freeman, and the Battle of Brandywine." *William and Mary Quarterly,* 3d ser., 37 (April 1979): 255–63.

Simler, Lucy. "Tenancy in Colonial Pennsylvania: The Case of Chester County." *William and Mary Quarterly,* 3d ser., 43 (October 1986): 542–60.

———. "The Landless Worker: An Index of Economic and Social Change in Chester County, Pennsylvania, 1750–1820," *Pennsylvania Magazine of History and Biography* 114 (April 1990): 163–99.

Simler, Lucy, and Paul G. E. Clemens. "Rural Labor and the Farm Household in Chester County, Pennsylvania, 1750–1820," in Stephen Innes, ed., *Work and Labor in Early America.* Chapel Hill: University of North Carolina Press, 1988. 106–43.

Soderlund, Jean. "Women's Authority in Pennsylvania and New Jersey Quaker Meetings, 1680–1760," *William and Mary Quarterly,* 3d ser., 44 (October 1987): 722–49.

Tiedemann, Joseph. "Communities in the Midst of the American Revolution: Queens County, New York, 1774–1775." *Journal of Social History* 18 (fall 1984): 57–78.

————. "Patriots by Default: Queens County, New York, and the British Army, 1776–1783." *William and Mary Quarterly,* 3d ser., 43 (January 1986): 35–63.

————. "A Revolution Foiled: Queens County, New York, 1775–1776." *Journal of American History* 75 (September 1988): 417–44.

Tully, Alan. "Ethnicity, Religion and Politics in Early America," *Pennsylvania Magazine of History and Biography* 107 (October 1983): 491–536.

————. "Quaker Party and Proprietary Policies: The Dynamics of Politics in Pre-Revolutionary Pennsylvania, 1730–1775," in Bruce C. Daniels, *Power and Status: Officeholding in Colonial America.* Middletown, Conn.: Wesleyan University Press, 1986. 75–105.

Van Buskirk, Judith. "They Didn't Join the Band: Disaffected Women in Revolutionary Pennsylvania." *Pennsylvania History* 62 (summer 1995): 306–29.

Books

Alden, John Richard. *The American Revolution, 1775–1783.* New York: Harper and Brothers, 1954.

Alexander, John K. *Render Them Submissive: Responses to Poverty in Philadelphia, 1760–1800.* Amherst: University of Massachusetts Press, 1980.

Anderson, Fred. *A People's Army: Massachusetts Soldiers and Society During the Seven Years' War.* Chapel Hill: University of North Carolina Press, 1984.

Anderson, Troyer S. *The Command of the Howe Brothers in the American Revolution.* New York: Oxford University Press, 1936.

Anderson, William G. *The Price of Liberty: The Public Debt of the American Revolution.* Charlottesville: University Press of Virginia, 1983.

Andrews, Dee. *The Methodists and Revolutionary America, 1760–1800: The Shaping of an Evangelical Culture.* Princeton: Princeton University Press, 2000.

Arnold, Douglas McNeil. *A Republican Revolution: Ideology and Politics in Pennsylvania.* New York: Garland, 1989.

Bailyn, Bernard. *The Ideological Origins of the American Revolution.* Cambridge: Harvard University Press, 1967.

Bailyn, Bernard, and Philip D. Morgan. *Strangers Within the Realm: Cultural Margins of the First British Empire.* Chapel Hill: University of North Carolina Press, 1991.

Becker, Carl L. *The History of Political Parties in the Colony of New York, 1760–1776.* Madison: University of Wisconsin Press, 1909, 1960.

Bezanson, Ann. *Prices and Inflation During the American Revolution: Pennsylvania, 1770–1790.* Philadelphia: University of Pennsylvania Press, 1951.

Bill, Alfred Hoyt. *Valley Forge: The Making of an Army.* New York: Harper and Row, 1952.

Bining, Arthur Cecil. *Pennsylvania Iron Manufacture in the Eighteenth Century.* Harrisburg: Pennsylvania Historical Commission, 1938.

Bolles, Albert S. *The Financial History of the United States from 1774 to 1789.* New York: 1879; rpt. New York: August M. Kelley, 1969.

Bowler, R. Arthur. *Logistics and the Failure of the British Army in America, 1775–1783.* Princeton: Princeton University Press, 1975.

Boyer, Charles S. *Early Forges and Furnaces in New Jersey.* Philadelphia: University of Pennsylvania Press, 1931.

Breen, T. H. *Tobacco Culture: The Mentality of the Great Tidewater Planters on the Eve of Revolution.* Princeton: Princeton University Press, 1985.

Brown, Gerald S. *The American Secretary: The Colonial Policy of Lord George Germain, 1775–1778.* Ann Arbor: University of Michigan Press, 1963.

Brown, Wallace. *The King's Friends: The Composition and Motives of the American Loyalist Claimants.* Providence: Brown University Press, 1965.

Brown, Weldon A. *Empire or Independence: A Study in the Failure of Reconciliation, 1774–1783.* Baton Rouge: Louisiana State University Press, 1941; rpt. Port Washington, N.Y.: Kennikat Press, 1966.

Brunhouse, Robert L. *The Counter-Revolution in Pennsylvania, 1776–1790.* Harrisburg: Pennsylvania Historical and Museum Commission, 1942, 1971.

Buel, Richard. *Dear Liberty: Connecticut's Mobilization for the Revolutionary War.* Middletown, Conn.: Wesleyan University Press, 1980.

Bullock, Charles J. *The Finances of the United States from 1775 to 1789, With Especial Reference to the Budget.* Madison, Wis., 1895; rpt. Philadelphia: Porcupine Press, 1979.

Burnett, Edmund C. *The Continental Congress.* New York: MacMillan, 1941.

Busch, Noel F. *Winter Quarters: George Washington and the Continental Army at Valley Forge.* New York: Liveright Press, 1974.

Bush, Martin H. *Revolutionary Enigma: A Reappraisal of General Philip Schuyler of New York.* Port Washington, N.Y.: I. J. Friedman, 1969.

Calhoon, Robert M. *The Loyalists in Revolutionary America, 1760–1781.* New York: Harcourt, Brace, Jovanovich, 1973.

Cappon, Lester J. et al., eds. *Atlas of Early American History: The Revolutionary Era, 1760–1790.* Princeton: Princeton University Press, 1976.

Carp, E. Wayne. *To Starve the Army at Pleasure: Continental Army Administration and American Political Culture, 1775–1783.* Chapel Hill: University of North Carolina Press, 1984.

Chidsey, Donald Barr. *Valley Forge.* New York: Crown, 1959.

Clemens, Paul G. E. *The Atlantic Economy and Colonial Maryland's Eastern Shore: From Tobacco to Grain.* Ithaca: Cornell University Press, 1980.

Colley, Linda. *Britons: Forging the Nation, 1707–1837.* New Haven: Yale University Press, 1992.

Cray, Robert E. *Paupers and Poor Relief in New York City and Its Rural Environs, 1700–1830.* Philadelphia: Temple University Press, 1988.

Cress, Lawrence Delbert. *Citizens in Arms: The Army and the Militia in American Society to the War of 1812.* Chapel Hill: University of North Carolina Press, 1982.

Crow, Jeffrey J., and Larry E. Tise, eds. *The Southern Experience in the American Revolution.* Chapel Hill: University of North Carolina Press, 1978.

Davidson, Robert L. D. *War Comes to Quaker Pennsylvania, 1682–1756.* New York: Columbia University Press, 1957.

Davis, W. W. H. *History of the Battle of Crooked Billet.* Doylestown, Pa.: Printed at the Democrat Office, 1860.

Doerflinger, Thomas M. *A Vigorous Spirit of Enterprise: Merchants and Economic Development in Revolutionary Philadelphia.* Chapel Hill: University of North Carolina Press, 1986.

Dwyer, William M. *The Day Is Ours! November 1776-January 1777: An Inside View of the Battles of Trenton and Princeton.* New York: Viking Press, 1983.

Ferguson, E. James. *The Power of the Purse: A History of American Public Finance, 1776–1790.* Chapel Hill: University of North Carolina Press, 1961.

Ferling, John E. *The First of Men: A Life of George Washington.* Knoxville: University of Tennessee Press, 1988.

Fischer, David Hackett. *Paul Revere's Ride.* New York: Oxford University Press, 1994.

Flexner, James Thomas. *George Washington in the American Revolution, 1775–1783.* Boston: Little, Brown, 1967.

Flower, Milton E. *John Dickinson, Conservative Revolutionary.* Charlottesville: University Press of Virginia, 1983.

Fogleman, Aaron Spencer. *Hopeful Journeys: German Immigration, Settlement, and Political Culture in Colonial America, 1717–1775.* Philadelphia: University of Pennsylvania Press, 1996.

Foner, Eric. *Tom Paine and Revolutionary America.* New York: Oxford University Press, 1976.

Foster, Joseph S. *In Pursuit of Equal Liberty: George Bryan and the American Revolution in Pennsylvania.* University Park: The Pennsylvania State University Press, 1994.

Frantz, John, and William Pencak, eds. *Beyond Philadelphia: The American Revolution in the Pennsylvania Hinterland.* University Park: The Pennsylvania State University Press, 1998.

Freeman, Douglas Southall. *George Washington.* New York: Charles Scribner's Sons, 1951.

French, Allen. *The Day of Concord and Lexington: The Nineteenth of April, 1775.* Boston: Little, Brown, 1925.

———. *The First Year of the American Revolution.* New York: Houghton Mifflin, 1934.

Furneaux, Rupert. *The Battle of Saratoga.* New York: Stein and Day, 1971.

Gilpin, Thomas. *Exiles in Virginia, With Observations on the Conduct of the Society of Friends During the Revolutionary War.* Philadelphia, 1848.

Greven, Philip. *Four Generations: Population, Land, and Family in Colonial Andover, Massachusetts.* Ithaca: Cornell University Press, 1970.

Griffin, Patrick. *The People with No Name: Ireland's Ulster Scots, America's Scots-Irish, and the Creation of a British Atlantic World, 1689–1764.* Princeton: Princeton University Press, 2001.

Gross, Robert A. *The Minutemen and Their World.* New York: Hill and Wang, 1976.

Gruber, Ira D. *The Howe Brothers and the American Revolution.* New York: Atheneum, 1972.

Hanna, William S. *Benjamin Franklin and Pennsylvania Politics.* Stanford: Stanford University Press, 1964.

Hatch, Nathan. *The Sacred Cause of Liberty.* New Haven: Yale University Press, 1977.

Hawke, David Freeman. *In The Midst of a Revolution.* Philadelphia: University of Pennsylvania Press, 1961.

Henderson, H. James. *Party Politics in the Continental Congress.* New York: McGraw-Hill, 1974.

Higginbotham, Don. *Daniel Morgan: Revolutionary Rifleman.* Chapel Hill: University of North Carolina Press, 1961.

———. *The War of American Independence: Military Attitudes, Policies, and Practice, 1763–1789.* New York: Macmillan, 1971.

———. *George Washington and the American Military Tradition.* Athens: University of Georgia Press, 1985.

Hoffman, Ronald, and Peter J. Albert., eds. *Sovereign States in an Age of Uncertainty.* Charlottesville: University Press of Virginia, 1981.

———. *Women in the Age of the American Revolution.* Charlottesville: University Press of Virginia, 1989.

Hoffman, Ronald, Peter J. Albert, and Thad Tate, eds. *An Uncivil War: The Southern Backcountry During the American Revolution.* Charlottesville: University Press of Virginia, 1985.

Humphrey, Carol Sue. *"This Popular Engine": New England Newspapers During the American Revolution.* Newark: University of Delaware Press, 1992.

Hutson, James H. *Pennsylvania Politics 1746–1770: The Movement for Royal Government and Its Consequences.* Princeton: Princeton University Press, 1972.

Illick, Joseph E. *Colonial Pennsylvania.* New York: Charles Scribner's Sons, 1976.

Jackson, Harvey H. *Lachlan McIntosh and the Politics of Revolutionary Georgia.* Athens: University of Georgia Press, 1979.

Jackson, John W. *The Pennsylvania Navy, 1775–1781: The Defense of the Delaware.* New Brunswick: Rutgers University Press, 1974.

———. *With the British Army in Philadelphia, 1777–1778.* San Rafael, Calif.: Presidio Press, 1979.

———. *Whitemarsh 1777: Impregnable Stronghold.* Norristown, Pa.: Historical Society of Fort Washington, 1984.

———. *Fort Mifflin: Valiant Defender of the Delaware.* Philadelphia: Old Fort Mifflin Historical Society, 1986.

Jedrey, Christopher M. *The World of John Cleaveland: Family and Community in Eighteenth Century New England.* New York: W. W. Norton, 1979.

Jillson, Calvin, and Rick K. Wilson. *Congressional Dynamics: Structure, Coordination, and Choice in the First American Congress, 1774–1789.* Stanford: Stanford University Press, 1994.

Jones, Douglas Lamar. *Village and Seaport: Migration and Society in Eighteenth Century Massachusetts.* Hanover, N.H.: University Press of New England, 1981.

Kashatus, William C., III. *Conflict of Convictions: A Reappraisal Quaker Involvement in the American Revolution.* Lanham, Md.: University Press of America, 1990.

Keegan, John. *The Face of Battle: A Study of Agincourt, Waterloo, and the Somme.* New York: Viking Press, 1976.

Kerber, Linda K. *Women of the Republic: Intellect and Ideology in Revolutionary America.* Chapel Hill: University of North Carolina Press, 1980.

Leiby, Adrian C. *The Revolutionary War in the Hackensack Valley: The Jersey Dutch and the Neutral Ground, 1775–1783.* New Brunswick: Rutgers University Press, 1962.

Lemon, James. *The Best Poor Man's Country: A Geographical Study of Early Southeastern Pennsylvania.* Baltimore: Johns Hopkins University Press, 1972.

Lesser, Charles S., ed. *The Sinews of Independence: Monthly Strength Reports of the Continental Army.* Chicago: University of Chicago Press, 1976.

Lincoln, Charles H. *The Revolutionary Movement in Pennsylvania, 1760–1776.* Philadelphia: University of Pennsylvania Press, 1901.

Lockridge, Kenneth A. *Literacy in Colonial New England: An Enquiry into the Social Context of Literacy in the Early Modern West.* New York: W. W. Norton, 1974.

Lucas, Stephen E. *Portents of Rebellion: Rhetoric and Revolution in Philadelphia, 1765–76.* Philadelphia: Temple University Press, 1976.

Lundin, Charles Leonard. *The Cockpit of the Revolution: The War for Independence in New Jersey.* Princeton: Princeton University Press, 1940.

Mackesy, Piers. *The War for America, 1775–1783.* Cambridge: Harvard University Press, 1964.

Martin, James Kirby. *Men in Rebellion: Higher Government Leaders and the Coming of the American Revolution.* New Brunswick: Rutgers University Press, 1973.

Martin, James Kirby, and Mark E. Lender. *A Respectable Army: The Military Origins of the Republic, 1763–1789.* Arlington Heights, Ill.: Harlan Davidson, 1982.

Mayer, Holly. *Belonging to the Army: Camp Followers and the American Revolution.* Columbia: University of South Carolina Press, 1996.

McGuire, Thomas J. *The Surprise of Germantown, or the Battle of Cliveden, October 4, 1777.* Philadelphia: Thomas Publications 1994.

————. *The Battle of Paoli* (Mechanicsburg, Pa.: Stackpole Books, 2000)

Mekeel, Arthur J. *The Quakers and the American Revolution.* York, Eng.: Sessions Book Trust, 1996.

Middlekauf, Robert. *The Glorious Cause: The American Revolution, 1763–1789.* New York: Oxford University Press, 1982.

Miller, John C. *The Triumph of Freedom, 1775–1783.* Boston: Little, Brown, 1948.

Mintz, Max M. *The Generals of Saratoga: John Burgoyne and Horatio Gates.* New Haven: Yale University Press, 1990.

Morgan, Edmund S. *American Slavery, American Freedom: The Ordeal of Colonial Virginia.* New York: W. W. Norton, 1975.

Munroe, John A. *Colonial Delaware: A History.* Millwood, N.Y.: KTO Press, 1978.

Nash, Gary B. *Quakers and Politics, 1681–1726.* Princeton: Princeton University Press, 1968.

————. *The Urban Crucible: Social Change, Political Consciousness, and the Origins of the American Revolution.* Cambridge: Harvard University Press, 1979.

Neimeyer, Charles. *America Goes to War: A Social History of the Continental Army.* New York: New York University Press, 1996.

Nelson, Paul David. *General Horatio Gates: A Biography.* Baton Rouge: Louisiana State University Press, 1976.

————. *General James Grant: Scottish Soldier and Royal Governor of East Florida.* Gainesville: University Press of Florida, 1993.

Newcomb, Benjamin H. *Franklin and Galloway: A Political Partnership.* New Haven: Yale University Press, 1972.

————. *Political Partisanship in the American Middle Colonies, 1700–1776.* Baton Rouge: Louisiana State University Press, 1995.

Norton, Mary Beth. *Liberty's Daughters: The Revolutionary Experience of American Women, 1750–1800.* Boston: Little, Brown, 1980.

Olton, Charles S. *Artisans for Independence: Philadelphia Mechanics and the American Revolution.* Syracuse: Syracuse University Press, 1975.

Ousterhout, Anne M. *A State Divided: Opposition in Pennsylvania to the American Revolution.* Westport, Conn.: Greenwood Press, 1987.

Palmer, Gregory. *Biographical Sketches of Loyalists of the American Revolution.* Westport, Conn.: Meckler Books, 1984.

Pancake, John S. *1777: The Year of The Hangman.* University: University of Alabama Press, 1977.

Peckham, Howard H. *The Toll of Independence: Engagements and Battle Casualties of the American Revolution.* Chicago: University of Chicago Press, 1974.

Rakove, Jack N. *The Beginnings of National Politics: An Interpretive History of the Continental Congress.* New York: Alfred A. Knopf, 1979.

Reed, John F. *Campaign to Valley Forge: July 1 to December 19, 1777.* Philadelphia: University of Pennsylvania Press, 1963.

————. *Valley Forge: Crucible of Victory.* Monmouth Beach, N.J.: Philip Freneau Press, 1969.

Roche, John F. *Joseph Reed: A Moderate in the American Revolution.* New York: Columbia University Press, 1957.

Rossie, Jonathan Gregory. *The Politics of Command in the American Revolution.* Syracuse: Syracuse University Press, 1975.

Rosswurm, Steven. *Arms, Country, and Class: The Philadelphia Militia and the "Lower Sort" During the American Revolution, 1775–1783.* New Brunswick: Rutgers University Press, 1987.

Royster, Charles A. *A Revolutionary People at War: The Continental Army and American Character, 1775–1782.* Chapel Hill: University of North Carolina Press, 1979.

———. *Light-Horse Harry Lee and the Legacy of the American Revolution.* New York: Alfred A. Knopf, 1981.

Ryerson, Richard Alan. *The Revolution Is Now Begun: The Radical Committees of Philadelphia, 1765–1776.* Philadelphia: University of Pennsylvania Press, 1978.

Scheer, George F., and Hugh F. Rankin. *Rebels and Redcoats.* Cleveland: World, 1957.

Schwartz, Sally. *A "Mixed Multitude": The Struggle for Toleration in Pennsylvania, 1681–1776.* New York: New York University Press, 1991.

Schweitzer, Mary M. *Custom and Contract: Household, Government, and the Economy in Colonial Pennsylvania.* New York: Columbia University Press, 1987.

Selesky, Harold E. "A Demographic Survey of the Continental Army That Wintered at Valley Forge, Pennsylvania, 1777–1778." Washington, D.C.: Government Printing Office, 1988.

———. *War and Society in Colonial Connecticut.* New Haven: Yale University Press, 1990.

Selsam, J. Paul. *The Pennsylvania Constitution of 1776: A Study in Revolutionary Democracy.* Harrisburg: Pennsylvania Historical Commission 1936.

Shy, John. *A People Numerous and Armed: Reflections on the Military Struggle for American Independence.* New York: Oxford University Press, 1976.

Smith, Billy G. *The 'Lower Sort': Philadelphia's Laboring People, 1750–1800.* Ithaca: Cornell University Press, 1990.

Splitter, Wolfgang. *Pastors People Politics: German Lutherans in Pennsylvania, 1740–1790.* Trier: Wissenschafter Verlag, 1998.

Stewart, Frank H. "Foraging for Valley Forge by General Anthony Wayne in Salem and Gloucester Counties, New Jersey, with Associated Happenings." Woodbury, N.J., 1929.

Sumner, William Graham. *The Financier and the Finances of the American Revolution.* New York: Burt Franklin, 1970.

Sutherland, Stella H. *Population Distribution in Colonial America.* New York, AMS Press, 1966.

Thayer, Theodore. *Pennsylvania Politics and the Growth of Democracy, 1740–1776.* Harrisburg: Pennsylvania Historical and Museum Commission, 1953.

Thibaut, Jacqueline. *This Fatal Crisis: Logistics, Supply, and the Continental Army at Valley Forge.* Vol. 2 of *Valley Forge Historical Research Project, 1777–1778.* Washington, D.C.: National Park Service, 1980.

———. *In the True Rustic Order: Material Aspects of the Valley Forge Encampment, 1777–1778.* Vol. 3 of *Valley Forge Historical Research Project.* Washington, D.C.: National Park Service, 1980.

Treese, Lorett. *Valley Forge: Making and Remaking a National Symbol.* University Park: The Pennsylvania State University Press, 1995.

Trussell, John B. B. *Birthplace of an Army: A Study of the Valley Forge Encampment.* Harrisburg: Pennsylvania Historical and Museum Commission, 1976.

Tully, Alan. *William Penn's Legacy: Politics and Social Structure in Provincial Pennsylvania, 1726–1755.* Baltimore: Johns Hopkins University Press, 1977.

———. *Forming American Politics: Ideas, Interests, and Institutions in Colonial New York and Pennsylvania.* Baltimore: Johns Hopkins University Press, 1994.

Van Buskirk, Judith. *Generous Enemies: Patriots and Loyalists in Revolutionary New York.* Philadelphia, University of Pennsylvania Press, 2002.

Vickers, Daniel F. *Farmers and Fishermen: Two Centuries of Work in Essex County, Massachusetts, 1630–1850.* Chapel Hill: University of North Carolina Press, 1994.

Wacker, Peter O. *Land and People: A Cultural Geography of Preindustrial New Jersey, Origins and Settlement Patterns.* New Brunswick: Rutgers University Press, 1975.

Wade, Herbert T., and Robert A. Lively, eds. *This Glorious Cause: The Adventures of Two Company Officers in General Washington's Army.* Princeton: Princeton University Press, 1958.

Ward, Christopher. *The War of the Revolution.* 2 Vols. New York: MacMillan, 1952.

Weber, Donald. *Rhetoric and History in Revolutionary New England.* New York: Oxford University Press, 1988.

White, Theodore. *In Search of History: A Personal Adventure.* New York: Harper and Row, 1978.

Wildes, Harry Emerson. *Valley Forge.* New York: MacMillan, 1938.

Wokeck, Marianne S. *Trade in Strangers: The Beginnings of Mass Migration to North America.* University Park: The Pennsylvania State University Press, 1999.

Wolf, Stephanie Grauman. *Urban Village: Population, Community, and Family Structure in Germantown, Pennsylvania, 1683–1800.* Princeton: Princeton University Press, 1976.

Wright, Robert K. *The Continental Army.* Washington, D.C.: Center of Military History, 1983.

Zuckerman, Michael, ed. *Friends and Neighbors: Group Life in America's First Plural Society.* Philadelphia: Temple University Press, 1982.

Dissertations

Aldrich, James M. "The Revolutionary Legislature in Pennsylvania: A Roll Call Analysis." Ph.D. diss., University of Maine at Orono, 1969.

Applegate, Howard Lewis. "Constitutions Like Iron: The Life of the American Revolutionary War Soldiers in the Middle Department, 1775–1783." Ph.D. diss., Syracuse University, 1964.

Becker, Laura Leff. "The American Revolution as a Community Experience: A Case Study of Reading, Pennsylvania." Ph.D. diss., University of Pennsylvania, 1978.

Berlin, Robert Harry. "The Administration of Military Justice in the Continental Army During the American Revolution." Ph.D. diss., University of California at Santa Barbara, 1976.

Bernstein, David Alan. "New Jersey in the American Revolution: The Establishment of a Government Amid Civil and Military Disorder, 1770–1781." Ph.D. diss., Rutgers University, 1970.

Bodle, Wayne K. "The Vortex of Small Fortunes: The Continental Army at Valley Forge, 1777–1778." Ph.D. diss., University of Pennsylvania, 1987.

Bradsher, James Gregory. "Preserving the Revolution: Civil-Military Relations During the American War for Independence, 1775–1783." Ph.D. diss., University of Massachusetts, 1984.

Branson, Susan. "Politics and Gender: The Political Consciousness of Philadelphia Women in the 1790s." Ph.D. diss., Northern Illinois University, 1992.

Brobeck, Stephen. "Changes in the Composition and Structure of Philadelphia Elite Groups, 1756–1790." Ph.D. diss., University of Pennsylvania, 1973.

Chase, Philander Dean. "Baron von Steuben in the War of Independence." Ph.D. diss., Duke University, 1973.

Conway, Stephen R. "Military-Civilian Crime and the British Army in North America, 1775–1781." Ph.D. diss., University College, London, 1981.

Doutrich, Paul E. "The Evolution of an Early American Town: Yorktown, Pennsylvania, 1740–1790." Ph.D. diss., University of Kentucky, 1985.

Geib, George Winthrop. "A History of Philadelphia: 1776–1789." Ph.D. diss., University of Wisconsin, 1969.

Gough, Robert James. "Towards a Theory of Class and Social Conflict: A Social History of Wealthy Philadelphians, 1775 and 1800." Ph.D. diss., University of Pennsylvania, 1977.

Henderson, Rodger C. "Community Development and the Revolutionary Transition in Eighteenth Century Lancaster County, Pennsylvania." Ph.D. diss., State University of New York at Binghamton, 1983.

High, John W. "The Philadelphia Loyalists, 1763–1783." Ph.D. diss., Temple University, 1975.

Jacobsen, Glenn W. "Politics, Parties, and Propaganda in Pennsylvania, 1776–1788," Ph.D. diss., University of Wisconsin, 1976.

Knouff, Gregory T. "The Common People's Revolution: Class, Race, Masculinity, and Locale in Pennsylvania, 1775–1783." Ph.D. diss., Rutgers University, 1996.

Lender, Mark Edward. "The Enlisted Line: The Continental Soldiers of New Jersey." Ph.D. diss., Rutgers University, 1975.

Levine, Michael Lewis. "The Transformation of a Radical Whig Under Republican Government: William Livingston, Governor of New Jersey, 1776–1790." Ph.D. diss., Rutgers University, 1975.

Mega, Thomas Burns. "Political and Constitutional Development in Pennsylvania, 1739–1780." Ph.D. diss., University of Minnesota, 1985.

Molovinsky, Lemuel David. "Pennsylvania's Legislative Efforts to Finance the War for Independence: A Study of the Continuity of Colonial Finance, 1775–1783." Ph.D. diss., Temple University, 1975.

Oaks, Robert Francis. "Philadelphia Merchants and the American Revolution, 1765–1776," Ph.D. diss., University of Southern California, 1970.

Powell, Barbara MacDonald. "The Most Celebrated Encampment: Valley Forge in American Culture." Ph.D. diss., Cornell University, 1883.

Powers, Ramon S. "Wealth and Poverty: Economic Base, Social Structure, and Attitudes in Revolutionary Pennsylvania, New Jersey, and Delaware." Ph.D. diss., University of Kansas, 1971.

Royer, Helen E. "The Role of the Continental Congress in the Prosecution of the American Revolution in Pennsylvania." Ph.D. diss., Pennsylvania State University, 1960.

Salay, David Lewis. "Arming for War: The Production of War Materiel in Pennsylvania for the American Armies During the Revolution." Ph.D. diss., University of Delaware, 1977.

Schaffel, Kenneth. "The American Board of War, 1776–1781." Ph.D. diss., City University of New York, 1983.

Seidel, John Lewis. "The Archaeology of the American Revolution: A Reappraisal and Case Study of the Continental Artillery Cantonment of 1778–1779, Pluckemin, New Jersey." Ph.D. diss., University of Pennsylvania, 1987.

Tiedemann, Joseph. "Response to Revolution: Queens County, New York, During the Era of the American Revolution." Ph.D. diss., City University of New York, 1977.

Warden, Rosemary Sweeney. "The Revolution in Political Leadership in Chester County, Pennsylvania, 1765–1785." Ph.D. diss., University of Wisconsin, 1979.

Weill, Barbara. "Democracy and Revolution: Democratic and Levelling Movements in Pennsylvania, 1760–1790." Ph.D. diss., New School for Social Research, 1977,

White, John Todd. "Standing Armies in Time of War: Republican Theory and Military Practice During the American Revolution." Ph.D. diss., George Washington University, 1978.

Wingo, Barbara Christine Gray. "Politics, Society, and Religion: The Presbyterian Clergy of Pennsylvania, New Jersey, and New York, and the Formation of the Nation, 1775–1808." Ph.D. diss., Tulane University, 1976.

Yalof, Helena Roberta. "British Military Theatricals in Philadelphia During the Revolutionary War." Ph.D. diss., New York University, 1972.

Index